THE GENE
1560 APOCRYPHA

The lost books from the 1560 Geneva Bible
Edition

Eternal Light Publishing

Table of content

The Geneva Bible 1560 Edition

The Geneva Bible, first printed in 1560, is notable for its foundational place in the pantheon of biblical translations and for the specific historical and cultural circumstances under which it was produced. This translation emerged from the tumultuous context of Protestant Reformation, which marked a significant schism from the Roman Catholic Church and fostered a burgeoning desire among new Protestant sects for scriptures that could be read and understood by ordinary believers. The Geneva Bible was the combined effort of English Protestant exiles who sought refuge in Geneva during the oppressive reign of Queen Mary I of England, famously dubbed "Bloody Mary" for her persecution of Protestants. Among these exiles were several scholars, including William Whittingham, who played a pivotal role in its translation and publication.

The Geneva Bible's creation was deeply influenced by the scholarly environment of Geneva, which had become a center of Reformation thought under leaders like John Calvin and Theodore Beza. The translation was distinctly designed to be accessible, with clear, concise English that could be easily understood by the public, differing significantly from earlier translations such as the Latin Vulgate, which was not readily comprehensible to the average layperson. This translation was revolutionary in several respects. It was the first English Bible to standardize verse numbers within the chapters, greatly facilitating the process of citation and cross-referencing, which was particularly useful for both preaching and scholarly study. Its format was also smaller, making it more portable and affordable, which was an innovation in an era when many Bibles were large, unwieldy volumes kept in churches. The Geneva Bible's influence extended well beyond its initial publication. It became the most widely used translation among English-speaking Protestants and was particularly dominant in the British Isles and later in the New World. The Pilgrims brought it with them on the Mayflower, and it remained influential in America throughout the early colonial period. Moreover, the linguistic style of the Geneva Bible has been credited with influencing English literature profoundly. Its phrases permeate the works of Shakespeare and other contemporary playwrights and poets, evidencing its widespread acceptance and use in public and private life.

However, the Geneva Bible was not without its controversies, particularly regarding its perceived ideological biases. The translation and its accompanying marginal notes were viewed by some, especially in the emerging Anglican Church and later under the Stuart monarchs, as politically and religiously charged. This perception led to the eventual commissioning of the King James Version in 1604, which sought to establish a more ecclesiastically neutral translation devoid of extensive commentary that could incite political or religious dissent. Despite being superseded by the King James Version in official use after 1611, the Geneva Bible remains a critical artifact in the study of biblical translations, Reformation history, and the development of early modern English literature. Its legacy underscores the complex interplay between religion, politics, and the dissemination of knowledge in shaping societal and cultural transformations.

The Apocrypha Section

The Apocrypha Section in the 1560 Geneva Bible represents a crucial and distinctive component of this seminal work, reflecting the complex interplay between Reformation theology, historical scholarship, and evolving religious practice. Its inclusion serves as a profound statement in the Protestant endeavor to reconcile the demands of a reformed doctrinal identity with the broader Christian heritage, illustrating the multifaceted implications for theology, liturgy, education, and historical understanding.

I. Theological Significance. The presence of the Apocrypha in the Geneva Bible embodies the intense debates over the canon of Scripture that animated the Reformation. Reformers associated with the Geneva Bible, deeply invested in purifying Christian practice through a return to scriptural foundations, grappled with the status of these texts. Unlike the texts of the Hebrew Bible, the Apocrypha was recognized for its moral and spiritual insights but was not universally accepted as canonical. The decision to include these books was not merely an acceptance of their historical use within

Christianity but a sophisticated acknowledgment of their potential to enrich Protestant theological discourse. By integrating the Apocrypha, the Geneva Bible provided a nuanced theological resource that offered expansive moral teachings and complex portrayals of faith under duress, which were seen as valuable for spiritual edification and ethical reflection.

II. Liturgical and Educational Impact

Liturgically, the Apocrypha had been integral to Christian worship within various traditions, notably within the Church of England. The Geneva Bible's inclusion of these texts helped maintain a liturgical continuity that was crucial for English exiles who were navigating the transition from traditional Catholic worship to reformed Protestant practice. This strategic inclusion helped soften the transition by preserving elements of the familiar spiritual and liturgical life, thus easing the cultural and spiritual shocks of reformation.

Educationally, the Apocrypha provided rich material for teaching a broad array of subjects from history and morality to sophisticated doctrinal concepts. Texts such as the Wisdom of Solomon and Sirach (Ecclesiasticus) complemented the canonical wisdom literature, offering layers of philosophical and ethical instruction that were valued in Protestant educational settings. Narratives like those found in Tobit and Judith, with their emphasis on piety, courage, and divine intervention, served as compelling pedagogical tools, offering narrative depth to the exploration of virtues in a way that resonated with contemporary experiences of persecution and moral challenge.

III. Historical and Cultural Context

The inclusion of the Apocrypha also mirrors the intellectual and cultural dynamism of the Renaissance, which influenced the Reformation's approach to scripture and tradition. This era was characterized by a critical reassessment of texts and traditions, fueled by humanistic scholarship and a more historiographical approach to ancient texts. Including the Apocrypha demonstrated the reformers' engagement with the full spectrum of Judeo-Christian tradition, asserting a continuity that validated the reformative project's historical and cultural legitimacy.

Broader Implications and Influence

For English Protestantism and beyond, the Geneva Bible, with its Apocrypha, became a cornerstone text, shaping the religious thoughts and practices of English-speaking Protestants globally. Its accessibility and the inclusion of these texts played a pivotal role in promoting biblical literacy and theological reflection among laypeople, offering a broader range of scriptural insights for personal devotion and communal worship.

In essence, the Apocrypha section of the Geneva Bible represents a vital engagement with the Christian textual tradition, reflecting both the reformative zeal of the new Protestant ethos and the continuity of older, broader Christian liturgical and educational practices. This balance not only contributed to the Geneva Bible's immense popularity and influence but also impacted the development of religious practice, education, and English literature, marking it as a key work in the religious and cultural history of the English-speaking world. This nuanced inclusion underscored the reformers' commitment to a faith that was both informed by tradition and invigorated by renewal, ensuring the Geneva Bible's status as a seminal text in Christian history.

The First Book of Esdras

The First Book of Esdras presents a unique rendition of Jewish history, particularly highlighting the epoch from the cessation of the Babylonian captivity to the nascent resettlement in Jerusalem under Cyrus the Great of Persia's edict. Regarded as apocryphal by the majority of Protestant denominations and all Jewish traditions, this text is nonetheless incorporated into the liturgies of the Eastern Orthodox Church and certain Anglican traditions, illustrating its diverse acceptance and canonical considerations. It revises and expands upon the narratives found in the canonical books of Ezra and Nehemiah by incorporating additional incidents and perspectives absent from the Hebrew Bible.

The narrative trajectory extends from the devout reforms instituted by King Josiah, through the calamitous devastation unleashed by Nebuchadnezzar, culminating in the Babylonian exile, and ultimately, the initial attempts to reconstruct the Temple in Jerusalem. This text serves not merely as a historical chronicle but also delves into profound theological themes of restoration and divine providence. It underscores the enduring mercy of God towards His people, in spite of their previous transgressions which precipitated their exile.

Theologically, the document explores the intricate dynamics of leadership and community life, epitomized by figures such as Zerubbabel and Ezra. These leaders spearhead the rejuvenation of the Jewish community and its religious observances. Within the liturgical context, especially noted during the Eastern Orthodox Church's Holy Week observances, it facilitates contemplations on repentance, spiritual renewal, and the symbiotic relationship between divine intervention and human action.

From a literary standpoint, the First Book of Esdras offers a comprehensive narrative that enriches our comprehension of the post-exilic Jewish community. It illuminates the ways Jewish sacred history was interpreted and reshaped in the Hellenistic milieu, providing critical insights into how Jewish traditions were transmitted and adapted beyond their initial Hebrew framework.

Historically, the inclusion of this text in the 1560 Geneva Bible marks it as a significant theological and cultural artifact, offering scholars and theologians a broader vista on a critical juncture in Jewish history and its subsequent interpretations. Its Greek origins and the editorial choices made in its composition reflect the complex interplay of cultural, religious, and political forces during its time of writing. This addition to the biblical canon enriches it by presenting an alternative perspective on pivotal events and theological themes fundamental to both Jewish and Christian traditions.

The First Book of Esdras

1 Josias held the Passover in Jerusalem to his Lord, and offered the Passover the fourteenth day of the first month, 2 having set the priests according to their daily courses, being arrayed in their vestments, in the Lord's temple. 3 He spoke to the Levites, the temple servants of Israel, that they should make themselves holy to the Lord, to set the holy ark of the Lord in the house that King Solomon the son of David had built. 4 He said, "You no longer need to carry it on your shoulders. Now therefore serve the Lord your God, and minister to his people Israel, and prepare yourselves by your fathers' houses and kindred, 5 according to the writing of King David of Israel, and according to the magnificence of Solomon his son. Stand in the holy place according to the divisions of your Levite families who minister in the presence of your kindred the descendants of Israel. 6 Offer the Passover in order, prepare the sacrifices for your kindred, and keep the Passover according to the Lord's commandment, which was given to Moses. 7 To the people which were present, Josias gave thirty thousand lambs and kids, and three thousand calves. These things were given from the king's possessions, as he promised, to the people and to the priests and Levites. 8 Helkias, Zacharias, and Esyelus, the rulers of the temple, gave to the priests for the Passover two thousand six hundred sheep, and three hundred calves. 9 Jeconias, Samaias, Nathanael his brother, Sabias, Ochielus, and Joram, captains over thousands, gave to the Levites for the Passover five thousand sheep and seven hundred calves. 10 When these things were done, the priests and Levites, having the unleavened bread, stood in proper order according to the kindred, 11 and according to the several divisions by fathers' houses, before the people, to offer to the Lord as it is written in the book of Moses. They did this in the morning. 12 They roasted the Passover lamb with fire, as required. They boiled the sacrifices in the brazen vessels and caldrons with a pleasing smell, 13 and set them before all the people. Afterward they prepared for themselves and for their kindred the priests, the sons of Aaron. 14 For the priests offered the fat until night. The

Levites prepared for themselves and for their kindred the priests, the sons of Aaron. ¹⁵ The holy singers also, the sons of Asaph, were in their order, according to the appointment of David: Asaph, Zacharias, and Eddinus, who represented the king. ¹⁶ Moreover the gatekeepers were at every gate. No one needed to depart from his daily duties, for their kindred the Levites prepared for them. ¹⁷ So the things that belonged to the Lord's sacrifices were accomplished in that day, in holding the Passover, ¹⁸ and offering sacrifices on the altar of the Lord, according to the commandment of King Josias. ¹⁹ So the children of Israel which were present at that time held the Passover and the feast of unleavened bread seven days. ²⁰ Such a Passover had not been held in Israel since the time of the prophet Samuel. ²¹ Indeed, none of the kings of Israel held such a Passover as Josias with the priests, the Levites, and the Jews, held with all Israel that were present in their dwelling place at Jerusalem. ²² This Passover was held in the eighteenth year of the reign of Josias. ²³ The works of Josias were upright before his Lord with a heart full of godliness. ²⁴ Moreover the things that came to pass in his days have been written in times past, concerning those who sinned and did wickedly against the Lord more than any other people or kingdom, and how they grieved him exceedingly, so that the Lord's words were confirmed against Israel. ²⁵ Now after all these acts of Josias, it came to pass that Pharaoh the king of Egypt came to make war at Carchemish on the Euphrates; and Josias went out against him. ²⁶ But the king of Egypt sent to him, saying, "What do I have to do with you, O king of Judea? ²⁷ I wasn't sent out from the Lord God against you, for my war is against the Euphrates. Now the Lord is with me, yes, the Lord is with me hastening me forward. Depart from me, and don't be against the Lord." ²⁸ However, Josias didn't turn back to his chariot, but tried to fight with him, not regarding the words of the prophet Jeremy from the Lord's mouth, ²⁹ but joined battle with him in the plain of Megiddo, and the commanders came down against King Josias. ³⁰ Then the king said to his servants, "Carry me away out of the battle, for I am very weak!" Immediately his servants carried him away out of the army. ³¹ Then he got into his second chariot. After he was brought back to Jerusalem he died, and was buried in the tomb of his ancestors. ³² All Judea mourned for Josias. Jeremy the prophet lamented for Josias, and the chief men with the women made lamentation for him to this day. This was given out for an ordinance to be done continually in all the nation of Israel. ³³ These things are written in the book of the histories of the kings of Judea, and every one of the acts that Josias did, and his glory, and his understanding in the law of the Lord, and the things that he had done before, and the things now told, are reported in the book of the kings of Israel and Judah. ³⁴ The people took Joachaz the son of Josias, and made him king instead of Josias his father, when he was twenty-three years old. ³⁵ He reigned in Judah and Jerusalem for three months Then the king of Egypt deposed him from reigning in Jerusalem. ³⁶ He set a tax upon the people of one hundred talents of silver and one talent of gold. ³⁷ The king of Egypt also made King Joakim his brother king of Judea and Jerusalem. ³⁸ And Joakim imprisoned the nobles and apprehended his brother Zarakes, and brought him up out of Egypt. ³⁹ Joakim was twenty-five years old when he began to reign in Judea and Jerusalem. He did that which was evil in the sight of the Lord. ⁴⁰ King Nabuchodonosor of Babylon came up against him, bound him with a chain of brass, and carried him to Babylon. ⁴¹ Nabuchodonosor also took some of the Lord's holy vessels, carried them away, and stored them in his own temple at Babylon. ⁴² But those things that are reported of him, and of his uncleanness and impiety, are written in the chronicles of the kings. ⁴³ Then Joakim his son reigned in his place. When he was made king, he was eighteen years old. ⁴⁴ He reigned three months and ten days in Jerusalem. He did that which was evil before the Lord. ⁴⁵ So after a year Nabuchodonosor sent and caused him to be brought to Babylon with the holy vessels of the Lord, ⁴⁶ and made Sedekias king of Judea and Jerusalem when he was twenty-one years old. He reigned eleven years. ⁴⁷ He also did that which was evil in the sight of the Lord, and didn't heed the words that were spoken by Jeremy the prophet from the Lord's mouth. ⁴⁸ After King Nabuchodonosor had made him to swear by the name of the Lord, he broke his oath and rebelled. Hardening his neck and his heart, he transgressed the laws of the Lord, the God of Israel. ⁴⁹ Moreover the governors of the people and of the priests did many things wickedly, exceeding all the defilements of all nations, and defiled the temple of the Lord, which was sanctified in Jerusalem. ⁵⁰ The God of their ancestors sent by his messenger to call them back, because he had compassion on them and on his dwelling place. ⁵¹ But they mocked his messengers. In the day when the Lord spoke, they scoffed at his prophets ⁵² until he, being angry with his people for their great ungodliness, commanded to bring up the kings of the Chaldeans against them. ⁵³ They killed their young men with the sword around their holy temple, and spared neither young man or young woman, old man or child; but he delivered all of them into their hands. ⁵⁴ They took all the holy vessels of the Lord, both great and small, with the treasure chests of the Lord's ark and the king's treasures, and carried them away to Babylon. ⁵⁵ They burned the Lord's house, broke down Jerusalem's walls, and burned its towers with fire. ⁵⁶ As for her glorious things, they didn't stop until they had brought them all to nothing. He carried the people who weren't slain with the sword to Babylon. ⁵⁷ They were servants to him and to his children until the Persians reigned, to fulfill the word of the Lord by the mouth of Jeremy: ⁵⁸ "Until the land has enjoyed its Sabbaths, the whole time of her desolation shall she keep Sabbath, to fulfil seventy years.

2

¹ In the first year of King Cyrus of the Persians, that the word of the Lord by the mouth of Jeremy might be accomplished, ² the Lord stirred up the spirit of King Cyrus of the Persians, and he made a proclamation throughout all his kingdom, and also by writing, ³ saying, "Cyrus king of the Persians says: The Lord of Israel, the Most High Lord, has made me king of the whole world, ⁴ and commanded me to build him a house at Jerusalem that is in Judea. ⁵ If therefore there are any of you that are of his people, let the Lord, even his Lord, be with him, and let him go up to Jerusalem that is in Judea, and build the house of the Lord of Israel. He is the Lord who dwells in Jerusalem. ⁶ Therefore, of those who dwell in various places, let those who are in his own place help each one with gold, with silver, ⁷ with gifts, with horses, and cattle, beside the

other things which have been added by vow for the temple of the Lord which is in Jerusalem. [8] Then the chief of the families of Judah and of the tribe of Benjamin stood up, with the priests, the Levites, and all whose spirit the Lord had stirred to go up, to build the house for the Lord which is in Jerusalem. [9] Those who lived around them helped them in all things with silver and gold, with horses and cattle, and with very many gifts that were vowed by a great number whose minds were so moved. [10] King Cyrus also brought out the holy vessels of the Lord, which Nabuchodonosor had carried away from Jerusalem and had stored in his temple of idols. [11] Now when King Cyrus of the Persians had brought them out, he delivered them to Mithradates his treasurer, [12] and by him they were delivered to Sanabassar the governor of Judea. [13] This was the number of them: one thousand gold cups, one thousand silver cups, twenty-nine silver censers, thirty gold bowls, two thousand four hundred ten silver bowls, and one thousand other vessels. [14] So all the vessels of gold and of silver were brought up, even five thousand four hundred seventy-nine, [15] and were carried back by Sanabassar, together with the returning exiles, from Babylon to Jerusalem. [16] In the time of King Artaxerxes of the Persians, Belemus, Mithradates, Tabellius, Rathumus, Beeltethmus, and Samellius the scribe, with their other associates, dwelling in Samaria and other places, wrote to him against those who lived in Judea and Jerusalem the following letter: [17] "To King Artaxerxes our Lord, from your servants, Rathumus the recorder, Samellius the scribe, and the rest of their council, and the judges who are in Coelesyria and Phoenicia: [18] Let it now be known to our lord the king, that the Jews that have come up from you to us, having come to Jerusalem, are building that rebellious and wicked city, and are repairing its marketplaces and walls, and are laying the foundation of a temple. [19] Now if this city is built and its walls are finished, they will not only refuse to give tribute, but will even stand up against kings. [20] Since the things pertaining to the temple are now in hand, we think it appropriate not to neglect such a matter, [21] but to speak to our lord the king, to the intent that, if it is your pleasure, search may be made in the books of your ancestors. 22 You will find in the chronicles what is written concerning these things, and will understand that that city was rebellious, troubling both kings and cities, 23 and that the Jews were rebellious, and kept starting wars there in the past. For this cause, this city was laid waste. 24 Therefore now we do declare to you, O lord the king, that if this city is built again, and its walls set up again, you will from then on have no passage into Coelesyria and Phoenicia." 25 Then the king wrote back again to Rathumus the recorder, Beeltethmus, Samellius the scribe, and to the rest that of their associates who lived in Samaria, Syria, and Phoenicia, as follows: 26 "I have read the letter which you have sent to me. Therefore I commanded to make search, and it has been found that that city of old time has fought against kings, 27 and the men were given to rebellion and war in it, and that mighty and fierce kings were in Jerusalem, who reigned and exacted tribute in Coelesyria and Phoenicia. 28 Now therefore I have commanded to prevent those men from building the city, and heed to be taken that there be nothing done contrary to this order, 29 and that those wicked doings proceed no further to the annoyance of kings." 30 Then King Artaxerxes, his letters being read, Rathumus, and Samellius the scribe, and the rest of their associates, went in haste to Jerusalem with cavalry and a multitude of people in battle array, and began to hinder the builders. So the building of the temple in Jerusalem ceased until the second year of the reign of King Darius of the Persians.

3

1 Now King Darius made a great feast for all his subjects, for all who were born in his house, for all the princes of Media and of Persia, 2 and for all the local governors and captains and governors who were under him, from India to Ethiopia, in the one hundred twenty-seven provinces. 3 They ate and drank, and when they were satisfied went home. Then King Darius went into his bedchamber slept, but awakened out of his sleep. 4 Then the three young men of the bodyguard, who guarded the king, spoke one to another: 5 "Let every one of us state what one thing is strongest. King Darius will give he whose statement seems wiser than the others great gifts and great honors in token of victory. 6 He shall be clothed in purple, drink from gold cups,

sleep on a gold bed, and have a chariot with bridles of gold, a fine linen turban, and a chain around his neck. ⁷ He shall sit next to Darius because of his wisdom, and shall be called cousin of Darius. ⁸ Then they each wrote his sentence, sealed them, and laid them under King Darius' pillow, ⁹ and said, "When the king wakes up, someone will give him the writing. Whoever the king and the three princes of Persia judge that his sentence is the wisest, to him shall the victory be given, as it is written." ¹⁰ The first wrote, "Wine is the strongest." ¹¹ The second wrote, "The king is strongest." ¹² The third wrote, "Women are strongest, but above all things Truth is the victor." ¹³ Now when the king woke up, they took the writing and gave it to him, so he read it. ¹⁴ Sending out, he called all the princes of Persia and of Media, the local governors, the captains, the governors, and the chief officers ¹⁵ and sat himself down in the royal seat of judgment; and the writing was read before them. ¹⁶ He said, "Call the young men, and they shall explain their own sentences. So they were called and came in. ¹⁷ They said to them, "Explain what you have written." Then the first, who had spoken of the strength of wine, began ¹⁸ and said this: "O sirs, how exceedingly strong wine is! It causes all men who drink it to go astray. ¹⁹ It makes the mind of the king and of the fatherless child to be the same, likewise of the bondman and of the freeman, of the poor man and of the rich. ²⁰ It also turns every thought into cheer and mirth, so that a man remembers neither sorrow nor debt. ²¹ It makes every heart rich, so that a man remembers neither king nor local governor. It makes people say things in large amounts. ²² When they are in their cups, they forget their love both to friends and kindred, and before long draw their swords. ²³ But when they awake from their wine, they don't remember what they have done. ²⁴ O sirs, isn't wine the strongest, seeing that it forces people to do this?" And when he had said this, he stopped speaking.

4

¹ Then the second, who had spoken of the strength of the king, began to say, ² "O sirs, don't men excel in strength who rule over the sea and land, and all things in them? ³ But yet the king is stronger. He is their lord and has dominion over them. In whatever he commands them,

they obey him. 4 If he tells them to make war the one against the other, they do it. If he sends them out against the enemies, they go, and conquer mountains, walls, and towers. 5 They kill and are killed, and don't disobey the king's commandment. If they win the victory, they bring everything to the king—all the plunder and everything else. 6 Likewise for those who are not soldiers, and don't have anything to do with wars, but farm, when they have reaped again that which they had sown, they bring some to the king and compel one another to pay tribute to the king. 7 He is just one man! If he commands people to kill, they kill. If he commands them to spare, they spare. 8 If he commands them to strike, they strike. If he commands them to make desolate, they make desolate. If he commands to build, they build. 9 If he commands them to cut down, they cut down. If he commands them to plant, they plant. 10 So all his people and his armies obey him. Furthermore, he lies down, he eats and drinks, and takes his rest; 11 and these keep watch around him. None of them may depart and do his own business. They don't disobey him in anything. 12 O sirs, how could the king not be the strongest, seeing that he is obeyed like this?" Then he stopped talking. 13 Then the third, who had spoken of women, and of truth, (this was Zorobabel) began to speak: 14 "O sirs, isn't the king great, and men are many, and isn't wine strong? Who is it then who rules them, or has the lordship over them? Aren't they women? 15 Women have given birth to the king and all the people who rule over sea and land. 16 They came from women. Women nourished up those who planted the vineyards, from where the wine comes. 17 Women also make garments for men. These bring glory to men. Without women, men can't exist. 18 Yes, and if men have gathered together gold and silver and any other beautiful thing, and see a woman who is lovely in appearance and beauty, 19 they let all those things go and gape at her, and with open mouth stare at her. They all have more desire for her than for gold, or silver, or any other beautiful thing. 20 A man leaves his own father who brought him up, leaves his own country, and joins with his wife. 21 With his wife he ends his days, with no thought for his father, mother, or country. 22 By this also you must know that women have dominion over you. Don't you labor and toil, and bring it all to give to women? 23 Yes, a man takes his sword and goes out to travel, to rob, to steal, and to sail on the sea and on rivers. 24 He sees a lion and walks in the darkness. When he has stolen, plundered, and robbed, he brings it to the woman he loves. 25 Therefore a man loves his wife better than father or mother. 26 Yes, there are many who have lost their minds for women, and become slaves for their sakes. 27 Many also have perished, have stumbled, and sinned, for women. 28 Now don't you believe me? Isn't the king great in his power? Don't all regions fear to touch him? 29 Yet I saw him and Apame the king's concubine, the daughter of the illustrious Barticus, sitting at the right hand of the king, 30 and taking the crown from the king's head, and setting it upon her own head. Yes, she struck the king with her left hand. 31 At this, the king gaped and gazed at her with open mouth. If she smiles at him, he laughs. But if she takes any displeasure at him, he flatters her, that she might be reconciled to him again. 32 O sirs, how can it not be that women are strong, seeing they do this?" 33 Then the king and the nobles looked at one another. So he began to speak concerning truth. 34 "O sirs, aren't women strong? The earth is great. The sky is high. The sun is swift in its course, for it circles around the sky, and returns on its course again in one day. 35 Isn't he who makes these things great? Therefore the truth is great, and stronger than all things. 36 All the earth calls upon truth, and the sky blesses truth. All works shake and tremble, but with truth there is no unrighteous thing. 37 Wine is unrighteous. The king is unrighteous. Women are unrighteous. All the children of men are unrighteous, and all their works are unrighteous. There is no truth in them. They shall also perish in their unrighteousness. 38 But truth remains, and is strong forever. Truth lives and conquers forevermore. 39 With truth there is no partiality toward persons or rewards, but truth does the things that are just, instead of any unrighteous or wicked things. All men approve truth's works. 40 In truth's judgment is not any unrighteousness. Truth is the strength, the kingdom, the power, and the majesty of all ages. Blessed be the God of truth!" 41 With that, he stopped speaking. Then all the people shouted and said, "Great is truth, and strong above all things!" 42 Then the king said to him, "Ask what you wish, even more than is appointed in writing, and we will give it to you, because you are found wisest. You shall sit next me, and shall be called my cousin." 43 Then he said to the king, "Remember your vow, which you vowed to build Jerusalem, in the day when you came to your kingdom, 44 and to send back all the vessels that were taken out of Jerusalem, which Cyrus set apart when he vowed to destroy Babylon, and vowed to send them back there. 45 You also vowed to build the temple which the Edomites burned when Judea was made desolate by the Chaldeans. 46 Now, O lord the king, this is what I request, and what I desire of you, and this is the princely generosity that may proceed from you: I ask therefore that you make good the vow, the performance of which you have vowed to the King of Heaven with your own mouth." 47 Then King Darius stood up, kissed him, and wrote letters for him to all the treasurers and governors and captains and local governors, that they should safely bring on their way both him, and all those who would go up with him to build Jerusalem. 48 He wrote letters also to all the governors who were in Coelesyria and Phoenicia, and to them in Libanus, that they should bring cedar wood from Libanus to Jerusalem, and that they should help him build the city. 49 Moreover he wrote for all the Jews who would go out of his realm up into Judea concerning their freedom, that no officer, no governor, no local governor, nor treasurer, should forcibly enter into their doors, 50 and that all the country which they occupied should be free to them without tribute, and that the Edomites should give up the villages of the Jews which they held at that time, 51 and that there should be given twenty talents yearly toward the building of the temple, until the time that it was built, 52 and another ten talents yearly for burnt offerings to be presented upon the altar every day, as they had a commandment to make seventeen offerings, 53 and that all those who would come from Babylonia to build the city should have their freedom—they and their descendants, and all the priests that came. 54 He wrote also to give them their support and the priests' vestments in which they minister. 55 For the Levites he wrote that their support should be given them until the day that the house was finished and Jerusalem built up. 56 He commanded that land and wages should be given to all who guarded the city. 57 He also sent away all the vessels from Babylon that Cyrus had set apart, and all that Cyrus had given in commandment, he commanded also to be done and to be sent to Jerusalem. 58 Now when this young man had gone out, he lifted up his face to heaven toward Jerusalem, and praised the King of heaven, 59 and said, "From you comes victory. From you comes wisdom. Yours is the glory, and I am your servant. 60 Blessed are you, who have given me wisdom. I give thanks to you, O Lord of our fathers. 61 So he took the letters, went out, came to Babylon, and told it all his kindred. 62 They praised the God of their ancestors, because he had given them freedom and liberty 63 to go up and to build Jerusalem and the temple which is called by his name. They feasted with instruments of music and gladness seven days.

5

1 After this, the chiefs of fathers' houses were chosen to go up according to their tribes, with their wives, sons, and daughters, with their menservants and maidservants, and their livestock. 2 Darius sent with them one thousand cavalry to bring them back to Jerusalem with peace, with musical instruments, drums, and flutes. 3 All their kindred were making merry, and he made them go up together with them. 4 These are the names of the men who went up, according to their families among their tribes after their several divisions. 5 The priests, the sons of Phinees, the sons of Aaron: Jesus the son of Josedek, the son of Saraias, and Joakim the son of Zorobabel, the son of Salathiel, of the house of David, of the lineage of Phares, of the tribe of Judah, 6 who spoke wise words before Darius the king of Persia in the second year of his reign, in the month Nisan, which is the first month. 7 These are the of Judeans who came up from the captivity, where they lived as foreigners, whom Nabuchodonosor the king of Babylon had carried away to Babylon. 8 They returned to Jerusalem and to the other parts of Judea, every man to his own city, who came with Zorobabel, with Jesus, Nehemias, Zaraias, Resaias, Eneneus, Mardocheus, Beelsarus, Aspharsus, Reelias, Roimus, and Baana, their leaders. 9 The number of them of the nation and their leaders: the sons of Phoros, two thousand one hundred seventy two; the sons of Saphat, four hundred seventy two; 10 the sons of Ares, seven

hundred fifty six; ¹¹ the sons of Phaath Moab, of the sons of Jesus and Joab, two thousand eight hundred twelve; ¹² the sons of Elam, one thousand two hundred fifty four; the sons of Zathui, nine hundred forty five; the sons of Chorbe, seven hundred five; the sons of Bani, six hundred forty eight; ¹³ the sons of Bebai, six hundred twenty three; the sons of Astad, one thousand three hundred twenty two; ¹⁴ the sons of Adonikam, six hundred sixty seven; the sons of Bagoi, two thousand sixty six; the sons of Adinu, four hundred fifty four; ¹⁵ the sons of Ater, of Ezekias, ninety two; the sons of Kilan and Azetas, sixty seven; the sons of Azaru, four hundred thirty two; ¹⁶ the sons off† Annis, one hundred one; the sons of Arom, the sons of Bassai, three hundred twenty three; the sons of Arsiphurith, one hundred twelve; ¹⁷ the sons of Baiterus, three thousand five; the sons of Bethlomon, one hundred twenty three; ¹⁸ those from Netophas, fifty five; those from Anathoth, one hundred fifty eight; those from Bethasmoth, forty two; ¹⁹ those from Kariathiarius, twenty five; those from Caphira and Beroth, seven hundred forty three; ²⁰ the Chadiasai and Ammidioi, four

hundred twenty two; those from Kirama and Gabbe, six hundred twenty one; ²¹ those from Macalon, one hundred twenty two; those from Betolion, fifty two; the sons of Niphis, one hundred fifty six; ²² the sons of Calamolalus and Onus, seven hundred twenty five; the sons of Jerechu, three hundred forty five; ²³ and the sons of Sanaas, three thousand three hundred thirty. ²⁴ The priests: the sons of Jeddu, the son of Jesus, among the sons of Sanasib, nine hundred seventy two; the sons of Emmeruth, one thousand fifty two; ²⁵ the sons of Phassurus, one thousand two hundred forty seven; and the sons of Charme, one thousand seventeen. ²⁶ The Levites: the sons of Jesus, Kadmiel, Bannas, and Sudias, seventy four. ²⁷ The holy singers: the sons of Asaph, one hundred twenty eight. ²⁸ The gatekeepers: the sons of Salum, the sons of Atar, the sons of Tolman, the sons of Dacubi, the sons of Ateta, the sons of Sabi, in all one hundred thirty nine. ²⁹ The temple servants: the sons of Esau, the sons of Asipha, the sons of Tabaoth, the sons of Keras, the sons of Sua, the sons of Phaleas, the sons of Labana, the sons of Aggaba. ³⁰ the sons of Acud, the sons of Uta, the sons of Ketab, the sons of Accaba, the sons of Subai, the sons of Anan, the sons of Cathua, the sons of Geddur, 31 the sons of Jairus, the sons of Daisan, the sons of Noeba, the sons of Chaseba, the sons of Gazera, the sons of Ozias, the sons of Phinoe, the sons of Asara, the sons of Basthai, the sons of Asana, the sons of Maani, the sons of Naphisi, the sons of Acub, the sons of Achipha, the sons of Asur, the sons of Pharakim, the sons of Basaloth, 32 the sons of Meedda, the sons of Cutha, the sons of Charea, the sons of Barchus, the sons of Serar, the sons of Thomei, the sons of Nasi, the sons of Atipha. 33 The sons of the servants of Solomon: the sons of Assaphioth, the sons of Pharida, the sons of Jeeli, the sons of Lozon, the sons of Isdael, the sons of Saphuthi, 34 the sons of Agia, the sons of Phacareth, the sons of Sabie, the sons of Sarothie, the sons of Masias, the sons of Gas, the sons of Addus, the sons of Subas, the sons of Apherra, the sons of Barodis, the sons of Saphat, the sons of Allon. 35 All the temple-servants and the sons of the servants of Solomon were three hundred seventy two. 36 These came up from Thermeleth, and Thelersas, Charaathalan leading them, and Allar; 37 and they could not show

their families, nor their stock, how they were of Israel: the sons of Dalan the son of Ban, the sons of Nekodan, six hundred fifty two. 38 Of the priests, those who usurped the office of the priesthood and were not found: the sons of Obdia, the sons of Akkos, the sons of Jaddus, who married Augia one of the daughters of Zorzelleus, and was called after his name. 39 When the description of the kindred of these men was sought in the register and was not found, they were removed from executing the office of the priesthood; 40 for Nehemias and Attharias told them that they should not be partakers of the holy things until a high priest wearing Urim and Thummim should arise. 41 So all those of Israel, from twelve years old and upward, beside menservants and women servants, were in number forty two thousand three hundred sixty. 42 Their menservants and handmaids were seven thousand three hundred thirty and seven; the minstrels and singers, two hundred forty five; 43 four hundred thirty and five camels, seven thousand thirty six horses, two hundred forty five mules, and five thousand five hundred twenty five beasts of burden. 44 And some of the chief men of their families, when they came to the temple of God that is in Jerusalem, vowed to set up the house again in its own place according to their ability, ⁴⁵ and to give into the holy treasury of the works one thousand minas of gold, five thousand minas of silver, and one hundred priestly vestments. ⁴⁶ The priests and the Levites and some of the people lived in Jerusalem and the country. The holy singers also and the gatekeepers and all Israel lived in their villages. ⁴⁷ But when the seventh month was at hand, and when the children of Israel were each in their own place, they all came together with one purpose into the broad place before the first porch which is toward the east. ⁴⁸ Then Jesus the son of Josedek, his kindred the priests, Zorobabel the son of Salathiel, and his kindred stood up and made the altar of the God of Israel ready ⁴⁹ to offer burned sacrifices upon it, in accordance with the express commands in the book of Moses the man of God. ⁵⁰ Some people joined them out of the other nations of the land, and they erected the altar upon its own place, because all the nations of the land were hostile to them and oppressed them; and they offered sacrifices at the proper times and burnt offerings to the Lord both morning and evening. ⁵¹ They also held the feast of tabernacles, as it is commanded in the law, and offered sacrifices daily, as appropriate. ⁵² After that, they offered the continual oblations and the sacrifices of the Sabbaths, of the new moons, and of all the consecrated feasts. ⁵³ All those who had made any vow to God began to offer sacrifices to God from the new moon of the seventh month, although the temple of God was not yet built. ⁵⁴ They gave money, food, and drink to the masons and carpenters. ⁵⁵ They also gave carts to the people of Sidon and Tyre, that they should bring cedar trees from Libanus, and convey them in rafts to the harbor of Joppa, according to the commandment which was written for them by Cyrus king of the Persians. ⁵⁶ In the second year after his coming to the temple of God at Jerusalem, in the second month, Zorobabel the son of Salathiel, Jesus the son of Josedek, their kindred, the Levitical priests, and all those who had come to Jerusalem out of the captivity began work. ⁵⁷ They laid the foundation of God's temple on the new moon of the second month, in the second year after they had come to Judea and

Jerusalem. [58] They appointed the Levites who were at least twenty years old over the Lord's works. Then Jesus, with his sons and kindred, Kadmiel his brother, the sons of Jesus, Emadabun, and the sons of Jada the son of Iliadun, and their sons and kindred, all the Levites, with one accord stood up and started the business, laboring to advance the works in the house of God. So the builders built the Lord's temple. [59] The priests stood arrayed in their vestments with musical instruments and trumpets, and the Levites the sons of Asaph with their cymbals, [60] singing songs of thanksgiving and praising the Lord, according to the directions of King David of Israel. [61] They sang aloud, praising the Lord in songs of thanksgiving, because his goodness and his glory are forever in all Israel. [62] All the people sounded trumpets and shouted with a loud voice, singing songs of thanksgiving to the Lord for the raising up of the Lord's house. [63] Some of the Levitical priests and of the heads of their families, the elderly who had seen the former house came to the building of this one with lamentation and great weeping. [64] But many with trumpets and joy shouted with a loud voice, [65] so that the people couldn't hear the trumpets for the weeping of the people, for the multitude sounded loudly, so that it was heard far away. [66] Therefore when the enemies of the tribe of Judah and Benjamin heard it, they came to know what that noise of trumpets meant. [67] They learned that those who returned from captivity built the temple for the Lord, the God of Israel. [68] So they went to Zorobabel and Jesus, and to the chief men of the families, and said to them, "We will build together with you. [69] For we, just like you, obey your Lord, and sacrifice to him from the days of King Asbasareth of the Assyrians, who brought us here." [70] Then Zorobabel, Jesus and the chief men of the families of Israel said to them, "It is not for you to build the house for the Lord our God. [71] We ourselves alone will build for the Lord of Israel, as King Cyrus of the Persians has commanded us." [72] But the heathen of the land pressed hard upon the inhabitants of Judea, cut off their supplies, and hindered their building. [73] By their secret plots, and popular persuasions and commotions, they hindered the finishing of the building all the time that King Cyrus lived. So they were hindered from building for two years, until the reign of Darius.

6

¹ Now in the second year of the reign of Darius, Aggaeus and Zacharius the son of Addo, the prophets, prophesied to the Jews in Judea and Jerusalem in the name of the Lord, the God of Israel. ² Then Zorobabel the son of Salathiel and Jesus the son of Josedek stood up and began to build the house of the Lord at Jerusalem, the prophets of the Lord being with them and helping them. ³ At the same time Sisinnes the governor of Syria and Phoenicia came to them, with Sathrabuzanes and his companions, and said to them, ⁴ "By whose authority do you build this house and this roof, and perform all the other things? Who are the builders who do these things?" ⁵ Nevertheless, the elders of the Jews obtained favor, because the Lord had visited the captives; ⁶ and they were not hindered from building until such time as communication was made to Darius concerning them, and his answer received. ⁷ A copy of the letter which Sisinnes, governor of Syria and Phoenicia, and Sathrabuzanes, with their companions, the rulers in Syria and Phoenicia, wrote and sent to Darius: ⁸ "To King Darius, greetings. Let it be fully known to our lord the king, that having come into the country of Judea, and entered into the city of Jerusalem, we found in the city of Jerusalem the elders of the Jews that were of the captivity ⁹ building a great new house for the Lord of hewn and costly stones, with timber laid in the walls. ¹⁰ Those works are being done with great speed. The work goes on prosperously in their hands, and it is being accomplished with all glory and diligence. ¹¹ Then asked we these elders, saying, 'By whose authority are you building this house and laying the foundations of these works?' ¹² Therefore, to the intent that we might give knowledge to you by writing who were the leaders, we questioned them, and we required of them the names in writing of their principal men. ¹³ So they gave us this answer, 'We are the servants of the Lord who made heaven and earth. ¹⁴ As for this house, it was built many years ago by a great and strong king of Israel, and was finished. ¹⁵ But when our fathers sinned against the Lord of Israel who is in heaven, and provoked him to wrath, he gave them over into the hands of King Nabuchodonosor of Babylon,

king of the Chaldeans. ¹⁶ They pulled down the house, burned it, and carried away the people captive to Babylon. ¹⁷ But in the first year that Cyrus reigned over the country of Babylon, King Cyrus wrote that this house should be rebuilt. ¹⁸ The holy vessels of gold and of silver that Nabuchodonosor had carried away out of the house at Jerusalem and had set up in his own temple, those King Cyrus brought out of the temple in Babylonia, and they were delivered to Zorobabel and to Sanabassarus the governor, ¹⁹ with commandment that he should carry away all these vessels, and put them in the temple at Jerusalem, and that the Lord's temple should be built on its site. ²⁰ Then Sanabassarus, having come here, laid the foundations of the Lord's house which is in Jerusalem. From that time to this we are still building. It is not yet fully completed.' ²¹ Now therefore, if it seems good, O king, let a search be made among the royal archives of our lord the king that are in Babylon. ²² If it is found that the building of the house of the Lord which is in Jerusalem has been done with the consent of King Cyrus, and it seems good to our lord the king, let him send us directions concerning these things." ²³ Then King Darius commanded that a search be made among the archives that were laid up at Babylon. So at Ekbatana the palace, which his in the country of Media, a scroll was found where these things were recorded: ²⁴ "In the first year of the reign of Cyrus, King Cyrus commanded to build up the house of the Lord which is in Jerusalem, where they sacrifice with continual fire. ²⁵ Its height shall be sixty cubits, and the breadth sixty cubits, with three rows of hewn stones, and one row of new wood from that country. Its expenses are to be given out of the house of King Cyrus. ²⁶ The holy vessels of the house of the Lord, both gold and silver, that Nabuchodonosor took out of the house at Jerusalem and carried away to Babylon, should be restored to the house at Jerusalem, and be set in the place where they were before." ²⁷ Also he commanded that Sisinnes the governor of Syria and Phoenicia, and Sathrabuzanes, and their companions, and those who were appointed rulers in Syria and Phoenicia, should be careful not to meddle with the place, but allow Zorobabel, the servant of the Lord, and governor of Judea, and the elders of the Jews, to build that house of the Lord in its place. 28 "I also command to have it built up whole again; and that they look diligently to help those who are of the captivity of Judea, until the house of the Lord is finished, 29 and that out of the tribute of Coelesyria and Phoenicia a portion shall be carefully given to these men for the sacrifices of the Lord, that is, to Zorobabel the governor for bulls, rams, and lambs, 30 and also corn, salt, wine and oil, and that continually every year without further question, according as the priests who are in Jerusalem may direct to be daily spent, 31 that drink offerings may be made to the Most High God for the king and for his children, and that they may pray for their lives." 32 He commanded that whoever should transgress, yes, or neglect anything written here, a beam shall be taken out of his own house, and he shall be hanged on it, and all his goods seized for the king. 33 "Therefore may the Lord, whose name is called upon there, utterly destroy every king and nation that stretches out his hand to hinder or damage that house of the Lord in Jerusalem. 34 I, King Darius have ordained that these things be done with diligence."

7

1 Then Sisinnes the governor of Coelesyria and Phoenicia, and Sathrabuzanes, with their companions, following the commandments of King Darius, 2 very carefully supervised the holy work, assisting the elders of the Jews and rulers of the temple. 3 So the holy work prospered, while Aggaeus and Zacharias the prophets prophesied. 4 They finished these things by the commandment of the Lord, the God of Israel, and with the consent of Cyrus, Darius, and Artaxerxes, kings of the Persians. 5 So the holy house was finished by the twenty-third day of the month Adar, in the sixth year of King Darius. 6 The children of Israel, the priests, the Levites, and the others who returned from captivity who joined them did what was written in the book of Moses. 7 For the dedication of the Lord's temple, they offered one hundred bulls, two hundred rams, four hundred lambs, 8 and twelve male goats for the sin of all Israel, according to the number of the twelve princes of the tribes of Israel. 9 The priests and the Levites stood arrayed in their vestments, according to their kindred, for the services of the Lord, the God of Israel,

according to the book of Moses. The gatekeepers were at every gate. [10] The children of Israel who came out of captivity held the Passover the fourteenth day of the first month, when the priests and the Levites were sanctified together, [11] with all those who returned from captivity; for they were sanctified. For the Levites were all sanctified together, [12] and they offered the Passover for all who returned from captivity, for their kindred the priests, and for themselves. [13] The children of Israel who came out of the captivity ate, even all those who had separated themselves from the abominations of the heathen of the land, and sought the Lord. [14] They kept the feast of unleavened bread seven days, rejoicing before the Lord, [15] because he had turned the counsel of the king of Assyria toward them, to strengthen their hands in the works of the Lord, the God of Israel.

8

[1] After these things, when Artaxerxes the king of the Persians reigned, Esdras came, who was the son of Azaraias, the son of Zechrias, the son of Helkias, the son of Salem, [2] the son of Sadduk, the son of Ahitob, the son of Amarias, the son of Ozias,† the son of Memeroth, the son of Zaraias, the son of Savias, the son of Boccas, the son of Abisne, the son of Phinees, the son of Eleazar, the son of Aaron, the chief priest. [3] This Esdras went up from Babylon as a skilled scribe in the law of Moses, which was given by the God of Israel. [4] The king honored him, for he found favor in his sight in all his requests. [5] There went up with him also some of the children of Israel, and of the priests, Levites, holy singers, gatekeepers, and temple servants to Jerusalem [6] in the seventh year of the reign of Artaxerxes, in the fifth month (this was the king's seventh year); for they left Babylon on the new moon of the first month and came to Jerusalem, by the prosperous journey which the Lord gave them‡ for his sake. [7] For Esdras had very great skill, so that he omitted nothing of the law and commandments of the Lord, but taught all Israel the ordinances and judgments. [8] Now the commission, which was written from King Artaxerxes, came to Esdras the priest and reader of the law of the Lord, was as follows: [9] "King Artaxerxes to Esdras the priest and reader of the law of the Lord, greetings. [10] Having determined to deal

graciously, I have given orders that those of the nation of the Jews, and of the priests and Levites, and of those within our realm who are willing and freely choose to, should go with you to Jerusalem. 11 As many therefore as are so disposed, let them depart with you, as it has seemed good both to me and my seven friends the counselors, 12 that they may look to the affairs of Judea and Jerusalem, in accordance with what is in the Lord's law, 13 and carry the gifts to the Lord of Israel to Jerusalem, which I and my friends have vowed, and that all the gold and silver that can be found in the country of Babylonia for the Lord in Jerusalem, 14 with that also which is given of the people for the temple of the Lord their God that is at Jerusalem, be collected: even the gold and silver for bulls, rams, and lambs, and what goes with them, 15 to the end that they may offer sacrifices to the Lord upon the altar of the Lord their God, which is in Jerusalem. 16 Whatever you and your kindred decide to do with gold and silver, do that according to the will of your God. 17 The holy vessels of the Lord, which are given you for the use of the temple of your God, which is in Jerusalem, 18 and whatever else

you shall remember for the use of the temple of your God, you shall give it out of the king's treasury. 19 I, King Artaxerxes, have also commanded the keepers of the treasures in Syria and Phoenicia, that whatever Esdras the priest and reader of the law of the Most High God shall send for, they should give it to him with all diligence, 20 to the sum of one hundred talents of silver, likewise also of wheat even to one hundred cors, and one hundred firkins of wine, and salt in abundance. 21 Let all things be performed after God's law diligently to the most high God, that wrath come not upon the kingdom of the king and his sons. 22 I command you also that no tax, nor any other imposition, be laid upon any of the priests, or Levites, or holy singers, or gatekeepers, or temple servants, or any that have employment in this temple, and that no man has authority to impose any tax on them. 23 You, Esdras, according to the wisdom of God, ordain judges and justices that they may judge in all Syria and Phoenicia all those who know the law of your God; and those who don't know it, you shall teach. 24 Whoever transgresses the law of your God and of the king shall be punished diligently, whether it be by death, or other punishment, by penalty of money, or by imprisonment." 25 Then Esdras the scribe said, "Blessed be the only Lord, the God of my fathers, who has put these things into the heart of the king, to glorify his house that is in Jerusalem, 26 and has honored me in the sight of the king, his counselors, and all his friends and nobles. 27 Therefore I was encouraged by the help of the Lord my God, and gathered together out of Israel men to go up with me. 28These are the chief according to their families and their several divisions, who went up with me from Babylon in the reign of King Artaxerxes: 29 of the sons of Phinees, Gerson; of the sons of Ithamar, Gamael; of the sons of David, Attus† the son of Sechenias; 30 of the sons of Phoros, Zacharais; and with him were counted one hundred fifty men; 31 of the sons of Phaath Moab, Eliaonias the son of Zaraias, and with him two hundred men; 32 of the sons of Zathoes, Sechenias the son of Jezelus, and with him three hundred men; of the sons of Adin, Obeth the son of Jonathan, and with him two hundred fifty men; 33 of the sons of Elam, Jesias son of Gotholias, and with him seventy men; 34 of the sons of Saphatias, Zaraias son of Michael, and with him seventy men; 35 of the sons of Joab, Abadias son of Jehiel. Jezelus, and with him two hundred twelve men; 36 of the sons of Banias, Salimoth son of Josaphias, and with him one hundred sixty men; 37 of the sons of Babi, Zacharias son of Bebai, and with him twenty-eight men; 38 of the sons of Azgad: Astath, Joannes son of Hakkatan Akatan, and with him one hundred ten men; 39 of the sons of Adonikam, the last, and these are the names of them, Eliphalat, Jeuel, and Samaias, and with them seventy men; 40 of the sons of Bago, Uthi the son of Istalcurus, and with him seventy men. 41 I gathered them together to the river called Theras. There we pitched our tents three days, and I inspected them. 42 When I had found there none of the priests and Levites, 43 then sent I to Eleazar, Iduel, Maasmas, 44 Elnathan, Samaias, Joribus, Nathan, Ennatan, Zacharias, and Mosollamus, principal men and men of understanding. 45 I asked them to go to Loddeus the captain, who was in the place of the treasury, 46 and commanded them that they should speak to Loddeus, to his kindred, and to the treasurers in that place, to send us such men as might execute the priests' office in our

Lord's house. ⁴⁷ By the mighty hand of our Lord, they brought to us men of understanding of the sons of Mooli the son of Levi, the son of Israel, Asebebias, and his sons, and his kindred, who were eighteen, ⁴⁸ and† Asebias, Annuus, and Osaias his brother, of the sons of Chanuneus, and their sons were twenty men; ⁴⁹ and of the temple servants whom David and the principal men had appointed for the servants of the Levites, two hundred twenty temple servants. The list of all their names was reported. ⁵⁰ There I vowed a fast for the young men before our Lord, to seek from him a prosperous journey both for us and for our children and livestock that were with us; ⁵¹ for I was ashamed to ask of the king infantry, cavalry, and an escort for protection against our adversaries. ⁵² For we had said to the king that the power of our Lord would be with those who seek him, to support them in all ways. ⁵³ Again we prayed to our lord about these things, and found him to be merciful. ⁵⁴ Then I set apart twelve men of the chiefs of the priests, Eserebias, Assamias, and ten men of their kindred with them. ⁵⁵ I weighed out to them the silver, the gold, and the holy vessels of the house of our Lord, which the king, his counselors, the nobles, and all Israel had given. ⁵⁶ When I had weighed it, I delivered to them six hundred fifty talents of silver, silver vessels weighing one hundred talents, one hundred talents of gold, ⁵⁷ twenty golden vessels, and twelve vessels of brass, even of fine brass, glittering like gold. ⁵⁸ I said to them, "You are holy to the Lord, the vessels are holy, and the gold and the silver are a vow to the Lord, the Lord of our fathers. ⁵⁹ Watch and keep them until you deliver them to the chiefs of the priests and Levites, and to the principal men of the families of Israel in Jerusalem, in the chambers of our Lord's house. ⁶⁰ So the priests and the Levites who received the silver, the gold, and the vessels which were in Jerusalem, brought them into the temple of the Lord. ⁶¹ We left the river Theras on the twelfth day of the first month. We came to Jerusalem by the mighty hand of our Lord which was upon us. The Lord delivered us from from every enemy on the way, and so we came to Jerusalem. ⁶² When we had been there three days, the silver and gold was weighed and delivered in our Lord's house on the fourth day to Marmoth the priest the son of† Urias. ⁶³ With him was Eleazar the son of

Phinees, and with them were Josabdus the son of Jesus and Moeth the son of Sabannus, the Levites. All was delivered to them by number and weight. 64 All the weight of them was recorded at the same hour. 65 Moreover those who had come out of captivity offered sacrifices to the Lord, the God of Israel, even twelve bulls for all Israel, ninety-six rams, 66 seventy-two lambs, and twelve goats for a peace offering—all of them a sacrifice to the Lord. 67 They delivered the king's commandments to the king's stewards and to the governors of Coelesyria and Phoenicia; and they honored the people and the temple of the Lord. 68 Now when these things were done, the principal men came to me and said, 69 "The nation of Israel, the princes, the priests, and the Levites haven't put away from themselves the foreign people of the land nor the uncleannesses of the Gentiles—the Canaanites, Hittites, Pherezites, Jebusites, Moabites, Egyptians, and Edomites. 70For both they and their sons have married with their daughters, and the holy seed is mixed with the foreign people of the land. From the beginning of this matter the rulers and the nobles have been partakers of this iniquity." 71 And as soon as I had heard these things, I tore my clothes and my holy garment, and plucked the hair from off my head and beard, and sat down sad and full of heaviness. 72 So all those who were moved at the word of the Lord, the God of Israel, assembled to me while I mourned for the iniquity, but I sat still full of heaviness until the evening sacrifice. 73 Then rising up from the fast with my clothes and my holy garment torn, and bowing my knees and stretching out my hands to the Lord, 74 I said, "O Lord, I am ashamed and confounded before your face, 75 for our sins are multiplied above our heads, and our errors have reached up to heaven 76 ever since the time of our fathers. We are in great sin, even to this day. 77 For our sins and our fathers' we with our kindred, our kings, and our priests were given up to the kings of the earth, to the sword, and to captivity, and for a prey with shame, to this day. 78 Now in some measure mercy has been shown to us from you, O Lord, that there should be left us a root and a name in the place of your sanctuary, 79 and to uncover a light in the house of the Lord our God, and to give us food in the time of our servitude. 80 Yes, when we were in bondage, we were not forsaken by our Lord, but he gave us favor before the kings of Persia, so that they gave us food, ⁸¹ glorified the temple of our Lord, and raised up the desolate Zion, to give us a sure dwelling in Judea and Jerusalem. ⁸² "Now, O Lord, what shall we say, having these things? For we have transgressed your commandments which you gave by the hand of your servants the prophets, saying, ⁸³ 'The land, which you enter into to possess as an inheritance, is a land polluted with the pollutions of the foreigners of the land, and they have filled it with their uncleanness. ⁸⁴ Therefore now you shall not join your daughters to their sons, neither shall you take their daughters for your sons. ⁸⁵ You shall never seek to have peace with them, that you may be strong, and eat the good things of the land, and that you may leave it for an inheritance to your children for evermore.' ⁸⁶ All that has happened is done to us for our wicked works and great sins, for you, O Lord, made our sins light, ⁸⁷ and gave to us such a root; but we have turned back again to transgress your law in mingling ourselves with the uncleanness of the heathen of the land. ⁸⁸ You weren't angry with us to destroy us until you had left us neither root, seed, nor name. ⁸⁹ O Lord of Israel, you are true, for we are left a root this day. ⁹⁰Behold, now we are before you in our iniquities, for we can't stand any longer before you because of these things." ⁹¹ As Esdras in his prayer made his confession, weeping, and lying flat on the ground before the temple, a very great throng of men, women, and children gathered to him from Jerusalem; for there was great weeping among the multitude. ⁹² Then Jechonias the son of Jeelus, one of the sons of Israel, called out, and said, "O Esdras, we have sinned against the Lord God, we have married foreign women of the heathen of the land, but there is still hope for Israel. ⁹³ Let's make an oath to the Lord about this, that we will put away all our foreign wives with their children, ⁹⁴ as seems good to you, and to as many as obey the Lord's Law. ⁹⁵ Arise, and take action, for this is your task, and we will be with you to do valiantly." ⁹⁶ So Esdras arose, and took an oath from the chief of the priests and Levites of all Israel to do these things; and they swore to it.

9

¹ Then Esdras rose up from the court of the temple and went to the chamber of Jonas the son of

Eliasib, 2 and lodged there, and ate no bread and drank no water, mourning for the great iniquities of the multitude. 3 A proclamation was made in all Judea and Jerusalem to all those who returned from captivity, that they should be gathered together at Jerusalem, 4 and that whoever didn't meet there within two or three days, in accordance with the ruling of the elders, that their livestock would be seized for the use of the temple, and they would be expelled from the multitude of those who returned from captivity 5 Within three days, all those of the tribe of Judah and Benjamin gathered together at Jerusalem. This was the ninth month, on the twentieth day of the month. 6 All the multitude sat together shivering in the broad place before the temple because of the present foul weather. 7 So Esdras arose up and said to them, "You have transgressed the law and married foreign wives, increasing the sins of Israel. 8 Now make confession and give glory to the Lord, the God of our fathers, 9 and do his will, and separate yourselves from the heat of the land, and from the foreign women." 10 Then the whole multitude cried out, and said with a loud voice, "Just as you have spoken, so we will do. 11 But because the multitude is great, and it is foul weather, so that we can't stand outside, and this is not a work of one day or two, seeing our sin in these things has spread far, 12 therefore let the rulers of the multitude stay, and let all those of our settlements that have foreign wives come at the time appointed, 13 and with them the rulers and judges of every place, until we turn away the wrath of the Lord from us for this matter." 14 So Jonathan the son of Azael and Ezekias the son of Thocanus took the matter on themselves. Mosollamus and Levis and Sabbateus were judges with them. 15 Those who returned from captivity did according to all these things. 16 Esdras the priest chose for himself principal men of their families, all by name. On the new moon of the tenth month they met together to examine the matter. 17 So their cases of men who had foreign wives was brought to an end by the new moon of the first month. 18 Of the priests who had come together and had foreign wives, there were found 19 of the sons of Jesus the son of Josedek, and his kindred, Mathelas, Eleazar, and Joribus, and Joadanus. 20 They gave their hands to put away their wives, and to offer rams to make reconciliation for their error. 21 Of the sons of Emmer: Ananias, Zabdeus, Manes, Sameus, Hiereel, and Azarias. 22 Of the sons of Phaisur: Elionas, Massias, Ishmael, Nathanael, Ocidelus, and Saloas. 23 Of the Levites: Jozabdus, Semeis, Colius who was called Calitas, Patheus, Judas, and Jonas. 24 Of the holy singers: Eliasibus and Bacchurus. 25 Of the gatekeepers: Sallumus and Tolbanes. 26 Of Israel, of the sons of Phoros: Hiermas, Ieddias, Melchias, Maelus, Eleazar, Asibas, and Banneas. 27 Of the sons of Ela: Matthanias, Zacharias, Jezrielus, Oabdius, Hieremoth, and Aedias. 28 Of the sons of Zamoth: Eliadas, Eliasimus, Othonias, Jarimoth, Sabathus, and Zardeus. 29 Of the sons of Bebai: Joannes, Ananias, Jozabdus, and Ematheis. 30 Of the sons of Mani: Olamus, Mamuchus, Jedeus, Jasubas, Jasaelus, and Hieremoth. 31 Of the sons of Addi: Naathus, Moossias, Laccunus, Naidus, Matthanias, Sesthel, Balnuus, and Manasseas. 32 Of the sons of Annas: Elionas, Aseas, Melchias, Sabbeus, and Simon Chosameus. 33 Of the sons of Asom: Maltanneus, Mattathias, Sabanneus, Eliphalat, Manasses, and Semei. 34 Of the sons of Baani: Jeremias, Momdis, Ismaerus, Juel, Mamdai, Pedias, Anos, Carabasion, Enasibus, Mamnitamenus, Eliasis, Bannus, Eliali, Someis, Selemias, and Nathanias. Of the sons of Ezora: Sesis, Ezril, Azaelus, Samatus, Zambri, and Josephus. 35 Of the sons of Nooma: Mazitias, Zabadeas, Edos, Juel, and Banaias. 36 All these had taken foreign wives, and they put them away with their children. 37 The priests and Levites, and those who were of Israel, lived in Jerusalem and in the country, on the new moon of the seventh month, and the children of Israel in their settlements. 38 The whole multitude gathered together with one accord into the broad place before the porch of the temple toward the east. 39 They said to Esdras the priest and reader, "Bring the law of Moses that was given by the Lord, the God of Israel." 40 So Esdras the chief priest brought the law to the whole multitude both of men and women, and to all the priests, to hear the law on the new moon of the seventh month. 41 He read in the broad place before the porch of the temple from morning until midday, before both men and women; and all the multitude gave attention to the law. 42 Esdras the priest and reader of the law stood up upon the pulpit of wood which had been prepared. ⁴³ Beside him stood Mattathias, Sammus, Ananias, Azarias, Urias, Ezekias, and Baalsamus on the right hand, ⁴⁴ and on his left hand, Phaldeus, Misael, Melchias, Lothasubus, Nabarias, and Zacharias. ⁴⁵ Then Esdras took the book of the law before the multitude, and sat honorably in the first place before all. ⁴⁶ When he opened the law, they all stood straight up. So Esdras blessed the Lord God Most High, the God of armies, the Almighty. ⁴⁷ All the people answered, "Amen." Lifting up their hands, they fell to the ground and worshiped the Lord. ⁴⁸ Also Jesus, Annus, Sarabias, Iadinus, Jacubus, Sabateus, Auteas, Maiannas, Calitas, Azarias, Jozabdus, Ananias, and Phalias, the Levites, taught the law of the Lord, ‡and read to the multitude the law of the Lord, explaining what was read. ⁴⁹ Then Attharates said to Esdras the chief priest and reader, and to the Levites who taught the multitude, even to all, ⁵⁰ "This day is holy to the Lord—now they all wept when they heard the law— ⁵¹ go then, eat the fat, drink the sweet, and send portions to those who have nothing; ⁵² for the day is holy to the Lord. Don't be sorrowful, for the Lord will bring you to honor." ⁵³ So the Levites commanded all things to the people, saying, "This day is holy. Don't be sorrowful." ⁵⁴ Then they went their way, every one to eat, drink, enjoy themselves, to give portions to those who had nothing, and to rejoice greatly, ⁵⁵ because they understood the words they were instructed with, and for which they had been assembled.

The Second Book of Esdras

The Second Book of Esdras, found within the Apocrypha of the Geneva Bible 1560, stands out as a profound narrative enriched with apocalyptic visions and theological reflections. This text, traditionally attributed to Ezra, a scribe and a priest, delves into profound questions concerning God's justice, the suffering of the righteous, and the hidden ways in which divine providence unfolds. It is composed in the aftermath of the Babylonian exile, offering a meditation on the challenges faced by the Jewish people during these tumultuous times.

The book is structured as a series of seven visions, which are both grand in scope and rich in symbolic imagery. These visions convey the deep inner turmoil of the prophet as he grapples with the destruction of Jerusalem, the desolation of the Holy Temple, and the moral decay he perceives within the community of the exiles. Through dialogues between Ezra and angelic beings, the text explores themes of judgment, redemption, and the eventual restoration of Israel.

Significantly, the Second Book of Esdras also addresses the broader human condition, pondering the purpose of human existence and the ultimate fate of the soul. It challenges believers to remain steadfast in their faith amidst adversity and to maintain hope in the promise of salvation. This eschatological focus is intertwined with practical wisdom and ethical imperatives, urging the community to adhere to the laws and statutes that govern righteous living according to the covenant.

In its entirety, the Second Book of Esdras not only serves as a theological anchor in times of crisis but also provides a bridge connecting prophetic traditions with the apocalyptic literature that influenced early Christian thought. Its inclusion in the Geneva Bible highlights its importance for contemporary spiritual reflection and its enduring appeal to readers seeking solace and understanding in the face of existential challenges.

The Second Book of Esdras

1 The second book of the prophet Esdras, the son of Saraias, the son of Azaraias, the son of Helkias, the son of Salemas, the son of Sadoc, the son of Ahitob, 2 the son of Achias, the son of Phinees, the son of Heli, the son of Amarias, the son of Aziei, the son of Marimoth, the son of Arna, the son of Ozias, the son of Borith, the son of Abissei, the son of Phinees, the son of Eleazar, 3 the son of Aaron, of the tribe of Levi, who was captive in the land of the Medes, in the reign of Artaxerxes king of the Persians. 4 The Lord's word came to me, saying, 5 "Go your way and show my people their sinful deeds, and their children their wickedness which they have done against me, that they may tell their children's children, 6 because the sins of their fathers have increased in them, for they have forgotten me, and have offered sacrifices to foreign gods. 7 Didn't I bring them out of the land of Egypt, out of the house of bondage? But they have provoked me to wrath and have despised my counsels. 8 So pull out the hair of your head and cast all evils upon them, for they have not been obedient to my law, but they are a rebellious people. 9 How long shall I endure them, to whom I have done so much good? 10 I have overthrown many kings for their sakes. I have struck down Pharoah with his servants and all his army. 11 I have destroyed all the nations before them. In the east, I have scattered the people of two provinces, even of Tyre and Sidon, and have slain all their adversaries. 12 Speak therefore to them, saying: 13 "The Lord says, truly I brought you through the sea, and where there was no path I made highways for you. I gave you Moses for a leader and Aaron for a priest. 14 I gave you light in a pillar of fire. I have done great wonders among you, yet you have forgotten me, says the Lord. 15 "The Lord Almighty says: The quails were for a token to you. I gave you a camp for your protection, but you complained there. 16 You didn't celebrate in my name for the destruction of your enemies, but even to this day you still complain. 17 Where are the benefits that I have given you? When you were hungry and thirsty in the wilderness, didn't you cry to me, 18 saying, 'Why have you brought us into this wilderness to kill us? It would

have been better for us to have served the Egyptians than to die in this wilderness.' 19 I had pity on your mourning and gave you manna for food. You ate angels' bread. 20 When you were thirsty, didn't I split the rock, and water flowed out in abundance? Because of the heat, I covered you with the leaves of the trees. 21 I divided fruitful lands among you. I drove out the Canaanites, the Pherezites, and the Philistines before you. What more shall I do for you?" says the Lord. 22 The Lord Almighty says, "When you were in the wilderness, at the bitter stream, being thirsty and blaspheming my name, 23 I gave you not fire for your blasphemies, but threw a tree in the water, and made the river sweet. 24 What shall I do to you, O Jacob? You, Judah, would not obey me. I will turn myself to other nations, and I will give my name to them, that they may keep my statutes. 25 Since you have forsaken me, I also will forsake you. When you ask me to be merciful to you, I will have no mercy upon you. 26 Whenever you call upon me, I will not hear you, for you have defiled your hands with blood, and your feet are swift to commit murder. 27 It is not as though you have forsaken me, but your own selves," says the Lord. 28 The Lord Almighty says, "Haven't I asked you as a father his sons, as a mother her daughters, and a nurse her young babies, 29 that you would be my people, and I would be your God, that you would be my children, and I would be your father? 30 I gathered you together, as a hen gathers her chicks under her wings. But now, what should I do to you? I will cast you out from my presence. 31 When you offer burnt sacrifices to me, I will turn my face from you, for I have rejected your solemn feast days, your new moons, and your circumcisions of the flesh. 32 I sent to you my servants the prophets, whom you have taken and slain, and torn their bodies in pieces, whose blood I will require from you," says the Lord. 33 The Lord Almighty says, "Your house is desolate. I will cast you out as the wind blows stubble. 34 Your children won't be fruitful, for they have neglected my commandment to you, and done that which is evil before me. 35 I will give your houses to a people that will come, which not having heard of me yet believe me. Those to whom I have shown no signs will do what I have commanded. 36 They have seen no prophets, yet they will remember their former condition. 37 I call to witness the gratitude of the people who will come, whose little ones rejoice with gladness. Although they see me not with bodily eyes, yet in spirit they will believe what I say." 38 And now, father, behold with glory, and see the people that come from the east: 39 to whom I will give for leaders, Abraham, Isaac, and Jacob, Oseas, Amos, and Micheas, Joel, Abdias, and Jonas, 40 Nahum, and Abacuc, Sophonias, Aggaeus, Zachary, and Malachy, who is also called the Lord's messenger.

2

1 The Lord says, "I brought this people out of bondage. I gave them my commandments by my servants the prophets, whom they would not listen to, but made my counsels void. 2 The mother who bore them says to them, 'Go your way, my children, for I am a widow and forsaken. 3 I brought you up with gladness, and I have lost you with sorrow and heaviness, for you have sinned before the Lord God, and done that which is evil before me. 4 But now what can I do for you? For I am a widow and forsaken.

Go your way, my children, and ask for mercy from the Lord.' 5 As for me, O father, I call upon you for a witness in addition to the mother of these children, because they would not keep my covenant, 6 that you may bring them to confusion, and their mother to ruin, that they may have no offspring. 7 Let them be scattered abroad among the heathen. Let their names be blotted out of the earth, for they have despised my covenant. 8 Woe to you, Assur, you who hide the unrighteous with you! You wicked nation, remember what I did to Sodom and Gomorrah, 9 whose land lies in lumps of pitch and heaps of ashes. That is what I will also do to those who have not listened to me," says the Lord Almighty. 10 The Lord says to Esdras, "Tell my people that I will give them the kingdom of Jerusalem, which I would have given to Israel. 11 I will also take their glory back to myself, and give these the everlasting tabernacles which I had prepared for them. 12 They will have the tree of life for fragrant perfume. They will neither labor nor be weary. 13 Ask, and you will receive. Pray that your days may be few, that they may be shortened. The kingdom is already prepared for you. Watch! 14 Call heaven and earth to witness. Call them to witness, for I have left out evil, and created the good, for I live, says the Lord. 15 "Mother, embrace your children. I will bring them out with gladness like a dove does. Establish their feet, for I have chosen you, says the Lord. 16 I will raise those who are dead up again from their places, and bring them out from their tombs, for I recognize my name in them. 17 Don't be afraid, you mother of children, for I have chosen you, says the Lord. 18 For your help, I will send my servants Esaias and Jeremy, after whose counsel I have sanctified and prepared for you twelve trees laden with various fruits, 19 and as many springs flowing with milk and honey, and seven mighty mountains, on which roses and lilies grow, with which I will fill your children with joy. 20 Do right to the widow. Secure justice for the fatherless. Give to the poor. Defend the orphan. Clothe the naked. 21 Heal the broken and the weak. Don't laugh a lame man to scorn. Defend the maimed. Let the blind man have a vision of my glory. 22 Protect the old and young within your walls. 23 Wherever you find the dead, set a sign upon them and commit them to the grave, and I will give you the first place in my resurrection. 24 Stay still, my people, and take your rest, for your rest will come. 25 Nourish your children, good nurse, and establish their feet. 26 As for the servants whom I have given you, not one of them will perish, for I will require them from among your number. 27 Don't be anxious, for when the day of suffering and anguish comes, others will weep and be sorrowful, but you will rejoice and have abundance. 28 The nations will envy you, but they will be able to do nothing against you, says the Lord. 29 My hands will cover you, so that your children don't see Gehenna. 30 Be joyful, mother, with your children, for I will deliver you, says the Lord. 31 Remember your children who sleep, for I will bring them out of the secret places of the earth and show mercy to them, for I am merciful, says the Lord Almighty. 32Embrace your children until I come, and proclaim mercy to them, for my wells run over, and my grace won't fail." 33 I, Esdras, received a command from the Lord on Mount Horeb to go to Israel, but when I came to them, they rejected me and rejected the Lord's commandment. 34 Therefore I say to you, O nations that hear and understand, "Look for your shepherd. He will give you everlasting rest, for he is near at hand who will come at the end of the age. 35 Be ready for the rewards of the kingdom, for the everlasting light will shine on you forevermore. 36 Flee the shadow of this world, receive the joy of your glory. I call to witness my savior openly. 37 Receive that which is given to you by the Lord, and be joyful, giving thanks to him who has called you to heavenly kingdoms. 38 Arise and stand up, and see the number of those who have been sealed at the Lord's feast. 39 Those who withdrew themselves from the shadow of the world have received glorious garments from the Lord. 40 Take again your full number, O Zion, and make up the reckoning of those of yours who are clothed in white, which have fulfilled the law of the Lord. 41 The number of your children, whom you long for, is fulfilled. Ask the power of the Lord, that your people, which have been called from the beginning, may be made holy." 42 I, Esdras, saw upon Mount Zion a great multitude, whom I could not number, and they all praised the Lord with songs. 43 In the midst of them, there was a young man of a high stature, taller than all the rest, and upon every one of their heads he set crowns, and he was more exalted than they were. I marveled greatly at this. 44 So I asked the angel, and said, "What are these, my Lord?" 45 He answered and said to me, "These are those who have put off the mortal clothing, and put on the immortal, and have confessed the name of God. Now are they crowned, and receive palms." 46 Then said I to the angel, "Who is the young man who sets crowns on them, and gives them palms in their hands?" 47 So he answered and said to me, "He is the Son of God, whom they have confessed in the world." Then I began to praise those who stood so valiantly for the name of the Lord. 48 Then the angel said to me, "Go your way, and tell my people what kind of things, and how great wonders of the Lord God you have seen."

3

1 In the thirtieth year after the ruin of the city, I Salathiel, also called Esdras, was in Babylon, and lay troubled upon my bed, and my thoughts came up over

my heart, 2 for I saw the desolation of Zion and the wealth of those who lived at Babylon. 3 My spirit was very agitated, so that I began to speak words full of fear to the Most High, and said, 4 "O sovereign Lord, didn't you speak at the beginning when you formed the earth—and that yourself alone—and commanded the dust 5 and it gave you Adam, a body without a soul? Yet it was the workmanship of your hands, and you breathed into him the breath of life, and he was made alive in your presence. 6 You led him into the garden which your right hand planted before the earth appeared. 7 You gave him your one commandment, which he transgressed, and immediately you appointed death for him and his descendants. From him were born nations, tribes, peoples, and kindred without number. 8 Every nation walked after their own will, did ungodly things in your sight, and despised your commandments, and you didn't hinder them. 9 Nevertheless, again in process of time, you brought the flood on those who lived in the world and destroyed them. 10 It came to pass that the same thing happened to them. Just as death came to Adam, so was the flood to these. 11 Nevertheless, you left one of them, Noah with his household, and all the righteous men who descended from him. 12 "It came to pass that when those who lived upon the earth began to multiply, they also multiplied children, peoples, and many nations, and began again to be more ungodly than their ancestors. 13 It came to pass, when they did wickedly before you, you chose one from among them, whose name was Abraham. 14 You loved, and to him only you showed the end of the times secretly by night, 15 and made an everlasting covenant with him, promising him that you would never forsake his descendants. To him, you gave Isaac, and to Isaac you gave Jacob and Esau. 16 You set apart Jacob for yourself, but rejected Esau. Jacob became a great multitude. 17 It came to pass that when you led his descendants out of Egypt, you brought them up to Mount Sinai. 18 You bowed the heavens also, shook the earth, moved the whole world, made the depths tremble, and troubled the age. 19 Your glory went through four gates, of fire, of earthquake, of wind, and of ice, that you might give the law to the descendants of Jacob, and the commandment to the descendants of Israel. 20 "Yet you didn't take away from them their wicked heart, that your law might produce fruit in them. 21 For the first Adam, burdened with a wicked heart transgressed and was overcome, as were all who are descended from him. 22 Thus disease was made permanent. The law was in the heart of the people along with the wickedness of the root. So the good departed away and that which was wicked remained. 23 So the times passed away, and the years were brought to an end. Then you raised up a servant, called David, 24 whom you commanded to build a city to your name, and to offer burnt offerings to you in it from what is yours. 25 When this was done many years, then those who inhabited the city did evil, 26 in all things doing as Adam and all his generations had done, for they also had a wicked heart. 27 So you gave your city over into the hands of your enemies. 28 "Then I said in my heart, 'Are their deeds of those who inhabit Babylon any better? Is that why it gained dominion over Zion?' 29 For it came to pass when I came here, that I also saw impietieswithout number, and my soul saw many sinners in this thirtieth year, so that my heart failed me. 30 For I have seen how you endure them sinning, and have spared those who act ungodly, and have destroyed your people, and have preserved your enemies; 31 and you have not shown how your way may be comprehended. Are the deeds of Babylon better than those of Zion? 32 Or is there any other nation that knows you beside Israel? Or what tribes have so believed your covenants as these tribes of Jacob? 33 Yet their reward doesn't appear, and their labor has no fruit, for I have gone here and there through the nations, and I see that they abound in wealth, and don't think about your commandments. 34 Weigh therefore our iniquities now in the balance, and theirs also who dwell in the world, and so will it be found which way the scale inclines. 35 Or when was it that they who dwell on the earth have not sinned in your sight? Or what nation has kept your commandments so well? 36 You will find some men by name who have kept your precepts, but you won't find nations."

4

1 The angel who was sent to me, whose name was Uriel, gave me an answer, 2 and said to me, "Your understanding has utterly

failed you regarding this world. Do you think you can comprehend the way of the Most High?" ³ Then I said, "Yes, my Lord." He answered me, "I have been sent to show you three ways, and to set before you three problems. ⁴ If you can solve one for me, I also will show you the way that you desire to see, and I will teach you why the heart is wicked." ⁵ I said, "Say on, my Lord." Then said he to me, "Go, weigh for me the weight of fire, or measure for me blast of wind, or call back for me the day that is past." ⁶ Then answered I and said, "Who of the sons of men is able to do this, that you should ask me about such things?" ⁷ He said to me, "If I had asked you, 'How many dwellings are there in the heart of the sea? Or how many springs are there at the fountain head of the deep? Or how many streams are above the firmament? Or which are the exits of hell? Or which are the entrances of paradise?' ⁸ Perhaps you would say to me, 'I never went down into the deep, or as yet into hell, neither did I ever climb up into heaven.' ⁹ Nevertheless now I have only asked you about the fire, wind, and the day, things which you have experienced, and from which you can't be separated, and yet have you given me no answer about them." ¹⁰ He said moreover to me, "You can't understand your own things that you grew up with. ¹¹ How then can your mind comprehend the way of the Most High? How can he who is already worn out with the corrupted world understand in corruption?" When I heard these things, I fell on my face ¹² and said to him, "It would have been better if we weren't here at all, than that we should come here and live in the midst of ungodliness, and suffer, and not know why." ¹³ He answered me, and said, §"A forest of the trees of the field went out, and took counsel together, ¹⁴ and said, 'Come! Let's go and make war against the sea, that it may depart away before us, and that we may make ourselves more forests.' ¹⁵ The waves of the sea also in like manner took counsel together, and said, 'Come! Let's go up and subdue the forest of the plain, that there also we may gain more territory.' ¹⁶ The counsel of the wood was in vain, for the fire came and consumed it. ¹⁷ Likewise also the counsel of the waves of the sea, for the sand stood up and stopped them. ¹⁸ If you were judge now between these two, which would you justify, or which would you condemn?" 19 I answered and said, "It is a foolish counsel that they both have taken, for the ground is given to the wood, and the place of the sea is given to bear its waves." 20 Then answered he me, and said, "You have given a right judgment. Why don't you judge your own case? 21 For just as the ground is given to the wood, and the sea to its waves, even so those who dwell upon the earth may understand nothing but what is upon the earth. Only he who dwells above the heavens understands the things that are above the height of the heavens." 22 Then answered I and said, "I beg you, O Lord, why has the power of understanding been given to me? 23 For it was not in my mind to be curious of the ways above, but of such things as pass by us daily, because Israel is given up as a reproach to the heathen. The people whom you have loved have been given over to ungodly nations. The law of our forefathers is made of no effect, and the written covenants are nowhere regarded. 24 We pass away out of the world like locusts. Our life is like a vapor, and we aren't worthy to obtain mercy. 25 What will he then do for his name by which we are called? I have asked about these things." 26 Then he answered me, and said, "If you are alive you will see, and if you live long, you will marvel, for the world hastens quickly to pass away. 27 For it is not able to bear the things that are promised to the righteous in the times to come; for this world is full of sadness and infirmities. 28 For the evil† about which you asked me has been sown, but its harvest hasn't yet come. 29 If therefore that which is sown isn't reaped, and if the place where the evil is sown doesn't pass away, the field where the good is sown won't come. 30 For a grain of evil seed was sown in the heart of Adam from the beginning, and how much wickedness it has produced to this time! How much more it will yet produce until the time of threshing comes! 31 Ponder now by yourself, how much fruit of wickedness a grain of evil seed has produced. 32 When the grains which are without number are sown, how great a threshing floor they will fill!" 33 Then I answered and said, "How long? When will these things come to pass? Why are our years few and evil?" 34 He answered me, and said, "Don't hurry faster than the Most High; for your haste is for your own self, but he who is above hurries on behalf of many. 35 Didn't the souls of the righteous ask question of these things in their chambers, saying, 'How long will we be here? When does the fruit of the threshing floor come?' 36 To them, Jeremiel the archangel answered, 'When the number is fulfilled of those who are like you. For he has weighed the world in the balance. 37 By measure, he has measured the times. By number, he has counted the seasons. He won't move or stir them until that measure is fulfilled." 38 Then I answered, "O sovereign Lord, all of us are full of ungodliness. 39 Perhaps it is for our sakes that the threshing time of the righteous is kept back—because of the sins of those who dwell on the earth." 40 So he answered me, "Go your way to a woman with child, and ask of her when she has fulfilled her nine months, if her womb may keep the baby any longer within her." 41 Then I said, "No, Lord, that can it not." He said to me, "In Hades, the chambers of souls are like the womb. 42 For just like a woman in labor hurries to escape the anguish of the labor pains, even so these places hurry to deliver those things that are committed to them from the beginning. 43 Then you will be shown those things which you desire to see." 44 Then I answered, "If I have found favor in your sight, and if it is possible, and if I am worthy, 45 show me this also, whether there is more to come than is past, or whether the greater part has gone over us. 46 For what is gone I know, but I don't know what is to come." 47 He said to me, "Stand up on my right side, and I will explain the parable to you." 48 So I stood, looked, and saw a hot burning oven passed by before me. It happened that when the flame had gone by I looked, and saw that the smoke remained. 49 After this, a watery cloud passed in front of me, and sent down much rain with a storm. When the stormy rain was past, the drops still remained in it." 50 Then said he to me, "Consider with yourself; as the rain is more than the drops, and the fire is greater than the smoke, so the quantity which is past was far greater; but the drops and the smoke still remained." 51 Then I prayed, and said, "Do you think that I will live until that time? Or who will be alive in those days?" 52 He answered me, "As for the signs you asked me about, I may tell you of them in part; but I wasn't sent to tell you about your life, for I don't know.

5

[1] "Nevertheless, concerning the signs, behold, the days will come when those who dwell on earth will be taken with great amazement, and the way of truth will be hidden, and the land will be barren of faith. [2] Iniquity will be increased above what now you see, and beyond what you have heard long ago. [3] The land that you now see ruling will be a trackless waste, and men will see it desolate. [4] But if the Most High grants you to live, you will see what is after the third period will be troubled. The sun will suddenly shine in the night, and the moon in the day. [5] Blood will drop out of wood, and the stone will utter its voice. The peoples will be troubled, and the stars will fall. [6] He will rule whom those who dwell on the earth don't expect, and the birds will fly away together. [7] The Sodomite sea will cast out fish, and make a noise in the night, which many have not known; but all will hear its voice. [8] There will also be chaos in many places. Fires will break out often, and the wild animals will change their places, and women will bring forth monsters. [9] Salt waters will be found in the sweet, and all friends will destroy one another. Then reason will hide itself, and understanding withdraw itself into its chamber. [10] It will be sought by many, and won't be found. Unrighteousness and lack of restraint will be multiplied on earth. [11] One country will ask another, 'Has righteousness, or a man that does righteousness, gone through you?' And it will say, 'No.' [12] It will come to pass at that time that men will hope, but won't obtain. They will labor, but their ways won't prosper. [13] I am permitted to show you such signs. If you will pray again, and weep as now, and fast seven days, you will hear yet greater things than these." [14] Then I woke up, and an extreme trembling went through my body, and my mind was so troubled that it fainted. [15] So the angel who had come to talk with me held me, comforted me, and set me on my feet. [16] In the second night, it came to pass that Phaltiel the captain of the people came to me, saying, "Where have you been? Why is your face sad? [17] Or don't you know that Israel is committed to you in the land of their captivity? [18] Get up then,

and eat some bread, and don't forsake us, like a shepherd who leaves the flock in the power of cruel wolves." 19 Then said I to him, "Go away from me and don't come near me for seven days, and then you shall come to me." He heard what I said and left me. 20 So I fasted seven days, mourning and weeping, like Uriel the angel had commanded me. 21 After seven days, the thoughts of my heart were very grievous to me again, 22 and my soul recovered the spirit of understanding, and I began to speak words before the Most High again. 23 I said, "O sovereign Lord of all the woods of the earth, and of all the trees thereof, you have chosen one vine for yourself. 24 Of all the lands of the world you have chosen one country for yourself. Of all the flowers of the world, you have chosen one lily for yourself. 25 Of all the depths of the sea, you have filled one river for yourself. Of all built cities, you have consecrated Zion for yourself. 26 Of all the birds that are created you have named for yourself one dove. Of all the livestock that have been made, you have provided for yourself one sheep. 27 Among all the multitudes of peoples you have gotten yourself one people. To this people, whom you loved, you gave a law that is approved by all. 28 Now, O Lord, why have you given this one people over to many, and have dishonored the one root above others, and have scattered your only one among many? 29 Those who opposed your promises have trampled down those who believed your covenants. 30 If you really do hate your people so much, they should be punished with your own hands." 31 Now when I had spoken these words, the angel that came to me the night before was sent to me, 32and said to me, "Hear me, and I will instruct you. Listen to me, and I will tell you more." 33 I said, "Speak on, my Lord." Then said he to me, "You are very troubled in mind for Israel's sake. Do you love that people more than he who made them?" 34 I said, "No, Lord; but I have spoken out of grief; for my heart is in agony every hour while I labor to comprehend the way of the Most High, and to seek out part of his judgment." 35 He said to me, "You can't." And I said, "Why, Lord? Why was I born? Why wasn't my mother's womb my grave, that I might not have seen the travail of Jacob, and the wearisome toil of the people of

Israel?" 36 He said to me, "Count for me those who haven't yet come. Gather together for me the drops that are scattered abroad, and make the withered flowers green again for me. 37 Open for me the chambers that are closed, and bring out the winds for me that are shut up in them. Or show me the image of a voice. Then I will declare to you the travail that you asked to see." 38 And I said, "O sovereign Lord, who may know these things except he who doesn't have his dwelling with men? 39 As for me, I lack wisdom. How can I then speak of these things you asked me about?" 40 Then said he to me, "Just as you can do none of these things that I have spoken of, even so you can't find out my judgment, or the end of the love that I have promised to my people." 41 I said, "But, behold, O Lord, you have made the promise to those who are alive at the end. What should they do who have been before us, or we ourselves, or those who will come after us?" 42 He said to me, "I will compare my judgment to a ring. Just as there is no slowness of those who are last, even so there is no swiftness of those who be first." 43 So I answered, "Couldn't you make them all at once that have been made, and that are now, and that are yet to come, that you might show your judgment sooner?" 44 Then he answered me, "The creature may not move faster than the creator, nor can the world hold them at once who will be created in it." 45 And I said, "How have you said to your servant, that you will surely make alive at once the creature that you have created? If therefore they will be alive at once, and the creation will sustain them, even so it might now also support them to be present at once." 46 And he said to me, "Ask the womb of a woman, and say to her, 'If you bear ten children, why do you it at different times? Ask her therefore to give birth to ten children at once." 47 I said, "She can't, but must do it each in their own time." 48 Then said he to me, "Even so, I have given the womb of the earth to those who are sown in it in their own times. 49 For just as a young child may not give birth, neither she who has grown old any more, even so have I organized the world which I created." 50 I asked, "Seeing that you have now shown me the way, I will speak before you. Is our mother, of whom you have told me, still young? Or does she now draw near to old age?" 51 He answered me, "Ask a woman who bears children, and she will tell you. 52 Say to her, 'Why aren't they whom you have now brought forth like those who were before, but smaller in stature?' 53 She also will answer you, 'Those who are born in the strength of youth are different from those who are born in the time of old age, when the womb fails.' 54 Consider therefore you also, how you are shorter than those who were before you. 55 So are those who come after you smaller than you, as born of the creature which now begins to be old, and is past the strength of youth." 56 Then I said, "Lord, I implore you, if I have found favor in your sight, show your servant by whom you visit your creation."

6

1 He said to me, "In the beginning, when the earth was made, before the portals of the world were fixed and before the gatherings of the winds blew, 2 before the voices of the thunder sounded and before the flashes of the lightning shone, before the foundations of paradise were laid, 3 before the fair flowers were seen, before the powers of the earthquake were established, before the innumerable army of angels were gathered together, 4 before the heights of the air were lifted up, before the measures of the firmament were named, before the footstool of Zion was established, 5 before the present years were reckoned, before the imaginations of those who now sin were estranged, and before they were sealed who have gathered faith for a treasure— 6 then I considered these things, and they all were made through me alone, and not through another; just as by me also they will be ended, and not by another." 7 Then I answered, "What will be the dividing of the times? Or when will be the end of the first and the beginning of the age that follows?" 8 He said to me, "From Abraham to Isaac, because Jacob and Esau were born to him, for Jacob's hand held Esau's heel from the beginning. 9 For Esau is the end of this age, and Jacob is the beginning of the one that follows. 10 The beginning of a man is his hand, and the end of a man is his heel. Seek nothing else between the heel and the hand, Esdras!" 11 Then I answered, "O sovereign Lord, if I have found favor in your sight, 12 I beg you, show your servant the end of your

signs which you showed me part on a previous night." 13 So he answered, "Stand up upon your feet, and you will hear a mighty sounding voice. 14 If the place you stand on is greatly moved 15 when it speaks don't be afraid, for the word is of the end, and the foundations of the earth will understand 16 that the speech is about them. They will tremble and be moved, for they know that their end must be changed." 17 It happened that when I had heard it, I stood up on my feet, and listened, and, behold, there was a voice that spoke, and its sound was like the sound of many waters. 18 It said, "Behold, the days come when I draw near to visit those who dwell upon the earth, 19 and when I investigate those who have caused harm unjustly with their unrighteousness, and when the affliction of Zion is complete, 20 and when the seal will be set on the age that is to pass away, then I will show these signs: the books will be opened before the firmament, and all will see together. 21 The children a year old will speak with their voices. The women with child will deliver premature children at three or four months, and they will live and dance. 22 Suddenly the sown places will appear unsown. The full storehouses will suddenly be found empty. 23 The trumpet will give a sound which when every man hears, they will suddenly be afraid. 24 At that time friends will make war against one another like enemies. The earth will stand in fear with those who dwell in it. The springs of the fountains will stand still, so that for three hours they won't flow. 25 "It will be that whoever remains after all these things that I have told you of, he will be saved and will see my salvation, and the end of my world. 26 They will see the men who have been taken up, who have not tasted death from their birth. The heart of the inhabitants will be changed and turned into a different spirit. 27 For evil will be blotted out and deceit will be quenched. 28 Faith will flourish. Corruption will be overcome, and the truth, which has been so long without fruit, will be declared." 29 When he talked with me, behold, little by little, the place I stood on rocked back and forth. 30 He said to me, "I came to show you these things tonight. 31 If therefore you will pray yet again, and fast seven more days, I will again tell you greater things than these. 32 For your voice has surely been heard before the Most High. For the Mighty has seen your righteousness. He has also seen your purity, which you have maintained ever since your youth. 33 Therefore he has sent me to show you all these things, and to say to you, 'Believe, and don't be afraid! 34 Don't be hasty to think vain things about the former times, that you may not hasten in the latter times." 35 It came to pass after this, that I wept again, and fasted seven days in like manner, that I might fulfill the three weeks which he told me. 36 On the eighth night, my heart was troubled within me again, and I began to speak in the presence of the Most High. 37 For my spirit was greatly aroused, and my soul was in distress. 38 I said, "O Lord, truly you spoke at the beginning of the creation, on the first day, and said this: 'Let heaven and earth be made,' and your word perfected the work. 39 Then the spirit was hovering, and darkness and silence were on every side. The sound of man's voice was not yet there. 40 Then you commanded a ray of light to be brought out of your treasuries, that your works might then appear. 41 "On the second day, again you made the spirit of the firmament and commanded it to divide and to separate the waters, that the one part might go up, and the other remain beneath. 42 "On the third day, you commanded that the waters should be gathered together in the seventh part of the earth. You dried up six parts and kept them, to the intent that of these some being both planted and tilled might serve before you. 43 For as soon as your word went out, the work was done. 44 Immediately, great and innumerable fruit grew, with many pleasant tastes, and flowers of inimitable color, and fragrances of most exquisite smell. This was done the third day. 45 "On the fourth day, you commanded that the sun should shine, the moon give its light, and the stars should be in their order; 46 and gave them a command to serve mankind, who was to be made. 47 "On the fifth day, you said to the seventh part, where the water was gathered together, that it should produce living creatures, fowls and fishes; and so it came to pass 48 that the mute and lifeless water produced living things as it was told, that the nations might therefore praise your wondrous works. 49 "Then you preserved two living creatures. The one you called Behemoth, and the other you called Leviathan. 50 You separated the one from the other; for the seventh part, namely, where the water was gathered together, might not hold them both. 51 To Behemoth, you gave one part, which was dried up on the third day, that he should dwell in it, in which are a thousand hills; 52 but to Leviathan you gave the seventh part, namely, the watery part. You have kept them to be devoured by whom you wish, when you wish. 53 "But on the sixth day, you commanded the earth to produce before you cattle, animals, and creeping things. 54 Over these, you ordained Adam as ruler over all the works that you have made. Of him came all of us, the people whom you have chosen. 55 "All this have I spoken before you, O Lord, because you have said that for our sakes you made this world. 56 As for the other nations, which also come from Adam, you have said that they are nothing, and are like spittle. You have likened the abundance of them to a drop that falls from a bucket. 57 Now, O Lord, behold these nations, which are reputed as nothing, being rulers over us and devouring us. 58 But we your people, whom you have called your firstborn, your only children, and your fervent lover, are given into their hands. 59 Now if the world is made for our sakes, why don't we possess our world for an inheritance? How long will this endure?"

7

1 When I had finished speaking these words, the angel which had been sent to me the nights before was sent to me. 2 He said to me, "Rise, Esdras, and hear the words that I have come to tell you." 3 I said, "Speak on, my Lord." Then he said to me, "There is a sea set in a wide place, that it might be broad and vast, 4 but its entrance is set in a narrow place so as to be like a river. 5 Whoever desires to go into the sea to look at it, or to rule it, if he didn't go through the narrow entrance, how could he come into the broad part? 6 Another thing also: There is a city built and set in a plain country, and full of all good things, 7 but its entrance is narrow, and is set in a dangerous place to fall, having fire on the right hand, and deep water on the left. 8 There is one only path between them both, even between the fire and the water, so that only one person can go there at once. 9 If this city is now given to a man for an

inheritance, if the heir doesn't pass the danger before him, how will he receive his inheritance?" 10 I said, "That is so, Lord." Then said he to me, "Even so also is Israel's portion. 11 I made the world for their sakes. What is now done was decreed when Adam transgressed my statutes. 12 Then the entrances of this world were made narrow, sorrowful, and toilsome. They are but few and evil, full of perils, and involved in great toils. 13 For the entrances of the greater world are wide and safe, and produce fruit of immortality. 14 So if those who live don't enter these difficult and vain things, they can never receive those that are reserved for them. 15 Now therefore why are you disturbed, seeing you are but a corruptible man? Why are you moved, since you are mortal? 16 Why haven't you considered in your mind that which is to come, rather than that which is present?" 17 Then I answered and said, "O sovereign Lord, behold, you have ordained in your law that the righteous will inherit these things, but that the ungodly will perish. 18 The righteous therefore will suffer difficult things, and hope for easier things, but those who have done wickedly have suffered the difficult things, and yet will not see the easier things." 19 He said to me, "You are not a judge above God, neither do you have more understanding than the Most High. 20 Yes, let many perish who now live, rather than that the law of God which is set before them be despised. 21 For God strictly commanded those who came, even as they came, what they should do to live, and what they should observe to avoid punishment. 22 Nevertheless, they weren't obedient to him, but spoke against him and imagined for themselves vain things. 23 They made cunning plans of wickedness, and said moreover of the Most High that he doesn't exist, and they didn't know his ways. 24 They despised his law and denied his covenants. They haven't been faithful to his statutes, and haven't performed his works. 25 Therefore, Esdras, for the empty are empty things, and for the full are the full things. 26 For behold, the time will come, and it will be, when these signs of which I told you before will come to pass, that the bride will appear, even the city coming forth, and she will be seen who now is withdrawn from the earth. 27 Whoever is delivered from the foretold evils will see my wonders. 28 For my son Jesus will be revealed with those who are with him, and those who remain will rejoice four hundred years. 29 After these years my son Christ will die, along with all of those who have the breath of life. 30 Then the world will be turned into the old silence seven days, like as in the first beginning, so that no human will remain. 31 After seven days the world that is not yet awake will be raised up, and what is corruptible will die. 32 The earth will restore those who are asleep in it, and the dust those who dwell in it in silence, and the secret places will deliver those souls that were committed to them. 33 The Most High will be revealed on the judgment seat, ‡ and compassion will pass away, and patience will be withdrawn. 34 Only judgment will remain. Truth will stand. Faith will grow strong. 35 Recompense will follow. The reward will be shown. Good deeds will awake, and wicked deeds won't sleep. 36 The pit of torment will appear, and near it will be the place of rest. The furnace of hell will be shown, and near it the paradise of delight. 37 Then the Most High will say to the nations that are raised from the dead, 'Look and understand whom you have denied, whom you haven't served, whose commandments you have despised. 38 Look on this side and on that. Here is delight and rest, and there fire and torments.' Thus he will speak to them in the day of judgment. 39 This is a day that has neither sun, nor moon, nor stars, 40 neither cloud, nor thunder, nor lightning, neither wind, nor water, nor air, neither darkness, nor evening, nor morning, 41 neither summer, nor spring, nor heat, nor winter, neither frost, nor cold, nor hail, nor rain, nor dew, 42 neither noon, nor night, nor dawn, neither shining, nor brightness, nor light, except only the splendor of the glory of the Most High, by which all will see the things that are set before them. 43 It will endure as though it were a week of years. 44 This is my judgment and its prescribed order; but I have only shown these things to you." 45 I answered, "I said then, O Lord, and I say now: Blessed are those who are now alive and keep your commandments! 46 But what about those for whom I prayed? For who is there of those who are alive who has not sinned, and who of the children of men hasn't transgressed your covenant? 47 Now I see that the world to come will bring delight to few, but torments to many. 48 For an evil heart has grown up in us, which has led us astray from these commandments and has brought us into corruption and into the ways of death. It has shown us the paths of perdition and removed us far from life— and that, not a few only, but nearly all who have been created." 49 He answered me, "Listen to me, and I will instruct you. I will admonish you yet again. 50 For this reason, the Most High has not made one world, but two. 51 For because you have said that the just are not many, but few, and the ungodly abound, hear the explanation. 52 If you have just a few precious stones, will you add them to lead and clay?" 53 I said, "Lord, how could that be?" 54 He said to me, "Not only that, but ask the earth, and she will tell you. Defer to her, and she will declare it to you. 55 Say to her, 'You produce gold, silver, and brass, and also iron, lead, and clay; 56 but silver is more abundant than gold, and brass than silver, and iron than brass, and lead than iron, and clay than lead.' 57 Judge therefore which things are precious and to be desired, what is abundant or what is rare?" 58 I said, "O sovereign Lord, that which is plentiful is of less worth, for that which is more rare is more precious." 59 He answered me, "Weigh within yourself the things that you have thought, for he who has what is hard to get rejoices over him who has what is plentiful. 60 So also is the judgment which I have promised; for I will rejoice over the few that will be saved, because these are those who have made my glory to prevail now, and through them, my name is now honored. 61 I won't grieve over the multitude of those who perish; for these are those who are now like mist, and have become like flame and smoke; they are set on fire and burn hotly, and are extinguished." 62 I answered, "O earth, why have you produced, if the mind is made out of dust, like all other created things? 63 For it would have been better that the dust itself had been unborn, so that the mind might not have been made from it. 64 But now the mind grows with us, and because of this we are tormented, because we perish and we know it. 65 Let the race of men lament and the animals of the field be glad. Let all who are born lament, but let the four-footed animals and the livestock rejoice. 66 For it is far better with them than with us; for they don't look forward to judgment, neither do they know of torments or of salvation promised to them after death. 67 For what does it profit us, that we will be preserved alive, but yet be afflicted with torment? 68 For all who are born are defiled with iniquities, and are full of sins and laden with transgressions. 69 If after death we were not to come into judgment, perhaps it would have been better for us." 70 He answered me, "When the Most High made the world and Adam and all those who came from him, he first prepared the judgment and the things that pertain to the judgment. 71 Now understand from your own words, for you have said that the mind grows with us. 72 They therefore who dwell on the earth will be tormented for this reason, that having understanding they have committed iniquity, and receiving commandments have not kept them, and having obtained a law they dealt unfaithfully with that which they received. 73 What then will they have to say in the judgment, or how will they answer in the last times? 74 For how long a time has the Most High been patient with those who inhabit the world, and not for their sakes, but because of the times which he has foreordained!" 75 I answered, "If I have found grace in your sight, O Lord, show this also to your servant, whether after death, even now when every one of us gives up his soul, we will be kept in rest until those times come, in which you renew the creation, or whether we will be tormented immediately." 76 He answered me, "I will show you this also; but don't join yourself with those who are scorners, nor count yourself with those who are tormented. 77 For you have a treasure of works laid up with the Most High, but it won't be shown you until the last times. 78 For concerning death the teaching is: When the decisive sentence has gone out from the Most High that a man shall die, as the spirit leaves the body to return again to him who gave it, it adores the glory of the Most High first of all. 79 And if it is one of those who have been scorners and have not kept the way of the Most High, and that have despised his law, and who hate those who fear God, 80 these spirits won't enter into habitations, but will wander and be in torments immediately, ever grieving and sad, in seven ways. ⁸¹ The first way, because they have despised the law of the Most High. ⁸² The second way, because they can't now make a good repentance that they may live. ⁸³ The third way, they will see the reward laid up for those who have believed the covenants of the Most High. ⁸⁴ The fourth way, they will consider the torment laid up for themselves in the last days. ⁸⁵ The fifth way, they will see the dwelling places of the others guarded by angels, with great quietness. ⁸⁶ The sixth way, they will see how immediately some of them will pass into torment. ⁸⁷ The seventh way, which is more grievous than all the aforesaid ways, because they will pine away in confusion and be consumed with shame, and will be withered up by fears, seeing the glory of the Most High before whom they have sinned while living, and before whom they will be judged in the last times. ⁸⁸ "Now this is the order of those who have kept the ways of the Most High, when they will be separated from their mortal body. ⁸⁹ In the time that they lived in it, they painfully served the Most High, and were in jeopardy every hour, that they might keep the law of the lawgiver perfectly. ⁹⁰ Therefore this is the teaching concerning them: ⁹¹ First of all they will see with great joy the glory of him who takes them up, for they will have rest in seven orders. ⁹² The first order, because they have labored with great effort to overcome the evil thought which was fashioned together with them, that it might not lead them astray from life into death. ⁹³ The second order, because they see the perplexity in which the souls of the ungodly wander, and the punishment that awaits them. ⁹⁴ The third order, they see the testimony which he who fashioned them gives concerning them, that while they lived they kept the law which was given them in trust. ⁹⁵ The fourth order, they understand the rest which, being gathered in their chambers, they now enjoy with great quietness, guarded by angels, and the glory that awaits them in the last days. ⁹⁶The fifth order, they rejoice that they have now escaped from that which is corruptible, and that they will inherit that which is to come, while they see in addition the difficulty and the pain from which they have been delivered, and the spacious liberty which they will receive with joy and immortality. ⁹⁷ The sixth order, when it is shown to them how their face will shine like the sun, and how they will be made like the light of the stars, being incorruptible from then on. [98] The seventh order, which is greater than all the previously mentioned orders, because they will rejoice with confidence, and because they will be bold without confusion, and will be glad without fear, for they hurry to see the face of him whom in their lifetime they served, and from whom they will receive their reward in glory. [99] This is the order of the souls of the just, as from henceforth is announced to them. Previously mentioned are the ways of torture which those who would not give heed will suffer from after this." [100] I answered, "Will time therefore be given to the souls after they are separated from the bodies, that they may see what you have described to me?" [101] He said, "Their freedom will be for seven days, that for seven days they may see the things you have been told, and afterwards they will be gathered together in their habitations." [102] I answered, "If I have found favor in your sight, show further to me your servant whether in the day of judgment the just will be able to intercede for the ungodly or to entreat the Most High for them, [103] whether fathers for children, or children for parents, or kindred for kindred, or kinsfolk for their next of kin, or friends for those who are most dear." [104] He answered me, "Since you have found favor in my sight, I will show you this also. The day of judgment is a day of decision, and displays to all the seal of truth. Even as now a father doesn't send his son, or a son his father, or a master his slave, or a friend him that is most dear, that in his place he may understand, or sleep, or eat, or be healed, [105] so no one will ever pray for another in that day, neither will one lay a burden on another, for then everyone will each bear his own righteousness or unrighteousness." [106] I answered, "How do we now find that first Abraham prayed for the people of Sodom, and Moses for the ancestors who sinned in the wilderness, [107] and Joshua after him for Israel in the days of *Achan, [108] and Samuel in the days of Saul, and David for the plague, and Solomon for those who would worship in the sanctuary, [109] and Elijah for those that received rain, and for the dead, that he might live, [110] and Hezekiah for the people in the days of Sennacherib, and many others prayed for many? [111] If therefore now, when corruption has grown and unrighteousness increased, the righteous have prayed for the ungodly, why will it not be so then also?" [112] He answered me, "This present world is not the end. The full glory doesn't remain in it. Therefore those who were able prayed for the weak. [113] But the day of judgment will be the end of this age, and the beginning of the immortality to come, in which corruption has passed away, [114] intemperance is at an end, infidelity is cut off, but righteousness has grown, and truth has sprung up. [115] Then no one will be able to have mercy on him who is condemned in judgment, nor to harm someone who is victorious." [116] I answered then, "This is my first and last saying, that it would have been better if the earth had not produced Adam, or else, when it had produced him, to have restrained him from sinning. [117] For what profit is it for all who are in this present time to live in heaviness, and after death to look for punishment? [118] O Adam, what have you done? For though it was you who sinned, the evil hasn't fallen on you alone, but on all of us who come from you. [119] For what profit is it to us, if an immortal time is promised to us, but we have done deeds that bring death? [120] And that there is promised us an everlasting hope, but we have most miserably failed? [121] And that there are reserved habitations of health and safety, but we have lived wickedly? [122] And that the glory of the Most High will defend those who have led a pure life, but we have walked in the most wicked ways of all? [123] And that a paradise will be revealed, whose fruit endures without decay, in which is abundance and healing, but we won't enter into it, [124] for we have lived in perverse ways? [125] And that the faces of those who have practiced selfcontrol will shine more than the stars, but our faces will be blacker than darkness? [126] For while we lived and committed iniquity, we didn't consider what we would have to suffer after death." [127] Then he answered, "This is the significance of the battle which humans born on the earth will fight: [128] if they are overcome, they will suffer as you have said, but if they get the victory, they will receive the thing that I say. [129] For this is the way that Moses spoke to the people while he lived, saying, 'Choose life, that you may live!' [130] Nevertheless they didn't believe him or the prophets after him, not even me, who have spoken to them. [131] Therefore there won't be such heaviness in their destruction, as there will be joy over those who are assured of salvation." [132] Then I answered, "I know, Lord, that the Most High is now called merciful, in that he has mercy upon those who have not yet come into the world; [133] and compassionate, in that he has compassion upon those who turn to his law; [134] and patient, in that he is patient with those who have sinned, since they are his creatures; [135] and bountiful, in that he is ready to give rather than to take away; [136] and very merciful, in that he multiplies more and more mercies to those who are present, and who are past, and also to those who are to come— [137] for if he wasn't merciful, the world wouldn't continue with those who dwell in it— [138] and one who forgives, for if he didn't forgive out of his goodness, that those who have committed iniquities might be relieved of them, not even one ten thousandth part of mankind would remain living; [139]and a judge, for if he didn't pardon those who were created by his word, and blot out the multitude of sins, [140] there would perhaps be very few left of an innumerable multitude."

8

[1] He answered me, "The Most High has made this world for many, but the world to come for few. [2] Now I will tell you a parable, Esdras. Just as when you ask the earth, it will say to you that it gives very much clay from which earthen vessels are made, but little dust that gold comes from. Even so is the course of the present world. [3] Many have been created, but few will be saved." [4] I answered, "Drink your fill of understanding then, O my soul, and let my heart devour wisdom. [5] For you have come here apart from your will, and depart against your will, for you have only been given a short time to live. [6] O Lord over us, grant to your servant that we may pray before you, and give us seed for our heart and cultivation for our understanding, that fruit may grow from it, by which everyone who is corrupt, who bears the likeness of a man, may live. [7] For you alone exist, and we all one workmanship of your hands, just as you have said. [8] Because you

give life to the body that is now fashioned in the womb, and give it members, your creature is preserved infire and water, and your workmanship endures nine months as your creation which is created in it. ⁹ But that which keeps and that which is kept will both be kept by your keeping. When the womb gives up again what has grown in it, ¹⁰ you have commanded that out of the parts of the body, that is to say, out of the breasts, be given milk, which is the fruit of the breasts, ¹¹ that the body that is fashioned may be nourished for a time, and afterwards you guide it in your mercy. ¹² Yes, you have brought it up in your righteousness, nurtured it in your law, and corrected it with your judgment. ¹³ You put it to death as your creation, and make it live as your work. ¹⁴ If therefore you lightly and suddenly destroy him which with so great labor was fashioned by your commandment, to what purpose was he made? ¹⁵ Now therefore I will speak. About man in general, you know best, but about your people for whose sake I am sorry, ¹⁶ and for your inheritance, for whose cause I mourn, for Israel, for whom I am heavy, and for the seed of Jacob, for whose sake I am troubled, ¹⁷ therefore I will begin to pray before you for myself and for them; for I see the failings of us who dwell in the land; ¹⁸ but I have heard the swiftness of the judgment which is to come. ¹⁹ Therefore hear my voice, and understand my saying, and I will speak before you." The beginning of the words of Esdras, before he was taken up. He said, ²⁰ "O Lord, you who remain forever, whose eyes are exalted, and whose chambers are in the air, ²¹ whose throne is beyond measure, whose glory is beyond comprehension, before whom the army of angels stand with trembling, ²² at whose bidding they are changed to wind and fire, whose word is sure, and sayings constant, whose ordinance is strong, and commandment fearful, ²³ whose look dries up the depths, and whose indignation makes the mountains to melt away, and whose truth bears witness— ²⁴ hear, O Lord, the prayer of your servant, and give ear to the petition of your handiwork. ²⁵ Attend to my words, for as long as I live, I will speak, and as long as I have understanding, I will answer. ²⁶ Don't look at the sins of your people, but on those who have served you in truth. ²⁷ Don't regard the doings of those who act wickedly, but of those who have kept your covenants in affliction. 28 Don't think about those who have lived wickedly before you, but remember those who have willingly known your fear. 29 Let it not be your will to destroy those who have lived like cattle, but look at those who have clearly taught your law. 30 Don't be indignant at those who are deemed worse than animals, but love those who have always put their trust in your glory. 31 For we and our fathers have passed our lives in ways that bring death, but you are called merciful because of us sinners. 32 For if you have a desire to have mercy upon us who have no works of righteousness, then you will be called merciful. 33 For the just, which have many good works laid up with you, will be rewarded for their own deeds. 34 For what is man, that you should take displeasure at him? Or what is a corruptible race, that you should be so bitter toward it? 35 For in truth, there is no man among those who are born who has not done wickedly, and among those who have lived, there is none which have not done wrong. 36 For in this, O Lord, your righteousness and your goodness will be declared, if you are merciful to those who have no store of good works." 37 Then he answered me, "Some things you have spoken rightly, and it will happen according to your words. 38 For indeed I will not think about the fashioning of those who have sinned, or about their death, their judgment, or their destruction; 39 but I will rejoice over the creation of the righteous and their pilgrimage, their salvation, and the reward that they will have. 40 Therefore as I have spoken, so it will be. 41 For as the farmer sows many seeds in the ground, and plants many trees, and yet not all that is sown will come up in due season, neither will all that is planted take root, even so those who are sown in the world will not all be saved." 42 Then I answered, "If I have found favor, let me speak before you. 43 If the farmer's seed doesn't come up because it hasn't received your rain in due season, or if it is ruined by too much rain and perishes, 44 likewise man, who is formed with your hands and is called your own image, because he is made like you, for whose sake you have formed all things, even him have you made like the farmer's seed. 45 Don't be angry with us, but spare your people and have mercy upon your inheritance, for you have mercy upon your own creation." ⁴⁶ Then he answered me, "Things present are for those who live now, and things to come for those who will live hereafter. ⁴⁷ For you come far short of being able to love my creature more than I. But you have compared yourself to the unrighteous. Don't do that! ⁴⁸ Yet in this will you be admirable to the Most High, ⁴⁹ in that you have humbled yourself, as it becomes you, and have not judged yourself among the righteous, so as to be much glorified. ⁵⁰ For many grievous miseries will fall on those who dwell in the world in the last times, because they have walked in great pride. ⁵¹ But understand for yourself, and for those who inquire concerning the glory of those like you, ⁵² because paradise is opened to you. The tree of life is planted. The time to come is prepared. Plenteousness is made ready. A city is built. Rest is †allowed. Goodness is perfected, and wisdom is perfected beforehand. ⁵³ The root of evil is sealed up from you. Weakness is done away from you, and death is hidden. Hell and corruption have fled into forgetfulness. ⁵⁴ Sorrows have passed away, and in the end, the treasure of immortality is shown. ⁵⁵ Therefore ask no more questions concerning the multitude of those who perish. ⁵⁶ For when they had received liberty, they despised the Most High, scorned his law, and forsook his ways. ⁵⁷ Moreover they have trodden down his righteous, ⁵⁸ and said in their heart that there is no God—even knowing that they must die. ⁵⁹ For as the things I have said will welcome you, so thirst and pain which are prepared for them. For the Most High didn't intend that men should be destroyed, ⁶⁰ but those who are created have themselves defiled the name of him who made them, and were unthankful to him who prepared life for them. ⁶¹ Therefore my judgment is now at hand, ⁶² which I have not shown to all men, but to you, and a few like you." Then I answered, ⁶³ "Behold, O Lord, now you have shown me the multitude of the wonders which you will do in the last times, but you haven't shown me when."

9

¹ He answered me, "Measure diligently within yourself. When you see that a certain part of the

signs are past, which have been told you beforehand, 2 then will you understand that it is the very time in which the Most High will visit the world which was made by him. 3 When earthquakes, tumult of peoples, plans of nations, wavering of leaders, and confusion of princes are seen in the world, 4 then will you understand that the Most High spoke of these things from the days that were of old, from the beginning. 5 For just as with everything that is made in the world, the beginning is evident and the end manifest, 6 so also are the times of the Most High: the beginnings are manifest in wonders and mighty works, and the end in effects and signs. 7 Everyone who will be saved, and will be able to escape by his works, or by faith by which they have believed, 8 will be preserved from the said perils, and will see my salvation in my land and within my borders, which I have sanctified for myself from the beginning. 9 Then those who now have abused my ways will be amazed. Those who have cast them away despitefully will live in torments. 10 For as many as in their life have received benefits, and yet have not known me, 11 and as many as have scorned my law, while they still had liberty and when an opportunity to repent was open to them, didn't understand, but despised it, 12 must know it in torment after death. 13 Therefore don't be curious any longer how the ungodly will be punished, but inquire how the righteous will be saved, those who the world belongs to, and for whom the world was created." 14 I answered, 15 "I have said before, and now speak, and will say it again hereafter, that there are more of those who perish than of those who will be saved, 16 like a wave is greater than a drop." 17 He answered me, "Just as the field is, so also the seed. As the flowers are, so are the colors. As the work is, so also is the judgment on it. As is the farmer, so also is his threshing floor. For there was a time in the world 18 when I was preparing for those who now live, before the world was made for them to dwell in. Then no one spoke against me, 19 for §no one existed. But now those who are created in this world that is prepared, both with a table that doesn't fail and a law which is unsearchable, are corrupted in their ways. 20 So I considered my world, and behold, it was destroyed, and my earth, and behold, it was in peril, because of the plans that had come into it. ²¹ I saw and spared them, but not greatly, and saved myself a grape out of a cluster, and a plant out of a great forest. ²² Let the multitude perish then, which were born in vain. Let my grape be saved, and my plant, for I have made them perfect with great labor. ²³ Nevertheless, if you will wait seven more days—however don't fast in them, ²⁴ but go into a field of flowers, where no house is built, and eat only of the flowers of the field, and you shall taste no flesh, and shall drink no wine, but shall eat flowers only— ²⁵ and pray to the Most High continually, then I will come and talk with you." ²⁶ So I went my way, just as he commanded me, into the field which is called Ardat. There I sat among the flowers, and ate of the herbs of the field, and this food satisfied me. ²⁷ It came to pass after seven days that I lay on the grass, and my heart was troubled again, like before. ²⁸ My mouth was opened, and I began to speak before the Lord Most High, and said, ²⁹ "O Lord, you showed yourself among us, to our fathers in the wilderness, when they went out of Egypt, and when they came into the wilderness, where no man treads and that bears no fruit. ³⁰ You said, 'Hear me, O Israel. Heed my words, O seed of Jacob. ³¹ For behold, I sow my law in you, and it will bring forth fruit in you, and you will be glorified in it forever.' ³² But our fathers, who received the law, didn't keep it, and didn't observe the statutes. The fruit of the law didn't perish, for it couldn't, because it was yours. ³³ Yet those who received it perished, because they didn't keep the thing that was sown in them. ³⁴ Behold, it is a custom that when the ground has received seed, or the sea a ship, or any vessel food or drink, and when it comes to pass that that which is sown, or that which is launched, ³⁵or the things which have been received, should come to an end, these come to an end, but the receptacles remain. Yet with us, it doesn't happen that way. ³⁶ For we who have received the law will perish by sin, along with our heart which received it. ³⁷ Notwithstanding the law doesn't perish, but remains in its honor." ³⁸ When I spoke these things in my heart, I looked around me with my eyes, and on my right side I saw a woman, and behold, she mourned and wept with a loud voice, and was much grieved in mind. Her clothes were torn, and she had ashes on her head. 39 Then let I my thoughts go in which I was occupied, and turned myself to her, 40 and said to her, "Why are you weeping? Why are you grieved in your mind?" 41 She said to me, "Leave me alone, my Lord, that I may weep for myself and add to my sorrow, for I am very troubled in my mind, and brought very low. 42 I said to her, "What ails you? Tell me." 43 She said to me, "I, your servant, was barren and had no child, though I had a husband thirty years. 44 Every hour and every day these thirty years I made my prayer to the Most High day and night. 45 It came to pass after thirty years that God heard me, your handmaid, and saw my low estate, and considered my trouble, and gave me a son. I rejoiced in him greatly, I and my husband, and all my neighbors. We gave great honor to the Mighty One. 46 I nourished him with great care. 47 So when he grew up, and I came to take him a wife, I made him a feast day.

10

1 "So it came to pass that when my son was entered into his wedding chamber, he fell down and died. 2 Then we all put out the lamps, and all my neighbors rose up to comfort me. I remained quiet until the second day at night. 3 It came to pass, when they had all stopped consoling me, encouraging me to be quiet, then rose I up by night, and fled, and came here into this field, as you see. 4 Now I don't intend to return into the city, but to stay here, and not eat or drink, but to continually mourn and fast until I die." 5 Then I left the reflections I was engaged in, and answered her in anger, 6 "You most foolish woman, don't you see our mourning, and what has happened to us? 7 For Zion the mother of us all is full of sorrow, and much humbled. 8 It is right now to mourn deeply, since we all mourn, and to be sorrowful, since we are all in sorrow, but you are mourning for one son. 9 Ask the earth, and she will tell you that it is she which ought to mourn for so many that grow upon her. 10 For out of her, all had their beginnings, and others will come; and, behold, almost all of them walk into destruction, and the multitude of them is utterly doomed. 11 Who then should mourn more, §she who has lost so great a multitude, or you, who are grieved but for one? 12 But if you say to me, 'My lamentation is not like the earth's,

for I have lost the fruit of my womb, which I brought forth with pains, and bare with sorrows;' ¹³ but it is with the earth after the manner of the earth. The multitude present in it has gone as it came. ¹⁴ Then say Ito you, 'Just as you have brought forth with sorrow, even so the earth also has given her fruit, namely, people, ever since the beginning to him who made her.' ¹⁵ Now therefore keep your sorrow to yourself, and bear with a good courage the adversities which have happened to you. ¹⁶ For if you will acknowledge the decree of God to be just, you will both receive your son in time, and will be praised among women. ¹⁷ Go your way then into the city to your husband." ¹⁸ She said to me, "I won't do that. I will not go into the city, but I will die here." ¹⁹ So I proceeded to speak further to her, and said, ²⁰ "Don't do so, but allow yourself to be persuaded by reason of the adversities of Zion; and be comforted by reason of the sorrow of Jerusalem. ²¹ For you see that our sanctuary has been laid waste, our altar broken down, our temple destroyed, ²² our lute has been brought low, our song is put to silence, our rejoicing is at an end, the light of our candlestick is put out, the ark of our covenant is plundered, our holy things are defiled, and the name that we are called is profaned. Our free men are despitefully treated, our priests are burned, our Levites have gone into captivity, our virgins are defiled and our wives ravished, our righteous men carried away, our little ones betrayed, our young men are brought into bondage, and our strong men have become weak. ²³ What is more than all, the seal of Zion has now lost the seal of her honor, and is delivered into the hands of those who hate us. ²⁴ Therefore shake off your great heaviness, and put away from yourself the multitude of sorrows, that the Mighty One may be merciful to you again, and the Most High may give you rest, even ease from your troubles." ²⁵ It came to pass while I was talking with her, behold, her face suddenly began to shine exceedingly, and her countenance glistered like lightning, so that I was very afraid of her, and wondered what this meant. ²⁶ Behold, suddenly she made a great and very fearful cry, so that the earth shook at the noise. ²⁷ I looked, and behold, the woman appeared to me no more, but there was a city built, and a place shown itself from large foundations. Then I was afraid, and cried with a loud voice, ²⁸ "Where is Uriel the angel, who came to me at the first? For he has caused me to fall into this great trance, and my end has turned into corruption, and my prayer a reproach!" ²⁹ As I was speaking these words, behold, the angel who had come to me at first came to me, and he looked at me. ³⁰ Behold, I lay as one who had been dead, and my understanding was taken from me. He took me by the right hand, and comforted me, and set me on my feet, and said to me, ³¹ "What ails you? Why are you so troubled? Why is your understanding and the thoughts of your heart troubled?" ³² I said, "Because you have forsaken me; yet I did according to your words, and went into the field, and, behold, I have seen, and still see, that which I am not able to explain." ³³ He said to me, "Stand up like a man, and I will instruct you." ³⁴ Then I said, "Speak on, my Lord; only don't forsake me, lest I die before my time. ³⁵ For I have seen what I didn't know, and hear what I don't know. ³⁶ Or is my sense deceived, or my soul in a dream? ³⁷ Now therefore I beg you to explain to your servant what this vision means." ³⁸ He answered me, "Listen to me, and I will inform you, and tell you about the things you are afraid of, for the Most High has revealed many secret things to you. ³⁹ He has seen that your way is righteous, because you are continually sorry for your people, and make great lamentation for Zion. ⁴⁰ This therefore is the meaning of the vision. ⁴¹ The woman who appeared to you a little while ago, whom you saw mourning, and began to comfort her, ⁴² but now you no longer see the likeness of the woman, but a city under construction appeared to you, ⁴³ and she told you of the death of her son, this is the interpretation: ⁴⁴ This woman, whom you saw, is Zion, whom you now see as a city being built. ⁴⁵ She told you that she had been barren for thirty years because there were three thousand years in the world in which there was no offering as yet offered in her. ⁴⁶ And it came to pass after three thousand years that Solomon built the city and offered offerings. It was then that the barren bore a son. ⁴⁷ She told you that she nourished him with great care. That was the dwelling in Jerusalem. ⁴⁸ When she said to you, 'My son died when he entered into his marriage chamber, and that misfortune befell her,' this was the destruction that came to Jerusalem. 49 Behold, you saw her likeness, how she mourned for her son, and you began to comfort her for what has happened to her. These were the things to be opened to you. 50 For now the Most High, seeing that you are sincerely grieved and suffer from your whole heart for her, has shown you the brightness of her glory and the attractiveness of her beauty. 51 Therefore I asked you to remain in the field where no house was built, 52 for I knew that the Most High would show this to you. 53 Therefore I commanded you to come into the field, where no foundation of any building was. 54 For no human construction could stand in the place in which the city of the Most High was to be shown. 55 Therefore don't be afraid nor let your heart be terrified, but go your way in and see the beauty and greatness of the building, as much as your eyes are able to see. 56 Then will you hear as much as your ears may comprehend. 57 For you are more blessed than many, and are called by name to be with the Most High, like only a few. 58 But tomorrow at night you shall remain here, 59 and so the Most High will show you those visions in dreams of what the Most High will do to those who live on the earth in the last days." So I slept that night and another, as he commanded me.

11

1 It came to pass the second night that I saw a dream, and behold, an eagle which had twelve feathered wings and three heads came up from the sea. 2 I saw, and behold, she spread her wings over all the earth, and all the winds of heaven blew on her, and the clouds were gathered together against her. 3 I saw, and out of her wings there grew other wings near them; and they became little, tiny wings. 4 But her heads were at rest. The head in the middle was larger than the other heads, yet rested it with them. 5 Moreover I saw, and behold, the eagle flew with her wings to reign over the earth and over those who dwell therein. 6 I saw how all things under heaven were subject to her, and no one spoke against her—no, not one creature on earth. 7 I saw, and behold, the eagle rose on her talons, and uttered her voice to

her wings, saying, 8 "Don't all watch at the same time. Let each one sleep in his own place and watch in turn; 9 but let the heads be preserved for the last." 10 I saw, and behold, the voice didn't come out of her heads, but from the midst of her body. 11 I counted her wings that were near the others, and behold, there were eight of them. 12 I saw, and behold, on the right side one wing arose and reigned over all the earth. 13 When it reigned, the end of it came, and it disappeared, so that its place appeared no more. The next wing rose up and reigned, and it ruled a long time. 14 It happened that when it reigned, its end came also, so that it disappeared, like the first. 15 Behold, a voice came to it, and said, 16 "Listen, you who have ruled over the earth all this time! I proclaim this to you, before you disappear, 17 none after you will rule as long as you, not even half as long." 18 Then the third arose, and ruled as the others before, and it also disappeared. 19 So it went with all the wings one after another, as every one ruled, and then disappeared. 20 I saw, and behold, in process of time the wings that followed were set up on the right side, that they might rule also.

Some of them ruled, but in a while they disappeared. 21 Some of them also were setup, but didn't rule. 22 After this I saw, and behold, the twelve wings disappeared, along with two of the little wings. 23 There was no more left on the eagle's body, except the three heads that rested, and six little wings. 24 I saw, and behold, two little wings divided themselves from the six and remained under the head that was on the right side; but four remained in their place. 25 I saw, and behold, these under wings planned to set themselves up and to rule. 26 I saw, and behold, there was one set up, but in a while it disappeared. 27 A second also did so, and it disappeared faster than the first. 28 I saw, and behold, the two that remained also planned between themselves to reign. 29 While they thought about it, behold, one of the heads that were at rest awakened, the one that was in the middle, for that was greater than the two other heads. 30 I saw how it joined the two other heads with it. 31 Behold, the head turned with those who were with it, and ate the two under wings that planned to reign. 32 But this head held the whole earth in possession, and ruled over those who dwell in it with much oppression. It had stronger governance over the world than all the wings that had gone before. 33 After this I saw, and behold, the head also that was in the middle suddenly disappeared, like the wings. 34 But the two heads remained, which also reigned the same way over the earth and over those who dwell in it. 35 I saw, and behold, the head on the right side devoured the one that was on the left side. 36 Then I heard a voice, which said to me, "Look in front of you, and consider the thing that you see." 37 I saw, and behold, something like a lion roused out of the woods roaring. I heard how he sent out a man's voice to the eagle, and spoke, saying, 38 "Listen and I will talk with you. The Most High will say to you, 39 'Aren't you the one that remains of the four animals whom I made to reign in my world, that the end of my times might come through them? 40 The fourth came and overcame all the animals that were past, and ruled the world with great trembling, and the whole extent of the earth with grievous oppression. He lived on the earth such a long time with deceit. 41 You have judged the earth, but not with truth. 42 For you have afflicted the meek, you have hurt the peaceful, you have hated those who speak truth, you have loved liars, destroyed the dwellings of those who produced fruit, and threw down the walls of those who did you no harm. 43 Your insolence has come up to the Most High, and your pride to the Mighty. 44 The Most High also has looked at his times, and behold, they are ended, and his ages are fulfilled. 45 Therefore appear no more, you eagle, nor your horrible wings, nor your evil little wings, nor your cruel heads, nor your hurtful talons, nor all your worthless body, 46 that all the earth may be refreshed and relieved, being delivered from your violence, and that she may hope for the judgment and mercy of him who made her."

12

1 It came to pass, while the lion spoke these words to the eagle, I saw, 2 and behold, the head that remained disappeared, and the two wings which went over to it arose and set themselves up to reign; and their kingdom was brief and full of uproar. 3 I saw, and behold, they disappeared, and the whole body of the eagle was burned, so that the earth was in great fear. Then I woke up

because of great perplexity of mind and great fear, and said to my spirit, 4 "Behold, you have done this to me, because you search out the ways of the Most High. 5 Behold, I am still weary in my mind, and very weak in my spirit. There isn't even a little strength in me, because of the great fear with which I was frightened tonight. 6 Therefore I will now ask the Most High that he would strengthen me to the end." 7 Then I said, "O sovereign Lord, if I have found favor in your sight, and if I am justified with you more than many others, and if my prayer has indeed come up before your face, 8 strengthen me then, and show me, your servant, the interpretation and plain meaning of this fearful vision, that you may fully comfort my soul. 9 For you have judged me worthy to show me the end of time and the last events of the times." 10 He said to me, "This is the interpretation of this vision which you saw: 11 The eagle, whom you saw come up from the sea, is the fourth kingdom which appeared in a vision to your brother Daniel. 12 But it was not explained to him, as I now explain it to you or have explained it. 13 Behold, the days come that a kingdom will rise up on earth, and it will be feared more than all the kingdoms that were before it. 14 Twelve kings will reign in it, one after another. 15 Of those, the second will begin to reign, and will reign a longer time than others of the twelve. 16 This is the interpretation of the twelve wings which you saw. 17 As for when you heard a voice which spoke, not going out from the heads, but from the midst of its body, this is the interpretation: 18 That after the time of that kingdom, there will arise no small contentions, and it will stand in peril of falling. Nevertheless, it won't fall then, but will be restored again to its former power. 19 You saw the eight under wings sticking to her wings. This is the interpretation: 20 That in it eight kings will arise, whose times will be short and their years swift. 21 Two of them will perish when the middle time approaches. Four will be kept for a while until the time of the ending of it will approach; but two will be kept to the end. 22 You saw three heads resting. This is the interpretation: 23 In its last days, the Most High will raise up three §kingdoms and renew many things in them. They will rule over the earth, 24 and over those who dwell in it, with much oppression, more than all those who were before them. Therefore they are called the heads of the eagle. 25 For these are those who will accomplish her wickedness, and who will finish her last actions. 26 You saw that the great head disappeared. It signifies that one of them will die on his bed, and yet with pain. 27 But for the two that remained, the sword will devour them. 28 For the sword of the one will devour him that was with him, but he will also fall by the sword in the last days. 29 You saw two under wings passing over to the head that is on the right side. 30 This is the interpretation: These are they whom the Most High has kept to his end. This is the brief reign that was full of trouble, as you saw. 31 "The lion, whom you saw rising up out of the forest, roaring, speaking to the eagle, and rebuking her for her unrighteousness, and all her words which you have heard, 32 this is the anointed one, whom the Most High has kept to the end of days, who will spring up out of the seed of David, and he will come and speak to them and reprove them for their wickedness and unrighteousness, and will heap up before them their contemptuous dealings. 33

For at first he will set them alive in his judgment, and when he has reproved them, he will destroy them. 34 For he will deliver the rest of my people with mercy, those who have been preserved throughout my borders, and he will make them joyful until the coming of the end, even the day of judgment, about which I have spoken to you from the beginning. 35 This is the dream that you saw, and this is its interpretation. 36 Only you have been worthy to know the secret of the Most High. 37 Therefore write all these things that you have seen in a book, and put it in a secret place. 38 You shall teach them to the wise of your people, whose hearts you know are able to comprehend and keep these secrets. 39 But wait here yourself seven more days, that you may be shown whatever it pleases the Most High to show you." Then he departed from me. 40 It came to pass, when all the people saw that the seven days were past, and I had not come again into the city, they all gathered together, from the least to the greatest, and came to me, and spoke to me, saying, 41 "How have we offended you? What evil have we done against you, that you have utterly forsaken us, and sit in this place? ⁴² For of all the prophets, only you are left to us, like a cluster of the vintage, and like a lamp in a dark place, and like a harbor for a ship saved from the tempest. ⁴³ Aren't the evils which have come to us sufficient? ⁴⁴ If you will forsake us, how much better had it been for us if we also had been consumed in the burning of Zion! ⁴⁵ For we are not better than those who died there." Then they wept with a loud voice. I answered them, ⁴⁶ "Take courage, O Israel! Don't be sorrowful, you house of Jacob; ⁴⁷ for the Most High remembers you. The Mighty has not forgotten you forever. ⁴⁸ As for me, I have not forsaken you. I haven't departed from you; but I have come into this place to pray for the desolation of Zion, and that I might seek mercy for the humiliation of your sanctuary. ⁴⁹ Now go your way, every man to his own house, and after these days I will come to you." ⁵⁰ So the people went their way into the city, as I told them to do. ⁵¹ But I sat in the field seven days, as the angel commanded me. In those days, I ate only of the flowers of the field, and my food was from plants.

13

¹ It came to pass after seven days, I dreamed a dream by night. ² Behold, a wind arose from the sea that moved all its waves. ³ I saw, and behold, this wind caused to come up from the midst of the sea something like the appearance of a man. I saw, and behold, that man flew with the clouds of heaven. When he turned his face to look, everything that he saw trembled. ⁴ Whenever the voice went out of his mouth, all who heard his voice melted, like the wax melts when it feels the fire. ⁵ After this I saw, and behold, an innumerable multitude of people was gathered together from the four winds of heaven to make war against the man who came out of the sea. ⁶ I saw, and behold, he carved himself a great mountain, and flew up onto it. ⁷ I tried to see the region or place from which the mountain was carved, and I couldn't. ⁸ After this I saw, and behold, all those who were gathered together to fight against him were very afraid, and yet they dared to fight. ⁹ Behold, as he saw the assault of the multitude that came, he didn't lift up his hand, or hold a spear or any weapon of war; ¹⁰ but I saw only how he sent out of his

mouth something like a flood of fire, and out of his lips a flaming breath, and out of his tongue he shot out a storm of sparks. 11 These were all mixed together: the flood of fire, the flaming breath, and the great storm, and fell upon the assault of the multitude which was prepared to fight, and burned up every one of them, so that all of a sudden an innumerable multitude was seen to be nothing but dust of ashes and smell of smoke. When I saw this, I was amazed. 12 Afterward, I saw the same man come down from the mountain, and call to himself another multitude which was peaceful. 13 Many people came to him. Some of them were glad. Some were sorry. Some of them were bound, and some others brought some of those as offerings. Then through great fear I woke up and prayed to the Most High, and said, 14 "You have shown your servant these wonders from the beginning, and have counted me worthy that you should receive my prayer. 15 Now show me also the interpretation of this dream. 16 For as I conceive in my understanding, woe to those who will be left in those days! Much more woe to those who are not left! 17 For those who were not left will be in heaviness, 18 understanding the things that are laid up in the latter days, but not attaining to them. 19 But woe to them also who are left, because they will see great perils and much distress, like these dreams declare. 20 Yet is it better for one to be in peril and to come into these things, than to pass away as a cloud out of the world, and not to see the things that will happen in the last days." He answered me, 21 "I will tell you the interpretation of the vision, and I will also open to you the things about which you mentioned. 22 You have spoken of those who are left behind. This is the interpretation: 23 He that will endure the peril in that time will protect those who fall into danger, even those who have works and faith toward the Almighty. 24 Know therefore that those who are left behind are more blessed than those who are dead. 25 These are the interpretations of the vision: Whereas you saw a man coming up from the midst of the sea, 26 this is he whom the Most High has been keeping for many ages, who by his own self will deliver his creation. He will direct those who are left behind. 27 Whereas you saw that out of his mouth came wind, fire, and storm, 28 and whereas he held neither spear, nor any weapon of war, but destroyed the assault of that multitude which came to fight against him, this is the interpretation: 29 Behold, the days come when the Most High will begin to deliver those who are on the earth. 30 Astonishment of mind will come upon those who dwell on the earth. 31 One will plan to make war against another, city against city, place against place, people against people, and kingdom against kingdom. 32 It will be, when these things come to pass, and the signs happen which I showed you before, then my Son will be revealed, whom you saw as a man ascending. 33 It will be, when all the nations hear his voice, every man will leave his own land and the battle they have against one another. 34 An innumerable multitude will be gathered together, as you saw, desiring to come and to fight against him. 35 But he will stand on the top of Mount Zion. 36 Zion will come, and will be shown to all men, being prepared and built, like you saw the mountain carved without hands. 37 My Son will rebuke the nations which have come for their wickedness, with plagues that are like a storm, 38 and will rebuke them to their face with their evil thoughts, and the torments with which they will be tormented, which are like a flame. He will destroy them without labor by the law, which is like fire. 39 Whereas you saw that he gathered to himself another multitude that was peaceful, 40 these are the ten tribes which were led away out of their own land in the time of Osea the king, whom Salmananser the king of the Assyrians led away captive, and he carried them beyond the River, and they were taken into another land. 41 But they made this plan among themselves, that they would leave the multitude of the heathen, and go out into a more distant region, where mankind had never lived, 42 that there they might keep their statutes which they had not kept in their own land. 43 They entered by the narrow passages of the river Euphrates. 44 For the Most High then did signs for them, and stopped the springs of the River until they had passed over. 45 For through that country there was a long way to go, namely, of a year and a half. The same region is called Arzareth. 46 Then they lived there until the latter time. Now when they begin to come again, 47 the Most High stops the springs of the River again, that they may go through. Therefore you saw the multitude gathered together with peace. ⁴⁸ But those who are left behind of your people are those who are found within my holy border. ⁴⁹ It will be therefore when he will destroy the multitude of the nations that are gathered together, he will defend the people who remain. ⁵⁰ Then will he show them very many wonders." ⁵¹ Then I said, "O sovereign Lord, explain this to me: Why have I seen the man coming up from the midst of the sea?" ⁵² He said to me, as no one can explore or know what is in the depths of the sea, even so no man on earth can see my Son, or those who are with him, except in the time of his day. ⁵³ This is the interpretation of the dream which you saw, and for this only you are enlightened about this, ⁵⁴ for you have forsaken your own ways, and applied your diligence to mine, and have searched out my law. ⁵⁵ You have ordered your life in wisdom, and have called understanding your mother. ⁵⁶ Therefore I have shown you this, for there is a reward laid up with the Most High. It will be, after another three days I will speak other things to you, and declare to you mighty and wondrous things." ⁵⁷ Then I went out and passed into the field, giving praise and thanks greatly to the Most High because of his wonders, which he did from time to time, ⁵⁸ and because he governs the time, and such things as happen in their seasons. So I sat there three days.

14

¹ It came to pass upon the third day, I sat under an oak, and, behold, a voice came out of a bush near me, and said, "Esdras, Esdras!" ² I said, "Here I am, Lord," and I stood up on my feet. ³ Then he said to me, "I revealed myself in a bush and talked with Moses when my people were in bondage in Egypt. ⁴ I sent him, and he led my people out of Egypt. I brought him up to Mount Sinai, where I kept him with me for many days. ⁵ I told him many wondrous things, and showed him the secrets of the times and the end of the seasons. I commanded him, saying, ⁶ 'You shall publish these openly, and these you shall hide.' ⁷ Now I say to you: ⁸ Lay up in your heart the signs that I have shown, the dreams that you have seen, and the interpretations which you have heard; ⁹ for you will be taken away from men, and from now

on you will live with my Son and with those who are like you, until the times have ended. 10 For the world has lost its youth, and the times begin to grow old. 11 For the age is divided into twelve parts, and ten parts of it are already gone, even the half of the tenth part. 12 There remain of it two parts after the middle of the tenth part. 13 Now therefore set your house in order, reprove your people, comfort the lowly among them, and instruct those of them who are wise, and now renounce the life that is corruptible, 14 and let go of the mortal thoughts, cast away from you the burdens of man, put off now your weak nature, 15 lay aside the thoughts that are most grievous to you, and hurry to escape from these times. 16 For worse evils than those which you have seen happen will be done after this. 17 For look how much the world will be weaker through age, so much that more evils will increase on those who dwell in it. 18 For the truth will withdraw itself further off, and falsehood will be near. For now the eagle which you saw in vision hurries to come." 19 Then I answered and said, "Let me speak in your presence, O Lord. 20 Behold, I will go, as you have commanded me, and reprove the people who now live, but who will warn those who will be born afterward? For the world is set in darkness, and those who dwell in it are without light. 21 For your law has been burned, therefore no one knows the things that are done by you, or the works that will be done. 22 But if I have found favor before you, send the Holy Spirit to me, and I will write all that has been done in the world since the beginning, even the things that were written in your law, that men may be able to find the path, and that those who would live in the latter days may live." 23 He answered me and said, "Go your way, gather the people together, and tell them not to seek you for forty days. 24 But prepare for yourself many tablets, and take with you Sarea, Dabria, Selemia, Ethanus, and Asiel, these five, which are ready to write swiftly; 25 and come here, and I will light a lamp of understanding in your heart which will not be put out until the things have ended about which you will write. 26 When you are done, some things you shall publish openly, and some things you shall deliver in secret to the wise. Tomorrow at this hour you will begin to write." 27 Then went I out, as he commanded me, and gathered all the people together, and said, 28 "Hear these words, O Israel! 29 Our fathers at the beginning were foreigners in Egypt, and they were delivered from there, 30 and received the law of life, which they didn't keep, which you also have transgressed after them. 31 Then the land of Zion was given to you for a possession; but you yourselves and your ancestors have done unrighteousness, and have not kept the ways which the Most High commanded you. 32 Becausehe is a righteous judge, in due time, he took from you what he had given you. 33 Now you are here, and your kindred are among you. 34 Therefore if you will rule over your own understanding and instruct your hearts, you will be kept alive, and after death you will obtain mercy. 35 For after death the judgment will come, when we will live again. Then the names of the righteous will become manifest, and the works of the ungodly will be declared. 36 Let no one therefore come to me now, nor seek me for forty days." 37 So I took the five men, as he commanded me, and we went out into the field, and remained there. 38 It came to pass on the next day that, behold, a voice called me, saying, "Esdras, open your mouth, and drink what I give you to drink." 39 Then opened I my mouth, and behold, a full cup was handed to me. It was full of something like water, but its color was like fire. 40 I took it, and drank. When I had drunk it, my heart uttered understanding, and wisdom grew in my chest, for my spirit retained its memory. 41 My mouth was opened, and shut no more. 42 The Most High gave understanding to the five men, and they wrote by course the things that were told them, in †characters which they didn't know, and they sat forty days. Now they wrote in the daytime, and at night they ate bread. 43 As for me, I spoke in the day, and by night I didn't hold my tongue. 44 So in forty days, ninety-four books were written. 45 It came to pass, when the forty days were fulfilled, that the Most High spoke to me, saying, "The first books that you have written, publish openly, and let the worthy and unworthy read them; 46 but keep the last seventy, that you may deliver them to those who are wise among your people; 47 for in them is the spring of understanding, the fountain of wisdom, and the stream of knowledge." 48 I did so.

15

¹ "Behold, speak in the ears of my people the words of prophecy which I will put in your mouth," says the Lord. ² "Cause them to be written on paper, for they are faithful and true. ³ Don't be afraid of their plots against you. Don't let the unbelief of those who speak against you trouble you. ⁴ For all the unbelievers will die in their unbelief. ⁵ "Behold," says the Lord, "I bring evils on the whole earth: sword, famine, death, and destruction. ⁶ For wickedness has prevailed over every land, and their hurtful works have reached their limit. ⁷ Therefore," says the Lord, ⁸ "I will hold my peace no more concerning their wickedness which they profanely commit, neither will I tolerate them in these things, which they wickedly practice. Behold, the innocent and righteous blood cries to me, and the souls of the righteous cry out continually. ⁹ I will surely avenge them," says the Lord, "and will receive to me all the innocent blood from among them. ¹⁰ Behold, my people is led like a flock to the slaughter. I will not allow them now to dwell in the land of Egypt, ¹¹ but I will bring them out with a mighty hand and with a high arm, and will strike Egypt with plagues, as before, and will destroy all its land." ¹² Let Egypt and its foundations mourn, for the plague of the chastisement and the punishment that God will bring upon it. ¹³ Let the farmers that till the ground mourn, for their seeds will fail and their trees will be ruined through the blight and hail, and a terrible tempest. ¹⁴ Woe to the world and those who dwell in it! ¹⁵ For the sword and their destruction draws near, and nation will rise up against nation to battle with weapons in their hands. ¹⁶ For there will be sedition among men, and growing strong against one another. In their might, they won't respect their king or the chief of their great ones. ¹⁷ For a man will desire to go into a city, and will not be able. ¹⁸ For because of their pride the cities will be troubled, the houses will be destroyed, and men will be afraid. ¹⁹ A man will have no pity on his neighbors, but will assault their houses with the sword and plunder their goods, because of the lack of bread, and for great suffering. ²⁰ "Behold," says God, "I call together all the kings of the earth to stir up those who are from the rising of the sun, from the south, from the east, and

Libanus, to turn themselves one against another, and repay the things that they have done to them. 21 Just as they do yet this day to my chosen, so I will do also, and repay into their bosom." The Lord God says: 22 "My right hand won't spare the sinners, and my sword won't cease over those who shed innocent blood on the earth. 23 A fire has gone out from his wrath and has consumed the foundations of the earth and the sinners, like burnt straw. 24 Woe to those who sin and don't keep my commandments!" says the Lord. 25 "I will not spare them. Go your way, you rebellious children! Don't defile my sanctuary!" 26 For the Lord knows all those who trespass against him, therefore he will deliver them to death and destruction. 27 For now evils have come upon the whole earth, and you will remain in them; for God will not deliver you, because you have sinned against him. 28 Behold, a horrible sight appearing from the east! 29 The nations of the dragons of Arabia will come out with many chariots. From the day that they set out, their hissing is carried over the earth, so that all those who will hear them may also fear and tremble. 30 Also the Carmonians, raging in wrath, will go out like the wild boars of the forest. They will come with great power and join battle with them, and will devastate a portion of the land of the Assyrians with their teeth. 31 Then the dragons will have the upper hand, remembering their nature. If they will turn themselves, conspiring together in great power to persecute them, 32 then these will be troubled, and keep silence through their power, and will turn and flee. 33 From the land of the Assyrians, an enemy in ambush will attack them and destroy one of them. Upon their army will be fear and trembling, and indecision upon their kings. 34 Behold, clouds from the east, and from the north to the south! They are very horrible to look at, full of wrath and storm. 35 They will clash against one another. They will pour out a heavy storm on the earth, even their own storm. There will be blood from the sword to the horse's belly, 36 and to the thigh of man, and to the camel's hock. 37 There will be fearfulness and great trembling upon earth. They who see that wrath will be afraid, and trembling will seize them. 38 After this, great storms will be stirred up from the south, from the north, and another part from the west. 39 Strong winds will arise from the east, and will shut it up, even the cloud which he raised up in wrath; and the storm that was to cause destruction by the east wind will be violently driven toward the south and west. 40 Great and mighty clouds, full of wrath, will be lifted up with the storm, that they may destroy all the earth and those who dwell in it. They will pour out over every high and lofty one a terrible storm, 41 fire, hail, flying swords, and many waters, that all plains may be full, and all rivers, with the abundance of those waters. 42 They will break down the cities and walls, mountains and hills, trees of the forest, and grass of the meadows, and their grain. 43 They will go on steadily to Babylon and destroy her. 44 They will come to it and surround it. They will pour out the storm and all wrath on her. Then the dust and smoke will go up to the sky, and all those who are around it will mourn for it. 45 Those who remain will serve those who have destroyed it. 46 You, Asia, who are partaker in the beauty of Babylon, and in the glory of her person— 47 woe to you, you wretch, because you have made yourself like her. You have decked out your daughters for prostitution, that they might please and glory in your lovers, which have always lusted after you! 48 You have followed her who is hateful in all her works and inventions. Therefore God says, 49 "I will send evils on you: widowhood, poverty, famine, sword, and pestilence, to lay waste your houses and bring you to destruction and death. 50 The glory of your power will be dried up like a flower when the heat rises that is sent over you. 51 You will be weakened like a poor woman who is beaten and wounded, so that you won't be able to receive your mighty ones and your lovers. 52 Would I have dealt with you with such jealousy," says the Lord, 53 "if you had not always slain my chosen, exalting and clapping of your hands, and saying over their dead, when you were drunk? 54 "Beautify your face! 55 The reward of a prostitute will be in your bosom, therefore you will be repaid. 56 Just as you will do to my chosen," says the Lord, "even so God will do to you, and will deliver you to your adversaries. 57 Your children will die of hunger. You will fall by the sword. Your cities will be broken down, and all your people in the field will perish by the sword. ⁵⁸ Those who are in the mountains will die of hunger, eat their own flesh, and drink their own blood, because of hunger for bread and thirst for water. ⁵⁹ You, unhappy above all others, will come and will again receive evils. ⁶⁰ In the passage, they will rush on the hateful city and will destroy some portion of your land, and mar part of your glory, and will return again to Babylon that was destroyed. ⁶¹ You will be cast down by them as stubble, and they will be to you as fire. ⁶² They will devour you, your cities, your land, and your mountains. They will burn all your forests and your fruitful trees with fire. ⁶³ They will carry your children away captive, and will plunder your wealth, and mar the glory of your face."

16

¹ Woe to you, Babylon, and Asia! Woe to you, Egypt and Syria! ² Put on sackcloth and garments of goats' hair, wail for your children and lament; for your destruction is at hand. ³ A sword has been sent upon you, and who is there to turn it back? ⁴ A fire has been sent upon you, and who is there to quench it? ⁵ Calamities are sent upon you, and who is there to drive them away? ⁶ Can one drive away a hungry lion in the forest? Can one quench a fire in stubble, once it has begun to burn? ⁷ Can one turn back an arrow that is shot by a strong archer? ⁸ The Lord God sends the calamities, and who will drive them away? ⁹ A fire will go out from his wrath, and who may quench it? ¹⁰ He will flash lightning, and who will not fear? He will thunder, and who wouldn't tremble? ¹¹ The Lord will threaten, and who will not be utterly broken in pieces at his presence? ¹² The earth and its foundations quake. The sea rises up with waves from the deep, and its waves will be troubled, along with the fish in them, at the presence of the Lord, and before the glory of his power. ¹³ For his right hand that bends the bow is strong, his arrows that he shoots are sharp, and will not miss when they begin to be shot into the ends of the world. ¹⁴ Behold, the calamities are sent out, and will not return again until they come upon the earth. ¹⁵ The fire is kindled and will not be put out until it consumes the foundations of the earth. ¹⁶ Just as an arrow which is shot by a mighty archer doesn't return backward, even so the calamities that are sent out upon earth won't return again. ¹⁷ Woe is me! Woe is me! Who will

deliver me in those days? 18 The beginning of sorrows, when there will be great mourning; the beginning of famine, and many will perish; the beginning of wars, and the powers will stand in fear; the beginning of calamities, and all will tremble! What will they do when the calamities come? 19 Behold, famine and plague, suffering and anguish! They are sent as scourges for correction. 20 But for all these things they will not turn them from their wickedness, nor be always mindful of the scourges. 21 Behold, food will be so cheap on earth that they will think themselves to be in good condition, and even then calamities will grow on earth: sword, famine, and great confusion. 22 For many of those who dwell on earth will perish of famine; and others who escape the famine, the sword will destroy. 23 The dead will be cast out like dung, and there will be no one to comfort them; for the earth will be left desolate, and its cities will be cast down. 24 There will be no farmer left to cultivate the earth or to sow it. 25 The trees will give fruit, but who will gather it? 26 The grapes will ripen, but who will tread them? For in all places there will be a great solitude; 27 for one man will desire to see another, or to hear his voice. 28 For of a city there will be ten left, and two of the field, who have hidden themselves in the thick groves, and in the clefts of the rocks. 29 As in an orchard of olives upon every tree there may be left three or four olives, 30 or as when a vineyard is gathered, there are some clusters left by those who diligently search through the vineyard, 31 even so in those days, there will be three or four left by those who search their houses with the sword. 32 The earth will be left desolate, and its fields will be for briers, and its roads and all her paths will grow thorns, because no sheep will pass along them. 33 The virgins will mourn, having no bridegrooms. The women will mourn, having no husbands. Their daughters will mourn, having no helpers. 34 Their bridegrooms will be destroyed in the wars, and their husbands will perish of famine. 35 Hear now these things, and understand them, you servants of the Lord. 36 Behold, the Lord's word: receive it. Don't doubt the things about which the Lord speaks. 37 Behold, the calamities draw near, and are not delayed. 38 Just as a woman with child in the ninth month, when the hour of her delivery draws near, within two or three hours great pains surround her womb, and when the child comes out from the womb, there will be no waiting for a moment, 39 even so the calamities won't delay coming upon the earth. The world will groan, and sorrows will seize it on every side. 40 "O my people, hear my word: prepare for battle, and in those calamities be like strangers on the earth. 41 He who sells, let him be as he who flees away, and he who buys, as one who will lose. 42 Let he who does business be as he who has no profit by it, and he who builds, as he who won't dwell in it, 43 and he who sows, as if he wouldn't reap, so also he who prunes the vines, as he who won't gather the grapes, 44 those who marry, as those who will have no children, and those who don't marry, as the widowed. 45 Because of this, those who labor, labor in vain; 46 for foreigners will reap their fruits, plunder their goods, overthrow their houses, and take their children captive, for in captivity and famine they will conceive their children. 47 Those who conduct business, do so only to be plundered. The more they adorn their cities, their houses, their possessions, and

their own persons, 48 the more I will hate them for their sins," says the Lord. 49 Just as a respectable and virtuous woman hates a prostitute, 50 so will righteousness hate iniquity, when she adorns herself, and will accuse her to her face, when he comes who will defend him who diligently searches out every sin on earth. 51 Therefore don't be like her or her works. 52 For yet a little while, and iniquity will be taken away out of the earth, and righteousness will reign over us. 53 Don't let the sinner say that he has not sinned; for God will burn coals of fire on the head of one who says "I haven't sinned before God and his glory." 54 Behold, the Lord knows all the works of men, their imaginations, their thoughts, and their hearts. 55 He said, "Let the earth be made," and it was made, "Let the sky be made," and it was made. 56 At his word, the stars were established, and he knows the number oft he stars. 57 He searches the deep and its treasures. He has measured the sea and what it contains. 58 He has shut the sea in the midst of the waters, and with his word, he hung the earth over the waters. 59 He has spread out the sky like a vault. He has founded it over the waters. 60 He has made springs of water in the desert and pools on the tops of the mountains to send out rivers from the heights to water the earth. ⁶¹ He formed man, and put a heart in the midst of the body, and gave him breath, life, and understanding, ⁶² yes, the spirit of God Almighty. He who made all things and searches out hidden things in hidden places, ⁶³ surely he knows your imagination, and what you think in your hearts. Woe to those who sin, and try to hide their sin! ⁶⁴ Because the Lord will exactly investigate all your works, and he will put you all to shame. ⁶⁵ When your sins are brought out before men, you will be ashamed, and your own iniquities will stand as your accusers in that day. ⁶⁶ What will you do? Or how will you hide your sins before God and his angels? ⁶⁷ Behold, God is the judge. Fear him! Stop sinning, and forget your iniquities, to never again commit them. So will God lead you out, and deliver you from all suffering. ⁶⁸ For, behold, the burning wrath of a great multitude is kindled over you, and they will take away some of you, and feed you with that which is sacrificed to idols. ⁶⁹ Those who consent to them will be held in derision and in contempt, and be trodden under foot. ⁷⁰ For there will be in various places, and in the next cities, a great insurrection against those who fear the Lord. ⁷¹ They will be like mad men, sparing none, but spoiling and destroying those who still fear the Lord. ⁷² For they will destroy and plunder their goods, and throw them out of their houses. ⁷³ Then the trial of my elect will be made known, even as the gold that is tried in the fire. ⁷⁴ Hear, my elect ones, says the Lord: "Behold, the days of suffering are at hand, and I will deliver you from them. ⁷⁵ Don't be afraid, and don't doubt, for God is your guide. ⁷⁶ You who keep my commandments and precepts," says the Lord God, "don't let your sins weigh you down, and don't let your iniquities lift themselves up." ⁷⁷ Woe to those who are choked with their sins and covered with their iniquities, like a field is choked with bushes, and its path covered with thorns, that no one may travel through! ⁷⁸ It is shut off and given up to be consumed by fire.

Tobit

The Book of Tobit stands out as a compelling narrative that weaves together themes of piety, righteousness, and divine providence, set against the backdrop of the Assyrian captivity of the Israelites. The story is centered on Tobit, a devout Israelite from the tribe of Naphtali, living in exile in Nineveh after the Assyrian conquest. Despite the adversities faced in exile, Tobit remains steadfast in his adherence to the law, demonstrating unwavering faith and charity by performing acts of kindness, such as burying the dead.

The narrative delves into themes of suffering and redemption, as Tobit loses his sight and seeks healing. Parallel to Tobit's story is that of his son, Tobias, who is sent on a journey to collect a debt, guided by the archangel Raphael, disguised as a human companion. This journey not only leads to Tobias retrieving the debt but also to his marriage to Sarah, a relative plagued by a demon that had killed her previous seven husbands on their wedding nights. Through divine intervention and adherence to instructions given by Raphael, Tobias is able to cure Sarah of her affliction and, upon his return, restore his father's sight. This text is rich in its portrayal of Jewish piety and law, emphasizing the importance of almsgiving, prayer, and fasting. It also highlights the role of angels as intermediaries between God and humans, illustrating the ways in which God intervenes in the lives of the faithful through angelic beings. The story is imbued with moral teachings and practical religious observances, making it a text of both spiritual and ethical instruction.

From a literary standpoint, this text is notable for its narrative richness and depth of character development, blending adventure, romance, and mystery. It provides profound insights into Jewish life during the exile, reflecting the struggles and hopes of the diasporic community in a foreign land. In the context of the Geneva Bible, the inclusion of the Book of Tobit offers readers a narrative that reinforces the themes of faithfulness to God's commands and reliance on divine guidance. It serves as an exemplar of how individual virtue and godliness can prevail despite the challenges of exile and oppression.

Tobit

[1] The book of the words of Tobit, the son of Tobiel, the son of Ananiel, the son of Aduel, the son of Gabael, of the seed of Asiel, of the tribe of Naphtali; [2] who in the days of Enemessar king of the Assyrians was carried away captive out of Thisbe, which is on the right hand of Kedesh Naphtali in Galilee above Asher. [3] I, Tobit walked in the ways of truth and righteousness all the days of my life, and I did many alms deeds to my kindred and my nation, who went with me into the land of the Assyrians, to Nineveh. [4] When I was in my own country, in the land of Israel, while I was yet young, all the tribe of Naphtali my father fell away from the house of Jerusalem, which was chosen out of all the tribes of Israel, that all the tribes should sacrifice there, and the temple of the habitation of the Most High was hallowed and built therein for all ages. [5] All the tribes which fell away together sacrificed to the heifer Baal, and so did the house of Naphtali my father. [6] I alone went often to Jerusalem at the feasts, as it has been ordained to all Israel by an everlasting decree, having the first fruits and the tenths of my increase, and that which was first shorn; and I gave them at the altar to the priests the sons of Aaron. [7] I gave a tenth part of all my increase to the sons of Levi, who ministered at Jerusalem. A second tenth part I sold away, and went, and spent it each year at Jerusalem. [8] A third tenth I gave to them to whom it was appropriate, as Deborah my father's mother had commanded me, because I was left an orphan by my father. [9] When I became a man, I took as wife Anna of the seed of our own family. With her, I became the father of Tobias. [10] When I was carried away captive to Nineveh, all my kindred and my relatives ate of the bread of the Gentiles; [11] but I kept myself from eating, [12] because I remembered God with all my soul. [13] So the Most High gave me grace and favor in the sight of Enemessar, and I was his purchasing agent. [14] And I went into Media, and left ten talents of silver in trust with Gabael, the brother of Gabrias, at Rages of Media. [15] And when Enemessar was dead, Sennacherib his son reigned in his place. In his time, the highways were troubled, and I could no longer go into Media. [16] In the days of Enemessar, I did

many alms deeds to my kindred: I gave my bread to the hungry, 17 and my garments to the naked. If I saw any of my race dead, and thrown out on the wall of Ninevah, I buried him. 18 If Sennacherib the king killed any, when he came fleeing from Judea, I buried them privately; for in his wrath he killed many; and the bodies were sought for by the king, and were not found. 19 But one of the Ninevites went and showed to the king concerning me, how I buried them, and hid myself; and when I knew that I was sought for to be putto death, I withdrew myself for fear. 20 And all my goods were forcibly taken away, and there was nothing left to me, save my wife Anna and my son Tobias. 21 No more than fifty five days passed before two of his sons killed him, and they fled into the mountains of Ararat. And Sarchedonus his son reigned in his place; and he appointed Achiacharus my brother Anael's son over all the accounts of his kingdom, and over all his affairs. 22 Achiacharus requested me, and I came to Nineveh. Now Achiacharus was cupbearer, keeper of the signet, steward, and overseer of the accounts. Sarchedonus appointed him next

to himself, but he was my brother's son.

2

1 Now when I had come home again, and my wife Anna was restored to me, and my son Tobias, in the feast of Pentecost, which is the holy feast of the seven weeks, there was a good dinner prepared for me, and I sat down to eat. 2 I saw abundance of meat, and I said to my son, "Go and bring whatever poor man you find of our kindred, who is mindful of the Lord. Behold, I wait for you." 3 Then he came, and said, "Father, one of our race is strangled, and has been cast out in the marketplace." 4 Before I had tasted anything, I sprang up, and took him up into a chamber until the sun had set. 5 Then I returned, washed myself, ate my bread in heaviness, 6 and remembered the prophecy of Amos, as he said, "Your feasts will be turned into mourning, and all your mirth into lamentation. 7 So I wept: and when the sun had set, I went and dug a grave, and buried him. 8 My neighbors mocked me, and said, "He is no longer afraid to be put to death for this matter; and yet he fled away. Behold, he buries the dead again." 9 The same night I returned from burying him, and

slept by the wall of my courtyard, being polluted; and my face was uncovered. [10] I didn't know that there were sparrows in the wall. My eyes were open and the sparrows dropped warm dung into my eyes, and white films came over my eyes. I went to the physicians, and they didn't help me; but Achiacharus nourished me, until I went into Elymais. [11] My wife Anna wove cloth in the women's chambers, [12] and sent the work back to the owners. They on their part paid her wages, and also gave her a kid. [13] But when it came to my house, it began to cry, and I said to her, "Where did this kid come from? Is it stolen? Give it back to the owners; for it is not lawful to eat anything that is stolen." [14] But she said, "It has been given to me for a gift more than the wages." I didn't believe her, and I asked her to return it to the owners; and I was ashamed of her. But she answered and said to me, "Where are your alms and your righteous deeds? Behold, you and all your works are known."

3
[1] I was grieved and wept, and prayed in sorrow, saying, [2] "O Lord, you are righteous, and all your works and all your ways are mercy and truth, and you judge true and righteous judgment forever. [3] Remember me, and look at me. Don't take vengeance on me for my sins and my ignorances, and the sins of my fathers who sinned before you. [4] For they disobeyed your commandments. You gave us as plunder, for captivity, for death, and for a proverb of reproach to all the nations among whom we are dispersed. [5] Now your judgments are many and true, that you should deal with me according to my sins and the sins of my fathers, because we didn't keep your commandments, for we didn't walk in truth before you. [6] Now deal with me according to that which is pleasing in your sight. Command my spirit to be taken from me, that I may be released, and become earth. For it is more profitable for me to die rather than to live, because I have heard false reproaches, and there is much sorrow in me. Command that I be released from my distress, now, and go to the everlasting place. Don't turn your face away from me." [7] The same day it happened to Sarah the daughter of Raguel in Ecbatana of Media, that she also was reproached by her father's

maidservants; [8] because that she had been given to seven husbands, and Asmodaeus the evil spirit killed them, before they had lain with her. And they said to her, "Do you not know that you strangle your husbands? You have had already seven husbands, and you haven't borne the name of any one of them. [9] Why do you scourge us? If they are dead, go your ways with them. Let us never see either son or daughter from you." [10] When she heard these things, she was grieved exceedingly, so that she thought about hanging herself. Then she said, "I am the only daughter of my father. If I do this, it will be a reproach to him, and I will bring down his old age with sorrow to the grave." [11] Then she prayed by the window, and said, "Blessed are you, O Lord my God, and blessed is your holy and honorable name forever! Let all your works praise you forever! [12] And now, Lord, I have set my eyes and my face toward you. [13] Command that I be released from the earth, and that I no longer hear reproach. [14] You know, Lord, that I am pure from all sin with man, [15] and that I never polluted my name or the name of my father in the land of my captivity. I am the only daughter of my father, and he has no child that will be his heir, nor brother near him, nor son belonging to him, that I should keep myself for a wife to him. Seven husbands of mine are dead already. Why should I live? If it doesn't please you to kill me, command some regard to be had of me, and pity taken of me, and that I hear no more reproach." [16] The prayer of both was heard before the glory of the great God. [17] Raphael also was sent to heal them both, to scale away the white films from Tobit's eyes, and to give Sarah the daughter of Raguel for a wife to Tobias the son of Tobit; and to bind Asmodaeus the evil spirit; because it belonged to Tobias that he should inherit her. At that very time, Tobit returned and entered into his house, and Sarah the daughter of Raguel came down from her upper chamber.

4

[1] In that day Tobit remembered the money which he had left in trust with Gabael in Rages of Media, [2] and he said to himself, I have asked for death; why do I not call my son Tobias, that I may explain to him about the money before I die? [3] And he called him, and said, "My child, if I die, bury

me. Don't despise your mother. Honor her all the days of your life, and do that which is pleasing to her, and don't grieve her. 4 Remember, my child, that she has seen many dangers for you, when you were in her womb. When she is dead, bury her by me in one grave. 5 My child, be mindful of the Lord our God all your days, and don't let your will be set to sin and to transgress his commandments: do righteousness all the days of your life, and don't follow the ways of unrighteousness. 6 For if you do what is true, your deeds will prosperously succeed for you, and for all those who do righteousness. 7 Give alms from your possessions. When you give alms, don't let your eye be envious. Don't turn away your face from any poor man, and the face of God won't be turned away from you. 8 As your possessions are, give alms of it according to your abundance. If you have little, don't be afraid to give alms according to that little; 9 for you lay up a good treasure for yourself against the day of necessity; 10 because alms giving delivers from death, and doesn't allow you to come into darkness. 11 Alms is a good gift in the sight of the Most High for all that give it. 12 Beware, my child, of all fornication, and take first a wife of the seed of your fathers. Don't take a strange wife, who is not of your father's tribe; for we are the descendants of the prophets. Remember, my child, that Noah, Abraham, Isaac, and Jacob, our fathers of old time, all took wives of their kindred, and were blessed in their children, and their seed will inherit the land. 13 And now, my child, love your kindred, and don't scorn your kindred and the sons and the daughters of your people in your heart, to take a wife of them; for in scornfulness is destruction and much trouble, and in idleness is decay and great lack; for idleness is the mother off a mine. 14 Don't let the wages of any man who works for you wait with you, but give it to him out of hand. If you serve God, you will be rewarded. Take heed to yourself, my child, in all your works, and be discreet in all your behavior. 15 And what you yourself hate, do to no man. Don't drink wine to drunkenness, and don't let drunkenness go with you on your way. 16 Give of your bread to the hungry, and of your garments to those who are naked. Give alms from all your abundance. Don't let your eye be envious when you give alms. [17] Pour out your bread on the burial of the just, and give nothing to sinners. [18] Ask counsel of every man who is wise, and don't despise any counsel that is profitable. [19] Bless the Lord your God at all times, and ask of him that your ways may be made straight, and that all your paths and counsels may prosper; for every nation has no counsel; but the Lord himself gives all good things, and he humbles whom he will, as he will. And now, my child, remember my commandments, and let them not be blotted out of your mind. [20] And now I explain to you about the ten talents of silver, which I left in trust with Gabael the son of Gabrias at Rages of Media. [21] And fear not, my child, because we are made poor. You have much wealth, if you fear God, and depart from all sin, and do that which is pleasing in his sight." [1] Then Tobias answered and said to him, "Father, I will do all things, whatever you have commanded me. [2] But how could I receive the money, since I don't know him?" [3] He gave him the handwriting, and said to him, "Seek a man who will go with you, and I will give him wages, while I still live; and go and receive the money." [4] He went to seek a man, and found Raphael who was an angel; [5] and he didn't know it. He said to him, "Can I go with you to Rages of Media? Do you know those places well?" [6] The angel said to him, "I will go with you. I know the way well. I have lodged with our brother Gabael." [7] Tobias said to him, "Wait for me, and I will tell my father." [8] He said to him, "Go, and don't wait. And he went in and said to his father, "Behold, I have found someone who will go with me." But he said, "Call him to me, that I may know of what tribe he is, and whether he be a trustworthy man to go with you." [9] So he called him, and he came in, and they saluted one another. [10] And Tobit said to him, "Brother, of what tribe and of what family are you? Tell me." [11] He said to him, "Do you seek a tribe and a family, or a hired man which will go with your son?" And Tobit said to him, "I want to know, brother, your kindred and your name." [12] And he said, "I am Azarias, the son of Ananias the great, of your kindred." [13] And he said to him, "Welcome, brother. Don't be angry with me, because I sought to know your tribe and family. You are my brother, of an honest and good lineage; for I knew Ananias and Jathan, the sons of Shemaiah the great, when we went together to Jerusalem to worship, and offered the firstborn, and the tenths of our increase; and they didn't go astray in the error of our kindred. My brother, you are of a great stock. 14 But tell me, what wages shall I give you? A drachma a day, and those things that be necessary for you, as to my son? 15 And moreover, if you both return safe and sound, I will add something to your wages." 16 And so they agreed. And he said to Tobias, "Prepare yourself for the journey. May God prosper you." So his son prepared what was needful for the journey, and his father said to him, "Go with this man; but God, who dwells in heaven, will prosper your journey. May his angel go with you." Then they both departed, and the young man's dog went with them. 17 But Anna his mother wept, and said to Tobit, "Why have you sent away our child? Isn't he the staff of our hand, ingoing in and out before us? 18 Don't be greedy to add money to money; but let it be as refuse compared to our child. 19 For what the Lord has given us to live is enough for us." 20 Tobit said to her, "Don't worry, my sister. He will return safe and sound, and your eyes will see him.

21 For a good angel will go with him. His journey will be prospered, and he will return safe and sound." 22 So she stopped weeping.

6

1 Now as they went on their journey, they came at evening to the river Tigris, and they lodged there. 2 But the young man went down to wash himself, and a fish leaped out of the river, and would have swallowed up the young man. 3 But the angel said to him, "Grab the fish!" So the young man grabbed the fish, and hauled it up onto the land. 4 And the angel said to him, "Cut the fish open, and take the heart, the liver, and the bile, and keep them with you." 5 And the young man did as the angel commanded him; but they roasted the fish, and ate it. And they both went on their way, till they drew near to Ecbatana. 6 The young man said to the angel, "Brother Azarias, of what use is the heart, the liver, and the bile of the fish?" 7 He said to him, "About the heart and the liver: If a demon or an evil spirit troubles anyone, we must burn those and make smoke of them before the man or the woman, and the affliction will flee. 8 But as for the bile, it is good to anoint a man that has white films in his eyes,

and he will be healed." 9 But when they drew near to Rages, 10 the angel said to the young man, "Brother, today we will lodge with Raguel. He is your kinsman. He has an only daughter named Sarah. I will speak about her, that she should be given to you for a wife. 11 For her inheritance belongs to you, and you only are of her kindred. 12 The maid is fair and wise. And now hear me, and I will speak to her father. When we return from Rages we will celebrate the marriage; for I know that Raguel may in no way marry her to another according to the law of Moses, or else he would be liable to death, because it belongs to you to take the inheritance, rather than any other." 13 Then the young man said to the angel, "Brother Azarias, I have heard that this maid has been given to seven men, and that they all perished in the bride-chamber. 14 Now I am the only son of my father, and I am afraid, lest I go in and die, even as those before me. For a demon loves her, which harms no man, but those which come to her. Now I fear lest I die, and bring my father's and my mother's life to the grave with sorrow because of me. They have no other son to bury them." 15

But the angel said to him, "Don't you remember the words which your father commanded you, that you should take a wife of your own kindred? Now hear me, brother; for she will be your wife. Don't worry about the demon; for this night she will be given you as wife. 16 And when you come into the bride-chamber, you shall take the ashes of incense, and shall lay upon them some of the heart and liver of the fish, and shall make smoke with them. 17 The demon will smell it, and flee away, and never come again any more. But when you go near to her, both of you rise up, and cry to God who is merciful. He will save you, and have mercy on you. Don't be afraid, for she was prepared for you from the beginning; and you will save her, and she will go with you. And I suppose that you will have children with her." When Tobias heard these things, he loved her, and his soul was strongly joined to her.

7

1 They came to Ecbatana, and arrived at the house of Raguel. But Sarah met them; and she greeted them, and they her. Then she brought them into the house. 2 Raguel said to Edna his wife, "This young man really

resembles Tobit my cousin!" ³ And Raguel asked them, "Where are you two from, kindred?" They said to him, "We are of the sons of Naphtali, who are captives in Nineveh." ⁴ He said to them, "Do you know Tobit our brother?" They said, "We know him." Then he said to them, "Is he in good health?" ⁵ They said, "He is both alive, and in good health." Tobias said, "He is my father." ⁶ And Raguel sprang up, and kissed him, wept, ⁷ blessed him, and said to him, "You are the son of an honest and good man." When he had heard that Tobit had lost his sight, he was grieved, and wept; ⁸ and Edna his wife and Sarah his daughter wept. They received them gladly; and they killed a ram of the flock, and served them meat. But Tobias said to Raphael, "Brother Azarias, speak of those things of which you talked about in the way, and let the matter be finished." ⁹ So he communicated the thing to Raguel. Raguel said to Tobias, "Eat, drink, and make merry: ¹⁰ for it belongs to you to take my child. However I will tell you the truth. ¹¹ I have given my child to seven men of our relatives, and whenever they came in to her, they died in the night. But for the present be merry." And Tobias said, "I will taste nothing here, until you all make a covenant and enter into that covenant with me." ¹² Raguel said, "Take her to yourself from now on according to custom. You are her relative, and she is yours. The merciful God will give all good success to you." ¹³ And he called his daughter Sarah, and took her by the hand, and gave her to be wife of Tobias, and said, "Behold, take her to yourself after the law of Moses, and lead her away to your father." And he blessed them. ¹⁴ He called Edna his wife, then took a book, wrote a contract, and sealed it. ¹⁵ Then they began to eat. ¹⁶ And Raguel called his wife Edna, and said to her, "Sister, prepare the other chamber, and bring her in there." ¹⁷ She did as he asked her, and brought her in there. She wept, and she received the tears of her daughter, and said to her, ¹⁸ "Be comforted, my child. May the Lord of heaven and earth give you favor for this your sorrow. Be comforted, my daughter."

8

¹ When they had finished their supper, they brought Tobias in to her. ² But as he went, he remembered the words of Raphael, and took the ashes of

the incense, and put the heart and the liver of the fish on them, and made smoke with them. ³ When the demon smelled that smell, it fled into the uppermost parts of Egypt, and the angel bound him. ⁴ But after they were both shut in together, Tobias rose up from the bed, and said, "Sister, arise, and let's pray that the Lord may have mercy on us." ⁵ And Tobias began to say, "Blessed are you, O God of our fathers, and blessed is your holy and glorious name forever. Let the heavens bless you, and all your creatures. ⁶ You made Adam, and gave him Eve his wife for a helper and support. From them came the seed of men. You said, it is not good that the man should be alone. Let's make him a helper like him. ⁷ And now, O Lord, I take not this my sister for lust, but in truth. Command that I may find mercy and grow old with her." ⁸ She said with him, "Amen." And they both slept that night. ⁹ Raguel arose, and went and dug a grave, ¹⁰ saying, "Lest he also should die." ¹¹ And Raguel came into his house, ¹² and said to Edna his wife, "Send one of the maidservants, and let them see if he is alive. If not, we will bury him, and no man will know it." ¹³ So the maidservant opened the door, and went in, and found them both sleeping, ¹⁴ and came out, and told them that he was alive. ¹⁵ Then Raguel blessed God, saying, "Blessed are you, O God, with all pure and holy blessing! Let your saints bless you, and all your creatures! Let all your angels and your elect bless you forever! ¹⁶ Blessed are you, because you have made me glad; and it has not happened to me as I suspected; but you have dealt with us according to your great mercy. ¹⁷ Blessed are you, because you have had mercy on two that were the only begotten children of their parents. Show them mercy, O Lord. Fulfill their life in health with gladness and mercy ¹⁸ He commanded his servants to fill the grave. ¹⁹ He kept the wedding feast for them fourteen days. ²⁰ Before the days of the wedding feast were finished, Raguel sware to him, that he should not depart till the fourteen days of the wedding feast were fulfilled; ²¹ and that then he should take half of his goods, and go in safety to his father; and the rest, said he, when my wife and I die.

9

¹ And Tobias called Raphael, and said to him, ² "Brother Azarias,

take with you a servant and two camels, and go to Rages of Media to Gabael, and receive the money for me, and bring him to the wedding feast, 3 because Raguel has sworn that I must not depart. 4 My father counts the days; and if I wait long, he will be very grieved. 5 So Raphael went on his way, and lodged with Gabael, and gave him the handwriting; so he brought forth the bags with their seals, and gave them to him. 6 Then they rose up early in the morning together, and came to the wedding feast. Tobias blessed his wife.

10

1 Tobit his father counted every day. When the days of the journey were expired, and they didn't come, 2 he said, "Is he perchance detained? Or is Gabael perchance dead, and there is no one to give him the money?" 3 He was very grieved. 4 But his wife said to him, "The child has perished, seeing he waits long." She began to bewail him, and said, 5 "I care about nothing, my child, since I have let you go, the light of my eyes." 6 Tobit said to her, "Hold your peace. Don't worry. He is in good health." 7 And she said to him, "Hold your peace. Don't deceive me. My

child has perished." And she went out every day into the way by which they went, and ate no bread in the day-time, and didn't stop bewailing her son Tobias for whole nights, until the fourteen days of the wedding feast were expired, which Raguel had sworn that he should spend there. Then Tobias said to Raguel, "Send me away, for my father and my mother look no more to see me." 8 But his father-in-law said to him, "Stay with me, and I will send to your father, and they will declare to him how things go with you." 9 Tobias said, "No. Send me away to my father." 10 Raguel arose, and gave him Sarah his wife, and half his goods, servants and cattle and money; 11 and he blessed them, and sent them away, saying, "The God of heaven will prosper you, my children, before I die." 12 And he said to his daughter, "Honor your father-in-law and your mother-in-law. They are now your parents. Let me hear a good report of you." Then he kissed her. Edna said to Tobias, "May the Lord of heaven restore you, dear brother, and grant to me that I may see your children of my daughter Sarah, that I may rejoice before the Lord. Behold, I commit my daughter to you in special trust. Don't cause her grief.

11

¹ After these things Tobias also went his way, blessing God because he had prospered his journey; and he blessed Raguel and Edna his wife. Then he went on his way until they drew near to Nineveh. ² Raphael said to Tobias, "Don't you know, brother, how you left your father? ³ Let's run forward before your wife, and prepare the house. ⁴ But take in your hand the bile of the fish." So they went their way, and the dog went after them. ⁵ Anna sat looking around toward the path for her son. ⁶ She saw him coming, and said to his father, "Behold, your son is coming with the man that went with him!" ⁷ Raphael said, "I know, Tobias, that your father will open his eyes. ⁸ Therefore anoint his eyes with the bile, and being pricked with it, he will rub, and will make the white films fall away. Then he will see you." ⁹ Anna ran to him, and fell upon the neck of her son, and said to him, "I have seen you, my child! I am ready to die." They both wept. ¹⁰ Tobit went toward the door and stumbled; but his son ran to him, ¹¹ and took hold of his father. He rubbed the bile on his father's eyes, saying, "Cheer up, my father." ¹² When his eyes began to hurt, he rubbed them. ¹³ Then the white films peeled away from the corners of his eyes; and he saw his son, and fell upon his neck. ¹⁴ He wept, and said, "Blessed are you, O God, and blessed is your name forever! Blessed are all your holy angels! ¹⁵ For you scourged, and had mercy on me. Behold, I see my son Tobias." And his son went in rejoicing, and told his father the great things that had happened to him in Media. ¹⁶ Tobit went out to meet his daughter-in-law at the gate of Nineveh, rejoicing and blessing God. Those who saw him go marveled, because he had received his sight. ¹⁷ Tobit gave thanks before them, because God had shown mercy on him. When Tobit came near to Sarah his daughter-in-law, he blessed her, saying, "Welcome, daughter! Blessed is God who has brought you to us, and blessed are your father and your mother." And there was joy among all his kindred who were at Nineveh. ¹⁸ Achiacharus and Nasbas his brother's son came. ¹⁹ Tobias' wedding feast was kept seven days with great gladness.

12

1 And Tobit called his son Tobias, and said to him, "See, my child, that the man which went with you have his wages, and you must give him more." 2 And he said to him, "Father, it is no harm to me to give him the half of those things which I have brought; 3 for he has led me for you in safety, and he cured my wife, and brought my money, and likewise cured you." 4 The old man said, "It is due to him. 5 And he called the angel, and said to him, "Take half of all that you have brought." 6 Then he called them both privately, and said to them, "Bless God, and give him thanks, and magnify him, and give him thanks in the sight of all that live, for the things which he has done with you. It is good to bless God and exalt his name, showing forth with honor the works of God. Don't be slack to give him thanks. 7 It is good to conceal the secret of a king, but to reveal gloriously the works of God. Do good, and evil won't find you. 8 Good is prayer with fasting, alms, and righteousness. A little with righteousness is better than much with unrighteousness. It is better to give alms than to lay up gold. 9 Alms delivers from death, and it purges away all sin. Those who give alms and do righteousness will be filled with life; 10 but those who sin are enemies to their own life. 11 Surely I will conceal nothing from you. I have said, 'It is good to conceal the secret of a king, but to reveal gloriously the works of God.' 12 And now, when you prayed, and Sarah your daughter-in-law, I brought the memorial of your prayer before the Holy One. When you buried the dead, I was with you likewise. 13 And when you didn't delay to rise up, and leave your dinner, that you might go and cover the dead, your good deed was not hidden from me. I was with you. 14 And now God sent me to heal you and Sarah your daughter-in-law. 15 I am Raphael, one of the seven holy angels which present the prayers of the saints and go in before the glory of the Holy One." 16 And they were both troubled, and fell upon their faces; for they were afraid. 17 And he said to them, "Don't be afraid. You will all have peace; but bless God forever. 18 For I came not of any favor of my own, but by the will of your God. Therefore bless him forever. 19 All these days I appeared to you. I didn't eat or drink, but you all saw a vision. 20 Now give God thanks, because I

ascend to him who sent me. Write in a book all the things which have been done." 21 Then they rose up, and saw him no more. 22 They confessed the great and wonderful works of God, and how the angel of the Lord had appeared to them.

13

1 And Tobit wrote a prayer for rejoicing, and said, "Blessed is God who lives forever! Blessed is his kingdom! 2 For he scourges, and shows mercy. He leads down to the grave,† and brings up again. There is no one who will escape his hand. 3 Give thanks to him before the Gentiles, all you children of Israel! For he has scattered us among them. 4 Declare his greatness, there. Extol him before all the living, because he is our Lord, and God is our Father forever. 5 He will scourge us for our iniquities, and will again show mercy, and will gather us out of all the nations among whom you are all scattered. 6 If you turn to him with your whole heart and with your whole soul, to do truth before him, then he will turn to you, and won't hide his face from you. See what he will do with you. Give him thanks with your whole mouth. Bless the Lord of righteousness. Exalt the everlasting King. I give him thanks in the land of my captivity, and show his strength and majesty to a nation of sinners. Turn, you sinners, and do righteousness before him. Who can tell if he will accept you and have mercy on you? 7 I exalt my God. My soul exalts the King of heaven, and rejoices in his greatness. 8 Let all men speak, and let them give him thanks in Jerusalem. 9 O Jerusalem, the holy city, he will scourge you for the works of your sons, and will again have mercy on the sons of the righteous. 10 Give thanks to the Lord with goodness, and bless the everlasting King, that his tabernacle may be built in you again with joy, and that he may make glad in you those who are captives, and love in you forever those who are miserable. 11 Many nations will come from afar to the name of the Lord God with gifts in their hands, even gifts to the King of heaven. Generations of generations will praise you, and sing songs of rejoicing. 12 All those who hate you are cursed. All those who love you forever will be blessed. 13 Rejoice and be exceedingly glad for the sons of the righteous; for they will be gathered together and will bless the Lord of the righteous. 14 Oh

blessed are those who love you. They will rejoice for your peace. Blessed are all those who mourned for all your scourges; because they will rejoice for you when they have seen all your glory. They will be made glad forever. 15 Let my soul bless God the great King. 16 For Jerusalem will be built with sapphires, emeralds, and precious stones; your walls and towers and battlements with pure gold. 17 The streets of Jerusalem will be paved with beryl, carbuncle, and stones of Ophir. 18 All her streets will say, "Hallelujah!" and give praise, saying, "Blessed be God, who has exalted you forever!

14

1 Then Tobit finished giving thanks. 2 He was fifty-eight years old when he lost his sight. After eight years, he received it again. He gave alms and he feared the Lord God more and more, and gave thanks to him. 3 Now he grew very old; and he called his son with the six sons of his son, and said to him, "My child, take your sons. Behold, I have grown old, and am ready to depart out of this life. 4 Go into Media, my child, for I surely believe all the things which Jonah the prophet spoke of Nineveh, that it will be overthrown, but in Media there will rather be peace for a season. Our kindred will be scattered in the earth from the good land. Jerusalem will be desolate, and the house of God in it will be burned up, and will be desolate for a time. 5 God will again have mercy on them, and bring them back into the land, and they will build the house, but not like to the former house, until the times of that age are fulfilled. Afterward they will return from the places of their captivity, and build up Jerusalem with honor. The house of God will be built in it forever with a glorious building, even as the prophets spoke concerning it. 6 And all the nations will turn to fear the Lord God truly, and will bury their idols. 7 All the nations will bless the Lord, and his people will give thanks to God, and the Lord will exalt his people; and all those who love the Lord God in truth and righteousness will rejoice, showing mercy to our kindred. 8 And now, my child, depart from Nineveh, because those things which the prophet Jonah spoke will surely come to pass. 9 But you must keep the law and the ordinances, and show yourself merciful and righteous, that it may be well with you. 10 Bury me

decently, and your mother with me. Don't stay at Nineveh. See, my child, what Aman did to Achiacharus who nourished him, how out of light he brought him into darkness, and all the recompense that he made him. Achiacharus was saved, but the other had his recompense, and he went down into darkness. Manasses gave alms, and escaped the snare of death which he set for him; but Aman fell into the snare, and perished. 11 And now, my children, consider what alms does, and how righteousness delivers." While he was saying these things, he gave up the ghost in the bed; but he was one hundred fifty eight years old. Tobias buried him magnificently. 12 When Anna died, he buried her with his father. But Tobias departed with his wife and his sons to Ecbatana to Raguel his father-in-law, 13 and he grew old in honor, and he buried his father in-law and mother-in-law magnificently, and he inherited their possessions, and his father Tobit's. 14 He died at Ecbatana of Media, being one hundred twenty seven years old. 15 Before he died, he heard of the destruction of Nineveh, which Nebuchadnezzar and Ahasuerus took captive.

Before his death, he rejoiced over Nineveh.

The book of Judith

The Book of Judith (Iudeth) is an evocative addition to the Apocrypha in the 1560 Geneva Bible, presenting a story of courage, faith, and divine intervention woven into a dramatic narrative. Set against the historical backdrop of Nebuchadnezzar's reign, although containing several historical inaccuracies, the story centers on Judith, a devout and heroic widow who lives in the besieged city of Bethulia. This narrative unfolds during a critical moment when the Israelites face severe threat from the Assyrian army led by the formidable general Holofernes, who seeks to conquer their land as part of a campaign to assert Assyrian dominance.

Judith stands out as a figure of both piety and political acumen; her story is a profound exploration of the themes of power and deliverance. Displaying remarkable bravery and faith, Judith devises a plan to save her people. She uses her wit and charm to infiltrate the enemy camp under the guise of a defector. Gaining the trust of Holofernes, she ultimately beheads him after he is incapacitated by alcohol, thereby decapitating the Assyrian leadership both literally and figuratively. Judith returns to Bethulia with the head of Holofernes, leading to the retreat of the Assyrian forces and delivering her people from imminent destruction.

The Book of Judith resonates deeply with its exploration of divine justice executed through unlikely means and individuals. Judith's actions are portrayed not just as acts of personal valor but as manifestations of God's ongoing involvement with His people, positioning her as an instrument of divine justice. This story challenges traditional roles and expectations of women in biblical times, presenting Judith as a model of virtue, strength, and strategic prowess. Theologically, the Book of Judith emphasizes themes such as the power of faith, the importance of loyalty to God, and the belief in deliverance from oppression. It encourages the faithful to trust in God's plans and timing, even in the face of overwhelming odds. The narrative also engages with the idea of sanctity in warfare, portraying the battle against the Assyrians as a fight not just for political survival but for religious preservation.

From a literary perspective, the Book of Judith is crafted with considerable sophistication, characterized by vivid descriptions, intense dialogues, and dramatic irony. Its inclusion in the Geneva Bible enriches the biblical text by offering a complex portrayal of heroism interlaced with theological and moral questions. The story of Judith has been influential not only in religious contexts but also in cultural and artistic domains, inspiring countless works of art, literature, and music, which interpret her tale as one of triumphant faith and divine providence.

The Book of Judith

1 In the twelfth year of the reign of Nabuchodonosor, who reigned in Nineve, the great city; in the days of Arphaxad, which reigned over the Medes in Ecbatane, 2 And built in Ecbatane walls round about of stones hewn three cubits broad and six cubits long, and made the height of the wall seventy cubits, and the breadth thereof fifty cubits: 3 And set the towers thereof upon the gates of it an hundred cubits high, and the breadth thereof in the foundation threescore cubits: 4 And he made the gates thereof, even gates that were raised to the height of seventy cubits, and the breadth of them was forty cubits, for the going forth of his mighty armies, and for the setting in array of his footmen: 5 Even in those days king Nabuchodonosor made war with king Arphaxad in the great plain, which is the plain in the borders of Ragau. 6 And there came unto him all they that dwelt in the hill country, and all that dwelt by Euphrates, and Tigris and Hydaspes, and the plain of Arioch the king of the Elymeans, and very many nations of the sons of Chelod, assembled themselves to the battle. 7 Then Nabuchodonosor king of the Assyrians sent unto all that dwelt in Persia, and to all that dwelt westward, and to those that dwelt in Cilicia, and Damascus, and Libanus, and Antilibanus, and to all that dwelt upon the sea coast, 8 And to those among the nations that were of Carmel, and Galaad, and the higher Galilee, and the great plain of Esdrelom, 9 And to all that were in Samaria and the cities thereof, and beyond Jordan unto Jerusalem, and Betane, and Chelus, and Kades, and the river of Egypt, and Taphnes, and Ramesse, and all the land of Gesem, 10 Until ye come beyond Tanis and Memphis, and to all the inhabitants of Egypt, until ye come to the borders of Ethiopia. 11 But all the inhabitants of the land made light of the commandment of Nabuchodonosor king of the Assyrians, neither went they with him to the battle; for they were not afraid of him: yea, he was before them as one man, and they sent away his ambassadors from them without effect, and with disgrace. 12 Therefore Nabuchodonosor was very angry with all this country, and sware by his throne and kingdom, that he would surely be avenged upon all those coasts of Cilicia, and Damascus, and Syria, and that he

would slay with the sword all the inhabitants of the land of Moab, and the children of Ammon, and all Judea, and all that were in Egypt, till ye come to the borders of the two seas. 13 Then he marched in battle array with his power against king Arphaxad in the seventeenth year, and he prevailed in his battle: for he overthrew all the power of Arphaxad, and all his horsemen, and all his chariots, 14 And became lord of his cities, and came unto Ecbatane, and took the towers, and spoiled the streets thereof, and turned the beauty thereof into shame. 15 He took also Arphaxad in the mountains of Ragau, and smote him through with his darts, and destroyed him utterly that day. 16 So he returned afterward to Nineve, both he and all his company of sundry nations being a very great multitude of men of war, and there he took his ease, and banqueted, both he and his army, a hundred and twenty days.

2

1 And in the eighteenth year, the two and twentieth day of the first month, there was talk in the house of Nabuchodonosor king of the Assyrians that he should, as he said, avenge himself on all the earth. 2 So he called unto him all his officers, and all his nobles, and communicated with them his secret counsel, and concluded the afflicting of the whole earth out of his own mouth. 3 Then they decreed to destroy all flesh, that did not obey the commandment of his mouth. 4 And when he had ended his counsel, Nabuchodonosor king of the Assyrians called Holofernes the chief captain of his army, which was next unto him, and said unto him. 5 Thus said the great king, the lord of the whole earth, Behold, thou shalt go forth from my presence, and take with them men that trust in their own strength, of footmen a hundred and twenty thousand; and the number of horses with their riders twelve thousand. 6 And thou shalt go against all the west country, because they disobeyed my commandment. 7 And thou shalt declare unto that they prepare for me earth and water: for I will go forth in my wrath against them and will cover the whole face of the earth with the feet of mine army, and I will give them for a spoil unto them: 8 So that their slain shall fill their valleys and brooks and the river shall be filled with their dead, till it overflow: 9 And I will lead them captives to the utmost parts of all

the earth. ¹⁰ Thou therefore shalt go forth. and take beforehand for me all their coasts: and if they will yield themselves unto thee, thou shalt reserve them for me till the day of their punishment. ¹¹ But concerning them that rebel, let not thine eye spare them; but put them to the slaughter, and spoil them wheresoever thou goest. ¹² For as I live, and by the power of my kingdom, whatsoever I have spoken, that will I do by mine hand. ¹³ And take thou heed that thou transgress none of the commandments of thy lord, but accomplish them fully, as I have commanded thee, and defer not to do them. ¹⁴ Then Holofernes went forth from the presence of his lord, and called all the governors and captains, and the officers of the army of Assur; ¹⁵ And he mustered the chosen men for the battle, as his lord had commanded him, unto an hundred and twenty thousand, and twelve thousand archers on horseback; ¹⁶ And he ranged them, as a great army is ordered for the war. ¹⁷ And he took camels and asses for their carriages, a very great number; and sheep and oxen and goats without number for their provision: ¹⁸ And plenty of victual for every man of the army, and very much gold and silver out of the king's house. ¹⁹ Then he went forth and all his power to go before king Nabuchodonosor in the voyage, and to cover all the face of the earth westward with their chariots, and horsemen, and their chosen footmen. ²⁰ A great number also sundry countries came with them like locusts, and like the sand of the earth: for the multitude was without number. ²¹ And they went forth of Nineve three days' journey toward the plain of Bectileth, and pitched from Bectileth near the mountain which is at the left hand of the upper Cilicia. ²² Then he took all his army, his footmen, and horsemen and chariots, and went from thence into the hill country; ²³ And destroyed Phud and Lud, and spoiled all the children of Rasses, and the children of Israel, which were toward the wilderness at the south of the land of the Chellians. ²⁴ Then he went over Euphrates, and went through Mesopotamia, and destroyed all the high cities that were upon the river Arbonai, till ye come to the sea. ²⁵ And he took the borders of Cilicia, and killed all that resisted him, and came to the borders of Japheth, which were toward the south, over against Arabia. ²⁶ He compassed also all the children of Madian, and burned up their tabernacles, and spoiled their sheepcotes. 27 Then he went down into the plain of Damascus in the time of wheat harvest, and burnt up all their fields, and destroyed their flocks and herds, also he spoiled their cities, and utterly wasted their countries, and smote all their young men with the edge of the sword. 28 Therefore the fear and dread of him fell upon all the inhabitants of the sea coasts, which were in Sidon and Tyrus, and them that dwelt in Sur and Ocina, and all that dwelt in Jemnaan; and they that dwelt in Azotus and Ascalon feared him greatly.

3

1 So they sent ambassadors unto him to treat of peace, saying, 2 Behold, we the servants of Nabuchodonosor the great king lie before thee; use us as shall be good in thy sight. 3 Behold, our houses, and all our places, and all our fields of wheat, and flocks, and herds, and all the lodges of our tents lie before thy face; use them as it pleased thee. 4 Behold, even our cities and the inhabitants thereof are thy servants; come and deal with them as seemed good unto thee.

5 So the men came to Holofernes, and declared unto him after this manner. 6 Then came he down toward the sea coast, both he and his army, and set garrisons in the high cities, and took out of them chosen men for aid. 7 So they and all the country round about received them with garlands, with dances, and with timbrels. 8 Yet he did cast down their frontiers, and cut down their groves: for he had decreed to destroy all the gods of the land, that all nations should worship Nabuchodonosor only, and that all tongues and tribes should call upon him as God. 9 Also he came over against Esdraelon near unto Judea, over against the great strait of Judea. 10 And he pitched between Geba and Scythopolis, and there he tarried a whole month, that he might gather together all the carriages of his army.

4

1 Now the children of Israel, that dwelt in Judea, heard all that Holofernes the chief captain of Nabuchodonosor king of the Assyrians had done to the nations, and after what manner he had spoiled all their temples, and brought them to naught. 2 Therefore they were exceedingly

afraid of him, and were troubled for Jerusalem, and for the temple of the Lord their God: ³For they were newly returned from the captivity, and all the people of Judea were lately gathered together: and the vessels, and the altar, and the house, were sanctified after the profanation. ⁴ Therefore they sent into all the coasts of Samaria, and the villages and to Bethoron, and Belmen, and Jericho, and to Choba, and Esora, and to the valley of Salem: ⁵ And possessed themselves beforehand of all the tops of the high mountains, and fortified the villages that were in them, and laid up victuals for the provision of war: for their fields were of late reaped. ⁶ Also Joacim the high priest, which was in those days in Jerusalem, wrote to them that dwelt in Bethulia, and Betomestham, which is over against Esdraelon toward the open country, near to Dothaim, ⁷ Charging them to keep the passages of the hill country: for by them there was an entrance into Judea, and it was easy to stop them that would come up, because the passage was straight, for two men at the most. ⁸ And the children of Israel did as Joacim the high priest had commanded them, with the ancients of all the people of Israel, which dwelt at Jerusalem. ⁹ Then every man of Israel cried to God with great fervency, and with great vehemency did they humble their souls: ¹⁰ Both they, and their wives and their children, and their cattle, and every stranger and hireling, and their servants bought with money, put sackcloth upon their loins. ¹¹ Thus every man and women, and the little children, and the inhabitants of Jerusalem, fell before the temple, and cast ashes upon their heads, and spread out their sackcloth before the face of the Lord: also they put sackcloth about the altar, ¹² And cried to the God of Israel all with one consent earnestly, that he would not give their children for a prey, and their wives for a spoil, and the cities of their inheritance to destruction, and the sanctuary to profanation and reproach, and for the nations to rejoice at. ¹³ So God heard their prayers, and looked upon their afflictions: for the people fasted many days in all Judea and Jerusalem before the sanctuary of the Lord Almighty. ¹⁴ And Joacim the high priest, and all the priests that stood before the Lord, and they which ministered unto the Lord, had their loins girt with sackcloth, and offered the daily burnt offerings, with the vows and free gifts of the people, 15 And had ashes on their mitres, and cried unto the Lord with all their power, that he would look upon all the house of Israel graciously.

5

1 Then was it declared to Holofernes, the chief captain of the army of Assur, that the children of Israel had prepared for war, and had shut up the passages of the hill country, and had fortified all the tops of the high hills and had laid impediments in the champaign countries: 2 Wherewith he was very angry, and called all the princes of Moab, and the captains of Ammon, and all the governors of the sea coast, 3 And he said unto them, Tell me now, ye sons of Chanaan, who this people is, that dwelleth in the hill country, and what are the cities that they inhabit, and what is the multitude of their army, and wherein is their power and strength, and what king is set over them, or captain of their army; 4 And why have they determined not to come and meet me, more than all the inhabitants of the west. 5 Then said Achior, the captain of all the sons of Ammon, Let my lord now hear a word from the mouth of thy servant, and I will declare unto thee the truth concerning this people, which dwelleth near thee, and inhabited the hill countries: and there shall no lie come out of the mouth of thy servant. 6 This people are descended of the Chaldeans: 7 And they sojourned heretofore in Mesopotamia, because they would not follow the gods of their fathers, which were in the land of Chaldea. 8 For they left the way of their ancestors, and worshipped the God of heaven, the God whom they knew: so they cast them out from the face of their gods, and they fled into Mesopotamia, and sojourned there many days. 9 Then their God commanded them to depart from the place where they sojourned, and to go into the land of Chanaan: where they dwelt, and were increased with gold and silver, and with very much cattle. 10 But when a famine covered all the land of Chanaan, they went down into Egypt, and sojourned there, while they were nourished, and became there a great multitude, so that one could not number their nation. 11 Therefore the king of Egypt rose up against them, and dealt subtilly with them, and brought them low with

labouring in brick, and made them slaves. 12 Then they cried unto their God, and he smote all the land of Egypt with incurable plagues: so the Egyptians cast them out of their sight. 13 And God dried the Red sea before them, 14 And brought them to mount Sina, and Cades Barne, and cast forth all that dwelt in the wilderness. 15 So they dwelt in the land of the Amorites, and they destroyed by their strength all them of Esebon, and passing over Jordan they possessed all the hill country. 16 And they cast forth before them the Chanaanite, the Pherezite, the Jebusite, and the Sychemite, and all the Gergesites, and they dwelt in that country many days. 17 And whilst they sinned not before their God, they prospered, because the God that hated iniquity was with them. 18 But when they departed from the way which he appointed them, they were destroyed in many battles very sore, and were led captives into a land that was not their's, and the temple of their God was cast to the ground, and their cities were taken by the enemies. 19 But now are they returned to their God, and are come up from the places where they were scattered, and have possessed Jerusalem, where their sanctuary is, and are seated in the hill country; for it was desolate. 20 Now therefore, my lord and governor, if there be any error against this people, and they sin against their God, let us consider that this shall be their ruin, and let us go up, and we shall overcome them. 21 But if there be no iniquity in their nation, let my lord now pass by, lest their Lord defend them, and their God be for them, and we become a reproach before all the world. 22 And when Achior had finished these sayings, all the people standing round about the tent murmured, and the chief men of Holofernes, and all that dwelt by the sea side, and in Moab, spoke that he should kill him. 23 For, say they, we will not be afraid of the face of the children of Israel: for, lo, it is a people that have no strength nor power for a strong battle 24 Now therefore, lord Holofernes, we will go up, and they shall be a prey to be devoured of all thine army.

6

1 And when the tumult of men that were about the council was ceased, Holofernes the chief captain of the army of Assur said unto Achior and all the Moabites

before all the company of other nations, 2 And who art thou, Achior, and the hirelings of Ephraim, that thou hast prophesied against us as to day, and hast said, that we should not make war with the people of Israel, because their God will defend them? and who is God but Nabuchodonosor? 3 He will send his power, and will destroy them from the face of the earth, and their God shall not deliver them: but we his servants will destroy them as one man; for they are not able to sustain the power of our horses. 4 For with them we will tread them under foot, and their mountains shall be drunken with their blood, and their fields shall be filled with their dead bodies, and their footsteps shall not be able to stand before us, for they shall utterly perish, saith king Nabuchodonosor, lord of all the earth: for he said, None of my words shall be in vain. 5 And thou, Achior, an hireling of Ammon, which hast spoken these words in the day of thine iniquity, shalt see my face no more from this day, until I take vengeance of this nation that came out of Egypt. 6 And then shall the sword of mine army, and the multitude of them that serve me, pass through thy sides, and thou shalt fall among their slain, when I return. 7 Now therefore my servants shall bring thee back into the hill country, and shall set thee in one of the cities of the passages: 8 And thou shalt not perish, till thou be destroyed with them. 9 And if thou persuade thyself in thy mind that they shall be taken, let not thy countenance fall: I have spoken it, and none of my words shall be in vain. 10 Then Holofernes commanded his servants, that waited in his tent, to take Achior, and bring him to Bethulia, and deliver him into the hands of the children of Israel. 11 So his servants took him, and brought him out of the camp into the plain, and they went from the midst of the plain into the hill country, and came unto the fountains that were under Bethulia. 12 And when the men of the city saw them, they took up their weapons, and went out of the city to the top of the hill: and every man that used a sling kept them from coming up by casting of stones against them. 13 Nevertheless having gotten privily under the hill, they bound Achior, and cast him down, and left him at the foot of the hill, and returned to their lord. 14 But the Israelites descended from their city, and came unto him, and loosed him, and brought him to Bethulia, and presented him to the governors of the city: 15 Which were in those days Ozias the son of Micha, of the tribe of Simeon, and Chabris the son of Gothoniel, and Charmis the son of Melchiel. 16 And they called together all the ancients of the city, and all their youth ran together, and their women, to the assembly, and they set Achior in the midst of all their people. Then Ozias asked him of that which was done. 17 And he answered and declared unto them the words of the council of Holofernes, and all the words that he had spoken in the midst of the princes of Assur, and whatsoever Holofernes had spoken proudly against the house of Israel. 18 Then the people fell down and worshipped God, and cried unto God. saying, 19 O Lord God of heaven, behold their pride, and pity the low estate of our nation, and look upon the face of those that are sanctified unto thee this day. 20 Then they comforted Achior, and praised him greatly. 21 And Ozias took him out of the assembly unto his house, and made a feast to the elders; and they called on the God of Israel all that night for help.

7

1 The next day Holofernes commanded all his army, and all his people which were come to take his part, that they should remove their camp against Bethulia, to take aforehand the ascents of the hill country, and to make war against the children of Israel. 2 Then their strong men removed their camps in that day, and the army of the men of war was a hundred and seventy thousand footmen, and twelve thousand horsemen, beside the baggage, and other men that were afoot among them, a very great multitude. 3 And they camped in the valley near unto Bethulia, by the fountain, and they spread themselves in breadth over Dothaim even to Belmaim, and in length from Bethulia unto Cynamon, which is over against Esdraelon. 4 Now the children of Israel, when they saw the multitude of them, were greatly troubled, and said every one to his neighbour, Now will these men lick up the face of the earth; for neither the high mountains, nor the valleys, nor the hills, are able to bear their weight. 5 Then every man took up his weapons

of war, and when they had kindled fires upon their towers, they remained and watched all that night. 6 But in the second day Holofernes brought forth all his horsemen in the sight of the children of Israel which were in Bethulia, 7 And viewed the passages up to the city, and came to the fountains of their waters, and took them, and set garrisons of men of war over them, and he himself removed toward his people. 8 Then came unto him all the chief of the children of Esau, and all the governors of the people of Moab, and the captains of the sea coast, and said, 9 Let our lord now hear a word, that there be not an overthrow in thine army. 10 For this people of the children of Israel do not trust in their spears, but in the height of the mountains wherein they dwell, because it is not easy to come up to the tops of their mountains. 11 Now therefore, my lord, fight not against them in battle array, and there shall not so much as one man of thy people perish. 12 Remain in thy camp, and keep all the men of thin army, and let thy servants get into their hands the fountain of water, which issued forth of the foot of the mountain: 13 For all the inhabitants of Bethulia have their water thence; so shall thirst kill them, and they shall give up their city, and we and our people shall go up to the tops of the mountains that are near, and will camp upon them, to watch that none go out of the city. 14 So they and their wives and their children shall be consumed with fire, and before the sword come against them, they shall be overthrown in the streets where they dwell. 15 Thus shalt thou render them an evil reward; because they rebelled, and met not thy person peaceably. 16 And these words pleased Holofernes and all his servants, and he appointed to do as they had spoken. 17 So the camp of the children of Ammon departed, and with them five thousand of the Assyrians, and they pitched in the valley, and took the waters, and the fountains of the waters of the children of Israel. 18 Then the children of Esau went up with the children of Ammon, and camped in the hill country over against Dothaim: and they sent some of them toward the south, and toward the east over against Ekrebel, which is near unto Chusi, that is upon the brook Mochmur; and the rest of the army of the Assyrians camped in the plain, and covered the face of the whole land; and their tents and carriages were pitched to a very great multitude. 19 Then the children of Israel cried unto the Lord their God, because their heart failed, for all their enemies had compassed them round about, and there was no way to escape out from among them. 20 Thus all the company of Assur remained about them, both their footmen, chariots, and horsemen, four and thirty days, so that all their vessels of water failed all the inhabitants of Bethulia. 21 And the cisterns were emptied, and they had not water to drink their fill for one day; for they gave them drink by measure. 22 Therefore their young children were out of heart, and their women and young men fainted for thirst, and fell down in the streets of the city, and by the passages of the gates, and there was no longer any strength in them. 23 Then all the people assembled to Ozias, and to the chief of the city, both young men, and women, and children, and cried with a loud voice, and said before all the elders, 24 God be judge between us and you: for ye have done us great injury, in that ye have not required peace of the children of Assur. 25 For now we have no helper: but God hath sold us into their hands, that we should be thrown down before them with thirst and great destruction. 26 Now therefore call them unto you, and deliver the whole city for a spoil to the people of Holofernes, and to all his army. 27 For it is better for us to be made a spoil unto them, than to die for thirst: for we will be his servants, that our souls may live, and not see the death of our infants before our eyes, nor our wives nor our children to die. 28 We take to witness against you the heaven and the earth, and our God and Lord of our fathers, which punished us according to our sins and the sins of our fathers, that he do not according as we have said this day. 29 Then there was great weeping with one consent in the midst of the assembly; and they cried unto the Lord God with a loud voice. 30 Then said Ozias to them, Brethren, be of good courage, let us yet endure five days, in the which space the Lord our God may turn his mercy toward us; for he will not forsake us utterly. 31 And if these days pass, and there come no help unto us, I will do according to your word. 32 And he dispersed the people, every one to their own charge; and they went unto the walls and towers of their city, and sent the women and children into their houses: and they were very low brought in the city.

8

¹ Now at that time Judith heard thereof, which was the daughter of Merari, the son of Ox, the son of Joseph, the son of Ozel, the son of Elcia, the son of Ananias, the son of Gedeon, the son of Raphaim, the son of Acitho, the son of Eliu, the son of Eliab, the son of Nathanael, the son of Samael, the son of Salasadal, the son of Israel. ² And Manasses was her husband, of her tribe and kindred, who died in the barley harvest. ³ For as he stood overseeing them that bound sheaves in the field, the heat came upon his head, and he fell on his bed, and died in the city of Bethulia: and they buried him with his fathers in the field between Dothaim and Balamo. ⁴ So Judith was a widow in her house three years and four months. ⁵ And she made her a tent upon the top of her house, and put on sackcloth upon her loins and ware her widow's apparel. ⁶ And she fasted all the days of her widowhood, save the eves of the sabbaths, and the sabbaths, and the eves of the new moons, and the new moons and the feasts and solemn days of the house of Israel. ⁷ She was also of a goodly countenance, and very beautiful to behold: and her husband Manasses had left her gold, and silver, and menservants and maidservants, and cattle, and lands; and she remained upon them. ⁸ And there was none that gave her an ill word; as she feared God greatly. ⁹ Now when she heard the evil words of the people against the governor, that they fainted for lack of water; for Judith had heard all the words that Ozias had spoken unto them, and that he had sworn to deliver the city unto the Assyrians after five days; ¹⁰ Then she sent her waiting woman, that had the government of all things that she had, to call Ozias and Chabris and Charmis, the ancients of the city. ¹¹ And they came unto her, and she said unto them, Hear me now, O ye governors of the inhabitants of Bethulia: for your words that ye have spoken before the people this day are not right, touching this oath which ye made and pronounced between God and you, and have promised to deliver the city to our enemies, unless within these days the Lord turn to help you. ¹² And now who are ye that have tempted God this

day, and stand instead of God among the children of men? 13 And now try the Lord Almighty, but ye shall never know anything. 14 For ye cannot find the depth of the heart of man, neither can ye perceive the things that he thinketh: then how can ye search out God, that hath made all these things, and know his mind, or comprehend his purpose? Nay, my brethren, provoke not the Lord our God to anger. 15 For if he will not help us within these five days, he hath power to defend us when he will, even every day, or to destroy us before our enemies. 16 Do not bind the counsels of the Lord our God: for God is not as man, that he may be threatened; neither is he as the son of man, that he should be wavering. 17 Therefore let us wait for salvation of him, and call upon him to help us, and he will hear our voice, if it pleases him. 18 For there arose none in our age, neither is there any now in these days neither tribe, nor family, nor people, nor city among us, which worship gods made with hands, as hath been aforetime. 19 For the which cause our fathers were given to the sword, and for a spoil, and had a great fall before our enemies. 20 But we know none other god,

therefore we trust that he will not despise us, nor any of our nation. 21 For if we be taken so, all Judea shall lie waste, and our sanctuary shall be spoiled; and he will require the profanation thereof at our mouth. 22 And the slaughter of our brethren, and the captivity of the country, and the desolation of our inheritance, will he turn upon our heads among the Gentiles, wheresoever we shall be in bondage; and we shall be an offence and a reproach to all them that possess us. 23 For our servitude shall not be directed to favour: but the Lord our God shall turn it to dishonour. 24 Now therefore, O brethren, let us shew an example to our brethren, because their hearts depend upon us, and the sanctuary, and the house, and the altar, rest upon us. 25 Moreover let us give thanks to the Lord our God, which tried us, even as he did our fathers. 26 Remember what things he did to Abraham, and how he tried Isaac, and what happened to Jacob in Mesopotamia of Syria, when he kept the sheep of Laban his mother's brother. 27 For he hath not tried us in the fire, as he did them, for the examination of their hearts, neither hath he taken vengeance on us: but the Lord doth scourge them that come near unto him, to admonish them. 28 Then said Ozias to her, All that thou hast spoken hast thou spoken with a good heart, and there is none that may gainsay thy words. 29 For this is not the first day wherein thy wisdom is manifested; but from the beginning of thy days all the people have known thy understanding, because the disposition of thine heart is good. 30 But the people were very thirsty, and compelled us to do unto them as we have spoken, and to bring an oath upon ourselves, which we will not break. 31Therefore now pray thou for us, because thou art a godly woman, and the Lord will send us rain to fill our cisterns, and we shall faint no more. 32 Then said Judith unto them, Hear me, and I will do a thing, which shall go throughout all generations to the children of our nation. 33 Ye shall stand this night in the gate, and I will go forth with my waiting woman: and within the days that ye have promised to deliver the city to our enemies the Lord will visit Israel by mine hand. 34 But enquire not ye of mine act: for I will not declare it unto you, till the things be finished that I do. 35 Then said Ozias and the princes unto her, Go in peace, and the Lord God be before thee, to take vengeance on our enemies. 36 So they returned from the tent, and went to their wards.

9

1 Judith fell upon her face, and put ashes upon her head, and uncovered the sackcloth wherewith she was clothed; and about the time that the incense of that evening was offered in Jerusalem in the house of the Lord Judith cried with a loud voice, and said, 2 O Lord God of my father Simeon, to whom thou gave a sword to take vengeance of the strangers, who loosened the girdle of a maid to defile her, and discovered the thigh to her shame, and polluted her virginity to her reproach; for thou said, It shall not be so; and yet they did so: 3 Wherefore thou gave their rulers to be slain, so that they dyed their bed in blood, being deceived, and smote the servants with their lords, and the lords upon their thrones; 4And hast given their wives for a prey, and their daughters to be captives, and all their spoils to be divided among thy dear children; which were moved with thy zeal, and abhorred the pollution of their blood, and called upon thee for aid: O God, O my God, hear me

also a widow. 5 For thou hast wrought not only those things, but also the things which fell out before, and which ensued after; thou hast thought upon the things which are now, and which are to come. 6 Yea, what things thou didst determine were ready at hand, and said, Lo, we are here: for all thy ways are prepared, and thy judgments are in thy foreknowledge. 7 For, behold, the Assyrians are multiplied in their power; they are exalted with horse and man; they glory in the strength of their footmen; they trust in shield, and spear, and bow, and sling; and know not that thou art the Lord that break the battles: the Lord is thy name. 8 Throw down their strength in thy power, and bring down their force in thy wrath: for they have purposed to defile thy sanctuary, and to pollute the tabernacle where thy glorious name rested and to cast down with sword the horn of thy altar. 9 Behold their pride, and send thy wrath upon their heads: give into mine hand, which am a widow, the power that I have conceived. 10 Smite by the deceit of my lips the servant with the prince, and the prince with the servant: break down their stateliness by the hand of a woman. 11 For thy power stood not in multitude nor thy might in strong men: for thou art a God of the afflicted, a helper of the oppressed, an upholder of the weak, a protector of the forlorn, a saviour of them that are without hope. 12 I pray thee, I pray thee, O God of my father, and God of the inheritance of Israel, Lord of the heavens and earth, Creator of the waters, king of every creature, hear thou my prayer: 13 And make my speech and deceit to be their wound and stripe, who have purposed cruel things against thy covenant, and thy hallowed house, and against the top of Sion, and against the house of the possession of thy children. 14 And make every nation and tribe to acknowledge that thou art the God of all power and might, and that there is none other that protected the people of Israel but thou.

10

1 Now after that she had ceased to cry unto the God of Israel, and had made an end of all these words. 2 She rose where she had fallen down, and called her maid, and went down into the house in the which she abode in the sabbath days, and in her feast days, 3 And pulled off the sackcloth which she had on, and

put off the garments of her widowhood, and washed her body all over with water, and anointed herself with precious ointment, and braided the hair of her head, and put on a tire upon it, and put on her garments of gladness, wherewith she was clad during the life of Manasses her husband. 4 And she took sandals upon her feet, and put about her her bracelets, and her chains, and her rings, and her earrings, and all her ornaments, and decked herself bravely, to allure the eyes of all men that should see her. 5 Then she gave her maid a bottle of wine, and a cruse of oil, and filled a bag with parched corn, and lumps of figs, and with fine bread; so she folded all these things together, and laid them upon her. 6 Thus they went forth to the gate of the city of Bethulia, and found standing there Ozias and the ancients of the city, Chabris and Charmis. 7 And when they saw her, that her countenance was altered, and her apparel was changed, they wondered at her beauty very greatly, and said unto her. 8 The God, the God of our fathers give thee favour, and accomplish thine enterprises to the glory of the children of Israel, and to the exaltation of Jerusalem. Then they worshipped God. 9 And she said unto them, Command the gates of the city to be opened unto me, that I may go forth to accomplish the things whereof ye have spoken with me. So they commanded the young men to open unto her, as she had spoken. 10 And when they had done so, Judith went out, she, and her maid with her; and the men of the city looked after her, until she was gone down the mountain, and till she had passed the valley, and could see her no more. 11 Thus they went straight forth in the valley: and the first watch of the Assyrians met her, 12 And took her, and asked her, Of what people art thou? and whence came thou? and whither goest thou? And she said, I am a woman of the Hebrews, and am fled from them: for they shall be given you to be consumed: 13 And I am coming before Holofernes the chief captain of your army, to declare words of truth; and I will shew him a way, whereby he shall go, and win all the hill country, without losing the body or life of any one of his men. 14 Now when the men heard her words, and beheld her countenance, they wondered greatly at her beauty, and said unto her, 15 Thou hast saved thy life, in that thou hast hasted to come down to the presence of our lord: now therefore come to his tent, and some of us shall conduct you, until they have delivered thee to his hands. ¹⁶ And when thou stand before him, be not afraid in thine heart, but shew unto him according to thy word; and he will entreat thee well. ¹⁷ Then they chose out of them a hundred men to accompany her and her maid; and they brought her to the tent of Holofernes. ¹⁸ Then was there a concourse throughout all the camp: for her coming was noised among the tents, and they came about her, as she stood without the tent of Holofernes, till they told him of her. ¹⁹ And they wondered at her beauty, and admired the children of Israel because of her, and every one said to his neighbour, Who would despise this people, that have among them such women? surely it is not good that one man of them be left who being let go might deceive the whole earth. ²⁰ And they that lay near Holofernes went out, and all his servants and they brought her into the tent. ²¹ Now Holofernes rested upon his bed under a canopy, which was woven with purple, and gold, and emeralds, and precious stones. ²² So they shewed him of her; and he came out before his tent with silver lamps going before him. ²³ And when Judith was come before him and his servants they all marvelled at the beauty of her countenance; and she fell down upon her face, and did reverence unto him: and his servants took her up.

11

¹ Then said Holofernes unto her, Woman, be of good comfort, fear not in thine heart: for I never hurt any that was willing to serve Nabuchodonosor, the king of all the earth. ² Now therefore, if thy people that dwelleth in the mountains had not set light by me, I would not have lifted up my spear against them: but they have done these things to themselves. ³ But now tell me wherefore thou art fled from them, and art come unto us: for thou art come for safeguard; be of good comfort, thou shalt live this night, and hereafter: ⁴ For none shall hurt thee, but entreat thee well, as they do the servants of king Nabuchodonosor my lord. ⁵ Then Judith said unto him, Receive the words of your servant, and suffer thine hand maid to speak in thy presence,

and I will declare no lie to my lord this night. 6 And if thou wilt follow the words of thine handmaid, God will bring the thing perfectly to pass by you; and my lord shall not fail of his purposes. 7 As Nabuchodonosor king of all the earth lived, and as his power lived, who had sent thee for the upholding of every living thing: for not only men shall serve him by thee, but also the beasts of the field, and the cattle, and the fowls of the air, shall live by thy power under Nabuchodonosor and all his house. 8 For we have heard of thy wisdom and thy policies, and it is reported in all the earth, that thou only art excellent in all the kingdom, and mighty in knowledge, and wonderful in feats of war. 9 Now as concerning the matter, which Achior did speak in thy council, we have heard his words; for the men of Bethulia saved him, and he declared unto them all that he had spoken unto you. 10 Therefore, O lord and governor, respect not his word; but lay it up in thine heart, for it is true: for our nation shall not be punished, neither can sword prevail against them, except they sin against their God. 11 And now, that my lord be not defeated and frustrate of his purpose, even death is now fallen upon them, and their sin hath overtaken them, wherewith they will provoke their God to anger whensoever they shall do that which is not fit to be done: 12bFor their victuals fail them, and all their water is scant, and they have determined to lay hands upon their cattle, and purposed to consume all those things, that God hath forbidden them to eat by his laws: 13 And are resolved to spend the first fruits of the tenths of wine and oil, which they had sanctified, and reserved for the priests that serve in Jerusalem before the face of our God; the which things it is not lawful for any of the people so much as to touch with their hands. 14 For they have sent some to Jerusalem, because they also that dwell there have done the like, to bring them a licence from the senate. 15 Now when they shall bring them word, they will forthwith do it, and they shall be given to thee to be destroyed the same day. 16 Wherefore I thine handmaid, knowing all this, am fled from their presence; and God hath sent me to work things with thee, whereat all the earth shall be astonished, and whosoever shall hear it. 17 For thy servant is religious, and served the God of heaven day and night: now therefore, my lord, I will remain with thee, and thy servant will go out by night into the valley, and I will pray unto God, and he will tell me when they have committed their sins: 18 And I will come and shew it unto thee: then thou shalt go forth with all thine army, and there shall be none of them that shall resist thee. 19 And I will lead thee through the midst of Judea, until thou come before Jerusalem; and I will set thy throne in the midst thereof; and thou shalt drive them as sheep that have no shepherd, and a dog shall not so much as open his mouth at thee: for these things were told me according to my foreknowledge, and they were declared unto me, and I am sent to tell thee. 20 Then her words pleased Holofernes and all his servants; and they marvelled at her wisdom, and said, 21 There is not such a woman from one end of the earth to the other, both for beauty of face, and wisdom of words. 22 Likewise Holofernes said unto her. God hath done well to send thee before the people, that strength might be in our hands and destruction upon them that lightly regard my lord. 23 And now thou art both beautiful in thy countenance, and witty in thy words: surely if thou do as thou hast spoken thy God shall be my God, and thou shalt dwell in the house of king Nabuchodonosor, and shalt be renowned through the whole earth.

12

1 Then he commanded to bring her in where his plate was set; and bade that they should prepare for her of his own meats, and that she should drink of his own wine. 2 And Judith said, I will not eat thereof, lest there be an offence: but provision shall be made for me of the things that I have brought. 3 Then Holofernes said unto her, If your provision should fail, how should we give thee the like? for there be none with us of thy nation. 4 Then said Judith unto him As thy soul lived, my lord, thine handmaid shall not spend those things that I have, before the Lord work by mine hand the things that he hath determined. 5 Then the servants of Holofernes brought her into the tent, and she slept till midnight, and she arose when it was toward the morning watch, 6 And sent to Holofernes, saying, Let my lord now command that thine handmaid may go forth unto prayer. 7 Then Holofernes

commanded his guard that they should not stay her: thus she abode in the camp three days, and went out in the night into the valley of Bethulia, and washed herself in a fountain of water by the camp. 8 And when she came out, she besought the Lord God of Israel to direct her way to the raising up of the children of her people. 9 So she came in clean, and remained in the tent, until she did eat her meat at evening. 10 And in the fourth day Holofernes made a feast to his own servants only, and called none of the officers to the banquet. 11 Then said he to Bagoas the eunuch, who had charge over all that he had, Go now, and persuade this Hebrew woman which is with thee, that she come unto us, and eat and drink with us. 12 For, lo, it will be a shame for our person, if we shall let such a woman go, not having had her company; for if we draw her not unto us, she will laugh us to scorn. 13 Then went Bagoas from the presence of Holofernes, and came to her, and he said, Let not this fair damsel fear to come to my lord, and to be honoured in his presence, and drink wine, and be merry with us and be made this day as one of the daughters of the Assyrians, which serve in the house of Nabuchodonosor. 14 Then said Judith unto him, Who am I now, that I should gainsay my lord? surely whatsoever pleased him I will do speedily, and it shall be my joy unto the day of my death. 15 So she arose, and decked herself with her apparel and all her woman's attire, and her maid went and laid soft skins on the ground for her over against Holofernes, which she had received of Bagoas for her daily use, that she might sit and eat upon them. 16 Now when Judith came in and sat down, Holofernes his heart was ravished with her, and his mind was moved, and he desired greatly her company; for he waited a time to deceive her, from the day that he had seen her. 17 Then said Holofernes unto her, Drink now, and be merry with us. 18 So Judith said, I will drink now, my lord, because my life is magnified in me this day more than all the days since I was born. 19 Then she took and ate and drank before him what her maid had prepared. 20 And Holofernes took great delight in her, and drank more wine than he had drunk at any time in one day since he was born.

13

¹ Now when the evening was come, his servants made haste to depart, and Bagoas shut his tent without, and dismissed the waiters from the presence of his lord; and they went to their beds: for they were all weary, because the feast had been long. ² And Judith was left alone in the tent, and Holofernes lying alone upon his bed: for he was filled with wine. ³ Now Judith had commanded her maid to stand without her bedchamber, and to wait for her. coming forth, as she did daily: for she said she would go forth to her prayers, and she spake to Bagoas according to the same purpose. ⁴ So all went forth and none was left in the bedchamber, neither little nor great. Then Judith, standing by his bed, said in her heart, O Lord God of all power, look at this present upon the works of mine hands for the exaltation of Jerusalem. ⁵ For now is the time to help thine inheritance, and to execute thine enterprizes to the destruction of the enemies which are risen against us. ⁶ Then she came to the pillar of the bed, which was at Holofernes' head, and took down his fauchion from thence, ⁷ And approached to his bed, and took hold of the hair of his head, and said, Strengthen me, O Lord God of Israel, this day. ⁸ And she smote twice upon his neck with all her might, and she took away his head from him. ⁹ And tumbled his body down from the bed, and pulled down the canopy from the pillars; and anon after she went forth, and gave Holofernes his head to her maid; ¹⁰ And she put it in her bag of meat: so they twain went together according to their custom unto prayer: and when they passed the camp, they compassed the valley, and went up the mountain of Bethulia, and came to the gates thereof. ¹¹ Then said Judith afar off, to the watchmen at the gate, Open, open now the gate: God, even our God, is with us, to shew his power yet in Jerusalem, and his forces against the enemy, as he hath even done this day. ¹² Now when the men of her city heard her voice, they made haste to go down to the gate of their city, and they called the elders of the city. ¹³And then they ran all together, both small and great, for it was strange unto them that she was come: so they opened the gate, and received them, and made a fire for a light, and stood round about them. ¹⁴ Then she said to them with a loud voice, Praise, praise God, praise God, I say, for

he hath not taken away his mercy from the house of Israel, but hath destroyed our enemies by mine hands this night. ¹⁵ So she took the head out of the bag, and shewed it, and said unto them, behold the head of Holofernes, the chief captain of the army of Assur, and behold the canopy, wherein he did lie in his drunkenness; and the Lord hath smitten him by the hand of a woman. ¹⁶ As the Lord lived, who hath kept me in my way that I went, my countenance hath deceived him to his destruction, and yet hath he not committed sin with me, to defile and shame me. ¹⁷ Then all the people were wonderfully astonished, and bowed themselves and worshipped God, and said with one accord, Blessed be thou, O our God, which hast this day brought to nought the enemies of thy people. ¹⁸ Then said Ozias unto her, O daughter, blessed art thou of the most high God above all the women upon the earth; and blessed be the Lord God, which hath created the heavens and the earth, which hath directed thee to the cutting off of the head of the chief of our enemies. ¹⁹ For this thy confidence shall not depart from the heart of men, which remember the power of God for ever. ²⁰ And God turn these things to thee for a perpetual praise, to visit thee in good things because thou hast not spared thy life for the affliction of our nation, but hast revenged our ruin, walking a straight way before our God. And all the people said; So be it, so be it.

14

¹ Then said Judith unto them, Hear me now, my brethren, and take this head, and hang it upon the highest place of your walls. ² And so soon as the morning shall appear, and the sun shall come forth upon the earth, take ye every one his weapons, and go forth every valiant man out of the city, and set ye a captain over them, as though ye would go down into the field toward the watch of the Assyrians; but go not down. ³ Then they shall take their armour, and shall go into their camp, and raise up the captains of the army of Assur, and shall run to the tent of Holofernes, but shall not find him: then fear shall fall upon them, and they shall flee before your face. ⁴ So ye, and all that inhabit the coast of Israel, shall pursue them, and overthrow them as they go. ⁵ But before ye

do these things, call me Achior the Ammonite, that he may see and know him that despised the house of Israel, and that sent him to us as it were to his death. 6 Then they called Achior out of the house of Ozias; and when he was come, and saw the head of Holofernes in a man's hand in the assembly of the people, he fell down on his face, and his spirit failed. 7 But when they had recovered him, he fell at Judith's feet, and reverenced her, and said, Blessed art thou in all the tabernacles of Juda, and in all nations, which hearing thy name shall be astonished. 8 Now therefore tell me all the things that thou hast done in these days. Then Judith declared unto him in the midst of the people all that she had done, from the day that she went forth until that hour she spake unto them. 9 And when she had left off speaking, the people shouted with a loud voice, and made a joyful noise in their city. 10 And when Achior had seen all that the God of Israel had done, he believed in God greatly, and circumcised the flesh of his foreskin, and was joined unto the house of Israel unto this day. 11 And as soon as the morning arose, they hanged the head of Holofernes upon the wall, and every man took his weapons, and they went forth by bands unto the straits of the mountain. 12 But when the Assyrians saw them, they sent to their leaders, which came to their captains and tribunes, and to every one of their rulers. 13 So they came to Holofernes' tent, and said to him that had the charge of all his things, Waken now our lord: for the slaves have been bold to come down against us to battle, that they may be utterly destroyed. 14 Then went in Bagoas, and knocked at the door of the tent; for he thought that he had slept with Judith. 15 But because none answered, he opened it, and went into the bedchamber, and found him cast upon the floor dead, and his head was taken from him. 16 Therefore he cried with a loud voice, with weeping, and sighing, and a mighty cry, and rent his garments. 17 After he went into the tent where Judith lodged: and when he found her not, he leaped out to the people, and cried, 18 These slaves have dealt treacherously; one woman of the Hebrews hath brought shame upon the house of king Nabuchodonosor: for, behold, Holofernes lieth upon the ground without a head. 19 When the captains of the Assyrians' army heard these words, they rent their coats and their minds were wonderfully troubled, and there was a cry and a very great noise throughout the camp

15

1 And when they that were in the tents heard, they were astonished at the thing that was done. 2 And fear and trembling fell upon them, so that there was no man that durst abide in the sight of his neighbour, but rushing out all together, they fled into every way of the plain, and of the hill country. 3 They also that had camped in the mountains round about Bethulia fled away. Then the children of Israel, every one that was a warrior among them, rushed out upon them. 4 Then sent Ozias to Betomasthem, and to Bebai, and Chobai, and Cola and to all the coasts of Israel, such as should tell the things that were done, and that all should rush forth upon their enemies to destroy them. 5 Now when the children of Israel heard it, they all fell upon them with one consent, and slew them unto Chobai: likewise also they that came from Jerusalem, and from all the hill country, (for men had told them what things were done in the camp of their enemies) and they that were in Galaad, and in Galilee, chased them with a great slaughter, until they were past Damascus and the borders thereof. 6 And the residue that dwelt at Bethulia, fell upon the camp of Assur, and spoiled them, and were greatly enriched. 7 And the children of Israel that returned from the slaughter had that which remained; and the villages and the cities, that were in the mountains and in the plain, gat many spoils: for the multitude was very great. 8 Then Joacim the high priest, and the ancients of the children of Israel that dwelt in Jerusalem, came to behold the good things that God had shewed to Israel, and to see Judith, and to salute her. 9 And when they came unto her, they blessed her with one accord, and said unto her, Thou art the exaltation of Jerusalem, thou art the great glory of Israel, thou art the great rejoicing of our nation: 10 Thou hast done all these things by thine hand: thou hast done much good to Israel, and God is pleased therewith: blessed be thou of the Almighty Lord for evermore. And all the people said, So be it. 11 And the people spoiled the camp the space of thirty days: and they gave unto

Judith Holofernes his tent, and all his plate, and beds, and vessels, and all his stuff: and she took it and laid it on her mule; and made ready her carts, and laid them thereon. 12 Then all the women of Israel ran together to see her, and blessed her, and made a dance among them for her: and she took branches in her hand, and gave also to the women that were with her. 13 And they put a garland of olive upon her and her maid that was with her, and she went before all the people in the dance, leading all the women: and all the men of Israel followed in their armour with garlands, and with songs in their mouths.

16

1 Then Judith began to sing this thanksgiving in all Israel, and all the people sang after her this song of praise. 2 And Judith said, Begin unto my God with timbrels, sing unto my Lord with cymbals: tune unto him a new psalm: exalt him, and call upon his name. 3 For God breaketh the battles: for among the camps in the midst of the people he hath delivered me out of the hands of them that persecuted me. 4 Assur came out of the mountains from the north, he came with ten thousands of his army, the multitude whereof stopped the torrents, and their horsemen have covered the hills. 5 He bragged that he would burn up my borders, and kill my young men with the sword, and dash the sucking children against the ground, and make mine infants as a prey, and my virgins as a spoil. 6 But the Almighty Lord hath disappointed them by the hand of a woman. 7 For the mighty one did not fall by the young men, neither did the sons of the Titans smite him, nor high giants set upon him: but Judith the daughter of Merari weakened him with the beauty of her countenance. 8 For she put off the garment of her widowhood for the exaltation of those that were oppressed in Israel, and anointed her face with ointment, and bound her hair in a tire, and took a linen garment to deceive him. 9 Her sandals ravished his eyes, her beauty took his mind prisoner, and the fauchion passed through his neck. 10 The Persians quaked at her boldness, and the Medes were daunted at her hardiness. 11 Then my afflicted shouted for joy, and my weak ones cried aloud; but they were astonished: these lifted up their voices, but they were overthrown. 12 The sons of the

damsels have pierced them through, and wounded them as fugatives' children: they perished by the battle of the Lord. 13 I will sing unto the Lord a new song: O Lord, thou art great and glorious, wonderful in strength, and invincible. 14 Let all creatures serve thee: for thou spakest, and they were made, thou didst send forth thy spirit, and it created them, and there is none that can resist thy voice. 15 For the mountains shall be moved from their foundations with the waters, the rocks shall melt as wax at thy presence: yet thou art merciful to them that fear thee. 16 For all sacrifice is too little for a sweet savour unto thee, and all the fat is not sufficient for thy burnt offering: but he that feareth the Lord is great at all times. 17 Woe to the nations that rise up against my kindred! the Lord Almighty will take vengeance of them in the day of judgment, in putting fire and worms in their flesh; and they shall feel them, and weep for ever. 18 Now as soon as they entered into Jerusalem, they worshipped the Lord; and as soon as the people were purified, they offered their burnt offerings, and their free offerings, and their gifts. 19 Judith also dedicated all the stuff of Holofernes, which the people had given her, and gave the canopy, which she had taken out of his bedchamber, for a gift unto the Lord. 20 So the people continued feasting in Jerusalem before the sanctuary for the space of three months and Judith remained with them. 21 After this time every one returned to his own inheritance, and Judith went to Bethulia, and remained in her own possession, and was in her time honourable in all the country. 22 And many desired her, but none knew her all the days of her life, after that Manasses her husband was dead, and was gathered to his people. 23 But she increased more and more in honour, and waxed old in her husband's house, being an hundred and five years old, and made her maid free; so she died in Bethulia: and they buried her in the cave of her husband Manasses. 24 And the house of Israel lamented her seven days: and before she died, she did distribute her goods to all them that were nearest of kindred to Manasses her husband, and to them that were the nearest of her kindred. 25 And there was none that made the children of Israel any more afraid in the days of Judith, nor a long time after her death.

Additions to Esther

This text, included in the Apocrypha of the 1560 Geneva Bible, enrich the canonical Book of Esther with additional scenes and religious elements that are not present in the Hebrew text. These additions significantly alter the tone and focus of the story, imbuing it with a more explicit spiritual dimension that emphasizes divine intervention, prayer, and piety.

Originating in the Greek Septuagint, these supplementary sections were likely composed during the period when many Jews lived under Hellenistic rule, and they reflect an attempt to express Jewish faith within a context that valued explicit expressions of religious devotion. The Additions to Esther include several key passages: a prologue that describes a dream of Mordecai, the prayers of Mordecai and Esther, an expansion on the decree against the Jews, and a triumphant conclusion that includes the interpretation of Mordecai's dream and additional details regarding his rise to power.

The Additions transform Esther from a narrative of political intrigue and personal courage into a more conventional Jewish tale of deliverance akin to those found in other biblical books like Daniel and Judith. For example, the prayers of Mordecai and Esther reveal their reliance on God, highlighting themes of providence and the power of prayer. Mordecai's dream and its interpretation introduce a prophetic element that underscores the story's themes of divine oversight and predetermined destiny. Theologically, these additions address the notable absence of God's name in the original Hebrew text by emphasizing God's implicit guidance and the importance of faith in Him. Mordecai and Esther's direct appeals to God through prayer align the story more closely with Jewish piety and the belief in an active, intervening deity.

In a literary sense, the Additions to Esther enhance the drama and complexity of the narrative, offering readers a richer, multi-layered text. They provide deeper insights into the characters' motivations and the religious dimensions of their struggles and victories. This not only heightens the story's emotional impact but also strengthens its function as a tool for religious and moral instruction.

Additions to Esther

10

4 And Mordecai said, These things be done of God. 5 I have mind on a dream, which I saw, signifying these same things, and nothing of those was void. 6 A little well, that waxed into a flood, and was turned into light, and sun, and turned again into full many waters, this well is Esther, whom the king took into wife, and would that she were his queen. 7 And the two dragons, I am, and Haman; 8 and folks that came together, be these, that enforced or endeavoured to do away the name of Jews. 9 But my folk Israel it is, that cried to the Lord; and the Lord made safe his people, and he hath delivered us from all evils, and he hath done great signs, or tokens, and wonders among heathen men 10 and he hath commanded two lots to be, one of God's people, and the other of all heathen men 11 And then ever either lot came into a day ordained, or determined, from that time before God and all folks. 12 And the Lord had mind on his people, and had mercy on his heritage. 13 And these days shall be kept in the month Adar, or March, in the fourteenth and the fifteenth day of the same month, with all busyness and joy of the people gathered into one company, into all the generations of the people of Israel afterward. *(In the Greek Esther, and likewise for the Hebrew Esther, the following verse serves as a postscript after the 10 new verses added to Chapter 10.)*

11

1 In the fourth year, when Ptolemy and Cleopatra reigned, Dositheus, that said himself to be a priest and of the kin of Levi, and Ptolemy, his son, brought this epistle of lots into Jerusalem, which epistle they said, that Lysimachus, the son of Ptolemy, translated. This is a rubric; for this beginning was in the common translation, which beginning is not told in Hebrew, neither at any of the translators. *(In the Greek Esther, verses 2-12 that follow, serve as a Prologue to Chapter 1; in the Hebrew Esther, they would be*

placed at verse 5 of Chapter 2.) 2 In the second year, when Artaxerxes the most reigned the mightiest king reigned, Mordecai, the son of Jair, the son of Shimei, the son of Kish, of the lineage of Benjamin, saw a dream in the first day of the month Nisan, that is, June; 3 and Mordecai was a man a Jew, that dwelled in the city of Susa, a great man, and among the chief men or the first men of the king's hall. 4 And he was of that number of prisoners, which Nebu-chadnezzar, the king of Babylon, had translated or brought over from Jerusalem with Jeconiah, king of Judah. And this was his dream. 5 He saw that voices, and noises, and thunders, and earth-movings, and great troubling appeared upon the earth. 6 And lo! two great dragons, and they were made ready against them-selves into battle; 7 at whose cry all nations were stirred together, to fight against the folk of just men. 8 And that was a day of darknesses, and of peril, of tribulation, and of anguish, and great dread was then upon the earth. 9 And the folk of just men, dreading their evils, was disturbed, and made ready to death. 10 And they cried to God; and when they cried, a little well increased into a full great flood, and it turned again into full many waters. 11 And then the light and the sun rose up; and meek men were enhanced, and devoured noble men. 12 And when Mordecai in his sleep had seen this thing, and had risen from his bed, he thought, what God would do, and he had fast set in his soul this vision, and coveted to know, what the dream signified. *(In the Greek Esther, verses 1-6 that follow conclude the Prologue to Chapter 1; in the Hebrew Esther, they would be placed at verse 21 of Chapter 2.)*

12

1 Forsooth Mordecai dwelled that time in the hall of the king, with Bigthan or Gabatha and Teresh or Tharra, the honest servants and chaste of the king, that were porters of the palace. 2 And when he had understood the thoughts of them, and had before-seen full diligently their busynesses, he learned that they endeavoured them to set their hands upon the king Ahasuerus, and he told of that thing to the king. 3 And when enquiring was had of ever either of them, the king commanded them, that acknowledged their treason, to be led to the death. 4 And the king wrote in books that

thing, that was done, and also Mordecai took mind of this thing to be written in letters. Forsooth the king wrote in books that, that was done, but also Mordecai betook the mind of the thing to letters. 5 And the king commanded Mordecai, that he should dwell in the hall of the palace, and he gave to him gifts for the telling. 6 Forsooth Haman, the son of Hammedatha, a Bougean, was most glorious before the king, and he would have annoyed Mordecai, and his people, for the twain honest and chaste servants of the king that were slain. Hitherto is the proem; those things, that pursue], were set[or put]in that place where it is written in the book, And they took away the goods, either the chattels of them; which things we found in the common translation. *(In the Greek Esther, verses 1-7 below follow verse 13 of Chapter 3; in the Hebrew Esther, these 7 verses would also follow verse 13 of Chapter 3.)*

13

1 Soothly this was the sampler of the epistle. The greatest king Ahasuerus, from India unto Ethiopia, saith health to the princes and dukes of an hundred and seven and twenty provinces, which princes and dukes be subjects to his empire. 2 When I was lord of full many folks, and I had made subject all the world to my lordship, I would not mis-use the greatness of power, but govern my subjects by mercy and softness, that they, leading their life in silence without any dread, should use peace coveted of all deadly men. 3 And when I asked of my counsellors, how this might be filled, one, Haman by name, that passed other men in wisdom and faithfulness, and was the second after the king, 4 showed to me, that a people was scattered in all the roundness of lands, the which people used new laws, and did against the custom of all folks, and despised the commandment of kings, and defouled by his dissention the according of all nations. 5 And when we had learned this thing, and saw, that one folk rebelled against all the kind of men, and that it used wayward laws, and was contrary to our commandments, and disturbed or troubled the peace and according of provinces subject to us, 6 we commanded, that whichever Haman showed, which is sovereign of all provinces, and is the second from the king, and whom we

honour in the place of father, they with their wives and children, be done away of their enemies, and no man have mercy upon them, in the fourteenth day of the twelfth month Adar, or March, of the present year; 7 that cursed [men go down to hell in one day, and yield peace to our empire, which they had troubled. Hitherto is the sampler of the epistle; these things, that pursue, I found written after that place, where it is read, And Mordecai went, and did all things, which Esther had commanded to him; nevertheless those things be not had in Hebrew, and utterly those be not said at any of the translators. *(In the Greek Esther, verses 8-19 below follow verse 17 of Chapter 4; in the Hebrew Esther, these 11 verses would also follow verse 17 of Chapter 4.)* 8 Forsooth Mordecai besought the Lord, and was mindful of all his works/and he was mindfuls of all the works of the Lord, 9 and said, Lord God, King Almighty, all things be set in thy lordship, either power, and there is none, that may against-stand thy will; if thou deemest for to save Israel, we shall be delivered anon. 10 Thou madest heaven and earth, and whatever thing is contained in the compass of heaven. 11 Thou art Lord of all things, and there is none that against-standeth thy majesty. 12 Thou knowest all things, and knowest, that not for pride and spite, neither for any covetousness of vain glory I did this thing, that I worshipped not Haman the most proud man 13 for I was ready willfully to kiss I was ready to have kissed willfully, yea, the steps of his feet for the health of Israel, 14 but I dreaded, lest I should bear over to a man, or to man, the honour of my God, and lest I should worship any man except my God. 15 And now, Lord King, God of Abraham, have thou mercy on thy people, for our enemies will lose us, and do away thine heritage; 16 despise not thy part, which thou again boughtest from Egypt. 17 Hear thou my prayer, and be thou merciful to the lot, and the part of thine heritage; and turn thou our mourning into joy, that we living praise thy name, Lord; and close thou not the mouths of men praising thee. 18 And all Israel with like mind and beseeching cried to the Lord, for cause that certain death nighed to them. *(In the Greek Esther, verses 1-19 below follow the preceding verses, prior to Chapter 5; in the Hebrew Esther, these 19 verses would also*

14

¹ Also queen Esther to the Lord, and dreaded the peril, that nighed. ² And when she had put away the king's clothes that pertained to the queen, she took clothes covenable to weepings and mourning; and for diverse ointments, she filled her head with ashes and drit, or vile power, or dust, and she meeked her body with fastings; and with braiding, or twisting, away of her hair, she filled all places, in which she was wont to be glad; ³ and she besought the Lord God of Israel, and said, My Lord, which alone art our King, help me a woman left alone, and of whom none other helper is except thee, ⁴ my peril is in my hands. ⁵ I have heard of my father, that thou, Lord, hast taken away Israel from all folks, and our fathers from all their greater men before, that thou shouldest wield an everlasting heritage; and thou hast done to them, as thou hast spoken, or promised. ⁶ We have sinned in thy sight, and therefore thou hast betaken us into the hands of our enemies; ⁷ for we worshipped the gods of them. Rightwise thou art, Lord; ⁸ and now it sufficeth not to them, that they oppress us with hardest servage, but they reckon the strength of their hands to the power of idols, ⁹ and therefore they will change thy behests, and do away thine heritage, and close the mouths of men praising thee, and quench the glory of thy temple and altar, ¹⁰ that they open the mouths of heathen men and they will open the mouths of heathen men, and praise the strength of idols, and preach a fleshly king without end. ¹¹ Lord, give thou not thy king's rod to them, that be nought, lest they laugh at our falling; but turn thou the counsel of them upon themselves, and destroy thou him, that began to be cruel against us. ¹² Lord, have thou mind, and show thee to us in the time of tribulation; and, Lord, King of gods, and King of all power, give thou trust to me; ¹³ give thou a word well addressed, in my mouth in the sight of the lion Ahasuerus, and turn over his heart into the hatred of our enemy, that both he perish, and other men that consented to him. ¹⁴ But deliver us in thine hand, and help me, having none other help but thee, ¹⁵ Lord, that hast the knowing of all things; and Lord, thou knowest that I hate

the glory of wicked men, and that I loathe the bed of uncircumcised men, and of each alien. [16] Lord, thou knowest my frailty and my need, that I hold abominable the sign of my pride and of my glory, which is on mine head in the days of my showing, and that I loathe it as the cloth of a woman having unclean blood, and I bear not, or use it, in the days of my stillness, [17] and that I ate not in the board of Haman, neither the feast of the king pleased me, and I drank not the wine of moist sacrifices, [18] and that thine handmaid was never glad, since I was translated hither till into present day, but in thee, Lord God of Abraham. [19] A! strong God above all, hear thou the voice of them, that have none other hope than thee, and deliver thou us from the hands of wicked men, and deliver thou me from my dread. *(In the Greek Esther, the next 2 verses would follow verse 8 of Chapter 4; in the Hebrew Esther, these 2 verses would also follow verse 8 of Chapter 4.)* [1'] And no doubt that Mordecai sent to Esther, that she should enter to the king, and pray for her people, and for her country. [1"] He said, Be thou mindful of the days of thy meekness, how thou were nourished in mine hand; for Haman, which is ordained the

second person in power from the king, hath spoken against us into death; therefore thou inwardly call the Lord, and speak thou to the king for us, and deliver us from death. *(In the Greek Esther, verses 1-16 below, follow Esther's prayer, which follows Mordecai's prayer, all of which precede Chapter 5; in the Hebrew Esther, these 16 verses would replace the first 2 verses of Chapter 5.)*

15

[1] Forsooth in the third day she putted off the clothes of her adorning, or of her mourning, and was encom-passed with her glory. [2] And when she shined in the king's clothing, and had inwardly called the Governor of all things and the Saviour God, she took two servantesses, [3] and soothly she leaned on one, as not sustaining to bear her body, for delights and full great tenderness; [4] but the other servantess pursued the lady, and bare up her clothes trailing down upon the earth. [5] And Esther in her face was coloured with rose colours, and with her pleasant and shining eyes she covered her sorrowful soul, that was drawn together with full much dread. [6] Therefore she entered through all the doors by order, and she stood against the king, where he sat upon the

seat of his realm, and was clothed in the king's clothes, and shined in gold and precious stones, and he was dreadful in sight. 7 And when he had raised up his face, and had showed the madness, or austereness, of his heart with burning eyes, the queen felled down before him; and when her colour was changed into paleness, she rested her head bowed down upon her handmaid. 8 And God turned the spirit of the king into mildness, and he hasted, and dreaded, and skipped out of the seat and the king hasting, and dreading, rose up anon of his seat; and he sustained her held up the queen with his arms, till she came again to herself; and he spake fair to her by these words, 9 Esther, what grief hast thou? I am thy brother; do not thou dread, 10 thou shalt not die, for this coming to me without calling; for this law is not made for thee, but for all men. Therefore nigh thou hither,11 and touch the sceptre, that is, the king's rod. And when she was still, took the golden rod, and putted on her neck; 12 and he kissed her, and said, Why speakest thou not to me? 13 And she answered, Lord, I saw thee as an angel of God, and mine heart was troubled for the dread of thy glory; 14 for, lord, thou art full wonderful, and thy face is full of graces. 15 And when she spake, again she felled down in a swoon, and was almost dead. 16 Soothly the king was troubled, and all his servants comforted her. *(In the Greek Esther, verses 1-24 below, follow verse 12 of Chapter 8; in the Hebrew Esther, these 24 verses would also follow verse 12 of Chapter 8.)* 1' The sampler of the letter of king Ahasuerus, which he sent for the Jews to all the provinces of his realm; and this same sampler is not had in the book of Hebrew.

16

1 The great king Ahasuerus, from India unto Ethiopia, saith health to the dukes and princes of an hundred and seven and twenty provinces, that obey to our commandment. 2 Many men misuse into pride the goodness and honour of princes, which is given to them; he 3 and not only they endeavor to oppress subjects to kings, but they bear not duly the glory given to them, and make ready treasons against them, that gave their glory to them. 4 And they be not appeased to do not thankings for benefices or goodnesses, and to defoul in themselves the laws of courtesy; but also they deem, that they may

flee the sentence of God seeing all things. 5 And they break out into so much madness, that they endeavor them with ropes, of leasings to destroy them, that keep diligently the offices betaken to them, and do so all things, that they be worthy the praising of all men; 6 while by subtle fraud false men deceive the simple ears of kings, and guessing other men by their own kind and while malicious men guessing other men by their own kind blameful by subtle fraud, they deceive the simple ears of kings. 7 Which thing is proved both by eld stories, and by these things that be done each day; how the studies of kings be made shrewd by evil suggestions of some men. 8 Wherefore it is to purvey for the peace of all provinces. 9 And though we command diverse things, ye owe not to guess, that this cometh of the unstableness of our soul or of our heart; but that we give sentence by our counsel for the manner and need of times, as the profit of the common thing asketh. 10 And that ye understand more openly that thing, that we say; Haman the son of Hammedatha, a man of Macedonia by soul and, and, and an alien from the blood of Persians, and defouling our piety with his cruelty, was a pilgrim, or a stranger, and was received of us; 11 and he feeled in himself so great courtesy of us, that he was called our father, and he was worshipped of all men as the second person after the king; 12 the which Haman was raised into so great swelling of pride, that he enforced to deprive us of the realm and of our life. 13 For by some new and unheard casts he asked into death Mordecai, by whose faith and benefices we live, and also the fellow of our realm, Esther, with all her folk; 14 and he thought these things, that when they were slain, he should set treason to our aloneness, that is, to us-self alone, and that he should translate the realm of Persians into the realm of the Macedonians. 15 Forsooth we found not the Jews in any guilt utterly that were ordained to death by him that is the worst of deadly men; but again-ward that the Jews, use just laws, 16 and be the sons of the highest and most God, and ever livingand be the sons of the highest and most, and of everlasting God, by whose benefice, or goodness, the realm was given both to our fathers and to us, and is kept unto this day. 17 Wherefore know ye, that those letters be void, which that Haman sent under our name. 18 For which great trespass both he that imagined it, and all his kindred, hangeth in gibbets before the gates of he city of Susa; for not we, but God yielded to him that, that he deserved. 19 Forsooth this commandment, which we send now, be set forth in all cities. Therefore this behest, that we send forth now, be it set up in all cities, that it be leaveful to the Jews to use their laws. 20 Which Jews ye owe to help, that they may slay them, that made themselves ready to the death of Jews, in the thirteenth day of the twelfth month, which is called Adar, or March; 21 for Almighty God hath turned this day of wailing and of mourning into joy to them. 22 Wherefore and ye have this day among other feast days, and hallow it with all gladness; 23 that it be known afterward, that all men, that obey faithfully to the kings of Persia, receive worthy meed for their faith; and that they, that set treason to the realm of them, perish for the felony. 24 And each province and city, that will not be partner of this solemnity, perish by sword and by fire; and be it so undone or destroyed, that not only it be without way to men, but also to beasts without end, for ensample of despising and unobedience.

The Wisdom of Solomon

This is an exemplary text that merges Hellenistic influences with Jewish theological traditions. Traditionally attributed to King Solomon, known for his wisdom in biblical lore, this book is considered a product of Hellenistic Judaism, written by an anonymous author in the 1st century BCE. This text offers profound reflections on wisdom, justice, and the immortality of the soul, showcasing a blend of philosophical inquiry and religious devotion.

The structure of "The Wisdom of Solomon" is designed to appeal to both Jewish and non-Jewish audiences, making a case for the superiority of godly wisdom over merely human knowledge. The book is divided into three main parts: an exhortation to rulers to seek divine wisdom, a discourse on wisdom as the guide of Israel during the Exodus, and a lengthy praise of wisdom by recounting the experiences of the ancestors of Israel. This sophisticated arrangement not only underscores the universal relevance of wisdom but also illustrates its practical implications through historical examples. Theologically, "The Wisdom of Solomon" emphasizes the concept of righteousness linked to immortality, presenting wisdom as a divine gift that offers insight into life's complexity and a moral compass by which to live. The text strongly advocates justice and portrays wisdom as an accessible, divine essence that shapes the world and enhances human understanding of divine law. It contrasts the fate of the righteous with that of the wicked, offering a vivid depiction of the rewards awaiting those who choose wisdom and the penalties for those who do not.

From a literary standpoint, the book employs an eloquent style, rich in poetic forms and rhetorical devices, making it one of the more stylistically sophisticated works found in biblical literature. Its language and imagery reflect a deep engagement with Greek philosophical concepts, particularly those found in Platonic and Stoic thought, yet the work remains firmly rooted in the Jewish tradition, replete with references to the Torah and prophetic writings.

This text provided a bridge between ancient wisdom literature and contemporary Christian thought, reflecting the Renaissance's burgeoning interest in integrating classical knowledge with Christian theology. It serves as a spiritual and intellectual resource, encouraging rulers and laypeople alike to seek divine wisdom as a guide in governance, personal conduct, and understanding the mysteries of life and death. Overall, "The Wisdom of Solomon" stands as a profound meditation on virtue, a manual for ethical conduct, and a theological treatise on the enduring relationship between divine justice and human morality. Its inclusion in the Geneva Bible enriches the Christian textual tradition by presenting a sophisticated articulation of wisdom's role in human affairs and the cosmic order.

The Wisdom of Solomon

[1] Love righteousness, ye that be judges of the earth: think of the Lord with a good (heart,) and in simplicity of heart seek him. [2] For he will be found of them that tempt him not; and sheweth himself unto such as do not distrust him. [3] For froward thoughts separate from God: and his power, when it is tried, reproveth the unwise. [4] For into a malicious soul wisdom shall not enter; nor dwell in the body that is subject unto sin. [5] For the holy spirit of discipline will flee deceit, and remove from thoughts that are without understanding, and will not abide when unrighteousness cometh in. [6] For wisdom is a loving spirit; and will not acquit a blasphemer of his words: for God is witness of his reins, and a true beholder of his heart, and a hearer of his tongue. [7] For the Spirit of the Lord filleth the world: and that which containeth all things hath knowledge of the voice. [8] Therefore he that speaketh unrighteous things cannot be hid: neither shall vengeance, when it punisheth, pass by him. [9] For inquisition shall be made into the counsels of the ungodly: and the sound of his words shall come unto the Lord for the manifestation of his wicked deeds. [10] For the ear of jealousy heareth all things: and the noise of murmurings is not hid. [11] Therefore beware of murmuring, which is unprofitable; and refrain your tongue from backbiting: for there is no word so secret, that shall go for nought: and the mouth that belieth slayeth the soul. [12] Seek not death in the error of your life: and pull not upon yourselves destruction with the works of your hands. [13] For God made not death: neither hath he pleasure in the destruction of the living. [14]For he created all things, that they might have their being: and the generations of the world were healthful; and there is no poison of destruction in them, nor the kingdom of death upon the earth: [15] (For righteousness is immortal:) [16] But ungodly men with their works and words called it to them: for when they thought to have it their friend, they consumed to nought, and made a covenant with it, because they are worthy to take part with it.

2

[1] For the ungodly said, reasoning with themselves, but not aright, Our life is short and tedious, and in the death of a man there is no remedy: neither was there any

man known to have returned from the grave. 2 For we are born at all adventure: and we shall be hereafter as though we had never been: for the breath in our nostrils is as smoke, and a little spark in the moving of our heart: 3 Which being extinguished, our body shall be turned into ashes, and our spirit shall vanish as the soft air, 4 And our name shall be forgotten in time, and no man shall have our works in remembrance, and our life shall pass away as the trace of a cloud, and shall be dispersed as a mist, that is driven away with the beams of the sun, and overcome with the heat thereof. 5 For our time is a very shadow that passeth away; and after our end there is no returning: for it is fast sealed, so that no man cometh again. 6 Come on therefore, let us enjoy the good things that are present: and let us speedily use the creatures like as in youth. 7 Let us fill ourselves with costly wine and ointments: and let no flower of the spring pass by us: 8 Let us crown ourselves with rosebuds, before they be withered: 9 Let none of us go without his part of our voluptuousness: let us leave tokens of our joyfulness in every place: for this is our portion, and our lot is this. 10 Let us oppress the poor righteous man, let us not spare the widow, nor reverence the ancient gray hairs of the aged. 11 Let our strength be the law of justice: for that which is feeble is found to be nothing worth. 12 Therefore let us lie in wait for the righteous; because he is not for our turn, and he is clean contrary to our doings: he upbraideth us with our offending the law, and objecteth to our infamy the transgressings of our education. 13 He professeth to have the knowledge of God: and he calleth himself the child of the Lord. 14 He was made to reprove our thoughts. 15 He is grievous unto us even to behold: for his life is not like other men's, his ways are of another fashion. 16 We are esteemed of him as counterfeits: he abstaineth from our ways as from filthiness: he pronounceth the end of the just to be blessed, and maketh his boast that God is his father. 17 Letus see if his words be true: and let us prove what shall happen in the end of him. 18 For if the just man be the son of God, he will help him, and deliver him from the hand of his enemies. 19 Let us examine him with despitefulness and torture, that we may know his meekness, and prove his patience. 20 Let us condemn him with a shameful death: for by his own saying he shall be respected. 21 Such things they did imagine, and were deceived: for their own wickedness hath blinded them. 22 As for the mysteries of God, they knew them not: neither hoped they for the wages of righteousness, nor discerned a reward for blameless souls. 23 For God created man to be immortal, and made him to be an image of his own eternity. 24 Nevertheless through envy of the devil came death into the world: and they that do hold of his side do find it.

3

1 But the souls of the righteous are in the hand of God, and there shall no torment touch them. 2 In the sight of the unwise they seemed to die: and their departure is taken for misery, 3 Andtheir going from us to be utter destruction: but they are in peace. 4 For though they be punished in the sight of men, yet is their hope full of immortality. 5 And having been a little chastised, they shall be greatly rewarded: for God proved them, and found them worthy for himself. 6 As gold in the furnace hath he tried them, and received them as a burnt offering. 7 And in the time of their visitation they shall shine, and run to and fro like sparks among the stubble. 8 They shall judge the nations, and have dominion over the people, and their Lord shall reign for ever. 9 They that put their trust in him shall understand the truth: and such as be faithful in love shall abide with him: for grace and mercy is to his saints, and he hath care for his elect. 10 But the ungodly shall be punished according to their own imaginations, which have neglected the righteous, and forsaken the Lord. 11 For whoso despiseth wisdom and nurture, he is miserable, and their hope is vain, their labours unfruitful, and their works unprofitable: 12 Their wives are foolish, and their children wicked: 13 Their offspring is cursed. Wherefore blessed is the barren that is undefiled, which hath not known the sinful bed: she shall have fruit in the visitation of souls. 14 And blessed is the eunuch, which with his hands hath wrought no iniquity, nor imagined wicked things against God: for unto him shall be given the special gift of faith, and an inheritance in the temple of the Lord more acceptable to his mind. 15 For glorious is the fruit of good labours: and the root of wisdom

shall never fall away. 16 As for the children of adulterers, they shall not come to their perfection, and the seed of an unrighteous bed shall be rooted out. 17 For though they live long, yet shall they be nothing regarded: and their last age shall be without honour. 18 Or, if they die quickly, they have no hope, neither comfort in the day of trial. 19 For horrible is the end of the unrighteous generation.

4

1 Better it is to have no children, and to have virtue: for the memorial thereof is immortal: because it is known with God, and with men. 2 When it is present, men take example at it; and when it is gone, they desire it: it weareth a crown, and triumpheth for ever, having gotten the victory, striving for undefiled rewards. 3 But the multiplying brood of the ungodly shall not thrive, nor take deep rooting from bastard slips, nor lay any fast foundation. 4 For though they flourish in branches for a time; yet standing not last, they shall be shaken with the wind, and through the force of winds they shall be rooted out. 5 The imperfect branches shall be broken off, their fruit unprofitable, not ripe to eat, yea, meet for nothing. 6 For children begotten of unlawful beds are witnesses of wickedness against their parents in their trial. 7 But though the righteous be prevented with death, yet shall he be in rest. 8 For honourable age is not that which standeth in length of time, nor that is measured by number of years. 9 But wisdom is the gray hair unto men, and an unspotted life is old age. 10 He pleased God, and was beloved of him: so that living among sinners he was translated. 11 Yea speedily was he taken away, lest that wickedness should alter his understanding, or deceit beguile his soul. 12 For the bewitching of naughtiness doth obscure things that arehonest; and the wandering of concupiscence doth undermine the simple mind. 13 He, being made perfect in a short time, fulfilled a long time: 14 For his soul pleased the Lord: therefore hasted he to take him away from among the wicked. 15 This the people saw, and understood it not, neither laid they up this in their minds, That his grace and mercy is with his saints, and that he hath respect unto his chosen. 16 Thus the righteous that is dead shall condemn the ungodly which are

living; and youth that is soon perfected the many years and old age of the unrighteous. ¹⁷ For they shall see the end of the wise, and shall not understand what God in his counsel hath decreed of him, and to what end the Lord hath set him in safety. ¹⁸ They shall see him, and despise him; but God shall laugh them to scorn: and they shall hereafter be a vile carcase, and a reproach among the dead for evermore. ¹⁹ For he shall rend them, and cast them down headlong, that they shall be speechless; and he shall shake them from the foundation; and they shall be utterly laid waste, and be in sorrow, and their memorial shall perish. ²⁰ And when they cast up the accounts of their sins, they shall come with fear: and their own iniquities shall convince them to their face.

5

¹ Then shall the righteous man stand in great boldness before the face of such as have afflicted him, and made no account of his labours. ² When they see it, they shall be troubled with terrible fear, and shall be amazed at the strangeness of his salvation, so far beyond all that they looked for. ³ And they repenting and groaning for anguish of spirit shall say within themselves, This was he, whom we had sometimes in derision, and a proverb of reproach: ⁴ We fools accounted his life madness, and his end to be without honour: ⁵ How is he numbered among the children of God, and his lot is among the saints! ⁶ Therefore have we erred from the way of truth, and the light of righteousness hath not shined unto us, and the sun of righteousness rose not upon us. ⁷ We wearied ourselves in the way of wickedness and destruction: yea, we have gone through deserts, where there lay no way: but as for the way of the Lord, we have not known it. ⁸ What hath pride profited us? or what good hath riches with our vaunting brought us? ⁹ All those things are passed away like a shadow, and as a post that hasted by; ¹⁰ And as a ship that passeth over the waves of the water, which when it is gone by, the trace thereof cannot be found, neither the pathway of the keel in the waves; ¹¹ Or as when a bird hath flown through the air, there is no token of her way to be found, but the light air being beaten with the stroke of her wings and parted with the violent noise and motion of them, is passed through, and therein afterwards no sign where

she went is to be found; 12 Or like as when an arrow is shot at a mark, it parteth the air, which immediately cometh together again, so that a man cannot know where it went through: 13 Even so we in like manner, as soon as we were born, began to draw to our end, and had no sign of virtue to shew; but were consumed in our own wickedness. 14 For the hope of the ungodly is like dust that is blown away with the wind; like a thin froth that is driven away with the storm; like as the smoke which is dispersed here and there with a tempest, and passeth away as the remembrance of a guest that tarrieth but a day. 15 But the righteous live for evermore; their reward also is with the Lord, and the care of them is with the most High. 16 Therefore shall they receive a glorious kingdom, and a beautiful crown from the Lord's hand: for with his right hand shall he cover them, and with his arm shall he protect them. 17 He shall take to him his jealousy for complete armour, and make the creature his weapon for the revenge of his enemies. 18 He shall put on righteousness as a breastplate, and true judgment instead of an helmet. 19 He shall take holiness for an invincible shield. 20 His severe wrath shall he sharpen for a sword, and the world shall fight with him against the unwise. 21 Then shall the right aiming thunderbolts go abroad; and from the clouds, as from a well drawn bow, shall they fly to the mark. 22 And hailstones full of wrath shall be cast as out of a stone bow, and the water of the sea shall rage against them, and the floods shall cruelly drown them. 23 Yea, a mighty wind shall stand up against them, and like a storm shall blow them away: thus iniquity shall lay waste the whole earth, and ill dealing shall overthrow the thrones of the mighty.

6

1 Hear therefore, O ye kings, and understand; learn, ye that be judges of the ends of the earth. 2 Give ear, ye that rule the people, and glory in the multitude of nations. 3 For power is given you of the Lord, and sovereignty from the Highest, who shall try your works, and search out your counsels. 4 Because, being ministers of his kingdom, ye have not judged aright, nor kept the law, nor walked after the counsel of God; 5Horribly and speedily shall he come upon you: for a sharp judgment shall be to them that be in high places. 6 For

mercy will soon pardon the meanest: but mighty men shall be mightily tormented. 7 For he which is Lord over all shall fear no man's person, neither shall he stand in awe of any man's greatness: for he hath made the small and great, and careth for all alike. 8 But a sore trial shall come upon the mighty. 9 Unto you therefore, O kings, do I speak, that ye may learn wisdom, and not fall away. 10 For they that keep holiness holily shall be judged holy: and they that have learned such things shall find what to answer. 11 Wherefore set your affection upon my words; desire them, and ye shall be instructed. 12 Wisdom is glorious, and never fadeth away: yea, she is easily seen of them that love her, and found of such as seek her. 13 She preventeth them that desire her, in making herself first known unto them. 14 Whoso seeketh her early shall have no great travail: for he shall find her sitting at his doors. 15 To think therefore upon her is perfection of wisdom: and whoso watcheth for her shall quickly be without care. 16 For she goeth about seeking such as are worthy of her, sheweth herself favourably unto them in the ways, and meeteth them in every thought. 17 For the very true beginning of her is the desire of discipline; and the care of discipline is love; 18 And love is the keeping of her laws; and the giving heed unto her laws is the assurance of incorruption; 19 And incorruption maketh us near unto God: 20 Therefore the desire of wisdom bringeth to a kingdom. 21 If your delight be then in thrones and sceptres, O ye kings of the people, honour wisdom, that ye may reign for evermore. 22 As for wisdom, what she is, and how she came up, I will tell you, and will not hide mysteries from you: but will seek her out from the beginning of her nativity, and bring the knowledge of her into light, and will not pass over the truth. 23 Neither will I go with consuming envy; for such a man shall have no fellowship with wisdom. 24 But the multitude of the wise is the welfare of the world: and a wise king is the upholding of the people. 25 Receive therefore instruction through my words, and it shall do you good.

7

1 I myself also am a mortal man, like to all, and the offspring of him that was first made of the earth, 2 And in my mother's womb was fashioned to be flesh

in the time of ten months, being compacted in blood, of the seed of man, and the pleasure that came with sleep. ³ And when I was born, I drew in the common air, and fell upon the earth, which is of like nature, and the first voice which I uttered was crying, as all others do. ⁴ I was nursed in swaddling clothes, and that with cares. ⁵ For there is no king that had any other beginning of birth. ⁶For all men have one entrance into life, and the like going out. ⁷ Wherefore I prayed, and understanding was given me: I called upon God, and the spirit of wisdom came to me. ⁸ I preferred her before sceptres and thrones, and esteemed riches nothing in comparison of her. ⁹ Neither compared I unto her any precious stone, because all gold in respect of her is as a little sand, and silver shall be counted as clay before her. ¹⁰ I loved her above health and beauty, and chose to have her instead of light: for the light that cometh from her never goeth out. ¹¹ All good things together came to me with her, and innumerable riches in her hands. ¹² And I rejoiced in them all, because wisdom goeth before them: and I knew not that she was the mother of them. ¹³ I learned diligently, and do communicate her liberally: I do not hide her riches. ¹⁴ For she is a treasure unto men that never faileth: which they that use become the friends of God, being commended for the gifts that come from learning. ¹⁵ God hath granted me to speak as I would, and to conceive as is meet for the things that are given me: because it is he that leadeth unto wisdom, and directeth the wise. ¹⁶ For in his hand are both we and our words; all wisdom also, and knowledge of workmanship. ¹⁷ For he hath given me certain knowledge of the things that are, namely, to know how the world was made, and the operation of the elements: ¹⁸ The beginning, ending, and midst of the times: the alterations of the turning of the sun, and the change of seasons: ¹⁹ The circuits of years, and the positions of stars: ²⁰ The natures of living creatures, and the furies of wild beasts: the violence of winds, and the reasonings of men: the diversities of plants and the virtues of roots: ²¹ And all such things as are either secret or manifest, them I know. ²² For wisdom, which is the worker of all things, taught me: for in her is an understanding spirit holy, one only, manifold, subtil, lively, clear, undefiled, plain, not subject to hurt, loving the thing that is good quick, which cannot be letted, ready to do good, 23 Kind to man, steadfast, sure, free from care, having all power, overseeing all things, and going through all understanding, pure, and most subtil, spirits. 24 For wisdom is more moving than any motion: she passeth and goeth through all things by reason of her pureness. 25 For she is the breath of the power of God, and a pure influence flowing from the glory of the Almighty: therefore can no defiled thing fall into her. 26 For she is the brightness of the everlasting light, the unspotted mirror of the power of God, and the image of his goodness. 27 And being but one, she can do all things: and remaining in herself, she maketh all things new: and in all ages entering into holy souls, she maketh them friends of God, and prophets. 28 For God loveth none but him that dwelleth with wisdom. 29 For she is more beautiful than the sun, and above all the order of stars: being compared with the light, she is found before it. 30 For after this cometh night: but vice shall not prevail against wisdom.

8

1 Wisdom reacheth from one end to another mightily: and sweetly doth she order all things. 2 I loved her, and sought her out from my youth, I desired to make her my spouse, and I was a lover of her beauty. 3 In that she is conversant with God, she magnifieth her nobility: yea, the Lord of all things himself loved her. 4 For she is privy to the mysteries of the knowledge of God, and a lover of his works. 5 If riches be a possession to be desired in this life; what is richer than wisdom, that worketh all things? 6 And if prudence work; who of all that are is a more cunning workman than she? 7 And if a man love righteousness her labours are virtues: for she teacheth temperance and prudence, justice and fortitude: which are such things, as men can have nothing more profitable in their life. 8 If a man desire much experience, she knoweth things of old, and conjectureth aright what is to come: she knoweth the subtilties of speeches, and can expound dark sentences: she foreseeth signs and wonders, and the events of seasons and times. 9 Therefore I purposed to take her to me to live with me, knowing that she would be a counsellor of

good things, and a comfort in cares and grief. 10 For her sake I shall have estimation among the multitude, and honour with the elders, though I be young. 11 I shall be found of a quick conceit in judgment, and shall be admired in the sight of great men. 12 When I hold my tongue, they shall bide my leisure, and when I speak, they shall give good ear unto me: if I talk much, they shall lay their hands upon their mouth. 13 Moreover by the means of her I shall obtain immortality, and leave behind me an everlasting memorial to them that come after me. 14 I shall set the people in order, and the nations shall be subject unto me. 15 Horrible tyrants shall be afraid, when they do but hear of me; I shall be found good among the multitude, and valiant in war. 16 After I am come into mine house, I will repose myself with her: for her conversation hath no bitterness; and to live with her hath no sorrow, but mirth and joy. 17 Now when I considered these things in myself, and pondered them in my heart, how that to be allied unto wisdom is immortality; 18 And great pleasure it is to have her friendship; and in the works of her hands are infinite riches; and

in the exercise of conference with her, prudence; and in talking with her, a good report; I went about seeking how to take her to me. 19 For I was a witty child, and had a good spirit. 20 Yea rather, being good, I came into a body undefiled. 21 Nevertheless, when I perceived that I could not otherwise obtain her, except God gave her me; and that was a point of wisdom also to know whose gift she was; I prayed unto the Lord, and besought him, and with my whole heart I said,

9

1 O God of my fathers, and Lord of mercy, who hast made all things with thy word, 2 And ordained man through thy wisdom, that he should have dominion over the creatures which thou hast made, 3 And order the world according to equity and righteousness, and execute judgment with an upright heart: 4 Give me wisdom, that sitteth by thy throne; and reject me not from among thy children: 5 For I thy servant and son of thine handmaid am a feeble person, and of a short time, and too young for the understanding of judgment and laws. 6 For though a man be never so perfect among the children of men, yet if

thy wisdom be not with him, he shall be nothing regarded. 7 Thou hast chosen me to be a king of thy people, and a judge of thy sons and daughters: 8 Thou hast commanded me to build a temple upon thy holy mount, and an altar in the city wherein thou dwellest, a resemblance of the holy tabernacle, which thou hast prepared from the beginning. 9 And wisdom was with thee: which knoweth thy works, and was present when thou madest the world, and knew what was acceptable in thy sight, and right in thy commandments. 10 O send her out of thy holy heavens, and from the throne of thy glory, that being present she may labour with me, that I may know what is pleasing unto thee. 11 For she knoweth and understandeth all things, and she shall lead me soberly in my doings, and preserve me in her power. 12 So shall my works be acceptable, and then shall judge thy people righteously, and be worthy to sit in my father's seat. 13 For what man is he that can know the counsel of God? or who can think what the will of the Lord is? 14 For the thoughts of mortal men are miserable, and our devices are but uncertain. 15 For the corruptible body presseth down the soul, and the earthy tabernacle weigheth down the mind that museth upon many things. 16 And hardly do we guess aright at things that are upon earth, and with labour do we find the things that are before us: but the things that are in heaven who hath searched out? 17 And thy counsel who hath known, except thou give wisdom, and send thy Holy Spirit from above? 18 For so the ways of them which lived on the earth were reformed, and men were taught the things that are pleasing unto thee, and were saved through wisdom.

10

1 She preserved the first formed father of the world, that was created alone, and brought him out of his fall, 2 And gave him power to rule all things. 3 But when the unrighteous went away from her in his anger, he perished also in the fury wherewith he murdered his brother. 4For whose cause the earth being drowned with the flood, wisdom again preserved it, and directed the course of the righteous in a piece of wood of small value. 5 Moreover, the nations in their wicked conspiracy being confounded, she found out the righteous, and preserved him

blameless unto God, and kept him strong against his tender compassion toward his son. 6 When the ungodly perished, she delivered the righteous man, who fled from the fire which fell down upon the five cities. 7 Of whose wickedness even to this day the waste land that smoketh is a testimony, and plants bearing fruit that never come to ripeness: and a standing pillar of salt is a monument of an unbelieving soul. 8 For regarding not wisdom, they gat not only this hurt, that they knew not the things which were good; but also left behind them to the world a memorial of their foolishness: so that in the things wherein they offended they could not so much as be hid. 9 But wisdom delivered from pain those that attended upon her. 10 When the righteous fled from his brother's wrath she guided him in right paths, shewed him the kingdom of God, and gave him knowledge of holy things, made him rich in his travels, and multiplied the fruit of his labours. 11 In the covetousness of such as oppressed him she stood by him, and made him rich. 12 She defended him from his enemies, and kept him safe from those that lay in wait, and in a sore conflict she gave him the victory; that he might know that goodness is stronger than all. 13 When the righteous was sold, she forsook him not, but delivered him from sin: she went down with him into the pit, 14 And left him not in bonds, till she brought him the sceptre of the kingdom, and power against those that oppressed him: as for them that had accused him, she shewed them to be liars, and gave him perpetual glory. 15 She delivered the righteous people and blameless seed from the nation that oppressed them. 16 She entered into the soul of the servant of the Lord, and withstood dreadful kings in wonders and signs; 17 Rendered to the righteous a reward of their labours, guided them in a marvellous way, and was unto them for a cover by day, and a light of stars in the night season; 18 Brought them through the Red sea, and led them through much water: 19 But she drowned their enemies, and cast them up out of the bottom of the deep. 20 Therefore the righteous spoiled the ungodly, and praised thy holy name, O Lord, and magnified with one accord thine hand, that fought for them. 21 For wisdom opened the mouth of the dumb, and made the tongues of them that cannot speak eloquent.

11

1 She prospered their works in the hand of the holy prophet. 2 They went through the wilderness that was not inhabited, and pitched tents in places where there lay no way. 3 They stood against their enemies, and were avenged of their adversaries. 4 When they were thirsty, they called upon thee, and water was given them out of the flinty rock, and their thirst was quenched out of the hard stone. 5 For by what things their enemies were punished, by the same they in their need were benefited. 6 For instead of a perpetual running river troubled with foul blood, 7 For a manifest reproof of that commandment, whereby the infants were slain, thou gavest unto them abundance of water by a means which they hoped not for: 8 Declaring by that thirst then how thou hadst punished their adversaries. 9 For when they were tried albeit but in mercy chastised, they knew how the ungodly were judged in wrath and tormented, thirsting in another manner than the just. 10 For these thou didst admonish and try, as a father: but the other, as a severe king, thou didst condemn and punish. 11 Whether they were absent or present, they were vexed alike. 12 For a double grief came upon them, and a groaning for the remembrance of things past. 13 For when they heard by their own punishments the other to be benefited, they had some feeling of the Lord. 14 For whom they respected with scorn, when he was long before thrown out at the casting forth of the infants, him in the end, when they saw what came to pass, they admired. 15 But for the foolish devices of their wickedness, wherewith being deceived they worshipped serpents void of reason, and vile beasts, thou didst send a multitude of unreasonable beasts upon them for vengeance; 16 That they might know, that wherewithal a man sinneth, by the same also shall he be punished. 17 For thy Almighty hand, that made the world of matter without form, wanted not means to send among them a multitude of bears or fierce lions, 18 Or unknown wild beasts, full of rage, newly created, breathing out either a fiery vapour, or filthy scents of scattered smoke, or shooting horrible sparkles out of their eyes: 19 Whereof not only the harm might dispatch them at

once, but also the terrible sight utterly destroy them. 20 Yea, and without these might they have fallen down with one blast, being persecuted of vengeance, and scattered abroad through the breath of thy power: but thou hast ordered all things in measure and number and weight. 21 For thou canst shew thy great strength at all times when thou wilt; and who may withstand the power of thine arm? 22 For the whole world before thee is as a little grain of the balance, yea, as a drop of the morning dew that falleth down upon the earth. 23 But thou hast mercy upon all; for thou canst do all things, and winkest at the sins of men, because they should amend. 24 For thou lovest all the things that are, and abhorrest nothing which thou hast made: for never wouldest thou have made any thing, if thou hadst hated it. 25 And how could any thing have endured, if it had not been thy will? or been preserved, if not called by thee? 26 But thous parest all: for they are thine, O Lord, thou lover of souls.

12

1 For thine incorruptible Spirit is in all things. 2 Therefore chastenest thou them by little and little that offend, and warnest them by putting them in remembrance wherein they have offended, that leaving their wickedness they may believe on thee, O Lord. 3 For it was thy will to destroy by the hands of our fathers both those old inhabitants of thy holy land, 4 Whom thou hatedst for doing most odious works of witchcrafts, and wicked sacrifices; 5 And also those merciless murderers of children, and devourers of man's flesh, and the feasts of blood, 6 With their priests out of the midst of their idolatrous crew, and the parents, that killed with their own hands souls destitute of help: 7 That the land, which thou esteemedst above all other, might receive a worthy colony of God's children. 8 Nevertheless even those thou sparedst as men, and didst send wasps, forerunners of thine host, to destroy them by little and little. 9 Not that thou wast unable to bring the ungodly under the hand of the righteous in battle, or to destroy them at once with cruel beasts, or with one rough word: 10 But executing thy judgments upon them by little and little, thou gavest them place of repentance, not being ignorant that they were a naughty

generation, and that their malice was bred in them, and that their cogitation would never be changed. ¹¹ For it was a cursed seed from the beginning; neither didst thou for fear of any man give them pardon for those things wherein they sinned. ¹² For who shall say, What hast thou done? or who shall withstand thy judgment? or who shall accuse thee for the nations that perish, whom thou made? or who shall come to stand against thee, to be revenged for the unrighteous men? ¹³ For neither is there any God but thou that careth for all, to whom thou mightest shew that thy judgment is not unright. ¹⁴ Neither shall king or tyrant be able to set his face against thee for any whom thou hast punished. ¹⁵ For so much then as thou art righteous thyself, thou orderest all things righteously: thinking it not agreeable with thy power to condemn him that hath not deserved to be punished. ¹⁶ For thy power is the beginning of righteousness, and because thou art the Lord of all, it maketh thee to be gracious unto all. ¹⁷ For when men will not believe that thou art of a full power, thou shewest thy strength, and among them that know it thou makest their boldness manifest. ¹⁸ But thou, mastering thy power, judgest with equity, and orderest us with great favour: for thou mayest use power when thou wilt. ¹⁹ But by such works hast thou taught thy people that the just man should be merciful, and hast made thy children to be of a good hope that thou givest repentance for sins. ²⁰ For if thou didst punish the enemies of thy children, and the condemned to death, with such deliberation, giving them time and place, whereby they might be delivered from their malice: ²¹ With how great circumspection didst thou judge thine own sons, unto whose fathers thou hast sworn, and made covenants of good promises? ²² Therefore, whereas thou dost chasten us, thou scourgest our enemies a thousand times more, to the intent that, when we judge, we should carefully think of thy goodness, and when we ourselves are judged, we should look for mercy. ²³ Wherefore, whereas men have lived dissolutely and unrighteously, thou hast tormented them with their own abominations. ²⁴ For they went astray very far in the ways of error, and held them for gods, which even among the beasts of their enemies were despised, being deceived, as children of no understanding. 25 Therefore unto them, as to children without the use of reason, thou didst send a judgment to mock them. 26 But they that would not be reformed by that correction, wherein he dallied with them, shall feel a judgment worthy of God. 27 For, look, for what things they grudged, when they were punished, that is, for them whom they thought to be gods; now being punished in them, when they saw it, they acknowledged him to be the true God, whom before they denied to know: and therefore came extreme damnation upon them.

13

1 Surely vain are all men by nature, who are ignorant of God, and could not out of the good things that are seen know him that is: neither by considering the works did they acknowledge the workmaster; 2 But deemed either fire, or wind, or the swift air, or the circle of the stars, or the violent water, or the lights of heaven, to be the gods which govern the world. 3 With whose beauty if they being delighted took them to be gods; let them know how much better the Lord of them is: for the first author of beauty hath created them. 4 But if they were astonished at their power and virtue, let them understand by them, how much mightier he is that made them. 5 For by the greatness and beauty of the creatures proportionably the maker of them is seen. 6 But yet for this they are the less to be blamed: for they peradventure err, seeking God, and desirous to find him. 7 For being conversant in his works they search him diligently, and believe their sight: because the things are beautiful that are seen. 8 Howbeit neither are they to be pardoned. 9 For if they were able to know so much, that they could aim at the world; how did they not sooner find out the Lord thereof? 10 But miserable are they, and in dead things is their hope, who call them gods, which are the works of men's hands, gold and silver, to shew art in, and resemblances of beasts, or a stone good for nothing, the work of an ancient hand. 11 Now a carpenter that felleth timber, after he hath sawn down a tree meet for the purpose, and taken off all the bark skilfully round about, and hath wrought it handsomely, and made a vessel thereof fit for the service of man's life; 12 And after spending the refuse of his work

to dress his meat, hath filled himself; 13 And taking the very refuse among those which served to no use, being a crooked piece of wood, and full of knots, hath carved it diligently, when he had nothing else to do, and formed it by the skill of his understanding, and fashioned it to the image of a man; 14 Or made it like some vile beast, laying it over with vermilion, and with paint colouring it red, and covering every spot therein; 15 And when he had made a convenient room for it, set it in a wall, and made it fast with iron: 16 For he provided for it that it might not fall, knowing that it was unable to help itself; for it is an image, and hath need of help: 17 Then maketh he prayer for his goods, for his wife and children, and is not ashamed to speak to that which hath no life. 18 For health he calleth upon that which is weak: for life prayeth to that which is dead; for aid humbly beseecheth that which hath least means to help: and for a good journey he asketh of that which cannot set a foot forward: 19 And for gaining and getting, and for good success of his hands, asketh ability to do of him, that is most unable to do any thing.

14

1 Again, one preparing himself to sail, and about to pass through the raging waves, calleth upon a piece of wood more rotten than the vessel that carrieth him 2 For verily desire of gain devised that, and the workman built it by his skill. 3 But thy providence, O Father, governeth it: for thou hast made a way in the sea, and a safe path in the waves; 4 Shewing that thou canst save from all danger: yea, though a man went to sea without art. 5 Nevertheless thou wouldest not that the works of thy wisdom should be idle, and therefore do men commit their lives to a small piece of wood, and passing the rough sea in a weak vessel are saved. 6 For in the old time also, when the proud giants perished, the hope of the world governed by thy hand escaped in a weak vessel, and left to all ages a seed of generation. 7 For blessed is the wood whereby righteousness cometh. 8 But that which is made with hands is cursed, as well it, as he that made it: he, because he made it; and it, because, being corruptible, it was called god. 9 For the ungodly and his ungodliness are both alike hateful unto God. 10 For that which is made shall be punished together with him that made it. 11

Therefore even upon the idols of the Gentiles shall there be a visitation: because in the creature of God they are become an abomination, and stumbling blocks to the souls of men, and a snare to the feet of the unwise. 12 For the devising of idols was the beginning of spiritual fornication, and the invention of them the corruption of life. 13 For neither were they from the beginning, neither shall they be for ever. 14 For by the vain glory of men they entered into the world, and therefore shall they come shortly to an end. 15 For a father afflicted with untimely mourning, when he hath made an image of his child soon taken away, now honoured him as a god, which was then a dead man, and delivered to those that were under him ceremonies and sacrifices. 16 Thus in process of time an ungodly custom grown strong was kept as a law, and graven images were worshipped by the commandments of kings. 17 Whom men could not honour in presence, because they dwelt far off, they took the counterfeit of his visage from far, and made an express image of a king whom they honored, to the end that by this their forwardness they might flatter him that was absent, as if he were present. 18 Also the singular diligence of the artificer did help to set forward the ignorant to more superstition. 19 For he, peradventure willing to please one in authority, forced all his skill to make the resemblance of the best fashion. 20 And so the multitude, allured by the grace of the work, took him now for a god, which a little before was but honoured. 21 And this was an occasion to deceive the world: for men, serving either calamity or tyranny, did ascribe unto stones and stocks the incommunicable name. 22 Moreover this was not enough for them, that they erred in the knowledge of God; but whereas they lived in the great war of ignorance, those so great plagues called they peace. 23 For whilst they slew their children in sacrifices, or used secret ceremonies, or made revellings of strange rites; 24 They kept neither lives nor marriages any longer undefiled: but either one slew another traiterously, or grieved him by adultery. 25 So that there reigned in all men without exception blood, manslaughter, theft, and dissimulation, corruption, unfaithfulness, tumults, perjury, 26 Disquieting of good men, forgetfulness of good turns, defiling of souls, changing of kind, disorder in marriages, adultery, and shameless uncleanness. 27 For the worshipping of idols not to be named is the beginning, the cause, and the end, of all evil. 28 For either they are mad when they be merry, or prophesy lies, or live unjustly, or else lightly forswear themselves. 29 For insomuch as their trust is in idols, which have no life; though they swear falsely, yet they look not to be hurt. 30 Howbeit for both causes shall they be justly punished: both because they thought not well of God, giving heed unto idols, and also unjustly swore in deceit, despising holiness. 31 For it is not the power of them by whom they swear: but it is the just vengeance of sinners, that punisheth always the offence of the ungodly.

15

1 But thou, O God, art gracious and true, longsuffering, and in mercy ordering all things, 2 For if we sin, we are thine, knowing thy power: but we will not sin, knowing that we are counted thine. 3 For to know thee is perfect righteousness: yea, to know thy power is the root of immortality. 4 For neither did the mischievous invention of men deceive us, nor an image spotted with divers colours, the painter's fruitless labour; 5 The sight whereof enticeth fools to lust after it, and so they desire the form of a dead image, that hath no breath. 6 Both they that make them, they that desire them, and they that worship them, are lovers of evil things, and are worthy to have such things to trust upon. 7 For the potter, tempering soft earth, fashioneth every vessel with much labour for our service: yea, of the same clay he maketh both the vessels that serve for clean uses, and likewise also all such as serve to the contrary: but what is the use of either sort, the potter himself is the judge. 8 And employing his labours lewdly, he maketh a vain god of the same clay, even he which a little before was made of earth himself, and within a little while after returneth to the same, out when his life which was lent him shall be demanded. 9 Notwithstanding his care is, not that he shall have much labour, nor that his life is short: but striveth to excel goldsmiths and silversmiths, and endeavoureth to do like the workers in brass, and counteth it his glory to make counterfeit things. 10 His heart is

ashes, his hope is more vile than earth, and his life of less value than clay: 11 Forasmuch as he knew not his Maker, and him that inspired into him an active soul, and breathed in a living spirit. 12 But they counted our life a pastime, and our time here a market for gain: for, say they, we must be getting every way, though it be by evil means. 13 For this man, that of earthly matter maketh brittle vessels and graven images, knoweth himself to offend above all others. 14 And all the enemies of thy people, that hold them in subjection, are most foolish, and are more miserable than very babes. 15 For they counted all the idols of the heathen to be gods: which neither have the use of eyes to see, nor noses to draw breath, nor ears to hear, nor fingers of hands to handle; and as for their feet, they are slow to go. 16 For man made them, and he that borrowed his own spirit fashioned them: but no man can make a god like unto himself. 17 For being mortal, he worketh a dead thing with wicked hands: for he himself is better than the things which he worshippeth: whereas he lived once, but they never. 18 Yea, they worshipped those beasts also that are most hateful: for being compared together, some are worse than others. 19 Neither are they beautiful, so much as to be desired in respect of beasts: but they went without the praise of God and his blessing.

16

1 Therefore by the like were they punished worthily, and by the multitude of beasts tormented. 2 Instead of which punishment, dealing graciously with thine own people, thou preparedst for them meat of a strange taste, even quails to stir up their appetite: 3 To the end that they, desiring food, might for the ugly sight of the beasts sent among them lothe even that, which they must needs desire; but these, suffering penury for a short space, might be made partakers of a strange taste. 4 For it was requisite, that upon them exercising tyranny should come penury, which they could not avoid: but to these it should only be shewed how their enemies were tormented. 5 For when the horrible fierceness of beasts came upon these, and they perished with the stings of crooked serpents, thy wrath endured not for ever: 6 But they were troubled for a small season, that they might be admonished,

having a sign of salvation, to put them in remembrance of the commandment of thy law. 7 For he that turned himself toward it was not saved by the thing that he saw, but by thee, that art the Saviour of all. 8 And in this thou madest thine enemies confess, that it is thou who deliverest from all evil: 9 For them the bitings of grasshoppers and flies killed, neither was there found any remedy for their life: for they were worthy to be punished by such. 10 But thy sons not the very teeth of venomous dragons overcame: for thy mercy was ever by them, and healed them. 11 For they were pricked, that they should remember thy words; and were quickly saved, that not falling into deep forgetfulness, they might be continually mindful of thy goodness. 12 For it was neither herb, nor mollifying plaister, that restored them to health: but thy word, O Lord, which healeth all things. 13 For thou hast power of life and death: thou leadest to the gates of hell, and bringest up again. 14 A man indeed killeth through his malice: and the spirit, when it is gone forth, returneth not; neither the soul received up cometh again. 15 But it is not possible to escape thine hand. 16 For the ungodly, that denied to know thee, were scourged by the strength of thine arm: with strange rains, hails, and showers, were they persecuted, that they could not avoid, and through fire were they consumed. 17 For, which is most to be wondered at, the fire had more force in the water, that quencheth all things: for the world fighteth for the righteous. 18 For sometime the flame was mitigated, that it might not burn up the beasts that were sent against the ungodly; but themselves might see and perceive that they were persecuted with the judgment of God. 19 And at another time it burneth even in the midst of water above the power of fire, that it might destroy the fruits of an unjust land. 20 Instead whereof thou feddest thine own people with angels' food, and didst send them from heaven bread prepared without their labour, able to content every man's delight, and agreeing to every taste. 21 For thy sustenance declared thy sweetness unto thy children, and serving to the appetite of the eater, tempered itself to every man's liking. 22 But snow and ice endured the fire, and melted not, that they might know that fire burning in the hail, and sparkling in the rain, did destroy the fruits of the enemies. 23 But this again did even forget his own strength, that the righteous might be nourished. 24 For the creature that serveth thee, who art the Maker increaseth his strength against the unrighteous for their punishment, and abateth his strength for the benefit of such as put their trust in thee. 25 Therefore even then was it altered into all fashions, and was obedient to thy grace, that nourisheth all things, according to the desire of them that had need: 26 That thy children, O Lord, whom thou lovest, might know, that it is not the growing of fruits that nourisheth man: but that it is thy word, which preserveth them that put their trust in thee. 27 For that which was not destroyed of the fire, being warmed with a little sunbeam, soon melted away: 28 That it might be known, that we must prevent the sun to give thee thanks, and at the dayspring pray unto thee. 29 For the hope of the unthankful shall melt away as the winter's hoar frost, and shall run away as unprofitable water.

17

1 For great are thy judgments, and cannot be expressed: therefore unnurtured souls have erred. 2 For when unrighteous men thought to oppress the holy nation; they being shut up in their houses, the prisoners of darkness, and fettered with the bonds of a long night, lay there exiled from the eternal providence. 3 For while they supposed to lie hid in their secret sins, they were scattered under a dark veil of forgetfulness, being horribly astonished, and troubled with strange apparitions. 4 For neither might the corner that held them keep them from fear: but noises as of waters falling down sounded about them, and sad visions appeared unto them with heavy countenances. 5 No power of the fire might give them light: neither could the bright flames of the stars endure to lighten that horrible night. 6 Only there appeared unto them a fire kindled of itself, very dreadful: for being much terrified, they thought the things which they saw to be worse than the sight they saw not. 7 As for the illusions of art magick, they were put down, and their vaunting in wisdom was reproved with disgrace. 8 For they, that promised to drive away terrors and troubles from a sick

soul, were sick themselves of fear, worthy to be laughed at. 9 For though no terrible thing did fear them; yet being scared with beasts that passed by, and hissing of serpents, 10 They died for fear, denying that they saw the air, which could of no side be avoided. 11 For wickedness, condemned by her own witness, is very timorous, and being pressed with conscience, always forecasteth grievous things. 12 For fear is nothing else but a betraying of the succours which reason offereth. 13 And the expectation from within, being less, counteth the ignorance more than the cause which bringeth the torment. 14 But they sleeping the same sleep that night, which was indeed intolerable, and which came upon them out of the bottoms of inevitable hell, 15 Were partly vexed with monstrous apparitions, and partly fainted, their heart failing them: for a sudden fear, and not looked for, came upon them. 16 So then whosoever there fell down was straitly kept, shut up in a prison without iron bars, 17 For whether he were husbandman, or shepherd, or a labourer in the field, he was overtaken, and endured that necessity, which could not be avoided: for they were all bound with one chain of darkness. 18 Whether it were a whistling wind, or a melodious noise of birds among the spreading branches, or a pleasing fall of water running violently, 19 Or a terrible sound of stones cast down, or a running that could not be seen of skipping beasts, or a roaring voice of most savage wild beasts, or a rebounding echo from the hollow mountains; these things made them to swoon for fear. 20 For the whole world shined with clear light, and none were hindered in their labour: 21 Over them only was spread an heavy night, an image of that darkness which should afterward receive them: but yet were they unto themselves more grievous than the darkness.

18

1 Nevertheless thy saints had a very great light, whose voice they hearing, and not seeing their shape, because they also had not suffered the same things, they counted them happy. 2 But for that they did not hurt them now, of whom they had been wronged before, they thanked them, and besought them pardon for that they had been enemies. 3 Instead whereof thou gavest them a

burning pillar of fire, both to be a guide of the unknown journey, and an harmless sun to entertain them honourably. 4 For they were worthy to be deprived of light and imprisoned in darkness, who had kept thy sons shut up, by whom the uncorrupt light of the law was to be given unto the world. 5 And when they had determined to slay the babes of the saints, one child being cast forth, and saved, to reprove them, thou tookest away the multitude of their children, and destroyedst them altogether in a mighty water. 6 Of that night were our fathers certified afore, that assuredly knowing unto what oaths they had given credence, they might afterwards be of good cheer. 7 So of thy people was accepted both the salvation of the righteous, and destruction of the enemies. 8 For wherewith thou didst punish our adversaries, by the same thou didst glorify us, whom thou hadst called. 9 For the righteous children of good men did sacrifice secretly, and with one consent made a holy law, that the saints should be like partakers of the same good and evil, the fathers now singing out the songs of praise. 10 But on the other side there sounded an ill according cry of the enemies, and a lamentable noise was carried abroad for children that were bewailed. 11 The master and the servant were punished after one manner; and like as the king, so suffered the common person. 12 So they all together had innumerable dead with one kind of death; neither were the living sufficient to bury them: for in one moment the noblest offspring of them was destroyed. 13 For whereas they would not believe any thing by reason of the enchantments; upon the destruction of the firstborn, they acknowledged this people to be the sons of God. 14 For while all things were in quiet silence, and that night was in the midst of her swift course, 15 Thine Almighty word leaped down from heaven out of thy royal throne, as a fierce man of war into the midst of a land of destruction, 16 And brought thine unfeigned commandment as a sharp sword, and standing up filled all things with death; and it touched the heaven, but it stood upon the earth. 17 Then suddenly visions of horrible dreams troubled them sore, and terrors came upon them unlooked for. 18 And one thrown here, and another there, half dead, shewed the cause of his death. 19 For the dreams that troubled them did foreshew this, lest they should perish, and not know why they were afflicted. 20 Yea, the tasting of death touched the righteous also, and there was a destruction of the multitude in the wilderness: but the wrath endured not long. 21 For then the blameless man made haste, and stood forth to defend them; and bringing the shield of his proper ministry, even prayer, and the propitiation of incense, set himself against the wrath, and so brought the calamity to an end, declaring that he was thy servant. 22 So he overcame the destroyer, not with strength of body, nor force of arms, but with a word subdued him that punished, alleging the oaths and covenants made with the fathers. 23 For when the dead were now fallen down by heaps one upon another, standing between, he stayed the wrath, and parted the way to the living. 24 For in the long garment was the whole world, and in the four rows of the stones was the glory of the fathers graven, and thy Majesty upon the diadem of his head. 25 Unto these the destroyer gave place, and was afraid of them: for it was enough that they only tasted of the wrath.

19

1 As for the ungodly, wrath came upon them without mercy unto the end: for he knew before what they would do; 2 How that having given them leave to depart, and sent them hastily away, they would repent and pursue them. 3 For whilst they were yet mourning and making lamentation at the graves of the dead, they added another foolish device, and pursued them as fugitives, whom they had intreated to be gone. 4 For the destiny, whereof they were worthy, drew them unto this end, and made them forget the things that had already happened, that they might fulfil the punishment which was wanting to their torments: 5 And that thy people might pass a wonderful way: but they might find a strange death. 6 For the whole creature in his proper kind was fashioned again anew, serving the peculiar commandments that were given unto them, that thy children might be kept without hurt: 7 As namely, a cloud shadowing the camp; and where water stood before, dry land appeared; and out of the Red sea a way without impediment; and out of the violent stream a green field: 8 Wherethrough all the people

went that were defended with thy hand, seeing thy marvellous strange wonders. ⁹ For they went at large like horses, and leaped like lambs, praising thee, O Lord, who hadst delivered them. ¹⁰ For they were yet mindful of the things that were done while they sojourned in the strange land, how the ground brought forth flies instead of cattle, and how the river cast up a multitude of frogs instead of fishes. ¹¹ But afterwards they saw a new generation of fowls, when, being led with their appetite, they asked delicate meats. ¹² For quails came up unto them from the sea for their contentment. ¹³ And punishments came upon the sinners not without former signs by the force of thunders: for they suffered justly according to their own wickedness, in so much as they used a more hard and hateful behaviour toward strangers. ¹⁴ For the Sodomites did not receive those, whom they knew not when they came: but these brought friends into bondage, that had well deserved of them. ¹⁵ And not only so, but peradventure some respect shall be had of those, because they used strangers not friendly: ¹⁶ But these very grievously afflicted them, whom they had received with feastings, and were already made partakers of the same laws with them. ¹⁷ Therefore even with blindness were these stricken, as those were at the doors of the righteous man: when, being compassed about with horrible great darkness, every one sought the passage of his own doors. ¹⁸ For the elements were changed in themselves by a kind of harmony, like as in a psaltery notes change the name of the tune, and yet are always sounds; which may well be perceived by the sight of the things that have been done. ¹⁹ For earthly things were turned into watery, and the things, that before swam in the water, now went upon the ground. ²⁰ The fire had power in the water, forgetting his own virtue: and the water forgat his own quenching nature. ²¹ On the other side, the flames wasted not the flesh of the corruptible living things, though they walked the rein; neither melted they the icy kind of heavenly meat that was of nature apt to melt. ²² For in all things, O Lord, thou didst magnify thy people, and glorify them, neither didst thou lightly regard them: but didst assist them in every time and place.

Ecclesiasticus

Ecclesiasticus, also known as the Wisdom of Sirach, is a distinguished text within the Apocrypha of the 1560 Geneva Bible, known for its deep insights into wisdom, ethics, and proper conduct. Authored by Jesus ben Sirach in the early 2nd century BCE, this work represents one of the most comprehensive treatments of Jewish wisdom literature from the Second Temple period. Unlike the canonical Proverbs, which comprises brief aphorisms, Ecclesiasticus offers extended reflections on themes ranging from practical advice on daily living to profound philosophical musings on life, death, and God.

Ecclesiasticus distinguishes itself through its systematic examination of how to live a virtuous life in the fear of the Lord, structured around themes such as humility, diligence, and the proper use of speech. It is divided into numerous discourses and proverbs that touch upon various aspects of daily life, including family relations, business dealings, and social interactions, making it a rich source of ethical instruction and wisdom for its readers.

Theologically, Ecclesiasticus emphasizes the fear of the Lord as the beginning of wisdom—a theme recurrent throughout the biblical wisdom literature. However, it uniquely combines this reverence with a strong endorsement of created wisdom, portraying it as an essential aspect of God's creation and an intrinsic part of human life. The book advocates for a life led in accordance with divine wisdom, which it sees as the path to honor, longevity, and prosperity.

From a literary perspective, Ecclesiasticus is noted for its eloquence and depth, employing a range of poetic forms to articulate its teachings. Its influence on both Jewish and Christian thought is considerable, as it was widely read and highly esteemed in the early Christian church as a source of moral instruction. In the Middle Ages, it continued to be used in theological education and personal devotion, especially within monastic communities.

Ecclesiaticus

1 All wisdom comes from the Lord, and is with him forever. 2 Who can count the sand of the seas, the drops of rain, and the days of eternity? 3 Who will search out the height of the sky, the breadth of the earth, the deep, and wisdom? 4 Wisdom has been created before all things, and the understanding of prudence from everlasting 6 To whom has the root of wisdom been revealed? Who has known her shrewd counsels? 7 The source of wisdom is God's word in the highest heaven, and her ways are the eternal commandments. 8 There is one wise, greatly to be feared, sitting upon his throne: the Lord. 9 He created her. He saw and measured her. He poured her out upon all his works. 10 She is with all flesh according to his gift. He gave her freely to those who love him. 11 The fear of the Lord is glory, exultation, gladness, and a crown of rejoicing. 12 The fear of the Lord will delight the heart, and will give gladness, joy, and length of days. 13 Whoever fears the Lord, it will go well with him at the last. He will be blessed in the day of his death. 14 To fear the Lord is the beginning of wisdom. It was created together with the faithful in the womb. 15 She laid an eternal foundation with men. She will be trusted among their offspring. 16 To fear the Lord is the fullness of wisdom. She inebriates men with her fruits. 17 She will fill all her house with desirable things, and her storehouses with her produce. 18 The fear of the Lord is the crown of wisdom, making peace and perfect health to flourish. 19 He both saw and measured her. He rained down skill and knowledge of understanding, and exalted the honor of those who hold her fast. 20 To fear the Lord is the root of wisdom. Her branches are length of days. 21 The fear of the Lord drives away sins. Where it resides, it will turn away all anger 22 Unjust wrath can never be justified, for his wrath tips the scale to his downfall. 23 A man that is patient will resist for a season, and afterward gladness will spring up to him. 24 He will hide his words until the right moment, and the lips of many will tell of his understanding. 25 A wise saying is in the treasures of wisdom; but godliness is an abomination to a sinner. 26 If you desire wisdom, keep the commandments and the Lord

will give her to you freely; 27 for the fear of the Lord is wisdom and instruction. Faith and humility are his good pleasure. 28 Don't disobey the fear of the Lord. Don't come to him with a double heart. 29 Don't be a hypocrite in men's sight. Keep watch over your lips. 30 Don't exalt yourself, lest you fall and bring dishonor upon your soul. The Lord will reveal your secrets and will cast you down in the midst of the congregation, because you didn't come to the fear of the Lord and your heart was full of deceit.

2

1 My son, if you come to serve the Lord, prepare your soul for temptation. 2 Set your heart aright, constantly endure, and don't make haste in time of calamity. 3 Cling to him, and don't depart, that you may be increased at your latter end. 4 Accept whatever is brought upon you, and be patient when you suffer humiliation. 5 For gold is tried in the fire, and acceptable men in the furnace of humiliation. 6 Put your trust in him, and he will help you. Make your ways straight, and set your hope on him. 7 All you who fear the Lord, wait for his mercy. Don't turn aside, lest you fall. 8 All you who fear the Lord, put your trust in him, and your reward will not fail. 9 All you who fear the Lord, hope for good things, and for eternal gladness and mercy. 10 Look at the generations of old, and see: Who ever put his trust in the Lord, and was ashamed? Or who remained in his fear, and was forsaken? Or who called upon him, and he neglected him? 11 For the Lord is full of compassion and mercy. He forgives sins and saves in time of affliction. 12 Woe to fearful hearts, to faint hands, and to the sinner who goes two ways! 13 Woe to the faint heart! For it doesn't believe. Therefore it won't be defended. 14 Woe to you who have lost your patience! And what will you all do when the Lord visits you? 15 Those who fear the Lord will not disobey his words. Those who love him will keep his ways. 16 Those who fear the Lord will seek his good pleasure. Those who love him will be filled with the law. 17 Those who fear the Lord will prepare their hearts, and will humble their souls in his sight. 18 We will fall into the hands of the Lord, and not into the hands of men; for as his majesty is, so also is his mercy.

3

¹ Hear me, your father, O my children, and do what you hear, that you all may be safe. ² For the Lord honors the father over the children, and has confirmed the judgment of the mother over her sons. ³ He who honors his father will make atonement for sins. ⁴ He who gives glory to his mother is as one who lays up treasure. ⁵ Whoever honors his father will have joy in his own children. He will be heard in the day of his prayer. ⁶ He who gives glory to his father will have length of days. He who listens to the Lord will bring rest to his mother, ⁷ and will serve under his parents, as to masters. ⁸ Honor your father in deed and word, that a blessing may come upon you from him. ⁹ For the blessing of the father establishes the houses of children, but the curse of the mother roots out the foundations. ¹⁰ Don't glorify yourself in the dishonor of your father, for your father's dishonor is no glory to you. ¹¹ For the glory of a man is from the honor of his father, and a mother in dishonor is a reproach to her children. ¹² My son, help your father in his old age, and don't grieve him as long as he lives. ¹³ If he fails in understanding, have patience with him. Don't dishonor him in your full strength. ¹⁴ For the kindness to your father will not be forgotten. Instead of sins it will be added to build you up. ¹⁵ In the day of your affliction it will be remembered for you, as fair weather upon ice, so your sins will also melt away. ¹⁶ He who forsakes his father is as a blasphemer. He who provokes his mother is cursed by the Lord. ¹⁷ My son, go on with your business in humility; so you will be loved by an acceptable man. ¹⁸ The greater you are, humble yourself the more, and you will find favor before the Lord. ¹⁹ d Many are lofty and renowned, but he reveals his secrets to the humble. ²⁰ For the power of the Lord is great, and he is glorified by those who are lowly. ²¹ Don't seek things that are too hard for you, and don't search out things that are above your strength. ²² Think about the things that have been commanded you, for you have no need of the things that are secret. ²³ Don't be overly busy in tasks that are beyond you, for more things are shown to you than men can understand. ²⁴ For the conceit of many has led them astray. Evil opinion has caused their judgment to slip. ²⁵ There is no light without eyes. There is no

wisdom without knowledge. 26 A stubborn heart will do badly at the end. He who loves danger will perish in it. 27 A stubborn heart will be burdened with troubles. The sinner will heap sin upon sins. 28 The calamity of the proud has no healing, for a weed of wickedness has taken root in him. 29 The heart of the prudent will understand a proverb. A wise man desires the ear of a listener. 30 Water will quench a flaming fire; almsgiving will make atonement for sins. 31 He who repays good turns is mindful of that which comes afterward. In the time of his falling he will find a support.

4

1 My son, don't deprive the poor of his living. Don't make the needy eyes wait long. 2 Don't make a hungry soul sorrowful, or provoke a man in his distress. 3 Don't add more trouble to a heart that is provoked. Don't put off giving to him who is in need. 4 Don't reject a suppliant in his affliction. Don't turn your face away from a poor man. 5 Don't turn your eye away from one who asks. Give no occasion to a man to curse you. 6 For if he curses you in the bitterness of his soul, he who made him will hear his supplication. 7 Endear yourself to the assembly. Bow your head to a great man. 8 Incline your ear to a poor man. Answer him with peaceful words in humility. 9 Deliver him who is wronged from the hand of him who wrongs him; Don't be hesitant in giving judgment. 10 Be as a father to the fatherless, and like a husband to their mother. So you will be as a son of the Most High, and he will love you more than your mother does. 11 Wisdom exalts her sons, and takes hold of those who seek her. 12 He who loves her loves life. Those who seek her early will be filled with gladness. 13 He who holds her fast will inherit glory. Where† he enters, the Lord will bless. 14 Those who serve her minister to the Holy One. The Lord loves those who love her. 15 He who listens to her will judge the nations. He who heeds her will dwell securely. 16 If he trusts her, he will inherit her, and his generations will possess her. 17 For at the first she will walk with him in crooked ways, and will bring fear and dread upon him, and torment him with her discipline, until she may trust his soul, and try him by her judgments. 18 Then she will return him again to the straight way, and will gladden him, and

reveal to him her secrets. ¹⁹ If he goes astray, she will forsake him, and hand him over to his fall. ²⁰ Watch for the opportunity, and beware of evil. Don't be ashamed of your soul. ²¹ For there is a shame that brings sin, and there is a shame that is glory and grace. ²² Don't show partiality, discrediting your soul. Don't revere any man to your falling. ²³ Don't refrain from speaking when it is for safety. Don't hide your wisdom for the sake of seeming fair. ²⁴ For wisdom will be known by speech, and instruction by the word of the tongue. ²⁵ Don't speak against the truth and be shamed for your ignorance. ²⁶ Don't be ashamed to confess your sins. Don't fight the river's current. ²⁷ Don't lay yourself down for a fool to tread upon. Don't be partial to one who is mighty. ²⁸ Strive for the truth to death, and the Lord God will fight for you. ²⁹ Don't be hasty with your tongue, or slack and negligent in your deeds. ³⁰ Don't be like a lion in your house, or suspicious of your servants. ³¹ Don't let your hand be stretched out to receive, and closed when you should repay.

5

¹ Don't set your heart upon your goods. Don't say, "They are sufficient for me." ² Don't follow your own mind and your strength to walk in the desires of your heart. ³ Don't say, "Who will have dominion over me?" for the Lord will surely take vengeance on you. ⁴ Don't say, "I sinned, and what happened to me?" for the Lord is patient. ⁵ Don't be so confident of atonement that you add sin upon sins. ⁶ Don't say, "His compassion is great. He will be pacified for the multitude of my sins," for mercy and wrath are with him, and his indignation will rest on sinners. ⁷ Don't wait to turn to the Lord. Don't put off from day to day; for suddenly the wrath of the Lord will come on you, and you will perish in the time of vengeance. ⁸ Don't set your heart upon unrighteous gains, for you will profit nothing in the day of calamity ⁹ Don't winnow with every wind. Don't walk in every path. This is what the sinner who has a double tongue does. ¹⁰ Be steadfast in your understanding. Let your speech be consistent. ¹¹ Be swift to hear and answer with patience. ¹² If you have understanding, answer your neighbor; but if not, put your hand over your mouth. ¹³ Glory and dishonor is in talk. A man's tongue may be his downfall. ¹⁴ Don't be called a

whisperer. Don't lie in wait with your tongue; for shame is on the thief, and an evil condemnation is on him who has a double tongue. 15 Don't be ignorant in a great or small matter.

6

1 Don't become an enemy instead of a friend; for an evil name will inherit shame and reproach. So it is with the sinner who has a double tongue. 2 Don't exalt yourself in the counsel of your soul, that your soul not be torn in pieces like a bull. 3 You will eat up your leaves, destroy your fruit, and leave yourself like a dry tree. 4 A wicked soul will destroy him who has it, and will make him a laughing stock to his enemies. 5 Sweet words will multiply a man's friends. A gracious tongue will multiply courtesies. 6 Let those that are at peace with you be many, but your advisers one of a thousand. 7 If you want to gain a friend, get him in a time of testing, and don't be in a hurry to trust him. 8 For there is a friend just for an occasion. He won't continue in the day of your affliction. 9 And there is a friend who turns into an enemy. He will discover strife to your reproach. 10 And there is a friend who is a companion at the table, but he won't continue in the day of your affliction. 11 In your prosperity he will be as yourself, and will be bold over your servants. 12 If you are brought low, he will be against you, and will hide himself from your face. 13 Separate yourself from your enemies, and beware of your friends. 14 A faithful friend is a strong defense. He who has found him has found a treasure. 15 There is nothing that can be taken in exchange for a faithful friend. His excellency is beyond price. 16 A faithful friend is a life-saving medicine. Those who fear the Lord will find him. 17 He who fears the Lord directs his friendship properly; for as he is, so is his neighbor also. 18 My son, gather instruction from your youth up. Even when you have gray hair you will find wisdom. 19 Come to her as one who plows and sows and wait for her good fruit; for your toil will be little in her cultivation, and you will soon eat of her fruit. 20 How exceedingly harsh she is to the unlearned! He who is without understanding will not remain in her. 21 She will rest upon him as a mighty stone of trial. He won't hesitate to cast her from him. 22 For wisdom is according to her name. She isn't manifest to many. 23 Give ear, my son, and accept

my judgment. Don't refuse my counsel. 24 Bring your feet into her fetters, and your neck into her chain. 25 Put your shoulder under her and bear her. Don't be grieved with her bonds. 26 Come to her with all your soul. Keep her ways with your whole power. 27 Search and seek, and she will be made known to you. When you get hold of her, don't let her go. 28 For at the last you will find her rest; and she will be turned for you into gladness 29 Her fetters will be to you for a covering of strength, and her chains for a robe of glory. 30 For there is a golden ornament upon her, and her bands are a purple cord. 31 You shall put her on as a robe of glory, and shall put her on as a crown of rejoicing. 32 My son, if you are willing, you will be instructed. If you will yield your soul, you will be prudent. 33 If you love to hear, you will receive. If you incline your ear, you will be wise. 34 Stand in the multitude of the elders. Attach yourself to whomever is wise. 35 Be willing to listen to every godly discourse. Don't let the proverbs of understanding escape you. 36 If you see a man of understanding, get to him early. Let your foot wear out the steps of his doors. 37 Let your mind dwell on the ordinances of the Lord and meditate continually on his commandments. He will establish your heart and your desire for wisdom will be given to you.

7

1 Do no evil, so no evil will overtake you. 2 Depart from wrong, and it will turn away from you. 3 My son, don't sow upon the furrows of unrighteousness, and you won't reap them sevenfold. 4 Don't seek preeminence from the Lord, nor the seat of honor from the king. 5 Don't justify yourself in the presence of the Lord, and don't display your wisdom before the king. 6 Don't seek to be a judge, lest you not be able to take away iniquities, lest perhaps you fear the person of a mighty man, and lay a stumbling block in the way of your uprightness. 7 Don't sin against the multitude of the city. Don't disgrace yourself in the crowd. 8 Don't commit a sin twice, for even in one you will not be unpunished. 9 Don't say, "He will look upon the multitude of my gifts. When I make an offering to the Most High God, he will accept it." 10 Don't be faint-hearted in your prayer. Don't neglect to give alms. 11

Don't laugh a man to scorn when he is in the bitterness of his soul, for there is one who humbles and exalts. 12 Don't devise a lie against your brother, or do the same to a friend. 13 Refuse to utter a lie, for that habit results in no good. 14 Don't babble in the assembly of elders. Don't repeat your words in your prayer. 15 Don't hate hard labor or farm work, which the Most High has created. 16 Don't number yourself among the multitude of sinners. Remember that wrath will not wait. 17 Humble your soul greatly, for the punishment of the ungodly man is fire and the worm. 18 Don't exchange a friend for something, neither a true brother for the gold of Ophir. 19 Don't deprive yourself of a wise and good wife, for her grace is worth more than gold. 20 Don't abuse a servant who works faithfully, or a hireling who gives you his life. 21 Let your soul love a wise servant. Don't defraud him of liberty. 22 Do you have cattle? Look after them. If they are profitable to you, let them stay by you. 23 Do you have children? Correct them, and make them obedient from their youth. 24 Do you have daughters? Take care of their bodies, and don't be overly indulgent toward them. 25 Give your daughter in marriage, and you will have accomplished a great matter. Give her to a man of understanding. 26 Do you have a wife who pleases you? Don't cast her out. But don't trust yourself to one who is hateful. 27 Honor your father with your whole heart, and don't forget the birth pangs of your mother. 28 Remember that you were born of them. What will you repay them for the things that they have done for you? 29 Fear the Lord with all your soul; and revere his priests. 30 With all your strength love him who made you. Don't forsake his ministers. 31 Fear the Lord and honor the priest. Give him his portion, evenas itis commanded you: the first fruits, the trespass offering, the gift of the shoulders, the sacrifice of sanctification, and the first fruits of holy things. 32 Also stretch out your hand to the poor man, that your blessing may be complete. 33 A gift has grace in the sight of every living man. Don't withhold grace for a dead man. 34 Don't avoid those who weep, and mourn with those who mourn. 35 Don't be slow to visit a sick man, for by such things you will gain love. 36 In all your words, remember eternity, and you will never sin.

8

1 Don't contend with a mighty man, lest perhaps you fall into his hands. 2 Don't strive with a rich man, lest perhaps he overpower you; for gold has destroyed many, and turned away the hearts of kings. 3 Don't argue with a loudmouthed man. Don't heap wood upon his fire. 4 Don't make fun of a rude man, lest your ancestors be dishonored. 5 Don't reproach a man when he turns from sin. Remember that we are all worthy of punishment. 6 Don't dishonor a man in his old age, for some of us are also growing old. 7 Don't rejoice over anyone's death. Remember that we all die. 8 Don't neglect the discourse of the wise. Be conversant with their proverbs; for from them you will learn discipline and how to serve great men. 9 Don't miss the discourse of the aged, for they also learned from their parents, because from them you will learn understanding, and to give an answer in time of need. 10 Don't kindle the coals of a sinner, lest you be burned with the flame of his fire. 11 Don't rise up from the presence of an insolent man, lest he lie in wait as an ambush for your mouth. 12 Don't lend to a man who is stronger than you; and if you lend, count it as a loss.

13 Don't be surety beyond your means. If you give surety, think as one who will have to pay. 14 Don't go to law with a judge; for according to his honor they will give judgment for him. 15 Don't travel with a reckless man, lest he be burdensome to you; for he will do as he pleases, and you will perish with his folly. 16 Don't fight with a wrathful man. Don't travel with him through the desert, for blood is as nothing in his sight. Where there is no help, he will overthrow you. 17 Don't consult with a fool, for he will not be able to keep a secret. 18 Do no secret thing before a stranger, for you don't know what it will cause. 19 Don't open your heart to every man. Don't let him return you a favor.

9

1 Don't be jealous over the wife of your bosom, and don't teach her an evil lesson against yourself. 2 Don't give your soul to a woman and let her trample down your strength. 3 Don't go to meet a woman who plays the prostitute, lest perhaps you fall into her snares. 4 Don't associate with a woman who is a singer, lest perhaps you be caught by her tricks. 5 Don't gaze at a virgin, lest perhaps you stumble and incur penalties for her. 6 Don't give

your soul to prostitutes, that you not lose your inheritance. [7] Don't look around in the streets of the city. Don't wander in its deserted places. [8] Turn your eye away from a beautiful woman, and don't gaze at another's beauty. Many have been led astray by the beauty of a woman; and with this, passion is kindled like a fire. [9] Don't dine at all with a woman who has a husband, or revel with her at wine, lest perhaps your soul turn away to her, and with your spirit you slide into destruction. [10] Don't forsake an old friend; for a new one is not comparable to him. A new friend is like new wine: if it becomes old, you will drink it with gladness. [11] Don't envy the success of a sinner; for you don't know what his end will be. [12] Don't delight in the delights of the ungodly. Remember they will not go unpunished to the grave. [13] Keep yourself far from the man who has power to kill, and you will not be troubled by the fear of death. If you come to him, commit no fault, lest he take away your life. Know surely that you go about in the midst of snares, and walk upon the battlements of a city. [14] As well as you can, aim to know your neighbors, and take counsel with the wise. [15] Let your conversation be with men of understanding. Let all your discourse be in the law of the Most High. [16] Let righteous people be companions at your table. Let your glorying be in the fear of the Lord. [17] A work is commended because of the skill of the artisan; so he who rules the people will be considered wise for his speech. [18] A loudmouthed man is dangerous in his city. He who is reckless in his speech will be hated.

10

[1] A wise judge will instruct his people. The government of a man of understanding will be well ordered. [2] As is the judge of his people, so are his officials. As the city's ruler is, so are all those who dwell in it. [3] An undisciplined king will destroy his people. A city will be established through the understanding of the powerful. [4] The government of the earth is in the Lord's hand. In due time, he will raise up over it the right person at the right time. [5] A man's prosperity is in the Lord's hand. He will lay his honor upon the person of the scribe. [6] Don't be angry with your neighbor for every wrong. Do nothing by works of violence. [7] Pride is hateful before the Lord and men. Arrogance is abhorrent

in the judgment of both. 8 Sovereignty is transferred from nation to nation because of injustice, violence, and greed for money 9 Why are dirt and ashes proud? Because in life, my body decays. 10 A long disease mocks the physician. The king of today will die tomorrow. 11 For when a man is dead, he will inherit maggots, vermin, and worms. 12 It is the beginning of pride when a man departs from the Lord. His heart has departed from him who made him. 13 For the beginning of pride is sin. He who keeps it will pour out abomination. For this cause the Lord brought upon them strange calamities and utterly overthrew them. 14 The Lord cast down the thrones of rulers and set the lowly in their place. 15 The Lord plucked up the roots of nations and planted the lowly in their place. 16 The Lord overthrew the lands of nations and destroyed them to the foundations of the earth. 17He took some of them away and destroyed them, and made their memory to cease from the earth. 18 Pride has not been created for men, nor wrathful anger for the offspring of women. 19 Whose offspring has honor? Human offspring who fear the Lord. Whose offspring has no honor? Human offspring who break the commandments. 20 In the midst of kindred he who rules them has honor. Those who fear the Lord have honor in his eyes. 21 Fear of the Lord is the beginning of acceptance, but obstinance and pride are the beginning of rejection 22 The rich man, the honorable, and the poor all glory in the fear of the Lord. 23 It is not right to dishonor a poor man who has understanding. Itis not fitting to glorify a man who is a sinner. 24 The prince, the judge, and the mighty man will be honored. There is not one of them greater than he who fears the Lord. 25 Free men will minister to a wise servant. A man who has knowledge will not complain. 26 Don't flaunt your wisdom in doing your work. Don't boast in the time of your distress. 27 Better is he who labors and abounds in all things, than he who boasts and lacks bread. 28 My son, glorify your soul in humility, and ascribe to yourself honor according to your worthiness. 29 Who will justify him who sins against his own soul? Who will honor him who dishonors his own life? 30 A poor man is honored for his knowledge. A rich man is honored for his riches. 31 But he who is honored in poverty, how much more in riches? He who is dishonored in riches, how much more in poverty?

11

1 The wisdom of the lowly will lift up his head, and make him sit in the midst of great men. 2 Don't commend a man for his good looks. Don't abhor a man for his outward appearance. 3 The bee is little among flying creatures, but what it produces is the best of confections. 4 Don't boast about the clothes you wear, and don't exalt yourself in the day of honor; for the Lord's works are wonderful, and his works are hidden among men. 5 Many kings have sat down upon the ground, but one who was never thought of has worn a crown. 6 Many mighty men have been greatly disgraced. Men of renown have been delivered into other men's hands. 7 Don't blame before you investigate. Understand first, and then rebuke. 8 Don't answer before you have heard. Don't interrupt while someone else is speaking. 9 Don't argue about a matter that doesn't concern you. Don't sit with sinners when they judge. 10 My son, don't be busy about many matters; for if you meddle much, you will not be unpunished. If you pursue, you will not overtake, and you will not escape by fleeing. 11 There is one who toils, labors, and hurries, and is even more behind. 12 There is one who is sluggish, and needs help, lacking in strength, and who abounds in poverty, but the Lord's eyes looked upon him for good, and he raised him up from his low condition, 13 and lifted up his head so that many marveled at him. 14 Good things and bad, life and death, poverty and riches, are from the Lord. 15 Wisdom and knowledge, and understanding of the Law are of the Lord: love and good works come of him 16 Errour and darkness are appointed for finners, and they that exalt themselves in evil, waxe olde in evil 17 The Lord's gift remains with the godly. His good pleasure will prosper forever. 18 One grows rich by his diligence and self-denial, and this is the portion of his reward: 19 when he says, "I have found rest, and now I will eat of my goods!" he doesn't know how much time will pass until he leaves them to others and dies. 20 Be steadfast in your covenant and be doing it, and grow old in your work. 21 Don't marvel at the works of a sinner, but trust the Lord and stay in your labor; for it is an easy thing in the sight of the Lord to

swiftly and suddenly make a poor man rich. 22 The Lord's blessing is in the reward of the godly. He makes his blessing flourish in an hour that comes swiftly. 23 Don't say, "What use is there of me? What further good things can be mine?" 24 Don't say, "I have enough. What harm could happen to me now?" 25 In the day of good things, bad things are forgotten. In the day of bad things, a man will not remember things that are good. 26 For it is an easy thing in the sight of the Lord to reward a man in the day of death according to his ways. 27 The affliction of an hour causes delights to be forgotten. In the end, a man's deeds are revealed. 28 Call no man happy before his death. A man will be known in his children. 29 Don't bring every man into your house, for many are the tricks of a deceitful man. 30 Like a decoy partridge in a cage, so is the heart of a proud man. Like a spy, he looks for your weakness. 31 For he lies in wait to turn things that are good into evil, and assigns blame in things that are praiseworthy 32 From a spark of fire, a heap of many coals is kindled, and a sinful man lies in wait to shed blood. 33 Take heed of an evil-doer, for he plans wicked things, lest perhaps he ruin your reputation forever. 34 Receive a stranger into your house, and he will distract you with arguments and estrange you from your own family.

12

1 If you do good, know to whom you do it, and your good deeds will have thanks. 2 Do good to a godly man, and you will find a reward— if not from him, then from the Most High. 3 No good will come to him who continues to do evil, nor to him who gives no alms. 4 Give to the godly man, and don't help the sinner. 5 Do good to one who is lowly. Don't give to an ungodly man. Keep back his bread, and don't give it to him, lest he subdue you with it; for you would receive twice as much evil for all the good you would have done to him. 6 For the Most High also hates sinners, and will repay vengeance to the ungodly. 7 Give to the good man, and don't help the sinner. 8 A man's friend won't be‡ fully tried in prosperity. His enemy won't be hidden in adversity. 9 In a man's prosperity, his enemies are grieved. In his adversity, even his friend leaves. 10 Never trust your enemy, for his wickedness is like corrosion in copper. 11 Though he humbles himself and walks bowed down, still be careful and

beware of him. You will be to him as one who has wiped a mirror, to be sure it doesn't completely tarnish. 12 Don't set him next to you, lest he overthrow you and stand in your place. Don't let him sit on your right hand, lest he seek to take your seat, and at the last you acknowledge my words, and be pricked with my sayings. 13 Who will pity a charmer that is bitten by a snake, or any who come near wild beasts? 14 Even so, who will pity him who goes to a sinner, and is associated with him in his sins? 15 For a while he will stay with you, and if you falter, he will not stay. 16 The enemy will speak sweetly with his lips, and in his heart plan to throw you into a pit. The enemy may weep with his eyes, but if he finds opportunity, he will want more blood. 17 If adversity meets you, you will find him there before you. Pretending to help you, he will trip you. 18 He will shake his head, clap his hands, whisper much, and change his countenance.

13

1 He who touches pitch will be defiled. He who has fellowship with a proud man will become like him. 2 Don't take up a burden above your strength. Have no fellowship with one who is mightier and richer than yourself. What fellowship would the earthen pot have with the kettle? The kettle will strike, and the pot will be dashed in pieces. 3 The rich man does a wrong and threatens. The poor is wronged and apologizes. 4 If you are profitable, he will exploit you. If you are in need, he will forsake you. 5 If you own something, he will live with you. He will drain your resources and will not be sorry. 6 Does he need you? Then he will deceive you, smile at you, and give you hope. He will speak kindly to you and say, "What do you need?" 7 He will shame you by his delicacies until he has made you bare twice or thrice, and in the end he will laugh you to scorn. Afterward he will see you, will forsake you, and shake his head at you. 8 Beware that you are not deceived and brought low in your enjoyment. 9 If a mighty man invites you, be reserved, and he will invite you more. 10 Don't press him, lest you be thrust back. Don't stand far off, lest you be forgotten. 11 Don't try to speak with him as an equal, and don't believe his many words; for he will test you with much talk, and will examine you in a smiling manner. 12 He who doesn't keep secrets to himself is unmerciful.

He won't hesitate to harm and to bind. 13 Keep them to yourself and be careful, for you walk in danger of falling. 14 Beware, and take good hede: for thou walk in peril of thine overthrowing: when thou hear this, awake in thy sleep 15 Every living creature loves its own kind, and every man loves his neighbor. 16 All flesh associates with their own kind. A man will stick to people like himself. 17 What fellowship would the wolf have with the lamb? So is the sinner to the godly. 18 What peace is there between a hyena and a dog? What peace is there between a rich man and the poor? 19 Wild donkeys are the prey of lions in the wilderness; likewise poor men are feeding grounds for the rich. 20 Lowliness is an abomination to a proud man; likewise a poor man is an abomination to the rich. 21 When a rich man is shaken, he is supported by his friends, but when the humble is down, he is pushed away even by his friends. 22 When a rich man falls, there are many helpers. He speaks things not to be spoken, and men justify him. A humble man falls, and men rebuke him. He utters wisdom, and is not listened to. 23 A rich man speaks, and all keep silence. They extol what he says to the clouds. A poor man speaks, and they say, "Who is this?" If he stumbles, they will help to overthrow him. 24 Riches are good if they have no sin. Poverty is evil only in the opinion of the ungodly. 25 The heart of a man changes his countenance, whether it is for good or for evil. 26 A cheerful countenance is a sign of a prosperous heart. Devising proverbs takes strenuous thinking.

14

1 Blessed is the man who has not slipped with his mouth, and doesn't suffer from sorrow for sins. 2 Blessed is he whose soul does not condemn him, and who has not given up hope. 3 Riches are not appropriate for a stingy person. What would a miser do with money? 4 He who gathers by denying himself gathers for others. Others will revel in his goods. 5 If one is mean to himself, to whom will he be good? He won't enjoy his possessions. 6 There is none more evil than he who is grudging to himself. This is a punishment for his wickedness. 7 Even if he does good, he does it in forgetfulness. In the end, he reveals his wickedness. 8 A miser is evil. He turns away and disregards souls. 9 A covetous

man's eye is not satisfied with his portion. Wicked injustice dries up his soul. 10 A miser begrudges bread, and it is lacking at his table. 11 My son, according to what you have, treat yourself well, and bring worthy offerings to the Lord. 12 Remember that death will not wait, and that the covenant of Hades hasn't been shown to you. 13 Do good to your friends before you die. According to your ability, reach out and give to them. 14 Don't deprive yourself of a good day. Don't let your share of a desired good pass you by. 15 Won't you leave your labors to another, and your toils be divided by lot? 16 Give, take, and treat yourself well, because there is no seeking of luxury in Hades. 17 All flesh grows old like a garment, for the covenant from the beginning is, "You must die!" 18 Like the leaves flourishing on a thick tree, some it sheds, and some grow, so also are the generations of flesh and blood: one comes to an end and another is born. 19 Every work rots and falls away, and its builder will depart with it. 20 Blessed is the man who meditates on wisdom, and who reasons by his understanding. 21 He who considers her ways in his heart will also have knowledge of her secrets. 22 Go after her like a hunter, and lie in wait in her paths. 23 He who peers in at her windows will also listen at her doors. 24 He who lodges close to her house will also fasten a nail in her walls. 25 He will pitch his tent near at hand to her, and will lodge in a lodging where good things are. 26 He will set his children under her shelter, and will rest under her branches. 27 By her he will be covered from heat, and will lodge in her glory

15

1 He who fears the Lord will do this. He who has possession of the law will obtain her. 2 She will meet him like a mother, and receive him like a wife married in her virginity. 3 She will feed him with bread of understanding and give him water of wisdom to drink. 4 He will be stayed upon her, and will not be moved. He will rely upon her, and will not be confounded. 5 She will exalt him above his neighbors. She will open his mouth in the midst of the congregation. 6 He will inherit joy, a crown of gladness, and an everlasting name. 7 Foolish men will not obtain her. Sinners will not see her. 8 She is far from pride. Liars will not remember her. 9 Praise is not attractive in the mouth of a sinner; for it was

not sent to him from the Lord. 10 For praise will be spoken in wisdom; The Lord will prosper it. 11 Don't say, "It is through the Lord that I fell away;" for you shall not do the things that he hates. 12 Don't say, "It is he that caused me to err;" for he has no need of a sinful man. 13 The Lord hates every abomination; and those who fear him don't love them. 14 He himself made man from the beginning and left him in the hand of his own counsel. 15 If you choose, you can keep the commandments. To be faithful is a matter of your choice. 16 He has set fire and water before you. You will stretch forth your hand to whichever you desire. 17 Before man is life and death. Whichever he likes, it will be given to him. 18 For the wisdom of the Lord is great. He is mighty in power, and sees all things. 19 His eyes are upon those who fear him. He knows every act of man. 20 He has not commanded any man to be ungodly. He has not given any man license to sin.

16

1 Don't desire a multitude of unprofitable children, neither delight in ungodly sons. 2 If they multiply, don't delight in them unless the fear of the Lord is in them. 3 Don't trust in their life. Don't rely on their numbers; for one can be better than a thousand, and to die childless than to have ungodly children. 4 For from one who has understanding, a city will be populated, but a race of wicked men will be made desolate. 5 I have seen many such things with my eyes. My ear has heard mightier things than these. 6 In a congregation of sinners, a fire will be kindled. In a disobedient nation, wrath is kindled. 7 He was not pacified toward the giants of old time, who revolted in their strength. 8 He didn't spare Lot's neighbors, whom he abhorred for their pride. 9 He didn't pity the people of perdition who were taken away in their sins, 10 or in like manner, the six hundred thousand footmen who were gathered together in the hardness of their hearts. 11 Even if there is one stiff-necked person, it is a marvel if he will be unpunished; for mercy and wrath are both with him who is mighty to forgive, and he pours out wrath. 12 As his mercy is great, so is his correction also. He judges a man according to his works. 13 The sinner will not escape with plunder. The perseverance of the godly will not be frustrated. 14 He will make room for every work of

mercy. Each man will receive according to his works. 15 The Lord hardened Pharao, that he should not know him, and that his works should be known upon the earth under the heaven 16 His mercy is known to all creatures: he had separate the light from the darkness 17 Don't say, "I will be hidden from the Lord," and "Who will remember me from on high?" I will not be known among so many people, for what is my soul in a boundless creation? 18 Behold, the heaven, the heaven of heavens, the deep, and the earth, will be moved when he visits. 19 The mountains and the foundations of the earth together are shaken with trembling when he looks at them. 20 No heart will think about these things. Who could comprehend his ways? 21 Like a tempest which no man can see, so, the majority of his works are hidden. 22 Who will declare his works of righteousness? Who will wait for them? For his covenant is afar off. 23 He who is lacking in understanding thinks about these things. An unwise and erring man thinks foolishly. 24 My son, listen to me, learn knowledge, and heed my words with your heart. 25 I will impart instruction with precision, and declare knowledge exactly. 26 In the judgment of the Lord are his works from the beginning. From the making of them he determined their boundaries. 27 He arranged his works for all time, and their beginnings to their generations. They aren't hungry or weary, and they don't cease from their works. 28 No one pushes aside his neighbor. They will never disobey his word. 29 After this also the Lord looked at the earth and filled it with his blessings. 30 All manner of living things covered its surface, and they return into it.

17

1 The Lord created mankind out of earth, and turned them back to it again. 2 He gave them days by number, and a set time, and gave them authority over the things that are on it. 3 He endowed them with strength proper to them, and made them according to his own image. 4 He put the fear of man upon all flesh, and gave him dominion over beasts and birds. 5 He created out of him an helper like unto himself, and gave them discretion and tongue, and eyes, ears, and an heart to understand, and he gave them a spirit, and he gave them speache to declare his works 6 He gave them counsel, tongue, eyes, ears, and heart to

have understanding. ⁷ He filled them with the knowledge of wisdom, and showed them good and evil. ⁸ He set his eye upon their hearts, to show them the majesty of his works. ⁹ Beside this, he gave them knowledge, and gave them the Law of life for an heritage, that they might now know that they were mortal. ¹⁰ And they will praise his holy name, that they may declare the majesty of his works. ¹¹ He added to them knowledge, and gave them a law of life for a heritage. ¹² He made an everlasting covenant with them, and showed them his decrees. ¹³ Their eyes saw the majesty of his glory. Their ears heard the glory of his voice. ¹⁴ He said to them, "Beware of all unrighteousness." So he gave them commandment, each man concerning his neighbor. ¹⁵ Their ways are ever before him. They will not be hidden from his eyes. ¹⁶ ¹⁷ For every nation he appointed a ruler, but Israel is the Lord's portion. ¹⁸ ¹⁹ All their works are as clear as the sun before him. His eyes are continually upon their ways. ²⁰ Their iniquities are not hidden from him. All their sins are before the Lord. ²¹ ²² With him the alms of a man is as a signet. He will keep a man's kindness as the pupil of the eye. ²³ Afterwards he will rise up and repay them, and render their repayment upon their head. ²⁴ However to those who repent he grants a return. He comforts those who are losing hope. ²⁵ Return to the Lord, and forsake sins. Make your prayer before his face offend less. ²⁶ Turn again to the Most High, and turn away from iniquity. Greatly hate the abominable thing. ²⁷ Who will give praise to the Most High in Hades, in place of the living who return thanks? ²⁸ Thanksgiving perishes from the dead, as from one who doesn't exist. He who is in life and health will praise the Lord. ²⁹ How great is the mercy of the Lord, and his forgiveness to those who turn to him! ³⁰ For humans are not capable of everything, because the son of man is not immortal. ³¹ What is brighter than the sun? Yet even this can be eclipsed. So flesh and blood devise evil. ³² He looks upon the power of the height of heaven, while all men are earth and ashes.

18

¹ He who lives forever created the whole universe. ² The Lord alone is just. ³ ⁴ He has given power to declare his works to no one. Who could trace out his mighty deeds? ⁵ Who could

measure the strength of his majesty? Who could also proclaim his mercies? ⁶ As for the wondrous works of the Lord, it is not possible to take from them nor add to them, neither is it possible to explore them. ⁷ When a man has finished, then he is just at the beginning. When he stops, then he will be perplexed. ⁸ What is mankind, and what purpose do they serve? What is their good, and what is their evil? ⁹ The number of man's days at the most are a hundred years. ¹⁰ As a drop of water from the sea, and a pebble from the sand, so are a few years in the day of eternity. ¹¹ For this cause the Lord was patient over them, and poured out his mercy upon them. ¹² He saw and perceived their end, that it is evil. Therefore he multiplied his forgiveness. ¹³ The mercy of a man is on his neighbor; but the mercy of the Lord is on all flesh: reproving, chastening, teaching, and bringing back, as a shepherd does his flock. ¹⁴ He has mercy on those who accept chastening, and that diligently seek after his judgments. ¹⁵ My son, don't add reproach to your good deeds, and no harsh words in any of your giving. ¹⁶ Doesn't the dew relieve the scorching heat? So a word is better than a gift. ¹⁷ Behold, isn't a word better than a gift? Both are with a gracious person. ¹⁸ A fool is ungracious and abusive. The gift of a grudging person consumes the eyes. ¹⁹ Learn before you speak. Take care of your health before you get sick. ²⁰ Before judgment, examine yourself, and in the hour of scrutiny you will find forgiveness. ²¹ Humble yourself before you get sick. In the time of sins, repent. ²² Let nothing hinder you to pay your vow in due time. Don't wait until death to be released. ²³ Before you make a vow, prepare yourself. Don't be like a man who tests the Lord. ²⁴ Think about the wrath coming in the days of the end, and the time of vengeance, when he turns away his face. ²⁵ In the days of fullness remember the time of hunger. Remember poverty and lack in the days of wealth. ²⁶ From morning until evening, the time changes. All things are speedy before the Lord. ²⁷ A wise man is cautious in everything. In days of sinning, he will beware of offense. ²⁸ Every man of understanding knows wisdom. He will give thanks to him who found her. ²⁹ They who were of understanding in sayings also became wise themselves, and poured out apt proverbs. ³⁰ Don't go after your lusts. Restrain your appetites. 31 If you give fully to your soul the delight of her desire, she will make you the laughing stock of your enemies. 32 Don't make merry in much luxury, and don't be tied to its expense. 33 Don't be made a beggar by banqueting with borrowed money when you have nothing in your purse.

19

1 A worker who is a drunkard will not become rich. He who despises small things will fall little by little. 2 Wine and women will make men of understanding go astray. He who joins with prostitutes is reckless. 3 Decay and worms will have him as their heritage. A reckless soul will be taken away. 4 He who is hasty to trust is shallow-hearted. He who sins offends against his own soul. 5 He who rejoices in wickedness will be condemned. 6 He who hates gossip has less wickedness. 7 Never repeat what is told you, and you won't lose anything. 8 Whether it is of friend or foe, don't tell it. Unless it is a sin to you, don't reveal it. 9 For if he has heard you and observed you, when the time comes, he will hate you. 10 Have you heard something? Let it die with you. Be brave: it will not make you burst! 11 A fool will travail in pain with a word, as a woman in labor with a child. 12 As an arrow that sticks in the flesh of the thigh, so is gossip in a fool. 13 Question a friend; it may be he didn't do it. If he did something, it may be that he may do it no more. 14 Question your neighbor; it may be he didn't say it. If he has said it, it may be that he may not say it again. 15 Question a friend; for many times there is slander. Don't trust every word. 16 There is one who slips, and not from the heart. Who is he who hasn't sinned with his tongue? 17 Reprove your neighbor before you threaten him; and give place to the law of the Most High. 18 19 20 All wisdom is the fear of the Lord. In all wisdom is the doing of the law. 21 22 The knowledge of wickedness is not wisdom. The prudence of sinners is not counsel. 23 There is a wickedness, and it is an abomination. There is a fool lacking in wisdom. 24 Better is one who has little understanding, and fears God, than one who has much intelligence and transgresses the law. 25 There is an exquisite subtlety, and it is unjust. And there is one who perverts favor to gain a judgment. 26 There is one who does wickedly, who hangs

down his head with mourning; but inwardly he is full of deceit, 27 bowing down his face, and pretending to be deaf in one ear. Where he isn't known, he will take advantage of you. 28 And if for lack of power he is hindered from sinning, if he finds opportunity, he will do mischief. 29 A man will be known by his appearance. One who has understanding will be known by his face when you meet him. 30 A man's attire, grinning laughter, and the way he walks show what he is.

20

1 There is a reproof that is not timely; and there is a person who is wise enough to keep silent. 2 How good is it to reprove, rather than to be angry. He who confesses will be kept back from harm. 3 4 As is the lust of a eunuch to deflower a virgin, so is he who executes judgments with violence. 5 There is one who keeps silent and is found wise; and there is one who is hated for his much talk. 6 There is one who keeps silent, for he has no answer to make; And there is one who keeps silent, knowing when to speak. 7 A wise man will be silent until his time has come, but the braggart and fool will miss his time. 8 He who uses many words will be abhorred. He who takes authority for himself will be hated in it. 9 There is a prosperity that a man finds in misfortunes; and there is a gain that turns to loss. 10 There is a gift that will not profit you; and there is a gift that pays back double. 11 There are losses because of glory; and there is one who has lifted up his head from a low estate. 12 There is one who buys much for a little, and pays for it again sevenfold. 13 He who is wise in words will make himself beloved; but the pleasantries of fools will be wasted. 14 The gift of a fool will not profit you, for he looks for repayment many times instead of one. 15 He will give little and insult much. He will open his mouth like a crier. Today he will lend, and tomorrow he will ask for it back. Such a one is a hateful man. 16 The fool will say, "I have no friend, and I have no thanks for my good deeds. Those who eat my bread have an evil tongue." 17 How often, and of how many, will he be laughed to scorn!§ 18 A slip on a pavement is better than a slip with the tongue. So the fall of the wicked will come speedily. 19 A man without grace is a tale out of season. It will be continually in the mouth of the ignorant. 20 A parable from a

fool's mouth will be rejected; for he won't tell it at the proper time. 21 There is one who is hindered from sinning through lack. When he rests, he will not be troubled. 22 There is one who destroys his soul through bashfulness. By a foolish countenance, he will destroy it. 23 There is one who for bashfulness makes promises to his friend; and he makes him his enemy for nothing. 24 A lie is an ugly blot on a person. It will be continually in the mouth of the ignorant. 25 A thief is better than a man who is continually lying, but they both will inherit destruction. 26 The destination of a liar is dishonor. His shame is with him continually. 27 He who is wise in words will advance himself. And one who is prudent will please great men. 28 He who tills his land will raise his harvest high. He who pleases great men will get pardon for iniquity. 29 Favors and gifts blind the eyes of the wise, and as a muzzle on the mouth, turn away reproofs. 30 Wisdom that is hidden, and treasure that is out of sight— what profit is in either of them? 31 Better is a man who hides his folly than a man who hides his wisdom.

21

1 My son, have you sinned? Do it no more; and ask forgiveness for your past sins. 2 Flee from sin as from the face of a snake; for if you go near, it will bite you. Its teeth are like lion's teeth, slaying people's souls. 3 All iniquity is as a two-edged sword. Its stroke has no healing. 4 Terror and violence will waste away riches. So the house of an arrogant man will be laid waste. 5 Supplication from a poor man's mouth reaches to the ears of God, and his judgment comes speedily. 6 One who hates reproof is in the path of the sinner. He who fears the Lord will repentin his heart. 7 He who is mighty in tongue is known far away; but the man of understanding knows when he slips. 8 He who builds his house with other men's money is like one who gathers stones for his own tomb. 9 The congregation of wicked men is as a bundle of tow with a flame of fire at the end of them. 10 The way of sinners is paved with stones; and at the end of it is the pit of Hades. 11 He who keeps the law becomes master of its intent. The fulfilment of the fear of the Lord is wisdom. 12 He who is not clever will not be instructed. There is a cleverness which

makes bitterness abound. 13 The knowledge of a wise man will be made to abound as a flood, and his counsel as a fountain of life 14 The inward parts of a fool are like a broken vessel. He will hold no knowledge. 15 If a man of knowledge hears a wise word, he will commend it and add to it. The wanton man hears it, and it displeases him, so he throws it away behind his back. 16 The chatter of a fool is like a burden in the way, but grace will be found on the lips of the wise. 17 The utterance of the prudent man will be sought for in the congregation. They will ponder his words in their heart. 18 As a house that is destroyed, so is wisdom to a fool. The knowledge of an unwise man is talk without sense. 19 Instruction is as fetters on the feet of an unwise man, and as manacles on the right hand. 20 A fool lifts up his voice with laughter, but a clever man smiles quietly. 21 Instruction is to a prudent man as an ornament of gold, and as a bracelet upon his right arm. 22 The foot of a fool rushes into a house, but a man of experience will be ashamed of entering. 23 A foolish man peers into the door of a house, but a man who is instructed will stand outside 24 It is rude for someone to listen at a door, but a prudent person will be grieved with the disgrace. 25 The lips of strangers will be grieved at these things, but the words of prudent man will be weighed in the balance. 26 The heart of fools is in their mouth, but the mouth of wise men is their heart. 27 When the ungodly curses an adversary, he curses his own soul. 28 A whisperer defiles his own soul, and will be hated wherever he travels.

22

1 A slothful man is compared to a stone that is defiled. Everyone will at hiss at him in his disgrace. 2 A slothful man is compared to the filth of a dunghill. Anyone who picks it up will shake it out of his hand. 3 An undisciplined child is a disgrace to his father, and a foolish daughter is born to his loss. 4 A prudent daughter will inherit a husband of her own. She who brings shame is the grief of her father. 5 She who is arrogant brings shame on father and husband. She will be despised by both of them. 6 Ill-timed conversation is like music in mourning, but stripes and correction are wisdom in every season. 7 He who teaches a fool is like one who glues potsherds together, even like one who wakes a sleeper out of a deep

sleep. 8 He who teaches a fool is as one who teaches a man who slumbers. In the end he will say, "What is it?" 9 10 11 Weep for the dead, for he lacks light. Weep for a fool, for he lacks understanding. Weep more sweetly for the dead, because he has found rest, but the life of the fool is worse than death. 12 Mourning for the dead lasts seven days, but for a fool and an ungodly man, it lasts all the days of his life. 13 Don't talk much with a foolish man, and don't go to one who has no understanding. Beware of him, lest you have trouble and be defiled in his onslaught. Turn away from him, and you will find rest, and you won't be wearied in his madness. 14 What would be heavier than lead? What is its name, but "Fool"? 15 Sand, salt, and a mass of iron is easier to bear than a man without understanding. 16 Timber girded and bound into a building will not be released with shaking. So a heart established in due season on well advised counsel will not be afraid. 17 A heart settled upon a thoughtful understanding is as an ornament of plaster on a polished wall. 18 Fences set on a high place will not stand against the wind; so a fearful heart in the imagination of a fool will not stand against any fear. 19 He who pricks the eye will make tears fall. He who pricks the heart makes it show feeling. 20 Whoever casts a stone at birds scares them away. He who insults a friend will dissolve friendship. 21 If you have drawn a sword against a friend, don't despair, for there may be a way back. 22 If you have opened your mouth against a friend, don't be afraid, for there may be reconciliation, unless it is for insulting, arrogance, disclosing of a secret, or a treacherous blow— for these things any friend will flee. 23 Gain trust with your neighbor in his poverty, that in his prosperity you may have gladness. Stay steadfast to him in the time of his affliction that you may be heir with him in his inheritance. 24 Before fire is the vapor and smoke of a furnace, so insults precede bloodshed. 25 I won't be ashamed to shelter a friend. I won't hide myself from his face. 26 If any evil happens to me because of him, everyone who hears it will beware of him. 27 Who will set a watch over my mouth, and a seal of shrewdness upon my lips, that I may not fall from it, and that my tongue may not destroy me?

23

¹ O Lord, Father and Master of my life, don't abandon me to their counsel. Don't let me fall because of them. ² Who will set scourges over my thought, and a discipline of wisdom over my heart, that they spare me not for my errors, and not overlook their sins? ³ Otherwise my errors might be multiplied, and my sins abound, I fall before my adversaries, and my enemy rejoice over me. ⁴ O Lord, Father and God of my life, don't give me a haughty eyes, ⁵ and turn away evil desire from me ⁶ Let neither gluttony nor lust overtake me. Don't give me over to a shameless mind. ⁷ Listen, my children, to the discipline of the mouth. He who keeps it will not be caught. ⁸ The sinner will be overpowered through his lips. By them, the insulter and the arrogant will stumble. ⁹ Don't accustom your mouth to an oath, and don't be accustomed to naming the Holy One, ¹⁰ for as a servant who is continually scourged will not lack bruises, so he also who swears and continually utters the Name will not be cleansed from sin. ¹¹ A man of many oaths will be filled with iniquity. The scourge will not depart from his house. If he offends, his sin will be upon him. If he disregards it, he has sinned doubly. If he has sworn falsely, he will not be justified, for his house will be filled with calamities. ¹² There is a manner of speech that is clothed with death. Let it not be found in the heritage of Jacob, for all these things will be far from the godly, and they will not wallow in sins. ¹³ Don't accustom your mouth to gross rudeness, for it involves sinful speech. ¹⁴ Remember your father and your mother, for you sit in the midst of great men, that you be not forgetful before them, and become a fool by your bad habit; so you may wish that you had not been born, and curse the day of your birth. ¹⁵ A man who is accustomed to abusive language won't be corrected all the days of his life. ¹⁶ Two sorts of people multiply sins, and the third will bring wrath: a hot passion, like a burning fire, will not be quenched until it is consumed; a fornicator in the body of his flesh will never cease until he has burned out the fire. ¹⁷ All bread is sweet to a fornicator. He will not cease until he dies. ¹⁸ A man who goes astray from his own marriage bed says in his heart, "Who sees me? Darkness is around me, and the walls hide

me. No one sees me. Of whom am I afraid? The Most High will not remember my sins." 19 The eyes of men are his terror. He doesn't know that the eyes of the Lord are ten thousand times brighter than the sun, seeing all the ways of men, and looking into secret places. 20 All things were known to him before they were created, and also after they were completed. 21 This man will be punished in the streets of the city. He will be seized where he least expects it. 22 So also is a wife who leaves her husband, and produces an heir by another man. 23 For first, she was disobedient in the law of the Most High. Second, she trespassed against her own husband. Third, she played the adulteress in fornication, and had children by another man. 24 She shall be brought out into the congregation. Her punishment will extend to her children. 25 Her children will not take root. Her branches will bear no fruit. 26 She will leave her memory for a curse. Her reproach won't be blotted out. 27 And those who are left behind will know that there is nothing better than the fear of the Lord, and nothing sweeter than to heed the commandments of the Lord

24

1 Wisdom will praise her own soul, and will proclaim her glory in the midst of her people. 2 She will open her mouth in the congregation of the Most High, and proclaim her glory in the presence of his power. 3 "I came out of the mouth of the Most High, and covered the earth as a mist. 4 I lived in high places, and my throne is in the pillar of the cloud. 5 Alone I surrounded the circuit of heaven, and walked in the depth of the abyss. 6 In the waves of the sea, and in all the earth, and in every people and nation, I obtained a possession. 7 With all these I sought rest. In whose inheritance shall I lodge? 8 Then the Creator of all things gave me a command. He who created me made my tent to rest, and said, 'Let your dwelling be in Jacob, and your inheritance in Israel.' 9 He created me from the beginning, before the ages. For all ages, I will not cease to exist. 10 In the holy tabernacle, I ministered before him. So I was established in Zion. 11 In the beloved city, likewise he gave me rest. In Jerusalem was my domain. 12 I took root in a people that was honored, even in the portion of the Lord's own inheritance. 13 I was exalted like a

cedar in Lebanon, And like a cypress tree on the mountains of Hermon. 14 I was exalted like a palm tree on the sea shore, like rose bushes in Jericho, and like a fair olive tree in the plain. I was exalted like a plane tree. 15 Like cinnamon and aspalathus, I have given a scent to perfumes. Like choice myrrh, I spread abroad a pleasant fragrance, like galbanum, onycha, stacte, and as the smell of frankincense in the tabernacle. 16 Like the terebinth, I stretched out my branches. My branches are glorious and graceful. 17 Like the vine, I put forth grace. My flowers are the fruit of glory and riches. 18 19 "Come to me, all you who desire me, and be filled with my fruits. 20 For my memory is sweeter than honey, and my inheritance than the honeycomb. 21 Those who eat me will be hungry for more. Those who drink me will be thirsty for more. 22 He who obeys me will not be ashamed. Those who work with me will not sin." 23 All these things are the book of the covenant of the Most High God, the law which Moses commanded us for an inheritance for the assemblies of Jacob. 24 25 It is he who makes wisdom abundant, as Pishon, and as Tigris in the days of first fruits. 26

He makes understanding full as the Euphrates, and as the Jordan in the days of harvest, 27 who makes instruction shine forth as the light, as Gihon in the days of vintage. 28 The first man didn't know her perfectly. In like manner, the last has not explored her. 29 For her thoughts are filled from the sea, and her counsels from the great deep. 30 I came out as a canal stream from a river, and as an irrigation ditch into a garden. 31 I said, "I will water my garden, and will drench my garden bed." Behold, my stream became a river, and my river became a sea. 32 I will yet bring instruction to light as the morning, and will make these things clear from far away. 33 I will continue to pour out teaching like prophecy, and leave it to all generations. 34 See that I have not labored for myself only, but for all those who diligently seek wisdom.

25

1 I enjoy three things, and they are beautiful before the Lord and men: the agreement of kindred, the friendship of neighbors, and a woman and her husband who walk together in agreement. 2 But my soul hates three sorts of people, and I am greatly offended at their life: a poor man who is

arrogant, a rich man who is a liar, and an old fool who is an adulterer. ³ If you gathered nothing in your youth, how could you find anything in your old age? ⁴ How beautiful a thing is judgment in the grayhaired, and for elders to know good counsel! ⁵ How beautiful is the wisdom of old men, and understanding and counsel to men who are in honor! ⁶ Much experience is the crown of the aged. Their glory is the fear of the Lord. ⁷ There are nine things that I have thought of, and in my heart counted happy, and the tenth I will utter with my tongue: a man who has joy with his children, and a man who lives and sees the fall of his enemies. ⁸ Happy is he who dwells with a wife of understanding, he who has not slipped with his tongue, and he who has not served a man who is unworthy of him. ⁹ Happy is he who has found prudence, and he who speaks in the ears of those who listen. ¹⁰ How great is he who has found wisdom! Yet is there none above him who fears the Lord. ¹¹ The fear of the Lord surpasses all things. To whom shall he who holds it be likened? ¹² ¹³ Any wound but a wound of the heart! Any wickedness but the wickedness of a woman! ¹⁴ Any calamity but a calamity from those who hate me! Any vengeance but the vengeance of enemies! ¹⁵ There is no venom worse than a snake's venom. There is no wrath worse than an enemy's wrath. ¹⁶ I would rather dwell with a lion and a dragon than keep house with a wicked woman. ¹⁷ The wickedness of a woman changes her appearance, and darkens her countenance like that of a bear. ¹⁸ Her husband will sit among his neighbors, and when he hears it, he sighs bitterly. ¹⁹ All malice is small compared to the malice of a woman. Let the portion of a sinner fall on her. ²⁰ As walking up a sandy hill is to the feet of the aged, so is a wife full of words to a quiet man. ²¹ Don't be ensnared by a woman's beauty. Don't desire a woman for her beauty. ²² There is anger, impudence, and great reproach if a woman supports her husband. ²³ A wicked woman is abasement of heart, sadness of countenance, and a wounded heart. A woman who won't make her husband happy is like hands that hang down, and weak knees. ²⁴ The beginning of sin came from a woman. Because of her, we all die. ²⁵ Don't give water an outlet, and don't give a wicked woman freedom of speech. ²⁶ If she doesn't go as you direct, cut her away from your flesh.

26

1 Happy is the husband of a good wife. The number of his days will be doubled. 2 A faithful wife gives joy to her husband. He will fulfill his years in peace. 3 A good wife is a great gift. She will be given to those who fear the Lord. 4 Whether a man is rich or poor, a good heart makes a cheerful face at all times. 5 Of three things my heart was afraid, and concerning the fourth kind I made supplication: The slander of a city, the assembly of a mob, and a false accusation. All these are more grievous than death. 6 A grief of heart and sorrow is a woman who is jealous of another woman. Her tongue-lashing makes it known to all. 7 A wicked woman is like a chafing yoke. He who takes hold of her is like one who grasps a scorpion. 8 A drunken woman causes great wrath. She will not cover her own shame. 9 The fornication of a woman is in the lifting up of her eyes; it will be known by her eyelids. 10 Keep strict watch on a headstrong daughter, lest she find liberty for herself, and use it. 11 Watch out for an impudent eye, and don't be surprised if it sins against you. 12 She will open her mouth like a thirsty traveller, and drink from every water that is near. She will sit down at every post, and open her quiver to any arrow. 13 The grace of a wife will delight her husband. Her knowledge will strengthen his bones. 14 A silent woman is a gift of the Lord. There is nothing worth so much as a well instructed soul. 15 A modest woman is grace upon grace. There are no scales that can weigh the value of a self-controlled soul. 16 As the sun when it arises in the highest places of the Lord, so is the beauty of a good wife in her well-organized home. 17 As the lamp that shines upon the holy lampstand, so is the beauty of the face on a well-proportioned body. 18 As the golden pillars are upon a base of silver, so are beautiful feet with the breasts of one who is steadfast. 19 27 28 For two things my heart is grieved, and for the third anger comes upon me: a warrior who suffers for poverty, men of understanding who are counted as garbage, and one who turns back from righteousness to sin—the Lord will prepare him for the sword! 29 It is difficult for a merchant to keep himself from

wrong doing, and for a retailer to be acquitted of sin.

27

¹ Many have sinned for profit. He who seeks to multiply wealth will turn his eye away. ² As a nail will stick fast between the joinings of stones, so sin will thrust itself in between buying and selling. ³ Unless a person holds on diligently to the fear of the Lord, his house will be overthrown quickly. ⁴ In the shaking of a sieve, the refuse remains, so does the filth of man in his thoughts. ⁵ The furnace tests the potter's vessels; so the test of a person is in his thoughts. ⁶ The fruit of a tree discloses its cultivation, so is the utterance of the thought of a person's heart. ⁷ Praise no man before you hear his thoughts, for this is how people are tested ⁸ If you follow righteousness, you will obtain it, and put it on like a long robe of glory. ⁹ Birds will return to their own kind, so truth will return to those who practice it. ¹⁰ The lion lies in wait for prey. So does sin for those who do evil. ¹¹ The discourse of a godly man is always wise, but the fool changes like the moon. ¹² Limit your time among people void of understanding, but persevere among the thoughtful. ¹³ The talk of fools is offensive. Their laughter is wantonly sinful. ¹⁴ Their talk with much swearing makes hair stand upright. Their strife makes others plug their ears. ¹⁵ The strife of the proud leads to bloodshed. Their abuse of each other is a grievous thing to hear. ¹⁶ He who reveals secrets destroys trust, and will not find a close friend. ¹⁷ Love a friend, and keep faith with him; but if you reveal his secrets, you shall not follow him; ¹⁸ for as a man has destroyed his enemy, so you have destroyed the friendship of your neighbor. ¹⁹ As a bird which you have released out of your hand, so you have let your neighbor go, and you will not catch him again. ²⁰ Don't pursue him, for he has gone far away, and has escaped like a gazelle out of the snare. ²¹ For a wound may be bound up, and after abuse there may be reconciliation; but he who reveals secrets is without hope. ²² One who winks the eye contrives evil things; and those who know him will keep their distance. ²³ When you are present, he will speak sweetly, and will admire your words; but afterward he will twist his speech and set a trap in your words. ²⁴ I have hated many things, but nothing like him. The Lord will hate him. ²⁵ One who casts a stone straight up casts it

on his own head. A deceitful blow opens wounds. 26 He who digs a pit will fall into it. He who sets a snare will be caught in it. 27 He who does evil things, they will roll back upon him, and he will not know where they came from. 28 Mockery and reproach are from the arrogant. Vengeance lies in wait for them like a lion. 29 Those who rejoice at the fall of the godly will be caught in a snare. Anguish will consume them before they die. 30 Wrath and anger, these also are abominations. A sinner will possess them.

28

1 He who takes vengeance will find vengeance from the Lord, and he will surely make his sins firm. 2 Forgive your neighbor the hurt that he has done, and then your sins will be pardoned when you pray. 3 Does anyone harbor anger against another and expect healing from the Lord? 4 Upon a man like himself he has no mercy, and does he make supplication for his own sins? 5 He himself, being flesh, nourishes wrath. Who will make atonement for his sins? 6 Remember your last end, and stop enmity. Remember corruption and death, and be true to the commandments. 7 Remember the commandments, and don't be angry with your neighbor. Remember the covenant of the Highest, and overlook ignorance. 8 Abstain from strife, and you will diminish your sins, for a passionate man will kindle strife. 9 A man who is a sinner will trouble friends and sow discord among those who are at peace. 10 As is the fuel of the fire, so it will burn; and as the stoutness of the strife is, so it will burn. As is the strength of the man, so will be his wrath; and as is his wealth, so he will exalt his anger. 11 A contention begun in haste kindles a fire, and hasty fighting sheds blood. 12 If you blow on a spark, it will burn; and if you spit upon it, it will be quenched. Both of these come out of your mouth. 13 Curse the whisperer and double-tongued, for he has destroyed many who were at peace. 14 A slanderer has shaken many, and dispersed them from nation to nation. It has pulled down strong cities and overthrown the houses of great men. 15 A slanderer has cast out brave women and deprived them of their labors. 16 He who listens to it will not find rest, nor will he live quietly. 17 The stroke of a whip makes a mark in the flesh, but the stroke of a tongue will

break bones. 18 Many have fallen by the edge of the sword, yet not so many as those who have fallen because of the tongue. 19 Happy is he who is sheltered from it, who has not passed through its wrath, who has not drawn its yoke, and has not been bound with its bands. 20 For its yoke is a yoke of iron, and its bands are bands of brass. 21 Its death is an evil death, and Hades is better than it. 22 It will not have rule over godly men. They will not be burned in its flame. 23 Those who forsake the Lord will fall into it. It will burn among them, and won't be quenched. It will be sent against them like a lion. It will destroy them like a leopard. 24 As you hedge your possession about with thorns, and secure your silver and your gold, 25 so make a balance and a weight for your words, and make a door and a bar for your mouth. 26 Take heed lest you slip with it, lest you fall before one who lies in wait.

29

1 He who shows mercy will lend to his neighbor. He who strengthens him with his hand keeps the commandments. 2 Lend to your neighbor in time of his need. Repay your neighbor on time. 3 Confirm your word, and keep faith with him; and at all seasons you will find what you need. 4 Many have considered a loan to be a windfall, and have given trouble to those who helped them. 5 Until he has received, he will kiss a man's hands. For his neighbor's money he will speak submissively. Then when payment is due, he will prolong the time, return excuses, and complain about the season. 6 If he prevails, the creditor will hardly receive half; and he will count it as a windfall. If not, he has deprived him of his money, and he has gotten him for an enemy without cause. He will pay him with cursing and railing. Instead of honor, he will pay him disgrace. 7 Many on account of fraud have turned away. They are afraid of being defrauded for nothing. 8 However be patient with a man in poor estate. Don't keep him waiting for your alms. 9 Help a poor man for the commandment's sake. According to his need don't send him empty away. 10 Lose your money for a brother and a friend. Don't let it rust under a stone and be lost. 11 Allocate your treasure according to the commandments of the Most High and it will profit you more than gold. 12 Store up almsgiving in your store-chambers and it will deliver you

out of all affliction. 13 It will fight for you against your enemy better than a mighty shield and a ponderous spear. 14 A good man will be surety for his neighbor. He who has lost shame will fail him. 15 Don't forget the kindness of your guarantor, for he has given his life for you. 16 A sinner will waste the property of his guarantor. 17 He who is thankless will fail him who delivered him. 18 Being surety has undone many who were prospering and shaken them as a wave of the sea. It has driven mighty men from their homes. They wandered among foreign nations. 19 A sinner who falls into suretiship and undertakes contracts for work will fall into lawsuits. 20 Help your neighbor according to your power, and be careful not to fall yourself. 21 The essentials of life are water, bread, a garment, and a house for privacy. 22 Better is the life of a poor man under a shelter of logs than sumptuous fare in another man's house. 23 With little or with much, be well satisfied. 24 It is a miserable life to go from house to house. Where you are a guest, you dare not open your mouth. 25 You will entertain, serve drinks, and have no thanks. In addition to this, you will hear bitter words. 26 "Come here, you sojourner, set a table, and if you have anything in your hand, feed me with it." 27 "Leave, you sojourner, for an honored guest is here. My brother has come to be my guest. I need my house." 28 These things are grievous to a man of understanding: The scolding about lodging and the insults of creditors.

30

1 He who loves his son will continue to lay stripes upon him, that he may have joy from him in the end. 2 He who chastises his son will have profit from him, and will brag about him among his acquaintances. 3 He who teaches his son will provoke his enemy to jealousy. Before friends, he will rejoice in him. 4 His father dies, and is as though he had not died; for he has left one behind him like himself. 5 In his life, he saw his son and rejoiced. When he died, it was without regret. 6 He left behind him an avenger against his enemies, and one to repay kindness to his friends. 7 He who makes too much of his son will bind up his wounds. His heart will be troubled at every cry. 8 An unbroken horse becomes stubborn. An unrestrained son becomes headstrong. 9 Pamper

your child, and he will make you afraid. Play with him, and he will grieve you. ¹⁰ Don't laugh with him, lest you have sorrow with him, and you gnash your teeth in the end. ¹¹ Give him no liberty in his youth, and don't ignore his follies. ¹² Bow down his neck in his youth, and beat him on the sides while he is a child, lest he become stubborn, and be disobedient to you, and there be sorrow to your soul. ¹³ Chastise your son, and give him work, lest his shameless behavior be an offense to you. ¹⁴ Better is a poor man who is healthy and fit, than a rich man who is afflicted in his body. ¹⁵ Health and fitness are better than all gold, and a strong body better than wealth without measure. ¹⁶ There is no wealth better than health of body. There is no gladness above the joy of the heart. ¹⁷ Death is better than a bitter life, and eternal rest than a continual sickness. ¹⁸ Good things poured out upon a mouth that is closed are like food offerings laid upon a grave. ¹⁹ What does an offering profit an idol? For it can't eat or smell. So is he who is punished by the Lord, ²⁰ seeing with his eyes and groaning, like a eunuch embracing a virgin and groaning. ²¹ Don't give your soul to sorrow.

Don't afflict yourself deliberately ²² Gladness of heart is the life of a man. Cheerfulness of a man lengthens his days. ²³ Love your own soul, and comfort your heart. Remove sorrow far from you, for sorrow has destroyed many, and there is no profit in it. ²⁴ Envy and wrath shorten life. Anxiety brings old age before its time. ²⁵ Those who are cheerful and merry will benefit from their food.

31

¹ Wakefulness that comes from riches consumes the flesh, and anxiety about it takes away sleep. ² Wakeful anxiety will crave slumber. In a severe disease, sleep will be broken. ³ A rich man toils in gathering money together. When he rests, he is filled with his good things. ⁴ A poor man toils in lack of substance. When he rests, he becomes needy. ⁵ He who loves gold won't be justified. He who follows destruction will himself have his fill of it. ⁶ Many have been given over to ruin for the sake of gold. Their destruction meets them face to face. ⁷ It is a stumbling block to those who sacrifice to it. Every fool will be taken by it. ⁸ Blessed is the rich person who is found blameless, and who doesn't go after gold ⁹ Who is he, that we

may call him blessed? For he has done wonderful things among his people. ¹⁰ Who has been tried by it, and found perfect? Then let him boast. Who has had the power to transgress, and has not transgressed? And to do evil, and has not done it? ¹¹ His prosperity will be made sure. The congregation will proclaim his alms. ¹² Do you sit at a great table? Don't be greedy there. Don't say, "There is a lot of food on it!" ¹³ Remember that a greedy eye is a wicked thing. What has been created more greedy than an eye? Therefore it sheds tears from every face. ¹⁴ Don't stretch your hand wherever it looks. Don't thrust yourself with it into the dish. ¹⁵ Consider your neighbor's feelings by your own. Be discreet in every point. ¹⁶ Eat like a human being those things which are set before you. Don't eat greedily, lest you be hated. ¹⁷ Be first to stop for manners' sake. Don't be insatiable, lest you offend. ¹⁸ And if you sit among many, Don't reach out your hand before them. ¹⁹ How sufficient to a well-mannered man is a very little. He doesn't breathe heavily in his bed. ²⁰ Healthy sleep comes from moderate eating. He rises early, and his wits are with him. The pain of wakefulness, colic, and griping are with an insatiable man. ²¹ And if you have been forced to eat, rise up in the middle of it, and you shall have rest. ²² Hear me, my son, and don't despise me, and in the end you will appreciate my words. In all your works be skillful, and no disease will come to you. ²³ People bless him who is liberal with his food. The testimony of his excellence will be believed. ²⁴ The city will murmur at him who is a stingy with his food. The testimony of his stinginess will be accurate. ²⁵ Don't show yourself valiant in wine, for wine has destroyed many. ²⁶ The furnace tests the temper of steel by dipping; so does wine test hearts in the quarreling of the proud. ²⁷ Wine is as good as life to men, if you drink it in moderation. What life is there to a man who is without wine? It has been created to make men glad. ²⁸ Wine drunk in season and in moderation is joy of heart and gladness of soul: ²⁹ Wine drunk excessively is bitterness of soul, with provocation and conflict. ³⁰ Drunkenness increases the rage of a fool to his hurt. It diminishes strength and adds wounds.

31

Don't rebuke your neighbor at a banquet of wine. Don't despise him in his mirth. Don't speak a word of reproach to him. Don't distress him by making demands of him. 32 1 Have they made you ruler of a feast? Don't be lifted up. Be among them as one of them. Take care of them first, and then sit down. 2 And when you have done all your duties, take your place, that you may be gladdened on their account, and receive a wreath for your good service. 3 Speak, you who are older, for it's your right, but with sound knowledge; and don't interrupt the music. 4 Don't pour out talk where there is a performance of music. Don't display your wisdom at the wrong time. 5 As a ruby signet in a setting of gold, so is a music concert at a wine banquet. 6 As an emerald signet in a work of gold, so is musical melody with pleasant wine. 7 Speak, young man, if you are obliged to, but no more than twice, and only if asked. 8 Sum up your speech, many things in few words. Be as one who knows and yet holds his tongue. 9 When among great men, don't behave as their equal. When another is speaking, don't babble. 10 Lightning speeds before thunder. Approval goes before one who is modest. 11 Rise up in good time, and don't be last. Go home quickly and don't loiter 12 Amuse yourself there and do what is in your heart. Don't sin by proud speech. 13 For these things bless your Maker, who gives you to drink freely of his good things. 14 He who fears the Lord will receive discipline. Those who seek him early will find favor. 15 He who seeks the law shall be filled with it, but the hypocrite will stumble at it. 16 Those who fear the Lord will find true judgment, and will kindle righteous acts like a light. 17 A sinful man shuns reproof, and will find a judgment according to his will. 18 A sensible person won't neglect a thought. An insolent and proud man won't crouch in fear, even after he has done a thing by himself without counsel. 19 Do nothing without counsel, 0 Don't go in a way of conflict. Don't stumble in stony places. 21 Don't be overconfident on a smooth road. 22 Beware of your own children. 23 In every work guard your own soul, for this is the keeping of the commandments. 24 He who believes the law gives heed to the commandment. He who trusts in the Lord will suffer no loss.

33

1 No evil will happen to him who fears the Lord, but in trials once

208

and again he will deliver him. 2 A wise man will not hate the law, but he who is a hypocrite about it is like a boat in a storm. 3 A man of understanding will put his trust in the law. And the law is faithful to him, as when one asks a divine oracle. 4 Prepare your speech, and so you will be heard. Bind up instruction, and make your answer. 5 The heart of a fool is like a cartwheel. His thoughts are like a rolling axle. 6 A stallion horse is like a mocking friend. He neighs under every one who sits upon him. 7 Why does one day excel another, when all the light of every day in the year is from the sun? 8 They were distinguished by the Lord's knowledge, and he varied seasons and feasts. 9 Some of them he exalted and hallowed, and some of them he has made ordinary days. 10 And all men are from the ground. Adam was created from dust. 11 In the abundance of his knowledge the Lord distinguished them, and made their ways different. 12 Some of them he blessed and exalted, and some of them he made holy and brought near to himself. Some of them he cursed and brought low, and overthrew them from their place. 13 As the clay of the potter in his hand, all his ways are according to his good pleasure, so men are in the hand of him who made them, to render to them according to his judgment. 14 Good is the opposite of evil, and life is the opposite of death; so† the sinner is the opposite of the godly. 15 Look upon all the works of the Most High like this, they come in pairs, one against another. 16 I was the last on watch, like one who gleans after the grape gatherers. 17 By the Lord's blessing I arrived before them, and filled my winepress like one who gathers grapes. 18 Consider that I labored not for myself alone, but for all those who seek instruction. 19 Hear me, you great men of the people, and listen with your ears, you rulers of the congregation. 20 To son and wife, to brother and friend, don't give power over yourself while you live, and don't give your goods to another, lest you regret it and must ask for them. 21 While you still live and breath is in you, don't give yourself over to anybody. 22 For it is better that your children should ask from you than that you should look to the hand of your children. 23 Excel in all your works. Don't bring a stain on your honor. 24 In the day that you end the days of your life, in the time of death, distribute your inheritance. 25 Fodder, a stick, and burdens are for a donkey. Bread, discipline, and work are for a servant. 26 Set your slave to work, and you will find rest. Leave his hands idle, and he will seek liberty. 27 Yoke and thong will bow the neck. For an evil slave there are racks and tortures. 28 Send him to labor, that he not be idle, for idleness teaches much mischief. 29 Set him to work, as is fit for him. If he doesn't obey, make his fetters heavy. 30 Don't be excessive toward any. Do nothing unjust. 31 If you have a slave, treat him like yourself, because you have bought him with blood. 32 If you have a slave, treat him like yourself. For like your own soul, you will need him. If you treat him ill, and he departs and runs away, 33 which way will you go to seek him?

34

1 Vain and false hopes are for a man void of understanding. Dreams give wings to fools. 2 As one who grasps at a shadow and follows after the wind, so is he who sets his mind on dreams. 3 The vision of dreams is a reflection, the likeness of a face near a face. 4 From an unclean thing what can be cleansed? From that which is false what can be true? 5 Divinations, and soothsayings, and dreams, are vain. The heart has fantasies like a woman in labor. 6 If they are not sent in a visitation from the Most High, don't give your heart to them. 7 For dreams have led many astray. They have failed by putting their hope in them. 8 Without lying the law will be fulfilled. Wisdom is complete in a faithful mouth. 9 A well-instructed man knows many things. He who has much experience will declare understanding. 10 He who has no experience knows few things. But he who has traveled increases cleverness. 11 I have seen many things in my travels. My understanding is more than my words. 12 I was often in danger even to death. I was preserved because of these experiences. 13 The spirit of those who fear the Lord will live, for their hope is in him who saves them. 14 Whoever fears the Lord won't be afraid, and won't be a coward, for he is his hope. 15 Blessed is the soul of him who fears the Lord. To whom does he give heed? Who is his support? 16 The eyes of the Lord are on those who love him, a mighty protection and strong support, a cover from the hot blast, a shade from the noonday

sun, a guard from stumbling, and a help from falling. 17 He raises up the soul, and enlightens the eyes. He gives health, life, and blessing. 18 He who sacrifices a thing wrongfully gotten, his offering is made in mockery. The mockery of wicked men are not acceptable. 19 The Most High has no pleasure in the offerings of the ungodly, Neither is he pacified for sins by the multitude of sacrifices. 20 Like one who kills a son before his father's eyes is he who brings a sacrifice from the goods of the poor. 21 The bread of the needy is the life of the poor. He who deprives him of it is a man of blood. 22 Like one who murders his neighbor is he who takes away his living. Like a shedder of blood is he who deprives a hireling of his hire. 23 When one builds, and another pulls down, what profit do they have but toil? 24 When one prays, and another curses, whose voice will the Lord listen to? 25 He who washes himself after touching a dead body, and touches it again, what does he gain by his washing? 26 Even so a man fasting for his sins, and going again, and doing the same, who will listen to his prayer? What profit does he have in his humiliation?

35

1 He who keeps the law multiplies offerings. He who heeds the commandments sacrifices a peace offering. 2 He who returns a kindness offers fine flour. He who gives alms sacrifices a thank offering. 3 To depart from wickedness pleases the Lord. To depart from unrighteousness is an atoning sacrifice 4 See that you don't appear in the presence of the Lord empty. 5 For all these things are done because of the commandment. 6 The offering of the righteous enriches the altar. The sweet fragrance of it is before the Most High. 7 The sacrifice of a righteous man is acceptable. It won't be forgotten. 8 Glorify the Lord with generosity. Don't reduce the first fruits of your hands. 9 In every gift show a cheerful countenance, And dedicate your tithe with gladness. 10 Give to the Most High according as he has given. As your hand has found, give generously. 11 For the Lord repays, and he will repay you sevenfold. 12 Don't plan to bribe him with gifts, for he will not receive them. Don't set your mind on an unrighteous sacrifice, For the Lord is the judge, and with him is no respect of persons. 13 He won't accept any person

against a poor man. He will listen to the prayer of him who is wronged. 14 He will in no way despise the supplication of the fatherless or the widow, when she pours out her tale. 15 Don't the tears of the widow run down her cheek Isn't her cry against him who has caused them to fall? 16 He who serves God according to his good pleasure will be accepted. His supplication will reach to the clouds. 17 The prayer of the humble pierces the clouds. until it comes near, he will not be comforted. He won't depart until the Most High visits and he judges righteously and executes judgment. 18 And the Lord will not be slack, neither will he be patient toward them, until he has crushed the loins of the unmerciful. He will repay vengeance to the heathen until he has taken away the multitude of the arrogant and broken in pieces the sceptres of the unrighteous, 19 until he has rendered to every man according to his deeds, and repaid the works of men according to their plans, until he has judged the cause of his people, and he will make them rejoice in his mercy. 20 Mercy is as welcome in the time of his affliction, as clouds of rain in the time of drought.

36

1 Have mercy upon us, O Lord the God of all, and look at us with favor; 2 and send your fear upon all the nations. 3 Lift up your hand against the foreign nations and let them see your mighty power. 4 As you showed your holiness in us before them, so be magnified in them before us. 5 Let them know you, as we also have known you, that there is no God but only you, O God. 6 Show new signs, and work various wonders. Glorify your hand and your right arm. 7 Raise up indignation and pour out wrath. Take away the adversary and destroy the enemy. 8 Hasten the time and remember your oath. Let them declare your mighty works. 9 Let him who escapes be devoured by raging fire. May those who harm your people find destruction. 10 Crush the heads of the rulers of the enemies who say, "There is no one but ourselves." 11 Gather all the tribes of Jacob together, and take them for your inheritance, as from the beginning. 12 O Lord, have mercy upon the people that is called by your name, and upon Israel, whom you likened to a firstborn. 13 Have compassion upon the city of your sanctuary, Jerusalem, the place of your rest.

14 Fill Zion. Exalt your oracles and fill your people with your glory. 15 Give testimony to those who were your creatures in the beginning, and fulfill the prophecies that have been spoken in your name. 16 Reward those who wait for you, and men will put their trust in your prophets. 17 Listen, O Lord, to the prayer of your servants, according to the blessing of Aaron concerning your people; and all those who are on the earth will know that you are the Lord, the eternal God. 18 The belly will eat any food, but one food is better than another. 19 The mouth tastes meats taken in hunting, so does an understanding heart detect false speech. 20 A contrary heart will cause heaviness. A man of experience will pay him back. 21 A woman will receive any man, but one daughter is better than another. 22 The beauty of a woman cheers the countenance. A man desires nothing more. 23 If kindness and humility are on her tongue, her husband is not like other sons of men. 24 He who gets a wife gets his richest treasure, a help meet for him and a pillar of support. 25 Where no hedge is, the property will be plundered. He who has no wife will mourn as he wanders. 26 For who would trust a nimble robber who skips from city to city? Even so, who would trust a man who has no nest, and lodges wherever he finds himself at nightfall?

37

1 Every friend will say, "I also am his friend"; but there is a friend which is only a friend in name. 2 Isn't there a grief in it even to death when a companion and friend is turned into an enemy? 3 O wicked imagination, why were you formed to cover the dry land with deceit? 4 There is a companion who rejoices in the gladness of a friend, but in time of affliction will be against him. 5 There is a companion who for the belly's sake labors with his friend, yet in the face of battle will carry his buckler. 6 Don't forget a friend in your soul. Don't be unmindful of him in your riches. 7 Every counselor extols counsel, but some give counsel in their own interest. 8 Let your soul beware of a counselor, and know in advance what is his interest (for he will take counsel for himself), lest he cast the lot against you, 9 and say to you, "Your way is good." Then he will stand near you, to see what will happen to you. 10 Don't take counsel with one who looks

askance at you. Hide your counsel from those who are jealous of you. ¹¹ Don't consult with a woman about her rival, with a coward about war, with a merchant about business, with a buyer about selling, with an envious man about thankfulness, with an unmerciful man about kindliness, with a sluggard about any kind of work, with a hireling in your house about finishing his work, or with an idle servant about much business. Pay no attention to these in any matter of counsel. ¹² But rather be continually with a godly man, whom you know to be a keeper of the commandments, who in his soul is as your own soul, and who will grieve with you, if you fail. ¹³ Make the counsel of your heart stand, for there is no one more faithful to you than it. ¹⁴ For a man's soul is sometimes inclined to inform him better than seven watchmen who sit on high on a watch-tower. ¹⁵ Above all this ask the Most High that he may direct your way in truth. ¹⁶ Let reason be the beginning of every work. Let counsel go before every action. ¹⁷ As a token of the changing of the heart, ¹⁸ four kinds of things rise up: good and evil, life and death. That which rules over them continually is the tongue. ¹⁹ There is one who is clever and the instructor of many, and yet is unprofitable to his own soul. ²⁰ There is one who is subtle in words, and is hated. He will be destitute of all food. ²¹ For grace was not given to him from the Lord, because he is deprived of all wisdom. ²² There is one who is wise to his own soul; and the fruits of his understanding are trustworthy in the mouth. ²³ A wise man will instruct his own people. The fruits of his understanding are trustworthy. ²⁴ A wise man will be filled with blessing. All those who see him will call him happy. ²⁵ The life of a man is counted by days. The days of Israel are innumerable. ²⁶ The wise man will inherit confidence among his people. His name will live forever. ²⁷ My son, test your soul in your life. See what is evil for it, and don't give in to it. ²⁸ For not all things are profitable for all men. Not every soul has pleasure in everything. ²⁹ Don't be insatiable in any luxury. Don't be greedy in the things that you eat. ³⁰ For overeating brings disease, and gluttony causes nausea. ³¹ Because of gluttony, many have perished, but he who takes heed shall prolong his life.

38

1 Honor a physician according to your need with the honors due to him, for truly the Lord has created him. 2 For healing comes from the Most High, and he shall receive a gift from the king. 3 The skill of the physician will lift up his head. He will be admired in the sight of great men. 4 The Lord created medicines out of the earth. A prudent man will not despise them. 5 Wasn't water made sweet with wood, that its power might be known? 6 He gave men skill that he might be glorified in his marvelous works. 7 With them he heals and takes away pain. 8 With these, the pharmacist makes a mixture. God's works won't be brought to an end. From him, peace is upon the face of the earth. 9 My son, in your sickness don't be negligent, but pray to the Lord, and he will heal you. 10 Put away wrong doing, and direct your hands in righteousness. Cleanse your heart from all sin. 11 Give a sweet savor and a memorial of fine flour and pour oil on your offering, according to your means. 12 Then give place to the physician, for truly the Lord has created him. Don't let him leave you, for you need him. 13 There is a time when in recovery is in their hands. 14 For they also shall ask the Lord to prosper them in diagnosis and in healing for the maintenance of life. 15 He who sins before his Maker, let him fall into the hands of the physician. 16 My son, let your tears fall over the dead, and as one who suffers grievously, begin lamentation. Wind up his body with due honor. Don't neglect his burial. 17 Make bitter weeping and make passionate wailing. Let your mourning be according to his merit, for one day or two, lest you be spoken evil of; and so be comforted for your sorrow. 18 For from sorrow comes death. Sorrow of heart saps one's strength. 19 In calamity, sorrow also remains. A poor man's life is grievous to the heart. 20 Don't give your heart to sorrow. Put it away, remembering the end. 21 Don't forget it, for there is no returning again. You do him no good, and you would harm yourself. 22 Remember his end, for so also will yours be: yesterday for me, and today for you. 23 When the dead is at rest, let his remembrance rest. Be comforted for him when his spirit departs from him. 24 The wisdom of the scribe comes by the opportunity of leisure. He who has little business can become wise. 25

How could he become wise who holds the plow, who glories in the shaft of the goad, who drives oxen and is occupied in their labors, and who mostly talks about bulls? 26 He will set his heart upon turning his furrows. His lack of sleep is to give his heifers their fodder. 27 So is every craftsman and master artisan who passes his time by night as by day, those who cut engravings of signets. His diligence is to make great variety. He sets his heart to preserve likeness in his portraiture, and is careful to finish his work. 28 So too is the smith sitting by the anvil and considering the unwrought iron. The smoke of the fire will waste his flesh. He toils in the heat of the furnace. The noise of the hammer deafens his ear. His eyes are upon the pattern of the object. He will set his heart upon perfecting his works. He will be careful to adorn them perfectly. 29 So is the potter sitting at his work and turning the wheel around with his feet, who is always anxiously set at his work. He produces his handiwork in quantity. 30 He will fashion the clay with his arm and will bend its strength in front of his feet. He will apply his heart to finish the glazing. He will be careful to clean the kiln. 31 All these put their trust in their hands. Each becomes skillful in his own work. 32 Without these no city would be inhabited. Men wouldn't reside as foreigners or walk up and down there. 33 They won't be sought for in the council of the people. They won't mount on high in the assembly. They won't sit on the seat of the judge. They won't understand the covenant of judgment. Neither will they declare instruction and judgment. They won't be found where parables are. 34 But they will maintain the fabric of the age. Their prayer is in the handiwork of their craft.

39

1 Not so he who has applied his soul and meditates in the law of the Most High. He will seek out the wisdom of all the ancients and will be occupied with prophecies. 2 He will keep the sayings of the men of renown and will enter in amidst the subtleties of parables. 3 He will seek out the hidden meaning of proverbs and be conversant in the dark sayings of parables. 4 He will serve among great men and appear before him who rules. He will travel through the land of foreign nations, for he has learned what is good and evil

among men. 5 He will apply his heart to return early to the Lord who made him, and will make supplication before the Most High, and will open his mouth in prayer, and will ask for pardon for his sins. 6 If the great Lord wills, he will be filled with the spirit of understanding; he will pour forth the words of his wisdom and in prayer give thanks to the Lord. 7 He will direct his counsel and knowledge, and he will meditate in his secrets. 8 He will show the instruction which he has been taught and will glory in the law of the covenant of the Lord. 9 Many will commend his understanding. So long as the world endures, it won't be blotted out. His memory won't depart. His name will live from generation to generation. 10 Nations will declare his wisdom. The congregation will proclaim his praise. 11 If he continues, he will leave a greater name than a thousand. If he finally rests, it is enough for him. 12 Yet more I will utter, which I have thought about. I am filled like the full moon. 13 Listen to me, you holy children, and bud forth like a rose growing by a brook of water. 14 Give a sweet fragrance like frankincense. Put forth flowers like a lily. Scatter a sweet smell and sing a song of praise. Bless the Lord for all his works! 15 Magnify his name and give utterance to his praise with the songs on your lips and with harps! Say this when you utter his praise: 16 All the works of the Lord are exceedingly good, and every command will be done in its time. 17 No one can say, "What is this?" "Why is that?" for at the proper time they will all be sought out. At his word, the waters stood as a heap, as did the reservoirs of water at the word of his mouth. 18 At his command all his good pleasure is fulfilled. There is no one who can hinder his salvation. 19 The works of all flesh are before him. It's impossible to be hidden from his eyes. 20 He sees from everlasting to everlasting. There is nothing too wonderful for him. 21 No one can say, "What is this?" "Why is that?" for all things are created for their own uses. 22 His blessing covered the dry land as a river and saturated it as a flood. 23 As he has made the waters salty, so the heathen will inherit his wrath. 24 His ways are plain to the holy. They are stumbling blocks to the wicked. 25 Good things are created from the beginning for the good. So are evil things for sinners. 26 The main things necessary for the life of man are water, fire, iron, salt, wheat flour, and honey, milk, the blood of the grape, oil, and clothing. 27 All these things are for good to the godly, but for sinners, they will be turned into evils. 28 There are winds that are created for vengeance, and in their fury they lay on their scourges heavily. In the time of reckoning, they pour out their strength, and will appease the wrath of him who made them. 29 Fire, hail, famine, and death— all these are created for vengeance— 30 wild beasts' teeth, scorpions, adders, and a sword punishing the ungodly to destruction. 31 They will rejoice in his commandment, and will be made ready upon earth when needed. In their seasons, they won't disobey his command. 32 Therefore from the beginning I was convinced, and I thought it through and left it in writing: 33 All the works of the Lord are good. He will supply every need in its time. 34 No one can say, "This is worse than that," for they will all be well approved in their time. 35 Now with all your hearts and voices, sing praises and bless the Lord's name!

40

1 Great travail is created for every man. A heavy yoke is upon the sons of Adam, from the day of their coming forth from their mother's womb, until the day for their burial in the mother of all things. 2 The expectation of things to come, and the day of death, trouble their thoughts, and cause fear in their hearts. 3 From him who sits on a throne of glory, even to him who is humbled in earth and ashes, 4 from him who wears purple and a crown, even to him who is clothed in burlap, 5 there is wrath, jealousy, trouble, unrest, fear of death, anger, and strife. In the time of rest upon his bed, his night sleep changes his knowledge. 6 He gets little or no rest, and afterward in his sleep, as in a day of keeping watch, he is troubled in the vision of his heart, as one who has escaped from the front of battle. 7 In the very time of his deliverance, he awakens, and marvels that the fear is nothing. 8 To all creatures, human and animal, and upon sinners sevenfold more, 9 come death, bloodshed, strife, sword, calamities, famine, suffering, and plague. 10 All these things were created for the wicked, and because of them the flood came. 11 All things that are of the earth turn to the earth again. All things that are of the waters return into the sea. 12 All bribery and

injustice will be blotted out. Good faith will stand forever. 13 The goods of the unjust will be dried up like a river, and like a great thunder in rain will go off in noise. 14 In opening his hands, a man will be made glad; so lawbreakers will utterly fail. 15 The children of the ungodly won't grow many branches, and are as unhealthy roots on a sheer rock. 16 The reeds by every water or river bank will be plucked up before all grass. 17 Kindness is like a garden of blessings. Almsgiving endures forever. 18 The life of one who labors and is content will be made sweet. He who finds a treasure is better than both. 19 Children and the building of a city establish a name. A blameless wife is better than both. 20 Wine and music rejoice the heart. The love of wisdom is better than both. 21 The pipe and the lute make pleasant melody. A pleasant tongue is better than both. 22 Your eye desires grace and beauty, but the green shoots of grain more than both. 23 A friend and a companion is always welcome, and a wife with her husband is better than both. 24 Relatives and helpers are for a time of affliction, but almsgiving rescues better than both. 25 Gold and silver will make the foot stand sure, and counsel is esteemed better than both. 26 Riches and strength will lift up the heart. The fear of the Lord is better than both. There is nothing lacking in the fear of the Lord. In it, there is no need to seek help. 27 The fear of the Lord is like a garden of blessing and covers a man more than any glory. 28 My son, don't lead a beggar's life. It is better to die than to beg. 29 A man who looks to the table of another, his life is not to be considered a life. He will pollute his soul with another person's food, but a wise and well-instructed person will beware of that. 30 Begging will be sweet in the mouth of the shameless, but it kindles a fire in his belly.

41

1 O death, how bitter is the memory of you to a man who is at peace in his possessions, to the man who has nothing to distract him and has prosperity in all things, and who still has strength to enjoy food! 2 O death, your sentence is acceptable to a man who is needy and who fails in strength, who is in extreme old age, is distracted about all things, is perverse, and has lost patience! 3 Don't be afraid of the sentence of death. Remember those who

have been before you and who come after. This is the sentence from the Lord over all flesh. 4 And why do you refuse when it is the good pleasure of the Most High? Whether life lasts ten, or a hundred, or a thousand years, there is no inquiry about life in Hades. 5 The children of sinners are abominable children and they frequent the dwellings of the ungodly. 6 The inheritance of sinners' children will perish and with their posterity will be a perpetual disgrace. 7 Children will complain of an ungodly father, because they suffer disgrace because of him. 8 Woe to you, ungodly men, who have forsaken the law of the Most High God! 9 If you are born, you will be born to a curse. If you die, a curse will be your portion. 10 All things that are of the earth will go back to the earth; so the ungodly will go from a curse to perdition. 11 The mourning of men is about their bodies; but the evil name of sinners will be blotted out. 12 Have regard for your name, for it continues with you longer than a thousand great treasures of gold. 13 A good life has its number of days, but a good name continues forever. 14 My children, follow instruction in peace. But wisdom that is hidden and a treasure that is not seen, what benefit is in them both? 15 Better is a man who hides his foolishness than a man who hides his wisdom. 16 Therefore show respect for my words; for it is not good to retain every kind of shame. Not everything is approved by all in good faith. 17 Be ashamed of sexual immorality before father and mother, of a lie before a prince and a mighty man, 18 of an offense before a judge and ruler, of iniquity before the congregation and the people, of unjust dealing before a partner and friend, 19 and of theft in the place where you sojourn. Be ashamed in regard of the truth of God and his covenant, of leaning on your elbow at dinner, of contemptuous behavior in the matter of giving and taking, 20 of silence before those who greet you, of looking at a woman who is a prostitute, 21 of turning away your face from a kinsman, of taking away a portion or a gift, of gazing at a woman who has a husband, 22 of meddling with his maid—and don't come near her bed, of abusive speech to friends—and after you have given, don't insult, 23 of repeating and speaking what you have heard, and of revealing of secrets. 24 So you will be ashamed of the right things and find favor in the sight of every man.

42

1 Don't be ashamed of these things, and don't sin to save face: 2 of the law of the Most High and his covenant, of judgment to do justice to the ungodly, 3 of reckoning with a partner and with travellers, of a gift from the inheritance of friends, 4 of exactness of scales and weights, of getting much or little, 5 of bargaining dealing with merchants, of frequent correction of children, and of making the back of an evil slave to bleed. 6 A seal is good where an evil wife is. Where there are many hands, lock things up. 7 Whatever you hand over, let it be by number and weight. In giving and receiving, let all be in writing. 8 Don't be ashamed to instruct the unwise and foolish, and one of extreme old age who contends with those who are young. So you will be well instructed indeed and approved in the sight of every living man. 9 A daughter is a secret cause of wakefulness to a father. Care for her takes away sleep— in her youth, lest she pass the flower of her age; when she is married, lest she should be hated; 10 in her virginity, lest she should be defiled and be with child in her father's house; when she has a husband, lest she should transgress; and when she is married, lest she should be barren. 11 Keep a strict watch over a headstrong daughter, lest she make you a laughingstock to your enemies, a byword in the city and notorious among the people, and shame you in public. 12 Don't gaze at every beautiful body. Don't sit in the midst of women. 13 For from garments comes a moth, and from a woman comes a woman's wickedness. 14 Better is the wickedness of a man than a pleasant woman, a woman who puts you to shame and disgrace. 15 I will make mention now of the works of the Lord, and will declare the things that I have seen. The Lord's works are in his words. 16 The sun that gives light looks at all things. The Lord's work is full of his glory. 17 The Lord has not given power to the saints to declare all his marvelous works, which the Almighty Lord firmly settled, that the universe might be established in his glory. 18 He searches out the deep and the heart. He has understanding of their secrets. For the Most High knows all knowledge. He sees the signs of the world. 19 He declares the things that are past

and the things that shall be, and reveals the traces of hidden things. ²⁰ No thought escapes him. There is not a word hidden from him. ²¹ He has ordered the mighty works of his wisdom. He is from everlasting to everlasting. Nothing has been added to them, nor diminished from them. He had no need of any counselor. ²² How desirable are all his works! One may see this even in a spark. ²³ All these things live and remain forever in all manner of uses. They are all obedient. ²⁴ All things are in pairs, one opposite the other. He has made nothing imperfect. ²⁵ One thing establishes the good things of another. Who could ever see enough of his glory?

43

¹ The pride of the heavenly heights is the clear sky, the appearance of heaven, in the spectacle of its glory. ² The sun, when it appears, bringing tidings as it rises, is a marvelous instrument, the work of the Most High. ³ At noon, it dries up the land. Who can stand against its burning heat? ⁴ A man tending a furnace is in burning heat, but the sun three times more, burning up the mountains, breathing out fiery vapors, and sending out bright beams, it blinds the eyes ⁵ Great is the Lord who made it. At his word, he hastens on its course. ⁶ The moon marks the changing seasons, declares times, and is a sign for the world. ⁷ From the moon is the sign of feast days, a light that wanes when it completes its course. ⁸ The month is called after its name, increasing wonderfully in its changing— an instrument of the army on high, shining in the structure of heaven, ⁹ the beauty of heaven, the glory of the stars, an ornament giving light in the highest places of the Lord. ¹⁰ At the word of the Holy One, they will stand in due order. They won't faint in their watches. ¹¹ Look at the rainbow, and praise him who made it. It is exceedingly beautiful in its brightness. ¹² It encircles the sky with its glorious circle. The hands of the Most High have stretched it out. ¹³ By his commandment, he makes the snow fall and swiftly sends the lightnings of his judgment. ¹⁴ Therefore the storehouses are opened, and clouds fly out like birds. ¹⁵ By his mighty power, he makes the clouds strong and the hailstones are broken in pieces. ¹⁶ At his appearing, the mountains will be shaken. At his will, the south wind will blow. ¹⁷ The voice of

his thunder rebukes the earth. So does the northern storm and the whirlwind. Like birds flying down, he sprinkles the snow. It falls down like the lighting of locusts. 18 The eye is dazzled at the beauty of its whiteness. The heart is amazed as it falls. 19 He also pours out frost on the earth like salt. When it is freezes, it has points like thorns. 20 The cold north wind blows and ice freezes on the water. It settles on every pool of water. The water puts it on like it was a breastplate. 21 It will devour the mountains, burn up the wilderness, and consume the green grass like fire. 22 A mist coming speedily heals all things. A dew coming after heat brings cheerfulness. 23 By his counsel, he has calmed the deep and planted islands in it. 24 Those who sail on the sea tell of its dangers. We marvel when we hear it with our ears. 25 There are also those strange and wondrous works in it— variety of all that has life and the huge creatures of the sea. 26 Because of him, his messengers succeed. By his word, all things hold together. 27 We may say many things, but couldn't say enough. The summary of our words is, "He is everything!" 28 How could we have strength to glorify him? For he is himself the greater than all his works. 29 The Lord is awesome and exceedingly great! His power is marvelous! 30 Glorify the Lord and exalt him as much as you can! For even yet, he will surpass that. When you exalt him, summon your full strength. Don't be weary, because you can't praise him enough. 31 Who has seen him, that he may describe him? Who can magnify him as he is? 32 Many things greater than these are hidden, for we have seen just a few of his works. 33 For the Lord made all things. He gave wisdom to the godly.

44

1 Let us now praise famous men, our ancestors in their generations. 2 The Lord created great glory in them— his mighty power from the beginning. 3 Some ruled in their kingdoms and were men renowned for their power, giving counsel by their understanding. Some have spoken in prophecies, 4 leaders of the people by their counsels, and by their understanding, giving instruction for the people. Their words in their instruction were wise. 5 Some composed musical tunes, and set forth verses in writing, 6 rich men endowed with ability, living peaceably in their homes. 7 All these were honored

in their generations, and were outstanding in their days. ⁸ Some of them have left a name behind them, so that others declare their praises. ⁹ But of others, there is no memory. They perished as though they had not been. They become as though they had not been born, they and their children after them. ¹⁰ But these were men of mercy, whose righteous deeds have not been forgotten. ¹¹ A good inheritance remains with their offspring. Their children are within the covenant. ¹² Their offspring stand fast, with their children, for their sakes. ¹³ Their offspring will remain forever. Their glory won't be blotted out. ¹⁴ Their bodies were buried in peace. Their name lives to all generations. ¹⁵ People will declare their wisdom. The congregation proclaims their praise. ¹⁶ Enoch pleased the Lord, and was taken up, an example of repentance to all generations. ¹⁷ Noah was found perfect and righteous. In the season of wrath, he kept the race alive. Therefore a remnant was left on the earth when the flood came. ¹⁸ Everlasting covenants were made with him, that all flesh should no more be blotted out by a flood. ¹⁹ Abraham was a great father of a multitude of nations.

There was none found like him in glory, ²⁰ who kept the law of the Most High, and was taken into covenant with him. In his flesh he established the covenant. When he was tested, he was found faithful. ²¹ Therefore he assured him by an oath that the nations would be blessed through his offspring, that he would multiply him like the dust of the earth, exalt his offspring like the stars, and cause them to inherit from sea to sea, and from the Euphrates River to the utmost parts of the earth. ²² In Isaac also, he established the same assurance for Abraham his father's sake, the blessing of all men, and the covenant. ²³ He made it rest upon the head of Jacob. He acknowledged him in his blessings, gave to him by inheritance, and divided his portions. He distributed them among twelve tribes.

45

¹ He brought out of him a man of mercy, who found favor in the sight of all people, a man loved by God and men, even Moses, whose memory is blessed. ² He made him equal to the glory of the saints, and magnified him in the fears of his enemies. ³ By his words he caused the wonders to cease. God glorified him in the

sight of kings. He gave him commandments for his people and showed him part of his glory. 4 He sanctified him in his faithfulness and meekness. He chose him out of all people. 5 He made him to hear his voice, led him into the thick darkness, and gave him commandments face to face, even the law of life and knowledge, that he might teach Jacob the covenant, and Israel his judgments. 6 He exalted Aaron, a holy man like Moses, even his brother, of the tribe of Levi. 7 He established an everlasting covenant with him, and gave him the priesthood of the people. He blessed him with stateliness, and dressed him in a glorious robe. 8 He clothed him in perfect splendor, and strengthened him with symbols of authority: the linen trousers, the long robe, and the ephod. 9 He encircled him with pomegranates; with many golden bells around him, to make a sound as he went, to make a sound that might be heard in the temple, for a reminder for the children of his people; 10 with a holy garment, with gold, blue, and purple, the work of the embroiderer; with an oracle of judgment—Urim and Thummim; 11 with twisted scarlet, the work of the craftsman; with precious stones engraved like a signet, in a setting of gold, the work of the jeweller, for a reminder engraved in writing, after the number of the tribes of Israel; 12 with a crown of gold upon the mitre, having engraved on it, as on a signet, "holiness", an ornament of honor, the work of an expert, the desires of the eyes, goodly and beautiful. 13 Before him there never have been anything like it. No stranger put them on, but only his sons and his offspring perpetually. 14 His sacrifices shall be wholly burned, twice every day continually. 15 Moses consecrated him, and anointed him with holy oil. It was an everlasting covenant with him and to his offspring, all the days of heaven, to minister to the Lord, to serve as a priest, and to bless his people in his name. 16 He chose him out of all living to offer sacrifice to the Lord— incense, and a sweet fragrance, for a memorial, to make atonement for your people. 17 He gave to him in his commandments, authority in the covenants of judgments, to teach Jacob the testimonies, and to enlighten Israel in his law. 18 Strangers conspired against him and envied him in the wilderness: Dathan and Abiram with their company, and the congregation of Korah, with wrath and anger. ¹⁹ The Lord saw it, and it displeased him. In the wrath of his anger, they were destroyed. He did wonders upon them, to consume them with flaming fire. ²⁰ He added glory to Aaron, and gave him a heritage. He divided to him the first fruits of the increase, and prepared bread of first fruits in abundance. ²¹ For they eat the sacrifices of the Lord, which he gave to him and to his offspring. ²² However, in the land of the people, he has no inheritance, and he has no portion among the people, for the Lord himself is your portion and inheritance. ²³ Phinehas the son of Eleazar is the third in glory, in that he was zealous in the fear of the Lord, and stood fast when the people turned away, and he made atonement for Israel. ²⁴ Therefore, a covenant of peace was established for him, that he should be leader of the sanctuary and of his people, that he and his offspring should have the dignity of the priesthood forever. ²⁵ Also he made a covenant with David the son of Jesse, of the tribe of Judah. The inheritance of the king is his alone from son to son. So the inheritance of Aaron is also to his seed. ²⁶ May God give you wisdom in your heart to judge his people in righteousness, that their good things may not be abolished, and that their glory may endure for all their generations.

46

¹ Joshua the son of Nun was valiant in war, and was the successor of Moses in prophecies. He was made great according to his name for the saving of God's elect, to take vengeance on the enemies that rose up against them, that he might give Israel their inheritance. ² How was he glorified in the lifting up his hands, and in stretching out his sword against the cities! ³Who before him stood so firm? For the Lord himself brought his enemies to him. ⁴ Didn't the sun go back by his hand? Didn't one day become as two? ⁵ He called upon the Most High, the Mighty One, when his foes pressed in all around him, and the great Lord heard him. ⁶ With hailstones of mighty power, he caused war to break violently upon the nation, and on the slope he destroyed those who resisted, so that the nations might know his armor, how he fought in the sight of the Lord; for he followed the Mighty

One. [7] Also in the time of Moses, he did a work of mercy— he and Caleb the son of Jephunneh— in that they withstood the adversary, hindered the people from sin, and stilled their wicked complaining. [8] And of six hundred thousand people on foot, they two alone were preserved to bring them into their inheritance, into a land flowing with milk and honey. [9] The Lord gave strength to Caleb, and it remained with him to his old age, so that he entered the hill country, and his offspring obtained it for an inheritance, [10] that all the children of Israel might see that it is good to follow the Lord. [11] Also the judges, every one by his name, all whose hearts didn't engage in immorality, and who didn't turn away from the Lord may their memory be blessed! [12] May their bones flourish again out of their place. May the name of those who have been honored be renewed in their children. [13] Samuel, the prophet of the Lord, loved by his Lord, established a kingdom and anointed princes over his people. [14] By the law of the Lord he judged the congregation, and the Lord watched over Jacob. [15] By his faithfulness he was proved to be a prophet. By his words he was known to be faithful in vision. [16] When his enemies pressed on him one very side, he called upon the Lord, the Mighty One, with the offering of the suckling lamb. [17] Then the Lord thundered from heaven. He made his voice heard with a mighty sound. [18] He utterly destroyed the rulers of the Tyrians and all the princes of the Philistines. [19] Before the time of his age-long sleep, he testified in the sight of the lord and his anointed, "I have not taken any man's goods, so much as a sandal;" and no one accused him. [20] Even after he fell asleep, he prophesied, and showed the king his end, and lifted up his voice from the earth in prophecy, to blot out the wickedness of the people.

47

[1] After him, Nathan rose up to prophesy in the days of David. [2] As is the fat when it is separated from the peace offering, so was David separated from the children of Israel. [3] He played with lions as with kids, and with bears as with lambs of the flock. [4] In his youth didn't he kill a giant, and take away reproach from the people when he lifted up his hand with a sling stone, and beat down the boasting

Goliath? 5 For he called upon the Most High Lord, and he gave him strength in his right hand to kill a man mighty in war, to exalt the horn of his people. 6 So they glorified him for his tens of thousands, and praised him for the blessings of the Lord, in that a glorious diadem was given to him. 7 For he destroyed the enemies on every side, and defeated the Philistines his adversaries. He broke their horn in pieces to this day. 8 In every work of his he gave thanks to the Holy One Most High with words of glory. He sang praise with his whole heart, and loved him who made him. 9 He set singers before the altar, to make sweet melody by their music. 10 He gave beauty to the feasts, and set in order the seasons to completion while they praised his holy name, and the sanctuary resounded from early morning. 11 The Lord took away his sins, and exalted his horn forever. He gave him a covenant of kings, and a glorious throne in Israel. 12 After him a wise son rose up, who because of him lived in security. 13 Solomon reigned in days of peace. God gave him rest all around, that he might set up a house for his name, and prepare a sanctuary forever. 14 How wise you were made in your youth, and filled as a river with understanding! 15 Your influence covered the earth, and you filled it with parables and riddles. 16 Your name reached to the far away islands, and you were loved for your peace. 17 For your songs, proverbs, parables, and interpretations, the countries marveled at you. 18 By the name of the Lord God, who is called the God of Israel, you gathered gold like tin, and multiplied silver like lead. 19 You bowed your loins to women, and in your body you were brought into subjection. 20 You blemished your honor, and defiled your offspring, to bring wrath upon your children. I was grieved for your folly, 21 because the sovereignty was divided, and a disobedient kingdom ruled out of Ephraim. 22 But the Lord will never forsake his mercy. He won't destroy any of his works, nor blot out the posterity of his elect. He won't take away the offspring him who loved him. He gave a remnant to Jacob, and to David a root from his own family. 23 So Solomon rested with his fathers. Of his offspring, he left behind him Rehoboam, the foolishness of the people, and one who lacked understanding, who made the people revolt by his counsel. Also Jeroboam the son of Nebat, who made Israel to sin, and gave a way of sin to Ephraim. 24 Their sins were multiplied exceedingly, until they were removed from their land. 25 For they sought out all manner of wickedness, until vengeance came upon them.

48

1 Then Elijah arose, the prophet like fire. His word burned like a torch. 2 He brought a famine upon them, and by his zeal made them few in number. 3 By the word of the Lord he shut up the heavens. He brought down fire three times. 4 How you were glorified, O Elijah, in your wondrous deeds! Whose glory is like yours? 5 You raised up a dead man from death, from Hades, by the word of the Most High. 6 You brought down kings to destruction, and honorable men from their sickbeds. 7 You heard rebuke in Sinai, and judgments of vengeance in Horeb. 8 You anointed kings for retribution, and prophets to succeed after you. 9 You were taken up in a tempest of fire, in a chariot of fiery horses. 10 You were recorded for reproofs in their seasons, to pacify anger, before it broke out into wrath, to turn the heart of the father to the son, and to restore the tribes of Jacob. 11 Blessed are those who saw you, and those who have been beautified with love; for we also shall surely live. 12 Elijah was wrapped in a whirlwind. Elisha was filled with his spirit. In his days he was not moved by the fear of any ruler, and no one brought him into subjection. 13 Nothing was too hard for him. When he was buried, his body prophesied. 14 As in his life he did wonders, so his works were also marvelous in death. 15 For all this the people didn't repent. They didn't depart from their sins, until they were carried away as a plunder from their land, and were scattered through all the earth. The people were left very few in number, but with a ruler from the house of David. 16 Some of them did that which was right, but some multiplied sins. 17 Hezekiah fortified his city, and brought water into its midst. He tunneled through rock with iron, and built cisterns for water. 18 In his days Sennacherib invaded, and sent Rabshakeh, and departed. He lifted up his hand against Zion, and boasted great things in his arrogance. 19 Then their hearts and their hands were shaken, and they were in pain, as women in labor. 20 But they called upon the Lord who is merciful, spreading

out their hands to him. The Holy One quickly heard them out of Heaven, and delivered them by the hand of Isaiah. 21 He struck the camp of the Assyrians, and his angel utterly destroyed them. 22 For Hezekiah did that which was pleasing to the Lord, and was strong in the ways of his ancestor David, which Isaiah the prophet commanded, who was great and faithful in his vision. 23 In his days the sun went backward. He prolonged the life of the king. 24 He saw by an excellent spirit what would come to pass in the future; and he comforted those who mourned in Zion. 25 He showed the things that would happen through the end of time, and the hidden things before they came. 49 1 The memory of Josiah is like the composition of incense prepared by the work of the perfumer. It will be sweet as honey in every mouth, and like music at a banquet of wine. 2 He did what was right in the reforming of the people, and took away the abominations of iniquity. 3 He set his heart right toward the Lord. In lawless days, he made godliness prevail. 4 Except David, Hezekiah, and Josiah, all were wicked, because they abandoned the law of the Most High. The kings of Judah came to an end. 5 They gave their power to others, and their glory to a foreign nation. 6 They set the chosen city of the sanctuary on fire and made her streets desolate, as it was written by the hand of Jeremiah. 7 For they mistreated him; yet he was sanctified in the womb to be a prophet, to root out, to afflict, to destroy and likewise to build and to plant. 8 Ezekiel saw the vision of glory, which God showed him on the chariot of the cherubim. 9 For truly he remembered the enemies in rainstorm, and to do good to those who directed their ways aright. 10 Also of the twelve prophets, may their bones flourish again out of their place. He comforted the people of Jacob, and delivered them by confident hope. 11 How shall we magnify Zerubbabel? He was like a signet ring on the right hand. 12 So was Jesus the son of Josedek, who in their days built the house, and exalted a‡ people holy to the Lord, prepared for everlasting glory. 13 Also of Nehemiah the memory is great. He raised up for us fallen walls, set up the gates and bars, and rebuilt our houses. 14 No man was created upon the earth like Enoch, for he was taken up from the earth. 15 Nor was there a man born like Joseph, a leader of his kindred, a supporter of the people. Even his bones were cared for. ¹⁶ Shem and Seth were honored among men, but above every living thing in the creation was Adam.

50

¹ It was Simon, the son of Onias, the high priest, who in his life repaired the house, and in his days strengthened the temple. ² The foundation was built by him to the height of the double walls, the lofty retaining walls of the temple enclosure. ³ In his days, a water cistern was dug, the brazen vessel like the sea in circumference. ⁴ He planned to save his people from ruin, and fortified the city against siege. ⁵ How glorious he was when the people gathered around him as he came out of the house of the veil! ⁶ He was like the morning star among clouds, like the full moon, ⁷ like the sunshining on the temple of the Most High, like the rainbow shining in clouds of glory, ⁸ like roses in the days of first fruits, like lilies by a water spring, like the shoot of the frankincense tree in summer time, ⁹ like fire and incense in the censer, like a vessel of beaten gold adorned with all kinds of precious stones, ¹⁰ like an olive tree loaded with fruit, and like a cypress growing high among the clouds. ¹¹ When he put on his glorious robe, and clothed himself in perfect splendor, ascending to the holy altar, he made the court of the sanctuary glorious. ¹² When he received the portions out of the priests' hands, as he stood by the hearth of the altar, with his kindred like a garland around him, he was like a young cedar in Lebanon surrounded by the trunks of palm trees. ¹³ All the sons of Aaron in their glory, held the Lord's offering in their hands before all the congregation of Israel. ¹⁴ Finishing the service at the altars, that he might arrange the offering of the Most High, the Almighty, ¹⁵ he stretched out his hand to the cup of libation, and poured out the cup of the grape. He poured it out at the foot of the altar, a sweet smelling fragrance to the Most High, the King of all. ¹⁶ Then the sons of Aaron shouted. They sounded the trumpets of beaten work. They made a great fanfare to be heard, for a reminder before the Most High. ¹⁷ Then all the people together hurried, and fell down to the ground on their faces to worship their Lord, the Almighty, God Most High. ¹⁸ The singers also praised him with their voices.

There was a sweet melody in the whole house. ¹⁹ And the people implored the Lord Most High, in prayer before him who is merciful, until the worship of the Lord was finished, and so they accomplished his service. ²⁰ Then he went down, and lifted up his hands over the whole congregation of the children of Israel, to give blessing to the Lord with his lips, and to glory in his name. ²¹ He bowed himself down in worship the second time, to declare the blessing from the Most High. ²² Now bless the God of all, who everywhere does great things, who exalts our days from the womb, and deals with us according to his mercy. ²³ May he grant us joyfulness of heart, and that peace may be in our days in Israel for the days of eternity, ²⁴ to entrust his mercy with us, and let him deliver us in his time! ²⁵ With two nations my soul is vexed, and the third is no nation: ²⁶ Those who sit on the mountain of Samaria, the Philistines, and the foolish people who live in Shechem. ²⁷ I have written in this book the instruction of understanding and knowledge, I Jesus, the son of Sirach Eleazar, of Jerusalem, who out of his heart poured forth wisdom. ²⁸ Blessed is he who will exercise

these things. He who lays them up in his heart will become wise. ²⁹ For if he does them, he will be strong in all things, for the light of the Lord is his guide.

51

A Prayer of Jesus the son of Sirach. ¹ I will give thanks to you, O Lord, O King, and will praise you, O God my Savior. I give thanks to your name, ² for you have been my protector and helper, and delivered my body out of destruction, and out of the snare of a slanderous tongue, from lips that fabricate lies. You were my helper before those who stood by, ³ and delivered me, according to the abundance of your mercy and of your name, from the gnashings of teeth ready to devour, out of the hand of those seeking my life, out of the many afflictions I endured, ⁴ from the choking of a fire on every side, and out of the midst of fire that I hadn't kindled, ⁵ out of the depth of the belly of Hades, from an unclean tongue, and from lying words— ⁶ the slander of an unrighteous tongue to the king. My soul drew near to death. My life was near to Hades. ⁷ They surrounded me on every side. There was no one to help me. I was looking for human help, and there was none. ⁸ Then

I remembered your mercy, O Lord, and your working which has been from everlasting, how you deliver those who wait for you, and save them out of the hand of their enemies. ⁹ I lifted up my prayer from the earth, and prayed for deliverance from death. ¹⁰ I called upon the Lord, the Father of my Lord, that he would not forsake me in the days of affliction, in the time when there was no help against the proud. ¹¹ I will praise your name continually. I will sing praise with thanksgiving. My prayer was heard. ¹² You saved me from destruction and delivered me from the evil time. Therefore I will give thanks and praise to you, and bless the name of the Lord. ¹³ When I was yet young, before I went abroad, I sought wisdom openly in my prayer. ¹⁴ Before the temple I asked for her. I will seek her out even to the end. ¹⁵ From the first flower to the ripening grape my heart delighted in her. My foot walked in uprightness. From my youth I followed her steps. ¹⁶ I inclined my ear a little, and received her, and found for myself much instruction. ¹⁷ I profited in her. I will give glory to him who gives me wisdom. ¹⁸ For I determined to practice her. I was zealous for that which is good. I will never be put to shame. ¹⁹ My soul has wrestled with her. In my conduct I was exact. I spread out my hands to the heaven above, and bewailed my ignorances of her. ²⁰ I directed my soul to her. In purity I found her. I got myself a heart joined with her from the beginning. Therefore I won't be forsaken. ²¹ My belly also was troubled to seek her. Therefore I have gained a good possession. ²² The Lord gave me a tongue for my reward. I will praise him with it. ²³ Draw near to me, all you who are uneducated, and live in the house of instruction. ²⁴ Why therefore are you all lacking in these things, and your souls are very thirsty? ²⁵ I opened my mouth and spoke, "Get her for yourselves without money." ²⁶ Put your neck under the yoke, and let your soul receive instruction. She is near to find. ²⁷ See with your eyes how that I labored just a little and found for myself much rest. ²⁸ Get instruction with a great sum of silver, and gain much gold by her. ²⁹ May your soul rejoice in his mercy, and may you all not be put to shame in praising him. ³⁰ Work your work before the time comes, and in his time he will give you your reward.

The Book of Baruch

This book is traditionally attributed to Baruch, the scribe and devoted follower of the prophet Jeremiah. This text serves as an important bridge connecting the prophetic literature of the Old Testament with the theological reflections emerging during and after the Babylonian Exile. Written in the late 6th century BCE or later, the Book of Baruch addresses the Jews in exile, offering a theological interpretation of their suffering and displacement as a consequence of their disobedience to God's commandments.

The book comprises a series of reflections, confessions, and exhortations, urging the people of Israel to repent and adhere steadfastly to the law of the Lord. It starts with a public reading of the text, followed by the people's confession of sins and acknowledgment of God's justice in their punishment. This framework highlights a central theme of the text: the idea that true wisdom and life come from God and adherence to His laws.

Baruch's writings also include a series of poems and prayers that lament the destruction of Jerusalem and the Temple, but also emphasize hope and divine mercy. These elements reflect a deep engagement with themes of exile and restoration that resonate throughout biblical prophetic literature. The text's poetic lament over Jerusalem is particularly poignant and serves as a focal point for its call to penitence and spiritual renewal.

In addition to its religious messages, the Book of Baruch also touches upon themes of wisdom, contrasting the idols of the nations with the wisdom of Israel's God. This theological discourse provides a broader context for understanding Israel's suffering and frames it within the wisdom tradition that seeks to elucidate the ways of God to humanity.

The inclusion of Baruch in the Apocrypha enriches the biblical canon by providing insights into the Jewish religious mindset during one of its most critical periods. It offers profound reflections on the nature of sin, the importance of repentance, and the enduring mercy of God, themes that are universal and perennial in the religious life of the community. The book not only contributes to the theological and liturgical life of the community but also enhances the literary and cultural heritage of biblical literature, making it a significant work for both historical study and contemporary reflection.

The Book of Baruch

1 And these are the words of the book, which Baruch the son of Nerias, the son of Maasias, the son of Sedecias, the son of Asadias, the son of Chelcias, wrote in Babylon, 2 In the fifth year, and in the seventh day of the month, what time as the Chaldeans took Jerusalem, and burnt it with fire. 3 And Baruch did read the words of this book in the hearing of Jechonias the son of Joachim king of Juda, and in the ears of all the people that came to hear the book, 4 And in the hearing of the nobles, and of the king's sons, and in the hearing of the elders, and of all the people, from the lowest unto the highest, even of all them that dwelt at Babylon by the river Sud. 5 Whereupon they wept, fasted, and prayed before the Lord. 6 They made also a collection of money according to every man's power: 7 And they sent it to Jerusalem unto Joachim the high priest, the son of Chelcias, son of Salom, and to the priests, and to all the people which were found with him at Jerusalem, 8 At the same time when he received the vessels of the house of the Lord, that were carried out of the temple, to return them into the land of Juda, the tenth day of the month Sivan, namely, silver vessels, which Sedecias the son of Josias king of Juda had made, 9 After that Nabuchodonosor king of Babylon had carried away Jechonias, and the princes, and the captives, and the mighty men, and the people of the land, from Jerusalem, and brought them unto Babylon. 10 And they said, Behold, we have sent you money to buy you burnt offerings, and sin offerings, and incense, and prepare ye manna, and offer upon the altar of the Lord our God; 11 And pray for the life of Nabuchodonosor king of Babylon, and for the life of Balthasar his son, that their days may be upon earth as the days of heaven: 12 And the Lord will giveus strength, and lighten our eyes, and we shall live under the shadow of Nabuchodonosor king of Babylon, and under the shadow of Balthasar his son, and we shall serve them many days, and find favour in their sight. 13 Pray for us also unto the Lord our God, for we have sinned against the Lord our God; and unto this day the fury of the Lord and his wrath is not turned from us. 14 And ye shall read this book which we have sent unto you, to make confession in the house of the Lord, upon the feasts and

solemn days. 15 And ye shall say, To the Lord our God belongeth righteousness, but unto us the confusion of faces, as it is come to pass this day, unto them of Juda, and to the inhabitants of Jerusalem, 16 And to our kings, and to our princes, and to our priests, and to our prophets, and to our fathers: 17 For we have sinned before the Lord, 18 And disobeyed him, and have not hearkened unto the voice of the Lord our God, to walk in the commandments that he gave us openly: 19 Since the day that the Lord brought our forefathers out of the land of Egypt, unto this present day, we have been disobedient unto the Lord our God, and we have been negligent in not hearing his voice. 20 Wherefore the evils cleaved unto us, and the curse, which the Lord appointed by Moses his servant at the time that he brought our fathers out of the land of Egypt, to give us a land that floweth with milk and honey, like as it is to see this day. 21 Nevertheless we have not hearkened unto the voice of the Lord our God, according unto all the words of the prophets, whom he sent unto us: 22 But every man followed the imagination of his own wicked heart, to serve strange gods, and to do evil in the sight of the Lord our God.

2

1 Therefore the Lord hath made good his word, which he pronounced against us, and against our judges that judged Israel, and against our kings, and against our princes, and against the men of Israel and Juda, 2 To bring upon us great plagues, such as never happened under the whole heaven, as it came to pass in Jerusalem, according to the things that were written in the law of Moses; 3 That a man should eat the flesh of his own son, and the flesh of his own daughter. 4 Moreover he hath delivered them to be in subjection to all the kingdoms that are round about us, to be as a reproach and desolation among all the people round about, where the Lord hath scattered them. 5 Thus we were cast down, and not exalted, because we have sinned against the Lord our God, and have not been obedient unto his voice. 6 To the Lord our God appertaineth righteousness: but unto us and to our fathers open shame, as appeareth this day. 7 For all these plagues are come upon us, which the Lord hath pronounced against us 8 Yet have we not prayed before the Lord,

that we might turn every one from the imaginations of his wicked heart. ⁹ Wherefore the Lord watched over us for evil, and the Lord hath brought it upon us: for the Lord is righteous in all his works which he hath commanded us. ¹⁰ Yet we have not hearkened unto his voice, to walk in the commandments of the Lord, that he hath set before us. ¹¹ And now, O Lord God of Israel, that hast brought thy people out of the land of Egypt with a mighty hand, and high arm, and with signs, and with wonders, and with great power, and hast gotten thyself a name, as appeareth this day: ¹² O Lord our God, we have sinned, we have done ungodly, we have dealt unrighteously in all thine ordinances. ¹³ Let thy wrath turn from us: for we are but a few left among the heathen, where thou hast scattered us. ¹⁴ Hear our prayers, O Lord, and our petitions, and deliver us for thine own sake, and give us favour in the sight of them which have led us away: ¹⁵ That all the earth may know that thou art the Lord our God, because Israel and his posterity is called by thy name. ¹⁶ O Lord, look down from thine holy house, and consider us: bow down thine ear, O Lord, to hear us. ¹⁷ Open thine eyes, and behold; for the dead that are in the graves, whose souls are taken from their bodies, will give unto the Lord neither praise nor righteousness: ¹⁸ But the soul that is greatly vexed, which goeth stooping and feeble, and the eyes that fail, and the hungry soul, will give thee praise and righteousness, O Lord. ¹⁹ Therefore we do not make our humble supplication before thee, O Lord our God, for the righteousness of our fathers, and of our kings. ²⁰ For thou hast sent out thy wrath and indignation upon us, as thou hast spoken by thy servants the prophets, saying, ²¹ Thus saith the Lord, Bow down your shoulders to serve the king of Babylon: so shall ye remain in the land that I gave unto your fathers. ²² But if ye will not hear the voice of the Lord, to serve the king of Babylon, ²³ I will cause to cease out of the cites of Judah, and from without Jerusalem, the voice of mirth, and the voice of joy, the voice of the bridegroom, and the voice of the bride: and the whole land shall be desolate of inhabitants. ²⁴ But we would not hearken unto thy voice, to serve the king of Babylon: therefore hast thou made good the words that thou spakest by thy servants the prophets, namely, that the bones of our kings, and the bones of our fathers, should be taken out of their place. 25 And, lo, they are cast out to the heat of the day, and to the frost of the night, and they died in great miseries by famine, by sword, and by pestilence. 26 And the house which is called by thy name hast thou laid waste, as it is to be seen this day, for the wickedness of the house of Israel and the house of Juda. 27 O Lord our God, thou hast dealt with us after all thy goodness, and according to all that great mercy of thine, 28 As thou spakest by thy servant Moses in the day when thou didst command him to write the law before the children of Israel, saying, 29 If ye will not hear my voice, surely this very great multitude shall be turned into a small number among the nations, where I will scatter them. 30 For I knew that they would not hear me, because it is a stiff necked people: but in the land of their captivities they shall remember themselves. 31 And shall know that I am the Lord their God: for I will give them an heart, and ears to hear: 32 And they shall praise me in the land of their captivity, and think upon my name, 33 And return from their stiff neck, and from their wicked deeds: for they shall remember the way of their fathers, which sinned before the Lord. 34 And I will bring them again into the land which I promised with an oath unto their fathers, Abraham, Isaac, and Jacob, and they shall be lords of it: and I will increase them, and they shall not be diminished. 35 And I will make an everlasting covenant with them to be their God, and they shall be my people: and I will no more drive my people of Israel out of the land that I have given them.

3

1 O Lord Almighty, God of Israel, the soul in anguish the troubled spirit, crieth unto thee. 2 Hear, O Lord, and have mercy; for thou art merciful: and have pity upon us, because we have sinned before thee. 3 For thou endurest for ever, and we perish utterly. 4 O Lord Almighty, thou God of Israel, hear now the prayers of the dead Israelites, and of their children, which have sinned before thee, and not hearkened unto the voice of thee their God: for the which cause these plagues cleave unto us. 5 Remember not the iniquities of our forefathers: but think upon thy power and thy name now at

this time. 6 For thou art the Lord our God, and thee, O Lord, will we praise. 7 And for this cause thou hast put thy fear in our hearts, to the intent that we should call upon thy name, and praise thee in our captivity: for we have called to mind all the iniquity of our forefathers, that sinned before thee. 8 Behold, we are yet this day in our captivity, where thou hast scattered us, for a reproach and a curse, and to be subject to payments, according to all the iniquities of our fathers, which departed from the Lord our God. 9 Hear, Israel, the commandments of life: give ear to understand wisdom. 10 How happeneth it Israel, that thou art in thine enemies' land, that thou art waxen old in a strange country, that thou art defiled with the dead, 11 That thou art counted with them that go down into the grave? 12 Thou hast forsaken the fountain of wisdom. 13 For if thou hadst walked in the way of God, thou shouldest have dwelled in peace for ever. 14 Learn where is wisdom, where is strength, where is understanding; that thou mayest know also where is length of days, and life, where is the light of the eyes, and peace. 15 Who hath found out her place? or who hath come into her treasures? 16 Where are the princes of the heathen become, and such as ruled the beasts upon the earth; 17 They that had their pastime with the fowls of the air, and they that hoarded up silver and gold, wherein men trust, and made no end of their getting? 18 For they that wrought in silver, and were so careful, and whose works are unsearchable, 19 They are vanished and gone down to the grave, and others are come up in their steads. 20 Young men have seen light, and dwelt upon the earth: but the way of knowledge have they not known, 21 Nor understood the paths thereof, nor laid hold of it: their children were far off from that way. 22 It hath not been heard of in Chanaan, neither hath it been seen in Theman. 23 The Agarenes that seek wisdom upon earth, the merchants of Meran and of Theman, the authors of fables, and searchers out of understanding; none of these have known the way of wisdom, or remember her paths. 24 O Israel, how great is the house of God! and how large is the place of his possession! 25 Great, and hath none end; high, and unmeasurable. 26 There were the giants famous from the beginning, that were of so great stature, and so expert in war. 27 Those did not the Lord choose, neither gave he the way of knowledge unto them: 28 But they were destroyed, because they had no wisdom, and perished through their own foolishness. 29 Who hath gone up into heaven, and taken her, and brought her down from the clouds? 30 Who hath gone over the sea, and found her, and will bring her for pure gold? 31 No man knoweth her way, nor thinketh of her path. 32 But he that knoweth all things knoweth her, and hath found her out with his understanding: he that prepared the earth for evermore hath filled it with four footed beasts: 33 He that sendeth forth light, and it goeth, calleth it again, and it obeyeth him with fear. 34 The stars shined in their watches, and rejoiced: when he calleth them, they say, Here we be; and so with cheerfulness they shewed light unto him that made them. 35 This is our God, and there shall none other be accounted of in comparison of him 36 He hath found out all the way of knowledge, and hath given it unto Jacob his servant, and to Israel his beloved. 37 Afterward did he shew himself upon earth, and conversed with men.

4

1 This is the book of the commandments of God, and the law that endureth for ever: all they that keep it shall come to life; but such as leave it shall die. 2 Turn thee, O Jacob, and take hold of it: walk in the presence of the light thereof, that thou mayest be illuminated. 3 Give not thine honour to another, nor the things that are profitable unto thee to a strange nation. 4 O Israel, happy are we: for things that are pleasing to God are made known unto us. 5 Be of good cheer, my people, the memorial of Israel. 6 Ye were sold to the nations, not for your destruction: but because ye moved God to wrath, ye were delivered unto the enemies. 7 For ye provoked him that made you by sacrificing unto devils, and not to God. 8 Ye have forgotten the everlasting God, that brought you up; and ye have grieved Jerusalem, that nursed you. 9 For when she saw the wrath of God coming uponyou, she said, Hearken, O ye that dwell about Sion: God hath brought upon me great mourning; 10 For I saw the captivity of my sons and daughters, which the Everlasting brought upon them. 11 With joy did I nourish them; but sent them

away with weeping and mourning. ¹² Let no man rejoice over me, a widow, and forsaken of many, who for the sins of my children am left desolate; because they departed from the law of God. ¹³ They knew not his statutes, nor walked in the ways of his commandments, nor trod in the paths of discipline in his righteousness. ¹⁴ Let them that dwell about Sion come, and remember ye the captivity of my sons and daughters, which the Everlasting hath brought upon them. ¹⁵ For he hath brought a nation upon them from far, a shameless nation, and of a strange language, who neither reverenced old man, nor pitied child. ¹⁶ These have carried away the dear beloved children of the widow, and left her that was alone desolate without daughters. ¹⁷ But what can I help you? ¹⁸ For he that brought these plagues upon you will deliver you from the hands of your enemies. ¹⁹ Go your way, O my children, go your way: for I am left desolate. ²⁰ I have put off the clothing of peace, and put upon me the sackcloth of my prayer: I will cry unto the Everlasting in my days. ²¹ Be of good cheer, O my children, cry unto the Lord, and he will deliver you from the power and hand of the enemies. ²² For my hope is in the Everlasting, that he will save you; and joy is come unto me from the Holy One, because of the mercy which shall soon come unto you from the Everlasting our Saviour. ²³ For I sent you out with mourning and weeping: but God will give you to me again with joy and gladness for ever. ²⁴ Like as now the neighbours of Sion have seen your captivity: so shall they see shortly your salvation from our God which shall come upon you with great glory, and brightness of the Everlasting. ²⁵ My children, suffer patiently the wrath that is come upon you from God: for thine enemy hath persecuted thee; but shortly thou shalt see his destruction, and shalt tread upon his neck. ²⁶ My delicate ones have gone rough ways, and were taken away as a flock caught of the enemies. ²⁷ Be of good comfort, O my children, and cry unto God: for ye shall be remembered of him that brought these things upon you. ²⁸ For as it was your mind to go astray from God: so, being returned, seek him ten times more. ²⁹ For he that hath brought these plagues upon you shall bring you everlasting joy with your salvation. ³⁰ Take a good heart, O

Jerusalem: for he that gave thee that name will comfort thee. ³¹ Miserable are they that afflicted thee, and rejoiced at thy fall. ³² Miserable are the cities which thy children served: miserable is she that received thy sons. ³³ For as she rejoiced at thy ruin, and was glad of thy fall: so shall she be grieved for her own desolation. ³⁴ For I will take away the rejoicing of her great multitude, and her pride shall be turned into mourning. ³⁵ For fire shall come upon her from the Everlasting, long to endure; and she shall be inhabited of devils for a great time. ³⁶ O Jerusalem, look about thee toward the east, and behold the joy that cometh unto thee from God. ³⁷ Lo, thy sons come, whom thou sentest away, they come gathered together from the east to the west by the word of the Holy One, rejoicing in the glory of God.

5

¹ Put off, O Jerusalem, the garment of mourning and affliction, and put on the comeliness of the glory that cometh from God for ever. ² Cast about thee a double garment of the righteousness which cometh from God; and set a diadem on thine head of the glory of the Everlasting. ³ For God will shew thy brightness unto every country under heaven. ⁴ For thy name shall be called of God for ever The peace of righteousness, and The glory of God's worship. ⁵ Arise, O Jerusalem, and stand on high, and look about toward the east, and behold thy children gathered from the west unto the east by the word of the Holy One, rejoicing in the remembrance of God. ⁶ For they departed from thee on foot, and were led away of their enemies: but God bringeth them unto thee exalted with glory, as children of the kingdom. ⁷ For God hath appointed that every high hill, and banks of long continuance, should be cast down, and valleys filled up, to make even the ground, that Israel may go safely in the glory of God, ⁸ Moreover even the woods and every sweetsmelling tree shall overshadow Israel by the commandment of God. ⁹ For God shall lead Israel with joy in the light of his glory with the mercy and righteousness that cometh from him.

A Copy of the Epistle of Jeremiah

A copy of an epistle, which Jeremy sent unto them which were to be led captives into Babylon by the king of the

¹ A copy of an epistle, which Jeremy sent unto them which were to be led captives into Babylon by the king of the Babylonians, to certify them, as it was commanded him of God. ² Because of the sins which ye have committed before God, ye shall be led away captives into Babylon by Nabuchodonosor king of the Babylonians. ³ So when ye be come unto Babylon, ye shall remain there many years, and for a long season, namely, seven generations: and after that I will bring you away peaceably from thence. ⁴ Now shall ye see in Babylon gods of silver, and of gold, and of wood, borne upon shoulders, which cause the nations to fear. ⁵ Beware therefore that ye in no wise be like to strangers, neither be ye afraid of them, when ye see the multitude before them and behind them, worshipping them. ⁶ But say ye in your hearts, O Lord, we must worship thee. ⁷ For mine angel is with you, and I myself caring for your souls. ⁸ As for their tongue, it is polished by the workman, and they themselves are gilded and laid over with silver; yet are they but false, and cannot speak. ⁹ And taking gold, as it were for a virgin that loveth to go gay, they make crowns for the heads of their gods. ¹⁰ Sometimes also the priests convey from their gods gold and silver, and bestow it upon themselves. ¹¹ Yea, they will give thereof to the common harlots, and deck them as men with garments, being gods of silver, and gods of gold, and wood. ¹² Yet cannot these gods save themselves from rust and moth, though they be covered with purple raiment. ¹³ They wipe their faces because of the dust of the temple, when there is much upon them. ¹⁴ And he that cannot put to death one that offendeth him holdeth a sceptre, as though he were a judge of the country. ¹⁵ He hath also in his right hand a dagger and an ax: but cannot deliver himself from war and thieves. ¹⁶ Whereby they are known not to be gods: therefore fear them not. ¹⁷ For like as a vessel that a man useth is nothing worth when it is broken; even so it is with their gods: when they be set up in the temple, their eyes be full of dust through the feet of them that come in. ¹⁸ And as the doors are made sure on every side upon him that offendeth the king, as being committed to suffer death: even so the priests

make fast their temples with doors, with locks, and bars, lest their gods be spoiled with robbers. 19 They light them candles, yea, more than for themselves, whereof they cannot see one. 20 They are as one of the beams of the temple, yet they say their hearts are gnawed upon by things creeping out of the earth; and when they eat them and their clothes, they feel it not. 21 Their faces are blacked through the smoke that cometh out of the temple. 22 Upon their bodies and heads sit bats, swallows, and birds, and the cats also. 23 By this ye may know that they are no gods: therefore fear them not. 24 Notwithstanding the gold that is about them to make them beautiful, except they wipe off the rust, they will not shine: for neither when they were molten did they feel it. 25 The things wherein there is no breath are bought for a most high price. 26 They are borne upon shoulders, having no feet whereby they declare unto men that they be nothing worth. 27 They also that serve them are ashamed: for if they fall to the ground at any time, they cannot rise up again of themselves: neither, if one set them upright, can they move of themselves: neither, if they be bowed down, can they make themselves straight: but they set gifts before them as unto dead men. 28 As for the things that are sacrificed unto them, their priests sell and abuse; in like manner their wives lay up part thereof in salt; but unto the poor and impotent they give nothing of it. 29 Menstruous women and women in childbed eat their sacrifices: by these things ye may know that they are no gods: fear them not. 30 For how can they be called gods? because women set meat before the gods of silver, gold, and wood. 31 And the priests sit in their temples, having their clothes rent, and their heads and beards shaven, and nothing upon their heads. 32 They roar and cry before their gods, as men do at the feast when one is dead. 33 The priests also take off their garments, and clothe their wives and children. 34 Whether it be evil that one doeth unto them, or good, they are not able to recompense it: they can neither set up a king, nor put him down. 35 In like manner, they can neither give riches nor money: though a man make a vow unto them, and keep it not, they will not require it. 36 They can save no man from death, neither deliver the weak from the mighty. 37 They cannot restore a blind man to his sight, nor help any man in his distress. 38 They can shew no mercy to the widow, nor do good to the fatherless. 39 Their gods of wood, and which are overlaid with gold and silver, are like the stones that be hewn out of the mountain: they that worship them shall be confounded. 40 How should a man then think and say that they are gods, when even the Chaldeans themselves dishonour them? 41 Who if they shall see one dumb that cannot speak, they bring him, and intreat Bel that he may speak, as though he were able to understand. 42 Yet they cannot understand this themselves, and leave them: for they have no knowledge. 43 The women also with cords about them, sitting in the ways, burn bran for perfume: but if any of them, drawn by some that passeth by, lie with him, she reproacheth her fellow, that she was not thought as worthy as herself, nor her cord broken. 44 Whatsoever is done among them is false: how may it then be thought or said that they are gods? 45 They are made of carpenters and goldsmiths: they can be nothing else than the workmen will have them to be. 46 And they themselves that made them can never continue long; how should then the things that are made of them be gods? 47 For they left lies and reproaches to them that come after. 48 For when there cometh any war or plague upon them, the priests consult with themselves, where they may be hidden with them. 49 How then cannot men perceive that they be no gods, which can neither save themselves from war, nor from plague? 50 For seeing they be but of wood, and overlaid with silver and gold, it shall be known hereafter that they are false: 51 And it shall manifestly appear to all nations and kings that they are no gods, but the works of men's hands, and that there is no work of God in them. 52 Who then may not know that they are no gods? 53 For neither can they set up a king in the land, nor give rain unto men. 54 Neither can they judge their own cause, nor redress a wrong, being unable: for they are as crows between heaven and earth. 55 Whereupon when fire falleth upon the house of gods of wood, or laid over with gold or silver, their priests will flee away, and escape; but they themselves shall be burned asunder like beams. 56 Moreover they cannot withstand any king or enemies:

how can it then be thought or said that they be gods? 57 Neither are those gods of wood, and laid over with silver or gold, able to escape either from thieves or robbers. 58 Whose gold, and silver, and garments wherewith they are clothed, they that are strong take, and go away withal: neither are they able to help themselves. 59 Therefore it is better to be a king that sheweth his power, or else a profitable vessel in an house, which the owner shall have use of, than such false gods; or to be a door in an house, to keep such things therein, than such false gods. or a pillar of wood in a a palace, than such false gods. 60 For sun, moon, and stars, being bright and sent to do their offices, are obedient. 61 In like manner the lightning when it breaketh forth is easy to be seen; and after the same manner the wind bloweth in every country. 62 And when God commandeth the clouds to go over the whole world, they do as they are bidden. 63 And the fire sent from above to consume hills and woods doeth as it is commanded: but these are like unto them neither in shew nor power. 64 Wherefore it is neither to be supposed nor said that they are gods, seeing, they are able neither to judge causes, nor to do good unto men. 65 Knowing therefore that they are no gods, fear them not, 66 For they can neither curse nor bless kings: 67 Neither can they shew signs in the heavens among the heathen, nor shine as the sun, nor give light as the moon. 68 The beasts are better than they: for they can get under a cover and help themselves. 69 It is then by no means manifest unto us that they are gods: therefore fear them not. 70 For as a scarecrow in a garden of cucumbers keepeth nothing: so are their gods of wood, and laid over with silver and gold. 71 And likewise their gods of wood, and laid over with silver and gold, are like to a white thorn in an orchard, that every bird sitteth upon; as also to a dead body, that is cast into the dark. 72 And ye shall know them to be no gods by the bright purple that rotteth upon them: and they themselves afterward shall be eaten, and shall be a reproach in the country. 73 Better therefore is the just man that hath none idols: for he shall be far from reproach.

The Song of the Three Holy Children

Also known as the "Prayer of Azariah and the Song of the Three Jews," is a captivating addition found in the Apocrypha of the 1560 Geneva Bible. This text is an expansion of the fiery furnace episode detailed in the Book of Daniel, where Shadrach, Meshach, and Abednego are cast into a blazing furnace for refusing to worship King Nebuchadnezzar's golden statue. Notably, this apocryphal addition is not found in the Jewish or Protestant canonical texts but is included in the Septuagint and traditionally used in the liturgy of the Eastern Orthodox and Catholic Churches.

This text is divided into two parts: the "Prayer of Azariah" which is recited while the three young men are in the furnace, and the "Song of the Three Jews," which they sing together after being joined by an angel who shields them from the flames. The prayer and song are profound expressions of faith and deliverance, illustrating the theme of divine intervention and the power of prayer. The "Prayer of Azariah" opens with a heartfelt appeal to God, acknowledging the justness of God's judgments and pleading for deliverance not based on the worthiness of the petitioners but on God's mercy and faithfulness. Azariah's prayer is a model of penitential prayer, acknowledging their exile as a consequence of Israel's collective sinfulness and a call for God's mercy based on His covenant promises. This text is a jubilant hymn of praise that all creation is invited to join, celebrating God's sovereignty and enduring mercies. This song mirrors many of the hymns found in the Psalms, calling upon the elements of creation—earth, air, fire, water, and all living things—to bless the Creator. The universality of the praise highlights the belief in God as the Lord of all nations and all creation, extending beyond the immediate context of Jewish worship.

The inclusion of this text in the Apocrypha enriches the biblical narrative by providing additional context to the famous furnace episode of Daniel, offering a deeper insight into the faith and prayers of the young men. It serves not only as a theological and liturgical resource but also as a literary work that underscores the power of faith and divine fidelity in the midst of persecution.

The song of the Three Holy Children

¹ And they walked in the midst of the fire, praising God, and blessing the Lord. ² Then Azarias stood up, and prayed on this manner; and opening his mouth in the midst of the fire said, ³ Blessed art thou, O Lord God of our fathers: thy name is worthy to be praised and glorified for evermore: ⁴ For thou art righteous in all the things that thou hast done to us: yea, true are all thy works, thy ways are right, and all thy judgments truth. ⁵ In all the things that thou hast brought upon us, and upon the holy city of our fathers, even Jerusalem, thou hast executed true judgment: for according to truth and judgment didst thou bring all these things upon us because of our sins. ⁶ For we have sinned and committed iniquity, departing from thee. ⁷ In all things have we trespassed, and not obeyed thy commandments, nor kept them, neither done as thou hast commanded us, that it might go well with us. ⁸ Wherefore all that thou hast brought upon us, and every thing that thou hast done to us, thou hast done in true judgment. ⁹ And thou didst deliver us into the hands of lawless enemies, most hateful forsakers of God, and to an unjust king, and the most wicked in all the world. ¹⁰ And now we cannot open our mouths, we are become a shame and reproach to thy servants; and to them that worship thee. ¹¹ Yet deliver us not up wholly, for thy name's sake, neither disannul thou thy covenant: ¹² And cause not thy mercy to depart from us, for thy beloved Abraham's sake, for thy servant Issac's sake, and for thy holy Israel's sake; ¹³ To whom thou hast spoken and promised, that thou wouldest multiply their seed as the stars of heaven, and as the sand that lieth upon the seashore. ¹⁴ For we, O Lord, are become less than any nation, and be kept under this day in all the world because of our sins. ¹⁵ Neither is there at this time prince, or prophet, or leader, or burnt offering, or sacrifice, or oblation, or incense, or place to sacrifice before thee, and to find mercy. ¹⁶ Nevertheless in a contrite heart and an humble spirit let us be accepted. ¹⁷ Like as in the burnt offerings of rams and bullocks, and like as in ten thousands of fat lambs: so let our sacrifice be in thy sight this day, and grant that we may wholly go after thee: for they shall not be confounded that put their trust in

thee. ¹⁸ And now we follow thee with all our heart, we fear thee, and seek thy face. ¹⁹ Put us not to shame: but deal with us after thy lovingkindness, and according to the multitude of thy mercies. ²⁰ Deliver us also according to thy marvellous works, and give glory to thy name, O Lord: and let all them that do thy servants hurt be ashamed; ²¹ And let them be confounded in all their power and might, and let their strength be broken; ²² And let them know that thou art God, the only God, and glorious over the whole world. ²³ And the king's servants, that put them in, ceased not to make the oven hot with rosin, pitch, tow, and small wood; ²⁴ So that the flame streamed forth above the furnace forty and nine cubits. ²⁵ And it passed through, and burned those Chaldeans it found about the furnace. ²⁶ But the angel of the Lord came down into the oven together with Azarias and his fellows, and smote the flame of the fire out of the oven; ²⁷ And made the midst of the furnace as it had been a moist whistling wind, so that the fire touched them not at all, neither hurt nor troubled them. ²⁸ Then the three, as out of one mouth, praised, glorified, and blessed, God in the furnace, saying, ²⁹ Blessed art thou, O Lord God of our fathers: and to be praised and exalted above all for ever. ³⁰ And blessed is thy glorious and holy name: and to be praised and exalted above all for ever. ³¹ Blessed art thou in the temple of thine holy glory: and to be praised and glorified above all for ever. ³² Blessed art thou that beholdest the depths, and sittest upon the cherubims: and to be praised and exalted above all for ever. ³³ Blessed art thou on the glorious throne of thy kingdom: and to be praised and glorified above all for ever. ³⁴ Blessed art thou in the firmament of heaven: and above all to be praised and glorified for ever. ³⁵ O all ye works of the Lord, bless ye the Lord: praise and exalt him above all for ever, ³⁶ O ye heavens, bless ye the Lord: praise and exalt him above all for ever. ³⁷ O ye angels of the Lord, bless ye the Lord: praise and exalt him above all for ever. ³⁸ O all ye waters that be above the heaven, bless ye the Lord: praise and exalt him above all for ever. ³⁹ O all ye powers of the Lord, bless ye the Lord: praise and exalt him above all for ever. ⁴⁰ O ye sun and moon, bless ye the Lord: praise and exalt him above all for ever. ⁴¹ O ye stars of heaven, bless ye the Lord: praise and exalt him above all for ever. 42 O every shower and dew, bless ye the Lord: praise and exalt him above all for ever. 43 O all ye winds, bless ye the Lord: praise and exalt him above all for ever, 44 O ye fire and heat, bless ye the Lord: praise and exalt him above all for ever. 45 O ye winter and summer, bless ye the Lord: praise and exalt him above all for ever. 46 O ye dews and storms of snow, bless ye the Lord: praise and exalt him above all for ever. 47 O ye nights and days, bless ye the Lord: bless and exalt him above all for ever. 48 O ye light and darkness, bless ye the Lord: praise and exalt him above all for ever. 49 O ye ice and cold, bless ye the Lord: praise and exalt him above all for ever. 50 O ye frost and snow, bless ye the Lord: praise and exalt him above all for ever. 51 O ye lightnings and clouds, bless ye the Lord: praise and exalt him above all for ever. 52 O let the earth bless the Lord: praise and exalt him above all for ever. 53 O ye mountains and little hills, bless ye the Lord: praise and exalt him above all for ever. 54 O all ye things that grow in the earth, bless ye the Lord: praise and exalt him above all for ever. 55 O ye mountains, bless ye the Lord: Praise and exalt him above all for ever. 56 O ye seas and rivers, bless ye the Lord: praise and exalt him above all for ever. 57 O ye whales, and all that move in the waters, bless ye the Lord: praise and exalt him above all for ever. 58 O all ye fowls of the air, bless ye the Lord: praise and exalt him above all for ever. 59 O all ye beasts and cattle, bless ye the Lord: praise and exalt him above all for ever. 60 O ye children of men, bless ye the Lord: praise and exalt him above all for ever. 61 O Israel, bless ye the Lord: praise and exalt him above all for ever. 62 O ye priests of the Lord, bless ye the Lord: praise and exalt him above all for ever. 63 O ye servants of the Lord, bless ye the Lord: praise and exalt him above all for ever. 64 O ye spirits and souls of the righteous, bless ye the Lord: praise and exalt him above all for ever. 65 O ye holy and humble men of heart, bless ye the Lord: praise and exalt him above all for ever. 66 O Ananias, Azarias, and Misael, bless ye the Lord: praise and exalt him above all for ever: for he hath delivered us from hell, and saved us from the hand of death, and delivered us out of the midst of the furnace and burning flame: even out of the midst of the fire hath he delivered us. 67 O give thanks unto the Lord, because he is gracious: for his mercy endureth for ever. [68] O all ye that worship the Lord, bless the God of gods, praise him, and give him thanks: for his mercy endureth for ever.

The Story of Susanna

The Story of Susanna, included in the Apocrypha of the 1560 Geneva Bible, is a compelling addition to the Book of Daniel. Known simply as Susanna or Shoshana in Hebrew, this narrative explores deep themes of virtue, justice, and divine intervention, standing out for its rich thematic content. It is particularly revered in the Septuagint and holds a significant place in the liturgies of the Eastern Orthodox and Catholic Churches.

Set against the backdrop of Babylon during the Jewish exile, the narrative centers around a righteous and beautiful woman, married to Joakim, a wealthy and respected member of the community. The plot unfolds in Joakim's orchard, where Susanna is confronted by two lecherous elders who threaten to accuse her of adultery if she refuses their advances. Embodying virtue and piety, she chooses the risk of death over sinning before God and rejects them.

Following through with their threat, the elders accuse her falsely. As she faces wrongful condemnation, her situation exemplifies the vulnerability of the righteous and the corruption that can pervade human justice systems. However, her fate takes a dramatic turn with the intervention of the young prophet Daniel. His astute cross-examination of the elders exposes their lies, using their conflicting testimonies about the supposed location of the incident to unveil their deceit. This leads to their condemnation and her exoneration.

This narrative serves as a profound meditation on the integrity of the judicial process and the dangers of false testimony, while celebrating the triumph of divine justice. It challenges the community's responsibility to seek truth and uphold justice, emphasizing the importance of individual courage and integrity in the face of wrongful accusations.

The Story of Susanna

¹ There dwelt a man in Babylon, and his name was Joakim: ² and he took a wife, whose name was Susanna, the daughter of Helkias, a very fair woman, and one that feared the Lord. ³ Her parents also were righteous, and taught their daughter according to the law of Moses. ⁴ Now Joakim was a great rich man, and had a fair garden joining unto his house: and to him resorted the Jews; because he was more honourable than all others. ⁵ And the same year there were appointed two of the ancients of the people to be judges, such as the Lord spake of, that wickedness came from Babylon from ancient judges, who were accounted to govern the people. ⁶ These kept much at Joakim's house: and all that had any suits in law came unto them. ⁷ Now when the people departed away at noon, Susanna went into her husband's garden to walk. ⁸ And the two elders beheld her going in every day, and walking; and they were inflamed with love for her. ⁹ And they perverted their own mind, and turned away their eyes, that they might not look unto heaven, nor remember just judgements. ¹⁰ And albeit they both were wounded with her love, yet durst not one shew another his grief. ¹¹ For they were ashamed to declare their lust, that they desired to have to do with her. ¹² Yet they watched jealously from day to day to see her. ¹³ And the one said to the other, Let us now go home: for it is dinner time. ¹⁴ So when they were gone out, they parted the one from the other, and turning back again they came to the same place; and after that they had asked one another the cause, they acknowledged their lust: and then appointed they a time both together, when they might find her alone. ¹⁵ And it fell out, as they watched a fit day, she went in as aforetime with two maids only, and she was desirous to wash herself in the garden: for it was hot. ¹⁶ And there was nobody there save the two elders, that had hid themselves, and watched her. ¹⁷ Then she said to her maids, Bring me oil and washing balls, and shut the garden doors, that I may wash me. ¹⁸ And they did as she bade them, and shut the garden doors, and went out themselves at the side doors to fetch the things that she had commanded them: and they saw not the elders, because they were hid. ¹⁹ Now when the maids were gone forth, the two elders rose up, and ran unto her, saying, ²⁰

Behold, the garden doors are shut, that no man can see us, and we are in love with thee; therefore consent unto us, and lie with us. 21 If thou wilt not, we will bear witness against thee, that a young man was with thee: and therefore thou didst send away thy maids from thee. 22 Then Susanna sighed, and said, I am straitened on every side: for if I do this thing, it is death unto me: and if I do it not, I cannot escape your hands. 23 It is better for me to fall into your hands, and not do it, than to sin in the sight of the Lord. 24 With that Susanna cried with a loud voice: and the two elders cried out against her. 25 Then ran the one, and opened the garden doors. 26 So when the servants of the house heard the cry in the garden, they rushed in at the side door, to see what had befallen her. 27 But when the elders had told their tale, the servants were greatly ashamed: for there was never such a report made of Susanna. 28 And it came to pass on the morrow, when the people assembled to her husband Joakim, the two elders came full of their wicked intent against Susanna to put her to death; 29 and said before the people, Send for Susanna, the daughter of Helkias, Joakim's wife. So they sent; 30 and she came with her father and mother, her children, and all her kindred. 31 Now Susanna was a very delicate woman, and beauteous to behold. 32 And these wicked men commanded her to be unveiled, (for she was veiled) that they might be filled with her beauty. 33 Therefore her friends and all that saw her wept. 34 Then the two elders stood up in the midst of the people, and laid their hands upon her head. 35 And she weeping looked up toward heaven: for her heart trusted in the Lord. 36 And the elders said, As we walked in the garden alone, this woman came in with two maids, and shut the garden doors, and sent the maids away. 37 Then a young man, who there was hid, came unto her, and lay with her. 38 And we, being in a corner of the garden, saw this wickedness, and ran unto them. 39 And when we saw them together, the man we could not hold: for he was stronger than we, and opened the doors, and leaped out. 40 But having taken this woman, we asked who the young man was, but she would not tell us: these things do we testify. 41 Then the assembly believed them, as those that were elders of the people and judges: so they condemned her to death. ⁴² Then Susanna cried out with a loud voice, and said, O everlasting God, that knowest the secrets, that knowest all things before they be: ⁴³ thou knowest that they have borne false witness against me, and, behold, I must die; whereas I never did such things as these men have maliciously invented against me. ⁴⁴ And the Lord heard her voice. ⁴⁵ Therefore when she was led away to be put to death, God raised up the holy spirit of a young youth, whose name was Daniel: ⁴⁶ and he cried with a loud voice, I am clear from the blood of this woman. ⁴⁷ Then all the people turned them toward him, and said, What mean these words that thou hast spoken? ⁴⁸ So he standing in the midst of them said, Are ye such fools, ye sons of Israel, that without examination or knowledge of the truth ye have condemned a daughter of Israel? ⁴⁹ Return again to the place of judgement: for these have borne false witness against her. ⁵⁰ Wherefore all the people turned again in haste, and the elders said unto him, Come, sit down among us, and shew it us, seeing God hath given thee the honour of an elder. ⁵¹ Then said Daniel unto them, Put them asunder one far from another, and I will examine them. ⁵² So when they were put asunder one from another, he called one of them, and said unto him, O thou that art waxen old in wickedness, now are thy sins come home to thee which thou hast committed aforetime, ⁵³ in pronouncing unjust judgement, and condemning the innocent, and letting the guilty go free; albeit the Lord saith, The innocent and righteous shalt thou not slay. ⁵⁴ Now then, if thou sawest her, tell me, Under what tree sawest thou them companying together? Who answered, Under a mastick tree. ⁵⁵ And Daniel said, Right well hast thou lied against thine own head; for even now the angel of God hath received the sentence of God and shall cut thee in two. ⁵⁶ So he put him aside, and commanded to bring the other, and said unto him, O thou seed of Canaan, and not of Judah, beauty hath deceived thee, and lust hath perverted thine heart. ⁵⁷ Thus have ye dealt with the daughters of Israel, and they for fear companied with you: but the daughter of Judah would not abide your wickedness. ⁵⁸ Now therefore tell me, Under what tree didst thou take them companying together? Who answered, Under a holm tree. ⁵⁹

Then said Daniel unto him, Right well hast thou also lied against thine own head: for the angel of God waiteth with the sword to cut thee in two, that he may destroy you. 60 With that all the assembly cried out with a loud voice, and blessed God, who saveth them that hope in him. 61 And they arose against the two elders, for Daniel had convicted them of false witness out of their own mouth: 62 and according to the law of Moses they did unto them in such sort as they maliciously intended to do to their neighbour: and they put them to death, and the innocent blood was saved the same day. 63 Therefore Helkias and his wife praised God for their daughter Susanna, with Joakim her husband, and all the kindred, because there was no dishonesty found in her. 64 And from that day forth was Daniel had in great reputation in the sight of the people.

Bel and the Dragon

This text is part of the additions to Daniel and is recognized in the Septuagint and in the liturgical traditions of the Eastern Orthodox and Catholic Churches. The narrative is composed of two distinct episodes that highlight the themes of idolatry, deceit, and divine justice, continuing the portrayal of Daniel as a figure of wisdom and piety.

The first part of the narrative deals with the Babylonian god Bel, worshipped through a statue. The Babylonians believe that Bel consumes large quantities of offerings left for him each night. Skeptical of Bel's divine nature, Daniel devises a plan to prove that the offerings are, in fact, deceitfully consumed by the priests of Bel and their families. By sprinkling ash on the temple floor after the doors are sealed, Daniel reveals the priests' secret passages used to enter the temple and consume the offerings, thereby exposing their fraud.

The second episode involves a dragon that is worshipped by the Babylonians. When Daniel is challenged to kill this creature without the use of a sword or staff, he ingeniously feeds the dragon a concoction of pitch, fat, and hair, causing the dragon to burst open upon consumption. This act further demonstrates the impotence of the idols and creatures the Babylonians worship compared to the power of the true God whom Daniel serves.

Through these narratives, the text critiques the practices of idol worship and highlights the cunning and resourcefulness of Daniel in uncovering deception. His actions serve not only to affirm the power of his God but also to challenge the misguided beliefs of the Babylonians. His wisdom and the miraculous outcomes of his challenges help to solidify the faith of the Jewish community while also appealing to the broader Hellenistic audience of the time, demonstrating the superiority of monotheism over pagan practices.

Bel and the Dragon

1 And king Astyages was gathered to his fathers, and Cyrus of Persia received his kingdom. 2 And Daniel conversed with the king, and was honored above all his friends. 3 Now the Babylonians had an idol, called Bel, and there were spent upon him every day twelve great measures of fine flour, and forty sheep, and six vessels of wine. 4 And the king worshipped it and went daily to adore it: but Daniel worshipped his own God. And the king said to him, Why do not you worship Bel? 5 Who answered and said, Because I may not worship idols made with hands, but the living God, who has created the heaven and the earth, and has sovereignty over all flesh. 6 Then said the king to him, Thinkest you not that Bel is a living God? see you not how much he eats and drinks every day? 7 Then Daniel smiled, and said, O king, be not deceived: for this is but clay within, and brass without, and did never eat or drink any thing. 8 So the king was angry, and called for his priests, and said to them, If you tell me not who this is that devours these expenses, you shall die. 9 But if you can certify me that Bel devours them, then Daniel shall die: for he has spoken blasphemy against Bel. And Daniel said to the king, Let it be according to your word. 10 Now the priests of Bel were threescore and ten, beside their wives and children. And the king went with Daniel into the temple of Bel. 11 So Bel's priests said, Behold, we go out: but you, O king, set on the meat, and make ready the wine, and shut the door fast and seal it with your own signet; 12 And to morrow when you come in, if you find not that Bel has eaten up all, we will suffer death: or else Daniel, that speaks falsely against us. 13 And they little regarded it: for under the table they had made a privy entrance, whereby they entered in continually, and consumed those things. 14 So when they were gone forth, the king set meats before Bel. Now Daniel had commanded his servants to bring ashes, and those they strewed throughout all the temple in the presence of the king alone: then they went out, and shut the door, and sealed it with the king's signet, and so departed. 15 Now in the night came the priests with their wives and children, as they were wont to do, and did eat and drink up all. 16 In the morning betime the king arose, and Daniel with him.

259

17 And the king said, Daniel, are the seals whole? And he said, Yes, O king, they be whole. 18 And as soon as he had opened the dour, the king looked upon the table, and cried with a loud voice, Great are you, O Bel, and with you is no deceit at all. 19 Then laughed Daniel, and held the king that he should not go in, and said, Behold now the pavement, and mark well whose footsteps are these. 20 And the king said, I see the footsteps of men, women, and children. And then the king was angry, 21 And took the priests with their wives and children, who showed him the privy doors, where they came in, and consumed such things as were upon the table. 22 Therefore the king killed them, and delivered Bel into Daniel's power, who destroyed him and his temple. 23 And in that same place there was a great dragon, which they of Babylon worshipped. 24 And the king said to Daniel, Will you also say that this is of brass? behold, he lives, he eats and drinks; you can not say that he is no living god: therefore worship him. 25 Then said Daniel to the king, I will worship the Lord my God: for he is the living God. 26 But give me leave, O king, and I shall kill this dragon without sword or staff. The king said, I give you leave. 27 Then Daniel took pitch, and fat, and hair, and did seethe them together, and made lumps thereof: this he put in the dragon's mouth, and so the dragon burst in sunder: and Daniel said, Behold, these are the gods you worship. 28 When they of Babylon heard that, they took great indignation, and conspired against the king, saying, The king is become a Jew, and he has destroyed Bel, he has slain the dragon, and put the priests to death. 29 So they came to the king, and said, Deliver us Daniel, or else we will destroy you and your house. 30 Now when the king saw that they pressed him sore, being constrained, he delivered Daniel to them: 31 Who cast him into the lions' den: where he was six days. 32 And in the den there were seven lions, and they had given them every day two carcasses, and two sheep: which then were not given to them, to the intent they might devour Daniel. 33 Now there was in Jewry a prophet, called Habbacuc, who had made pottage, and had broken bread in a bowl, and was going into the field, for to bring it to the reapers. 34 But the angel of the Lord said to Habbacuc,

Go, carry the dinner that you have into Babylon to Daniel, who is in the lions' den. 35 And Habbacuc said, Lord, I never saw Babylon; neither do I know where the den is. 36 Then the angel of the Lord took him by the crown, and bare him by the hair of his head, and through the vehemency of his spirit set him in Babylon over the den. 37 And Habbacuc cried, saying, O Daniel, Daniel, take the dinner which God has sent you. 38 And Daniel said, You have remembered me, O God: neither have you forsaken them that seek you and love you. 39 So Daniel arose, and did eat: and the angel of the Lord set Habbacuc in his own place again immediately. 40 Upon the seventh day the king went to bewail Daniel: and when he came to the den, he looked in, and behold, Daniel was sitting. 41 Then cried the king with a loud voice, saying, Great are you Lord God of Daniel, and there is none other beside you. 42 And he drew him out, and cast those that were the cause of his destruction into the den: and they were devoured in a moment before his face.

The First Book of Maccabees

The First Book of Maccabees is a pivotal text within the Apocrypha of the 1560 Geneva Bible, providing a detailed historical account of the Jewish struggle for religious freedom and political independence during the 2nd century BCE. This narrative focuses on the revolt against the Seleucid Empire and the Hellenistic cultural imposition led by the Maccabee family, particularly under the leadership of Judas Maccabeus.

Originating as a Hebrew document, though now extant only in Greek, the book serves as a crucial source for understanding the complex socio-political landscape of Judea under Hellenistic rule. The narrative begins with the reign of Alexander the Great and traces the division of his empire among his generals, setting the stage for the ensuing conflicts that affected Judea. The heart of the story documents the rise of the Hellenistic king Antiochus IV Epiphanes, who desecrated the Temple in Jerusalem and outlawed Jewish practices, leading to the Maccabean revolt. The text is highly detailed in its coverage of military campaigns, political maneuvers, and diplomatic efforts. It celebrates the Maccabees' valor, strategic prowess, and their commitment to the Torah, portraying their struggle as not only a fight for national sovereignty but also for the preservation of Jewish religion and way of life. Through its narrative, the First Book of Maccabees also reflects on themes of leadership, fidelity, and the divine right of resistance against tyranny, echoing the Biblical narratives of deliverance.

Structurally, the book is meticulous in its chronological account, providing not only a historical record but also a testament to the resilience of the Jewish people. Its portrayal of the Maccabees as both national heroes and devout adherents to their faith made the text an inspirational and edifying read for both Jewish and Christian audiences. Overall, the First Book of Maccabees is not only a historical document but a profound narrative of faith, heroism, and the perpetual fight for religious freedom. Its inclusion in the Geneva Bible enriches the historical depth and theological diversity of the scriptural canon, offering readers insights into the enduring nature of faith amidst trials.

The First Book of the Maccabees

1 And it happened, after that Alexander son of Philip, the Macedonian, who came out of the land of Chettiim, had smitten Darius king of the Persians and Medes, that he reigned in his stead, the first over Greece, 2 And made many wars, and won many strong holds, and slew the kings of the earth, 3 And went through to the ends of the earth, and took spoils of many nations, insomuch that the earth was quiet before him; whereupon he was exalted and his heart was lifted up. 4 And he gathered a mighty strong host and ruled over countries, and nations, and kings, who became tributaries unto him. 5 And after these things he fell sick, and perceived that he should die. 6 Wherefore he called his servants, such as were honourable, and had been brought up with him from his youth, and parted his kingdom among them, while he was yet alive. 7 So Alexander reigned twelve years, and then died. 8 And his servants bare rule every one in his place. 9 And after his death they all put crowns upon themselves; so did their sons after them many years: and evils were multiplied in the earth. 10 And there came out of them a wicked root Antiochus surnamed Epiphanes, son of Antiochus the king, who had been an hostage at Rome, and he reigned in the hundred and thirty and seventh year of the kingdom of the Greeks. 11 In those days went there out of Israel wicked men, who persuaded many, saying, Let us go and make a covenant with the heathen that are round about us: for since we departed from them we have had much sorrow. 12 So this device pleased them well. 13 Then certain of the people were so forward herein, that they went to the king, who gave them licence to do after the ordinances of the heathen: 14 Whereupon they built a place of exercise at Jerusalem according to the customs of the heathen: 15 And made themselves uncircumcised, and forsook the holy covenant, and joined themselves to the heathen, and were sold to do mischief. 16 Now when the kingdom was established before Antiochus, he thought to reign over Egypt that he might have the dominion of two realms. 17 Wherefore he entered into Egypt with a great multitude, with chariots, and elephants, and horsemen, and a great navy, 18

And made war against Ptolemee king of Egypt: but Ptolemee was afraid of him, and fled; and many were wounded to death. 19 Thus they got the strong cities in the land of Egypt and he took the spoils thereof. 20 And after that Antiochus had smitten Egypt, he returned again in the hundred forty and third year, and went up against Israel and Jerusalem with a great multitude, 21 And entered proudly into the sanctuary, and took away the golden altar, and the candlestick of light, and all the vessels thereof, 22 And the table of the shewbread, and the pouring vessels, and the vials. and the censers of gold, and the veil, and the crown, and the golden ornaments that were before the temple, all which he pulled off. 23 He took also the silver and the gold, and the precious vessels: also he took the hidden treasures which he found. 24 And when he had taken all away, he went into his own land, having made a great massacre, and spoken very proudly. 25 Therefore there was a great mourning in Israel, in every place where they were; 26 So that the princes and elders mourned, the virgins and young men were made feeble, and the beauty of women was changed. 27 Every bridegroom took up lamentation, and she that sat in the marriage chamber was in heaviness, 28 The land also was moved for the inhabitants thereof, and all the house of Jacob was covered with confusion. 29 And after two years fully expired the king sent his chief collector of tribute unto the cities of Juda, who came unto Jerusalem with a great multitude, 30 And spake peaceable words unto them, but all was deceit: for when they had given him credence, he fell suddenly upon the city, and smote it very sore, and destroyed much people of Israel. 31 And when he had taken the spoils of the city, he set it on fire, and pulled down the houses and walls thereof on every side. 32 But the women and children took they captive, and possessed the cattle. 33 Then builded they the city of David with a great and strong wall, and with mighty towers, and made it a strong hold for them. 34 And they put therein a sinful nation, wicked men, and fortified themselves therein. 35 They stored it also with armour and victuals, and when they had gathered together the spoils of Jerusalem, they laid them up there, and so they became a sore snare: 36 For it was a place to lie in wait against the sanctuary, and an evil adversary to Israel. 37 Thus they shed innocent blood on every side of the sanctuary, and defiled it: 38 Insomuch that the inhabitants of Jerusalem fled because of them: whereupon the city was made an habitation of strangers, and became strange to those that were born in her; and her own children left her. 39 Her sanctuary was laid waste like a wilderness, her feasts were turned into mourning, her sabbaths into reproach her honour into contempt. 40 As had been her glory, so was her dishonour increased, and her excellency was turned into mourning. 41 Moreover king Antiochus wrote to his whole kingdom, that all should be one people, 42 And every one should leave his laws: so all the heathen agreed according to the commandment of the king. 43 Yea, many also of the Israelites consented to his religion, and sacrificed unto idols, and profaned the sabbath. 44 For the king had sent letters by messengers unto Jerusalem and the cities of Juda that they should follow the strange laws of the land, 45 And forbid burnt offerings, and sacrifice, and drink offerings, in the temple; and that they should profane the sabbaths and festival days: 46 And pollute the sanctuary and holy people: 47 Set up altars, and groves, and chapels of idols, and sacrifice swine's flesh, and unclean beasts: 48 That they should also leave their children uncircumcised, and make their souls abominable with all manner of uncleanness and profanation: 49 To the end they might forget the law, and change all the ordinances. 50 And whosoever would not do according to the commandment of the king, he said, he should die. 51 In the selfsame manner wrote he to his whole kingdom, and appointed overseers over all the people, commanding the cities of Juda to sacrifice, city by city. 52 Then many of the people were gathered unto them, to wit every one that forsook the law; and so they committed evils in the land; 53 And drove the Israelites into secret places, even wheresoever they could flee for succour. 54 Now the fifteenth day of the month Casleu, in the hundred forty and fifth year, they set up the abomination of desolation upon the altar, and builded idol altars throughout the cities of Juda on every side; 55 And burnt incense at the doors of their houses, and in the streets. 56 And when they had rent in pieces the books of the law which they found, they burnt them with fire. 57 And whosoever was found with any the book of the testament, or if any committed to the law, the king's commandment was, that they should put him to death. 58 Thus did they by their authority unto the Israelites every month, to as many as were found in the cities. 59 Now the five and twentieth day of the month they did sacrifice upon the idol altar, which was upon the altar of God. 60 At which time according to the commandment they put to death certain women, that had caused their children to be circumcised. 61 And they hanged the infants about their necks, and rifled their houses, and slew them that had circumcised them. 62 Howbeit many in Israel were fully resolved and confirmed in themselves not to eat any unclean thing. 63 Wherefore they chose rather to die, that they might not be defiled with meats, and that they might not profane the holy covenant: so then they died. 64 And there was very great wrath upon Israel.

2

1 In those days arose Mattathias the son of John, the son of Simeon, a priest of the sons of Joarib, from Jerusalem, and dwelt in Modin. 2 And he had five sons, Joannan, called Caddis: 3 Simon; called Thassi: 4 Judas, who was called Maccabeus: 5 Eleazar, called Avaran: and Jonathan, whose surname was Apphus. 6 And when he saw the blasphemies that were committed in Juda and Jerusalem, 7 He said, Woe is me! wherefore was I born to see this misery of my people, and of the holy city, and to dwell there, when it was delivered into the hand of the enemy, and the sanctuary into the hand of strangers? 8 Her temple is become as a man without glory. 9 Her glorious vessels are carried away into captivity, her infants are slain in the streets, her young men with the sword of the enemy. 10 What nation hath not had a part in her kingdom and gotten of her spoils? 11 All her ornaments are taken away; of a free woman she is become a bondslave. 12 And, behold, our sanctuary, even our beauty and our glory, is laid waste, and the Gentiles have profaned it. 13 To what end therefore shall we live any longer? 14 Then Mattathias and his sons rent their clothes, and put on sackcloth, and mourned very sore. 15 In the mean while the king's officers, such as compelled the people to

revolt, came into the city Modin, to make them sacrifice. 16 And when many of Israel came unto them, Mattathias also and his sons came together. 17 Then answered the king's officers, and said to Mattathias on this wise, Thou art a ruler, and an honourable and great man in this city, and strengthened with sons and brethren: 18 Now therefore come thou first, and fulfil the king's commandment, like as all the heathen have done, yea, and the men of Juda also, and such as remain at Jerusalem: so shalt thou and thy house be in the number of the king's friends, and thou and thy children shall be honoured with silver and gold, and many rewards. 19 Then Mattathias answered and spake with a loud voice, Though all the nations that are under the king's dominion obey him, and fall away every one from the religion of their fathers, and give consent to his commandments: 20 Yet will I and my sons and my brethren walk in the covenant of our fathers. 21 God forbid that we should forsake the law and the ordinances. 22 We will not hearken to the king's words, to go from our religion, either on the right hand, or the left. 23 Now when he had left speaking these words, there came one of the Jews in the sight of all to sacrifice on the altar which was at Modin, according to the king's commandment. 24 Which thing when Mattathias saw, he was inflamed with zeal, and his reins trembled, neither could he forbear to shew his anger according to judgment: wherefore he ran, and slew him upon the altar. 25 Also the king's commissioner, who compelled men to sacrifice, he killed at that time, and the altar he pulled down. 26 Thus dealt he zealously for the law of God like as Phinees did unto Zambri the son of Salom. 27 And Mattathias cried throughout the city with a loud voice, saying, Whosoever is zealous of the law, and maintaineth the covenant, let him follow me. 28 So he and his sons fled into the mountains, and left all that ever they had in the city. 29 Then many that sought after justice and judgment went down into the wilderness, to dwell there: 30 Both they, and their children, and their wives; and their cattle; because afflictions increased sore upon them. 31 Now when it was told the king's servants, and the host that was at Jerusalem, in the city of David, that certain men, who had broken the king's commandment, were gone down into the secret places in the wilderness, 32 They pursued after them a great number, and having overtaken them, they camped against them, and made war against them on the sabbath day. 33 And they said unto them, Let that which ye have done hitherto suffice; come forth, and do according to the commandment of the king, and ye shall live. 34 But they said, We will not come forth, neither will we do the king's commandment, to profane the sabbath day. 35 So then they gave them the battle with all speed. 36 Howbeit they answered them not, neither cast they a stone at them, nor stopped the places where they lay hid; 37 But said, Let us die all in our innocency: heaven and earth will testify for us, that ye put us to death wrongfully. 38 So they rose up against them in battle on the sabbath, and they slew them, with their wives and children and their cattle, to the number of a thousand people. 39 Now when Mattathias and his friends understood hereof, they mourned for them right sore. 40 And one of them said to another, If we all do as our brethren have done, and fight not for our lives

and laws against the heathen, they will now quickly root us out of the earth. 41 At that time therefore they decreed, saying, Whosoever shall come to make battle with us on the sabbath day, we will fight against him; neither will we die all, as our brethren that were murdered in the secret places. 42 Then came there unto him a company of Assideans who were mighty men of Israel, even all such as were voluntarily devoted unto the law. 43 Also all they that fled for persecution joined themselves unto them, and were a stay unto them. 44 So they joined their forces, and smote sinful men in their anger, and wicked men in their wrath: but the rest fled to the heathen for succour. 45 Then Mattathias and his friends went round about, and pulled down the altars: 46 And what children soever they found within the coast of Israel uncircumcised, those they circumcised valiantly. 47 They pursued also after the proud men, and the work prospered in their hand. 48 So they recovered the law out of the hand of the Gentiles, and out of the hand of kings, neither suffered they the sinner to triumph. 49 Now when the time drew near that Mattathias should die, he said unto his sons, Now hath pride and rebuke gotten strength, and the time of destruction, and the wrath of indignation: 50 Now therefore, my sons, be ye zealous for the law, and give your lives for the covenant of your fathers. 51 Call to remembrance what acts our fathers did in their time; so shall ye receive great honour and an everlasting name. 52 Was not Abraham found faithful in temptation, and it was imputed unto him for righteousness? 53 Joseph in the time of his distress kept the commandment and was made lord of Egypt. 54 Phinees our father in being zealous and fervent obtained the covenant of an everlasting priesthood. 55 Jesus for fulfilling the word was made a judge in Israel. 56 Caleb for bearing witness before the congregation received the heritage of the land. 57 David for being merciful possessed the throne of an everlasting kingdom. 58 Elias for being zealous and fervent for the law was taken up into heaven. 59 Ananias, Azarias, and Misael, by believing were saved out of the flame. 60 Daniel for his innocency was delivered from the mouth of lions. 61 And thus consider ye throughout all ages, that none that put their trust in him shall be overcome. 62 Fear not then the words of a sinful man: for his glory shall be dung and worms. 63 To day he shall be lifted up and to morrow he shall not be found, because he is returned into his dust, and his thought is come to nothing. 64 Wherefore, ye my sons, be valiant and shew yourselves men in the behalf of the law; for by it shall ye obtain glory. 65 And behold, I know that your brother Simon is a man of counsel, give ear unto him alway: he shall be a father unto you. 66 As for Judas Maccabeus, he hath been mighty and strong, even from his youth up: let him be your captain, and fight the battle of the people. 67 Take also unto you all those that observe the law, and avenge ye the wrong of your people. 68 Recompense fully the heathen, and take heed to the commandments of the law. 69 So he blessed them, and was gathered to his fathers. 70 And he died in the hundred forty and sixth year, and his sons buried him in the sepulchres of his fathers at Modin, and all Israel made great lamentation for him.

3

1 Then his son Judas, called Maccabeus, rose up in his stead. 2 And all his brethren helped him, and so did all they that held with

his father, and they fought with cheerfulness the battle of Israel. ³ So he gat his people great honour, and put on a breastplate as a giant, and girt his warlike harness about him, and he made battles, protecting the host with his sword. ⁴ In his acts he was like a lion, and like a lion's whelp roaring for his prey. ⁵ For He pursued the wicked, and sought them out, and burnt up those that vexed his people. ⁶ Wherefore the wicked shrunk for fear of him, and all the workers of iniquity were troubled, because salvation prospered in his hand. ⁷ He grieved also many kings, and made Jacob glad with his acts, and his memorial is blessed for ever. ⁸ Moreover he went through the cities of Juda, destroying the ungodly out of them, and turning away wrath from Israel: ⁹ So that he was renowned unto the utmost part of the earth, and he received unto him such as were ready to perish. ¹⁰ Then Apollonius gathered the Gentiles together, and a great host out of Samaria, to fight against Israel. ¹¹ Which thing when Judas perceived, he went forth to meet him, and so he smote him, and slew him: many also fell down slain, but the rest fled. ¹² Wherefore Judas took their spoils, and Apollonius' sword also, and therewith he fought all his life long. ¹³ Now when Seron, a prince of the army of Syria, heard say that Judas had gathered unto him a multitude and company of the faithful to go out with him to war; ¹⁴ He said, I will get me a name and honour in the kingdom; for I will go fight with Judas and them that are with him, who despise the king's commandment. ¹⁵ So he made him ready to go up, and there went with him a mighty host of the ungodly to help him, and to be avenged of the children of Israel. ¹⁶ And when he came near to the going up of Bethhoron, Judas went forth to meet him with a small company: ¹⁷ Who, when they saw the host coming to meet them, said unto Judas, How shall we be able, being so few, to fight against so great a multitude and so strong, seeing we are ready to faint with fasting all this day? ¹⁸ Unto whom Judas answered, It is no hard matter for many to be shut up in the hands of a few; and with the God of heaven it is all one, to deliver with a great multitude, or a small company: ¹⁹ For the victory of battle standeth not in the multitude of an host; but strength cometh from heaven. ²⁰ They come against us in much pride and iniquity to destroy us, and our wives and children, and to spoil us: 21 But we fight for our lives and our laws. 22 Wherefore the Lord himself will overthrow them before our face: and as for you, be ye not afraid of them. 23 Now as soon as he had left off speaking, he leapt suddenly upon them, and so Seron and his host was overthrown before him. 24 And they pursued them from the going down of Bethhoron unto the plain, where were slain about eight hundred men of them; and the residue fled into the land of the Philistines. 25 Then began the fear of Judas and his brethren, and an exceeding great dread, to fall upon the nations round about them: 26 Insomuch as his fame came unto the king, and all nations talked of the battles of Judas. 27 Now when king Antiochus heard these things, he was full of indignation: wherefore he sent and gathered together all the forces of his realm, even a very strong army. 28 He opened also his treasure, and gave his soldiers pay for a year, commanding them to be ready whensoever he should need them. 29 Nevertheless, when he saw that the money of his treasures failed and that the tributes in the country were small, because of the dissension and plague, which he had brought upon the land in taking away the laws which had been of old time; 30 He feared that he should not be able to bear the charges any longer, nor to have such gifts to give so liberally as he did before: for he had abounded above the kings that were before him. 31 Wherefore, being greatly perplexed in his mind, he determined to go into Persia, there to take the tributes of the countries, and to gather much money. 32 So he left Lysias, a nobleman, and one of the blood royal, to oversee the affairs of the king from the river Euphrates unto the borders of Egypt: 33 And to bring up his son Antiochus, until he came again. 34 Moreover he delivered unto him the half of his forces, and the elephants, and gave him charge of all things that he would have done, as also concerning them that dwelt in Juda and Jerusalem: 35 To wit, that he should send an army against them, to destroy and root out the strength of Israel, and the remnant of Jerusalem, and to take away their memorial from that place; 36 And that he should place strangers in all their quarters, and divide their land by lot. 37 So the king took the half of the forces that remained, and departed from Antioch, his royal city, the hundred forty and seventh year; and having passed the river Euphrates, he went through the high countries. ³⁸ Then Lysias chose Ptolemee the son of Dorymenes, Nicanor, and Gorgias, mighty men of the king's friends: ³⁹ And with them he sent forty thousand footmen, and seven thousand horsemen, to go into the land of Juda, and to destroy it, as the king commanded. ⁴⁰ So they went forth with all their power, and came and pitched by Emmaus in the plain country. ⁴¹ And the merchants of the country, hearing the fame of them, took silver and gold very much, with servants, and came into the camp to buy the children of Israel for slaves: a power also of Syria and of the land of the Philistines joined themselves unto them. ⁴² Now when Judas and his brethren saw that miseries were multiplied, and that the forces did encamp themselves in their borders: for they knew how the king had given commandment to destroy the people, and utterly abolish them; ⁴³ They said one to another, Let us restore the decayed fortune of our people, and let us fight for our people and the sanctuary. ⁴⁴ Then was the congregation gathered together, that they might be ready for battle, and that they might pray, and ask mercy and compassion. ⁴⁵ Now Jerusalem lay void as a wilderness, there was none of her children that went in or out: the sanctuary also was trodden down, and aliens kept the strong hold; the heathen had their habitation in that place; and joy was taken from Jacob, and the pipe with the harp ceased. ⁴⁶ Wherefore the Israelites assembled themselves together, and came to Maspha, over against Jerusalem; for in Maspha was the place where they prayed aforetime in Israel. ⁴⁷ Then they fasted that day, and put on sackcloth, and cast ashes upon their heads, and rent their clothes, ⁴⁸ And laid open the book of the law, wherein the heathen had sought to paint the likeness of their images. ⁴⁹ They brought also the priests' garments, and the firstfruits, and the tithes: and the Nazarites they stirred up, who had accomplished their days. ⁵⁰ Then cried they with a loud voice toward heaven, saying, What shall we do with these, and whither shall we carry them away? 51 For thy sanctuary is trodden down and profaned, and thy priests are in heaviness, and brought low. 52 And lo, the heathen are assembled together against us to destroy us: what things they imagine against us, thou knowest. 53 How shall we be able to stand against them, except thou, O God, be our help? 54 Then sounded they with trumpets, and cried with a loud voice. 55 And after this Judas ordained captains over the people, even captains over thousands, and over hundreds, and over fifties, and over tens. 56 But as for such as were building houses, or had betrothed wives, or were planting vineyards, or were fearful, those he commanded that they should return, every man to his own house, according to the law. 57 So the camp removed, and pitched upon the south side of Emmaus. 58 And Judas said, arm yourselves, and be valiant men, and see that ye be in readiness against the morning, that ye may fight with these nations, that are assembled together against us to destroy us and our sanctuary: 59 For it is better for us to die in battle, than to behold the calamities of our people and our sanctuary. 60

Nevertheless, as the will of God is in heaven, so let him do.

4

1 Then took Gorgias five thousand footmen, and a thousand of the best horsemen, and removed out of the camp by night; 2 To the end he might rush in upon the camp of the Jews, and smite them suddenly. And the men of the fortress were his guides. 3 Now when Judas heard thereof he himself removed, and the valiant men with him, that he might smite the king's army which was at Emmaus, 4 While as yet the forces were dispersed from the camp. 5 In the mean season came Gorgias by night into the camp of Judas: and when he found no man there, he sought them in the mountains: for said he, These fellows flee from us 6 But as soon as it was day, Judas shewed himself in the plain with three thousand men, who nevertheless had neither armour nor swords to their minds. 7 And they saw the camp of the heathen, that it was strong and well harnessed, and compassed round about with horsemen; and these were expert of war. 8 Then said Judas to the men that were with him, Fear ye not their multitude, neither be ye afraid of their assault. 9

Remember how our fathers were delivered in the Red sea, when Pharaoh pursued them with an army. ¹⁰ Now therefore let us cry unto heaven, if peradventure the Lord will have mercy upon us, and remember the covenant of our fathers, and destroy this host before our face this day: ¹¹ That so all the heathen may know that there is one who delivereth and saveth Israel. ¹² Then the strangers lifted up their eyes, and saw them coming over against them. ¹³ Wherefore they went out of the camp to battle; but they that were with Judas sounded their trumpets. ¹⁴ So they joined battle, and the heathen being discomfited fled into the plain. ¹⁵ Howbeit all the hindmost of them were slain with the sword: for they pursued them unto Gazera, and unto the plains of Idumea, and Azotus, and Jamnia, so that there were slain of them upon a three thousand men. ¹⁶ This done, Judas returned again with his host from pursuing them, ¹⁷ And said to the people, Be not greedy of the spoil inasmuch as there is a battle before us, ¹⁸ And Gorgias and his host are here by us in the mountain: but stand ye now against our enemies, and overcome them, and after this ye may boldly take the spoils. ¹⁹ As Judas was yet speaking these words, there appeared a part of them looking out of the mountain: ²⁰ Who when they perceived that the Jews had put their host to flight and were burning the tents; for the smoke that was seen declared what was done: ²¹ When therefore they perceived these things, they were sore afraid, and seeing also the host of Judas in the plain ready to fight, ²² They fled every one into the land of strangers. ²³ Then Judas returned to spoil the tents, where they got much gold, and silver, and blue silk, and purple of the sea, and great riches. ²⁴ After this they went home, and sung a song of thanksgiving, and praised the Lord in heaven: because it is good, because his mercy endureth forever. ²⁵ Thus Israel had a great deliverance that day. ²⁶ Now all the strangers that had escaped came and told Lysias what had happened: ²⁷ Who, when he heard thereof, was confounded and discouraged, because neither such things as he would were done unto Israel, nor such things as the king commanded him were come to pass. ²⁸ The next year therefore following Lysias gathered together threescore thousand choice men of foot, and five thousand horsemen, that he might subdue them. ²⁹ So they came into Idumea, and pitched their tents at Bethsura, and Judas met them with ten thousand men. ³⁰ And when he saw that mighty army, he prayed and said, Blessed art thou, O Saviour of Israel, who didst quell the violence of the mighty man by the hand of thy servant David, and gavest the host of strangers into the hands of Jonathan the son of Saul, and his armourbearer; ³¹ Shut up this army in the hand of thy people Israel, and let them be confounded in their power and horsemen: ³² Make them to be of no courage, and cause the boldness of their strength to fall away, and let them quake at their destruction: ³³ Cast them down with the sword of them that love thee, and let all those that know thy name praise thee with thanksgiving. ³⁴ So they joined battle; and there were slain of the host of Lysias about five thousand men, even before them were they slain. ³⁵ Now when Lysias saw his army put to flight, and the manliness of Judas' soldiers, and how they were ready either to live or die valiantly, he went into Antiochia, and gathered together a company of strangers, and having made his army greater than it was, he purposed to come again into Judea. ³⁶ Then said Judas and his brethren, Behold, our enemies are discomfited: let us go up to cleanse and dedicate the sanctuary. ³⁷ Upon this all the host assembled themselves together, and went up into mount Sion. ³⁸ And when they saw the sanctuary desolate, and the altar profaned, and the gates burned up, and shrubs growing in the courts as in a forest, or in one of the mountains, yea, and the priests' chambers pulled down; ³⁹ They rent their clothes, and made great lamentation, and cast ashes upon their heads, ⁴⁰ And fell down flat to the ground upon their faces, and blew an alarm with the trumpets, and cried toward heaven. ⁴¹ Then Judas appointed certain men to fight against those that were in the fortress, until he had cleansed the sanctuary. ⁴² So he chose priests of blameless conversation, such as had pleasure in the law: ⁴³ Who cleansed the sanctuary, and bare out the defiled stones into an unclean place. ⁴⁴ And when as they consulted what to do with the altar of burnt offerings, which was profaned; ⁴⁵ They thought it best to pull it down, lest it should be a reproach to them, because the heathen had defiled it: wherefore they pulled it down, 46 And laid up the stones in the mountain of the temple in a convenient place, until there should come a prophet to shew what should be done with them. 47 Then they took whole stones according to the law, and built a new altar according to the former; 48 And made up the sanctuary, and the things that were within the temple, and hallowed the courts. 49 They made also new holy vessels, and into the temple they brought the candlestick, and the altar of burnt offerings, and of incense, and the table. 50 And upon the altar they burned incense, and the lamps that were upon the candlestick they lighted, that they might give light in the temple. 51 Furthermore they set the loaves upon the table, and spread out the veils, and finished all the works which they had begun to make. 52 Now on the five and twentieth day of the ninth month, which is called the month Casleu, in the hundred forty and eighth year, they rose up betimes in the morning, 53 And offered sacrifice according to the law upon the new altar of burnt offerings, which they had made. 54 Look, at what time and what day the heathen had profaned it, even in that was it dedicated with songs, and citherns, and harps, and cymbals. 55 Then all the people fell upon their faces, worshipping and praising the God of heaven, who had given them good success. 56 And so they kept the dedication of the altar eight days and offered burnt offerings with gladness, and sacrificed the sacrifice of deliverance and praise. 57 They decked also the forefront of the temple with crowns of gold, and with shields; and the gates and the chambers they renewed, and hanged doors upon them. 58 Thus was there very great gladness among the people, for that the reproach of the heathen was put away. 59 Moreover Judas and his brethren with the whole congregation of Israel ordained, that the days of the dedication of the altar should be kept in their season from year to year by the space of eight days, from the five and twentieth day of the month Casleu, with mirth and gladness. 60 At that time also they builded up the mount Sion with high walls and strong towers round about, lest the Gentiles should come and tread it down as they had done before. 61 And they set there a garrison to keep it, and fortified Bethsura to preserve it; that the people might have a defence against Idumea.

5

1 Now when the nations round about heard that the altar was built and the sanctuary renewed as before, it displeased them very much. 2 Wherefore they thought to destroy the generation of Jacob that was among them, and thereupon they began to slay and destroy the people. 3 Then Judas fought against the children of Esau in Idumea at Arabattine, because they besieged Gael: and he gave them a great overthrow, and abated their courage, and took their spoils. 4 Also he remembered the injury of the children of Bean, who had been a snare and an offence unto the people, in that they lay in wait for them in the ways. 5 He shut them up therefore in the towers, and encamped against them, and destroyed them utterly, and burned the towers of that place with fire, and all that were therein. 6 Afterward he passed over to the children of Ammon, where he found a mighty power, and much people, with Timotheus their captain. 7 So he fought many battles with them, till at length they were discomfited before him; and he smote them. 8 And when he had taken Jazar, with the towns belonging thereto, he returned into Judea. 9 Then the heathen that were at Galaad assembled themselves together against the Israelites that were in their quarters, to destroy them; but they fled to the fortress of Dathema. 10 And sent letters unto Judas and his brethren, The heathen that are round about us are assembled together against us to destroy us: 11 And they are preparing to come and take the fortress whereunto we are fled, Timotheus being captain of their host. 12 Come now therefore, and deliver us from their hands, for many of us are slain: 13 Yea, all our brethren that were in the places of Tobie are put to death: their wives and their children also they have carried away captives, and borne away their stuff; and they have destroyed there about a thousand men. 14 While these letters were yet reading, behold, there came other messengers from Galilee with their clothes rent, who reported on this wise, 15 And said, They of Ptolemais, and of Tyrus, and Sidon, and all Galilee of the Gentiles, are assembled together against us to consume us. 16 Now when Judas

and the people heard these words, there assembled a great congregation together, to consult what they should do for their brethren, that were in trouble, and assaulted of them. ¹⁷ Then said Judas unto Simon his brother, Choose thee out men, and go and deliver thy brethren that are in Galilee, for I and Jonathan my brother will go into the country of Galaad. ¹⁸ So he left Joseph the son of Zacharias, and Azarias, captains of the people, with the remnant of the host in Judea to keep it. ¹⁹ Unto whom he gave commandment, saying, Take ye the charge of this people, and see that ye make not war against the heathen until the time that we come again. ²⁰ Now unto Simon were given three thousand men to go into Galilee, and unto Judas eight thousand men for the country of Galaad. ²¹ Then went Simon into Galilee, where he fought many battles with the heathen, so that the heathen were discomfited by him. ²² And he pursued them unto the gate of Ptolemais; and there were slain of the heathen about three thousand men, whose spoils he took. ²³ And those that were in Galilee, and in Arbattis, with their wives and their children, and all that they

had took he away with him, and brought them into Judea with great joy. ²⁴ Judas Maccabeus also and his brother Jonathan went over Jordan, and travelled three days' journey in the wilderness, ²⁵ Where they met with the Nabathites, who came unto them in a peaceable manner, and told them every thing that had happened to their brethren in the land of Galaad: ²⁶ And how that many of them were shut up in Bosora, and Bosor, and Alema, Casphor, Maked, and Carnaim; all these cities are strong and great: ²⁷ And that they were shut up in the rest of the cities of the country of Galaad, and that against to morrow they had appointed to bring their host against the forts, and to take them, and to destroy them all in one day. ²⁸ Hereupon Judas and his host turned suddenly by the way of the wilderness unto Bosora; and when he had won the city, he slew all the males with the edge of the sword, and took all their spoils, and burned the city with fire, ²⁹ From whence he removed by night, and went till he came to the fortress. ³⁰ And betimes in the morning they looked up, and, behold, there was an innumerable people bearing ladders and other engines of war, to take the fortress: for they assaulted them. 31 When Judas therefore saw that the battle was begun, and that the cry of the city went up to heaven, with trumpets, and a great sound, 32 He said unto his host, Fight this day for your brethren. 33 So he went forth behind them in three companies, who sounded their trumpets, and cried with prayer. 34 Then the host of Timotheus, knowing that it was Maccabeus, fled from him: wherefore he smote them with a great slaughter; so that there were killed of them that day about eight thousand men. 35 This done, Judas turned aside to Maspha; and after he had assaulted it he took and slew all the males therein, and received the spoils thereof and and burnt it with fire. 36 From thence went he, and took Casphon, Maged, Bosor, and the other cities of the country of Galaad. 37 After these things gathered Timotheus another host and encamped against Raphon beyond the brook. 38 So Judas sent men to espy the host, who brought him word, saying, All the heathen that be round about us are assembled unto them, even a very great host. 39 He hath also hired the Arabians to help them and they have pitched their tents beyond the brook, ready to come and fight against thee. Upon this Judas went to meet them. 40 Then Timotheus said unto the captains of his host, When Judas and his host come near the brook, if he pass over first unto us, we shall not be able to withstand him; for he will mightily prevail against us: 41 But if he be afraid, and camp beyond the river, we shall go over unto him, and prevail against him. 42 Now when Judas came near the brook, he caused the scribes of the people to remain by the brook: unto whom he gave commandment, saying, Suffer no man to remain in the camp, but let all come to the battle. 43 So he went first over unto them, and all the people after him: then all the heathen, being discomfited before him, cast away their weapons, and fled unto the temple that was at Carnaim. 44 But they took the city, and burned the temple with all that were therein. Thus was Carnaim subdued, neither could they stand any longer before Judas. 45 Then Judas gathered together allthe Israelites that were in the country of Galaad, from the least unto the greatest, even their wives, and their children, and their stuff, a very great host, to the end they might come into the land of Judea. ⁴⁶ Now when they came unto Ephron, (this was a great city in the way as they should go, very well fortified) they could not turn from it, either on the right hand or the left, but must needs pass through the midst of it. ⁴⁷ Then they of the city shut them out, and stopped up the gates with stones. ⁴⁸ Whereupon Judas sent unto them in peaceable manner, saying, Let us pass through your land to go into our own country, and none shall do you any hurt; we will only pass through on foot: howbeit they would not open unto him. ⁴⁹ Wherefore Judas commanded a proclamation to be made throughout the host, that every man should pitch his tent in the place where he was. ⁵⁰ So the soldiers pitched, and assaulted the city all that day and all that night, till at the length the city was delivered into his hands: ⁵¹ Who then slew all the males with the edge of the sword, and rased the city, and took the spoils thereof, and passed through the city over them that were slain. ⁵² After this went they over Jordan into the great plain before Bethsan. ⁵³ And Judas gathered together those that came behind, and exhorted the people all the way through, till they came into the land of Judea. ⁵⁴ So they went up to mount Sion with joy and gladness, where they offered burnt offerings, because not one of them were slain until they had returned in peace. ⁵⁵ Now what time as Judas and Jonathan were in the land of Galaad, and Simon his brother in Galilee before Ptolemais, ⁵⁶ Joseph the son of Zacharias, and Azarias, captains of the garrisons, heard of the valiant acts and warlike deeds which they had done. ⁵⁷ Wherefore they said, Let us also get us a name, and go fight against the heathen that are round about us. ⁵⁸ So when they had given charge unto the garrison that was with them, they went toward Jamnia. ⁵⁹ Then came Gorgias and his men out of the city to fight against them. ⁶⁰ And so it was, that Joseph and Azarias were put to flight, and pursued unto the borders of Judea: and there were slain that day of the people of Israel about two thousand men. ⁶¹ Thus was there a great overthrow among the children of Israel, because they were not obedient unto Judas and his brethren, but thought to do some valiant act. ⁶² Moreover these men came not of the seed of those, by whose hand deliverance was given unto Israel. 63 How be it the man Judas and his brethren were greatly renowned in the sight of all Israel, and of all the heathen, wheresoever their name was heard of; 64 Insomuch as the people assembled unto them with joyful acclamations. 65 Afterward went Judas forth with his brethren, and fought against the children of Esau in the land toward the south, where he smote Hebron, and the towns thereof, and pulled down the fortress of it, and burned the towers thereof round about. 66 From thence he removed to go into the land of the Philistines, and passed through Samaria. 67 At that time certain priests, desirous to shew their valour, were slain in battle, for that they went out to fight unadvisedly. 68 So Judas turned to Azotus in the land of the Philistines, and when he had pulled down their altars, and burned their carved images with fire, and spoiled their cities, he returned into the land of Judea.

6

1 About that time king Antiochus travelling through the high countries heard say, that Elymais in the country of Persia was a city greatly renowned for riches, silver, and gold; 2 And that there was in it a very rich temple, wherein were coverings of gold, and breastplates, and shields, which Alexander, son of Philip, the Macedonian king, who reigned first among the Grecians, had left there. 3 Wherefore he came and sought to take the city, and to spoil it; but he was not able, because they of the city, having had warning thereof, 4 Rose up against him in battle: so he fled, and departed thence with great heaviness, and returned to Babylon. 5 Moreover there came one who brought him tidings into Persia, that the armies, which went against the land of Judea, were put to flight: 6 And that Lysias, who went forth first with a great power was driven away of the Jews; and that they were made strong by the armour, and power, and store of spoils, which they had gotten of the armies, whom they had destroyed: 7 Also that they had pulled down the abomination, which he had set up upon the altar in Jerusalem, and that they had compassed about the sanctuary with high walls, as before, and his city Bethsura. 8 Now when the king heard these words, he was astonished and sore moved: whereupon he laid

him down upon his bed, and fell sick for grief, because it had not befallen him as he looked for. 9 And there he continued many days: for his grief was ever more and more, and he made account that he should die. 10 Wherefore he called for all his friends, and said unto them, The sleep is gone from mine eyes, and my heart faileth for very care. 11 And I thought with myself, Into what tribulation am I come, and how great a flood of misery is it, wherein now I am! for I was bountiful and beloved in my power. 12 But now I remember the evils that I did at Jerusalem, and that I took all the vessels of gold and silver that were therein, and sent to destroy the inhabitants of Judea without a cause. 13 I perceive therefore that for this cause these troubles are come upon me, and, behold, I perish through great grief in a strange land. 14 Then called he for Philip, one of his friends, who he made ruler over all his realm, 15 And gave him the crown, and his robe, and his signet, to the end he should bring up his son Antiochus, and nourish him up for the kingdom. 16 So king Antiochus died there in the hundred forty and ninth year. 17 Now when Lysias knew that the king was dead, he set up Antiochus his son, whom he had brought up being young, to reign in his stead, and his name he called Eupator. 18 About this time they that were in the tower shut up the Israelites round about the sanctuary, and sought always their hurt, and the strengthening of the heathen. 19 Wherefore Judas, purposing to destroy them, called all the people together to besiege them. 20 So they came together, and besieged them in the hundred and fiftieth year, and he made mounts for shot against them, and other engines. 21 Howbeit certain of them that were besieged got forth, unto whom some ungodly men of Israel joined themselves: 22 And they went unto the king, and said, How long will it be ere thou execute judgment, and avenge our brethren? 23 We have been willing to serve thy father, and to do as he would have us, and to obey his commandments; 24 For which cause they of our nation besiege the tower, and are alienated from us: moreover as many of us as they could light on they slew, and spoiled our inheritance. 25 Neither have they stretched out their hand against us only, but also against their borders. 26 And, behold, this day are they besieging the tower at Jerusalem, to take it: the sanctuary also and Bethsura have they fortified. 27 Wherefore if thou dost not prevent them quickly, they will do the greater things than these, neither shalt thou be able to rule them. 28 Now when the king heard this, he was angry, and gathered together all his friends, and the captains of his army, and those that had charge of the horse. 29 There came also unto him from other kingdoms, and from isles of the sea, bands of hired soldiers. 30 So that the number of his army was an hundred thousand footmen, and twenty thousand horsemen, and two and thirty elephants exercised in battle. 31 These went through Idumea, and pitched against Bethsura, which they assaulted many days, making engines of war; but they of Bethsura came out, and burned them with fire, and fought valiantly. 32 Upon this Judas removed from the tower, and pitched in Bathzacharias, over against the king's camp. 33 Then the king rising very early marched fiercely with his host toward Bathzacharias, where his armies made them ready to battle, and sounded the trumpets. 34 And to the end they might provoke the elephants to fight, they shewed them the blood of grapes and mulberries. 35 Moreover they divided the beasts among the armies, and for every elephant they appointed a thousand men, armed with coats of mail, and with helmets of brass on their heads; and beside this, for every beast were ordained five hundred horsemen of the best. 36 These were ready at every occasion: wheresoever the beast was, and whithersoever the beast went, they went also, neither departed they from him. 37 And upon the beasts were there strong towers of wood, which covered every one of them, and were girt fast unto them with devices: there were also upon every one two and thirty strong men, that fought upon them, beside the Indian that ruled him. 38 As for the remnant of the horsemen, they set them on this side and that side at the two parts of the host giving them signs what to do, and being harnessed all over amidst the ranks. 39 Now when the sun shone upon the shields of gold and brass, the mountains glistered therewith, and shined like lamps of fire. 40 So part of the king's army being spread upon the high mountains, and part on the valleys below, they marched on safely and in order. ⁴¹ Wherefore all that heard the noise of their multitude, and the marching of the company, and the rattling of the harness, were moved: for the army was very great and mighty. ⁴² Then Judas and his host drew near, and entered into battle, and there were slain of the king's army six hundred men. ⁴³ Eleazar also, surnamed Savaran, perceiving that one of the beasts, armed with royal harness, was higher than all the rest, and supposing that the king was upon him, ⁴⁴ Put himself in jeopardy, to the end he might deliver his people, and get him a perpetual name: ⁴⁵ Wherefore he ran upon him courageously through the midst of the battle, slaying on the right hand and on the left, so that they were divided from him on both sides. ⁴⁶ Which done, he crept under the elephant, and thrust him under, and slew him: whereupon the elephant fell down upon him, and there he died. ⁴⁷ Howbeit the rest of the Jews seeing the strength of the king, and the violence of his forces, turned away from them. ⁴⁸ Then the king's army went up to Jerusalem to meet them, and the king pitched his tents against Judea, and against mount Sion. ⁴⁹ But with them that were in Bethsura he made peace: for they came out of the city, because they had no victuals there to endure the siege, it being a year of rest to the land. ⁵⁰ So the king took Bethsura, and set a garrison there to keep it. ⁵¹ As for the sanctuary, he besieged it many days: and set there artillery with engines and instruments to cast fire and stones, and pieces to cast darts and slings. ⁵² Whereupon they also made engines against their engines, and held them battle a long season. ⁵³ Yet at the last, their vessels being without victuals, (for that it was the seventh year, and they in Judea that were delivered from the Gentiles, had eaten up the residue of the store;) ⁵⁴ There were but a few left in the sanctuary, because the famine did so prevail against them, that they were fain to disperse themselves, every man to his own place. ⁵⁵ At that time Lysias heard say, that Philip, whom Antiochus the king, whiles he lived, had appointed to bring up his son Antiochus, that he might be king, ⁵⁶ Was returned out of Persia and Media, and the king's host also that went with him, and that he sought to take unto him the ruling of the affairs. ⁵⁷ Wherefore he went in all haste, and said to the king and the captains of the host and the company, We decay daily, and our victuals are but small, and the place we lay siege unto is strong, and the affairs of the kingdom lie upon us: 58 Now therefore let us be friends with these men, and make peace with them, and with all their nation; 59 And covenant with them, that they shall live after their laws, as they did before: for they are therefore displeased, and have done all these things, because we abolished their laws. 60 So the king and the princes were content: wherefore he sent unto them to make peace; and they accepted thereof. 61 Also the king and the princes made an oath unto them: whereupon they went out of the strong hold. 62 Then the king entered into mount Sion; but when he saw the strength of the place, he broke his oath that he had made, and gave commandment to pull down the wall round about. 63 Afterward departed he in all haste, and returned unto Antiochia, where he found Philip to be master of the city: so he fought against him, and took the city by force.

7

1 In the hundred and one and fiftieth year Demetrius the son of Seleucus departed from Rome, and came up with a few men unto a city of the sea coast, and reigned there. 2 And as he entered into the palace of his ancestors, so it was, that his forces had taken Antiochus and Lysias, to bring them unto him. 3 Wherefore, when he knew it, he said, Let me not see their faces. 4 So his host slew them. Now when Demetrius was set upon the throne of his kingdom, 5 There came unto him all the wicked and ungodly men of Israel, having Alcimus, who was desirous to be high priest, for their captain: 6 And they accused the people to the king, saying, Judas and his brethren have slain all thy friends, and driven us out of our own land. 7 Now therefore send some man whom thou trustest, and let him go and see what havock he hath made among us, and in the king's land, and let him punish them with all them that aid them. 8 Then the king chose Bacchides, a friend of the king, who ruled beyond the flood, and was a great man in the kingdom, and faithful to the king, 9 And him he sent with that wicked Alcimus, whom he made high priest, and commanded that he should take vengeance of the children of Israel. 10 So they departed, and came with a great

power into the land of Judea, where they sent messengers to Judas and his brethren with peaceable words deceitfully. [11]But they gave no heed to their words; for they saw that they were come with a great power. [12] Then did there assemble unto Alcimus and Bacchides a company of scribes,to require justice. [13] Now the Assideans were the first among the children of Israel that sought peace of them: [14] For said they, One that is a priest of the seed of Aaron is come with this army, and he will do us no wrong. [15] So he spake unto them, peaceably, and sware unto them, saying, we will procure the harm neither of you nor your friends. [16] Whereupon they believed him: howbeit he took of them threescore men, and slew them in one day, according to the words which he wrote, [17] The flesh of thy saints have they cast out, and their blood have they shed round about Jerusalem, and there was none to bury them. [18] Wherefore the fear and dread of them fell upon all the people, who said, There is neither truth nor righteousness in them; for they have broken the covenant and oath that they made. [19] After this, removed Bacchides from Jerusalem, and pitched his tents in Bezeth, where he sent and took many of the men that had forsaken him, and certain of the people also, and when he had slain them, he cast them into the great pit. [20] Then committed he the country to Alcimus, and left with him a power to aid him: so Bacchides went to the king. [21] But Alcimus contended for the high priesthood. [22] And unto him resorted all such as troubled the people, who, after they had gotten the land of Juda into their power, did much hurt in Israel. [23] Now when Judas saw all the mischief that Alcimus and his company had done among the Israelites, even above the heathen, [24] He went out into all the coasts of Judea round about, and took vengeance of them that had revolted from him, so that they durst no more go forth into the country. [25] On the other side, when Alcimus saw that Judas and his company had gotten the upper hand, and knew that he was not able to abide their force, he went again to the king, and said all the worst of them that he could. [26] Then the king sent Nicanor, one of his honourable princes, a man that bare deadly hate unto Israel, with commandment to destroy the people. 27 So Nicanor came to Jerusalem with a great force; and sent unto Judas and his brethren deceitfully with friendly words, saying, 28 Let there be no battle between me and you; I will come with a few men, that I may see you in peace. 29 He came therefore to Judas, and they saluted one another peaceably. Howbeit the enemies were prepared to take away Judas by violence. 30 Which thing after it was known to Judas, to wit, that he came unto him with deceit, he was sore afraid of him, and would see his face no more. 31 Nicanor also, when he saw that his counsel was discovered, went out to fight against Judas beside Capharsalama: 32 Where there were slain of Nicanor's side about five thousand men, and the rest fled into the city of David. 33 After this went Nicanor up to mount Sion, and there came out of the sanctuary certain of the priests and certain of the elders of the people, to salute him peaceably, and to shew him the burnt sacrifice that was offered for the king. 34 But he mocked them, and laughed at them, and abused them shamefully, and spake proudly, 35 And sware in his wrath, saying, Unless Judas and his host be now delivered into my hands, if ever I come again in safety, I will burn up this house: and with that he went out in a great rage. 36 Then the priests entered in, and stood before the altar and the temple, weeping, and saying, 37 Thou, O Lord, didst choose this house to be called by thy name, and to be a house of prayer and petition for thy people: 38 Be avenged of this man and his host, and let them fall by the sword: remember their blasphemies, and suffer them not to continue any longer. 39 So Nicanor went out of Jerusalem, and pitched his tents in Bethhoron, where an host out of Syria met him. 40 But Judas pitched in Adasa with three thousand men, and there he prayed, saying, 41 O Lord, when they that were sent from the king of the Assyrians blasphemed, thine angel went out, and smote an hundred fourscore and five thousand of them. 42 Even so destroy thou this host before us this day, that the rest may know that he hath spoken blasphemously against thy sanctuary, and judge thou him according to his wickedness. 43 So the thirteenth day of the month Adar the hosts joined battle: but Nicanor's host was discomfited, and he himself was first slain in the battle. ⁴⁴ Now when Nicanor's host saw that he was slain, they cast away their weapons, and fled. ⁴⁵ Then they pursued after them a day's journey, from Adasa unto Gazera, sounding an alarm after them with their trumpets. ⁴⁶ Whereupon they came forth out of all the towns of Judea round about, and closed them in; so thatthey, turning back upon them that pursued them, were all slain with the sword, andnot one of them was left. ⁴⁷ Afterwards they took the spoils, and the prey, and smote off Nicanors head, and his right hand, which he stretched out so proudly, and brought them away, and hanged them up toward Jerusalem. ⁴⁸ For this cause the people rejoiced greatly, and they kept that day a day of great gladness. ⁴⁹ Moreover they ordained to keep yearly this day, being the thirteenth of Adar. ⁵⁰ Thus the land of Juda was in rest a little while.

8

¹ Now Judas had heard of the Romans, that they were mighty and valiant men, and such as would lovingly accept all that joined themselves unto them, and make a league of amity with all that came unto them; ² And that they were men of great valour. It was told him also of their wars and noble acts which they had done among the Galatians, and how they had conquered them, and brought them under tribute; ³ And what they had done in the country of Spain, for the winning of the mines of the silver and gold which is there; ⁴ And that by their policy and patience they had conquered all the place, though it were very far from them; and the kings also that came against them from the uttermost part of the earth, till they had discomfited them, and given them a great overthrow, so that the rest did give them tribute every year: ⁵ Beside this, how they had discomfited in battle Philip, and Perseus, king of the Citims, with others that lifted up themselves against them, and had overcome them: ⁶ How also Antiochus the great king of Asia, that came against them in battle, having an hundred and twenty elephants, with horsemen, and chariots, and a very great army, was discomfited by them; ⁷ And how they took him alive, and covenanted that he and such as reigned after him should pay a great tribute, and give hostages, and that which was agreed upon, ⁸ And the country of India, and

Media and Lydia and of the goodliest countries, which they took of him, and gave to king Eumenes: ⁹ Moreover how the Grecians had determined to come and destroy them; ¹⁰ And that they, having knowledge thereof sent against them a certain captain, and fighting with them slew many of them, and carried away captives their wives and their children, and spoiled them, and took possession of their lands, and pulled down their strong holds, and brought them to be their servants unto this day: ¹¹ It was told him besides, how they destroyed and brought under their dominion all other kingdoms and isles that at any time resisted them; ¹² But with their friends and such as relied upon them they kept amity: and that they had conquered kingdoms both far and nigh, insomuch as all that heard of their name were afraid of them: ¹³ Also that, whom they would help to a kingdom, those reign; and whom again they would, they displace: finally, that they were greatly exalted: ¹⁴ Yet for all this none of them wore a crown or was clothed in purple, to be magnified thereby: ¹⁵ Moreover how they had made for themselves a senate house, wherein three hundred and twenty men sat in council daily, consulting alway for the people, to the end they might be well ordered: ¹⁶ And that they committed their government to one man every year, who ruled over all their country, and that all were obedient to that one, and that there was neither envy nor emmulation among them. ¹⁷ In consideration of these things, Judas chose Eupolemus the son of John, the son of Accos, and Jason the son of Eleazar, and sent them to Rome, to make a league of amity and confederacy with them, ¹⁸ And to intreat them that they would take the yoke from them; for they saw that the kingdom of the Grecians did oppress Israel with servitude. ¹⁹ They went therefore to Rome, which was a very great journey, and came into the senate, where they spake and said. ²⁰ Judas Maccabeus with his brethren, and the people of the Jews, have sent us unto you, to make a confederacy and peace with you, and that we might be registered your confederates and friends. ²¹ So that matter pleased the Romans well. ²² And this is the copy of the epistle which the senate wrote back again in tables of brass, and sent to Jerusalem, that there they might have by them a memorial of peace and confederacy: 23 Good success be to the Romans, and to the people of the Jews, by sea and by land for ever: the sword also and enemy be far from them, 24 If there come first any war upon the Romans or any of their confederates throughout all their dominion, 25 The people of the Jews shall help them, as the time shall be appointed, with all their heart: 26 Neither shall they give any thing unto them that make war upon them, or aid them with victuals, weapons, money, or ships, as it hath seemed good unto the Romans; but they shall keep their covenants without taking any thing therefore. 27 In the same manner also, if war come first upon the nation of the Jews, the Romans shall help them with all their heart, according as the time shall be appointed them: 28 Neither shall victuals be given to them that take part against them, or weapons, or money, or ships, as it hath seemed good to the Romans; but they shall keep their covenants, and that without deceit. 29 According to these articles did the Romans make a covenant with the people of the Jews. 30 Howbeit if hereafter the one party or the other shall think to meet to add or diminish any thing, they may do it at their pleasures, and whatsoever they shall add or take away shall be ratified. 31 And as touching the evils that Demetrius doeth to the Jews, we have written unto him, saying, Wherefore thou made thy yoke heavy upon our friends and confederates the Jews? 32 If therefore they complain any more against thee, we will do them justice, and fight with thee by sea and by land.

9

1 Furthermore, when Demetrius heard the Nicanor and his host were slain in battle, he sent Bacchides and Alcimus into the land of Judea the second time, and with them the chief strength of his host: 2 Who went forth by the way that leadeth to Galgala, and pitched their tents before Masaloth, which is in Arbela, and after they had won it, they slew much people. 3 Also the first month of the hundred fifty and second year they encamped before Jerusalem: 4 From whence they removed, and went to Berea, with twenty thousand footmen and two thousand horsemen. 5 Now Judas had pitched his tents at Eleasa, and three thousand chosen men with him: 6 Who seeing the multitude of the other

army to be so great were sore afraid; whereupon many conveyed themselves out of the host, insomuch as abode of them no more but eight hundred men. 7 When Judas therefore saw that his host slipt away, and that the battle pressed upon him, he was sore troubled in mind, and much distressed, for that he had no time to gather them together. 8 Nevertheless unto them that remained he said, Let us arise and go up against our enemies, if peradventure we may be able to fight with them. 9 But they dehorted him, saying, We shall never be able: let us now rather save our lives, and hereafter we will return with our brethren, and fight against them: for we are but few. 10 Then Judas said, God forbid that I should do this thing, and flee away from them: if our time be come, let us die manfully for our brethren, and let us not stain our honour. 11 With that the host of Bacchides removed out of their tents, and stood over against them, their horsemen bein divided into two troops, and their slingers and archers going before the host and they that marched in the foreward were all mighty men. 12 As for Bacchides, he was in the right wing: so the host drew near on the two parts, and sounded their trumpets. 13 They also of Judas' side, even they sounded their trumpets also, so that the earth shook at the noise of the armies, and the battle continued from morning till night. 14 Now when Judas perceived that Bacchides and the strength of his army were on the right side, he took with him all the hardy men, 15 Who discomfited the right wing, and pursued them unto the mount Azotus. 16 But when they of the left wing saw that they of the right wing were discomfited, they followed upon Judas and those that were with him hard at the heels from behind: 17 Where upon there was a sorebattle, insomuch as many were slain on both parts. 18 Judas also was killed, and the remnant fled. 19 Then Jonathan and Simon took Judas their brother, and buried him in the sepulchre of his fathers in Modin. 20 Moreover they bewailed him, and all Israel made great lamentation for him, and mourned many days, saying, 21 How is the valiant man fallen, that delivered Israel! 22 As for the other things concerning Judas and his wars, and the noble acts which he did, and his greatness, they are not written: for they were very many. 23 Now after the death of Judas the wicked began to put forth their heads in all the coasts of Israel, and there arose up all such as wrought iniquity. 24 In those days also was there a very great famine, by reason whereof the country revolted, and went with them. 25 Then Bacchides chose the wicked men, and made them lords of the country. 26 And they made enquiry and search for Judas' friends, and brought them unto Bacchides, who took vengeance of them, and used them despitefully. 27 So was there a great affliction in Israel, the like whereof was not since the time that a prophet was not seen among them. 28 For this cause all Judas' friends came together, and said unto Jonathan, 29 Since thy brother Judas died, we have no man like him to go forth against our enemies, and Bacchides, and against them of our nation that are adversaries to us. 30 Now therefore we have chosen thee this day to be our prince and captain in his stead, that thou mayest fight our battles. 31 Upon this Jonathan took the governance upon him at that time, and rose up instead of his brother Judas. 32 But when Bacchides gat knowledge thereof, he sought for to slay him 33 Then Jonathan, and Simon his brother, and all that were with him, perceiving that, fled into the wilderness of Thecoe, and pitched their tents by the water of the pool Asphar. 34 Which when Bacchides understood, he came near to Jordan with all his host upon the sabbath day. 35 Now Jonathan had sent his brother John, a captain of the people, to pray his friends the Nabathites, that they might leave with them their carriage, which was much. 36 But the children of Jambri came out of Medaba, and took John, and all that he had, and went their way with it. 37 After this came word to Jonathan and Simon his brother, that the children of Jambri made a great marriage, and were bringing the bride from Nadabatha with a great train, as being the daughter of one of the great princes of Chanaan. 38 Therefore they remembered John their brother, and went up, and hid themselves under the covert of the mountain: 39 Where they lifted up their eyes, and looked, and, behold, there was much ado and great carriage: and the bridegroom came forth, and his friends and brethren, to meet them with drums, and instruments of musick, and many weapons. 40 Then Jonathan and they that were with him rose up against them from the place where they lay in ambush, and made a slaughter of them in such sort, as many fell down dead, and the remnant fled into the mountain, and they took all their spoils. 41 Thus was the marriage turned into mourning, and the noise of their melody into lamentation. 42 So when they had avenged fully the blood of their brother, they turned again to the marsh of Jordan. 43 Now when Bacchides heard hereof, he came on the sabbath day unto the banks of Jordan with a great power. 44 Then Jonathan said to his company, Let us go up now and fight for our lives, for it standeth not with us to day, as in time past: 45 For, behold, the battle is before us and behind us, and the water of Jordan on this side and that side, the marsh likewise and wood, neither is there place for us to turn aside. 46 Wherefore cry ye now unto heaven, that ye may be delivered from the hand of your enemies. 47 With that they joined battle, and Jonathan stretched forth his hand to smite Bacchides, but he turned back from him. 48 Then Jonathan and they that were with him leapt into Jordan, and swam over unto the other bank: howbeit the other passed not over Jordan unto them. 49 So there were slain of Bacchides' side that day about a thousand men. 50 Afterward returned Bacchides to Jerusalem and repaired the strong cites in Judea; the fort in Jericho, and Emmaus, and Bethhoron, and Beth-el, and Thamnatha, Pharathoni, and Taphon, these did he strengthen with high walls, with gates and with bars. 51 And in them he set a garrison, that they might work malice upon Israel. 52 He fortified also the city Bethsura, and Gazera, and the tower, and put forces in them, and provision of victuals. 53 Besides, he took the chief men's sons in the country for hostages, and put them into the tower at Jerusalem to be kept. 54 Moreover in the hundred fifty and third year, in the second month, Alcimus commanded that the wall ofthe inner court ofthe sanctuary should be pulled down; he pulled down also the works of the prophets 55 And as he began to pull down, even at that time was Alcimus plagued, and his enterprizes hindered: for his mouth was stopped, and he was taken with a palsy, so that he could no more speak any thing, nor give order concerning his house. 56 So Alcimus died at that time with great torment. 57 Now when Bacchides saw that Alcimus was dead, he returned to the king: whereupon the land of Judea was in rest two years. 58 Then all the ungodly men held a council, saying, Behold, Jonathan and his company are at ease, and dwell without care: now therefore we will bring Bacchides hither, who shall take them all in one night. 59 So they went and consulted with him. 60 Then removed he, and came with a great host, and sent letters privily to his adherents in Judea, that they should take Jonathan and those that were with him: howbeit they could not, because their counsel was known unto them. 61 Wherefore they took of the men of the country, that were authors of that mischief, about fifty persons, and slew them. 62 Afterward Jonathan, and Simon, and they that were with him, got them away to Bethbasi, which is in the wilderness, and they repaired the decays thereof, and made it strong. 63 Which thing when Bacchides knew, he gathered together all his host, and sent word to them that were of Judea. 64 Then went he and laid siege against Bethbasi; and they fought against it a long season and made engines of war. 65 But Jonathan left his brother Simoninthe city, and went forth himself into the country, and with a certain number went he forth. 66 And he smote Odonarkes and his brethren, and the children of Phasiron in their tent. 67 And when he began to smite them, and came up with his forces, Simon and his company went out of the city, and burned up the engines of war, 68 And fought against Bacchides, who was discomfited by them, and they afflicted him sore: for his counsel and travail was in vain. 69 Wherefore he was very wroth at the wicked men that gave him counsel to come into the country, inasmuch as he slew many of them, and purposed to return into his own country. 70 Whereof when Jonathan had knowledge, he sent ambassadors unto him, to the end he should make peace with him, and deliver them the prisoners. 71 Which thing he accepted, and did according to his demands, and sware unto him that he would never do him harm all the days of his life. 72 When therefore he had restored unto him the prisoners that he had taken aforetime out of the land of Judea, he returned and went his way into his own land, neither came he any more into their borders. 73 Thus the sword ceased from Israel: but Jonathan dwelt at Machmas, and began to govern the people; and he destroyed the ungodly men out of Israel.

10

1 In the hundred and sixtieth year Alexander, the son of Antiochus surnamed Epiphanes, went up and took Ptolemais: for the people had received him, by means whereof he reigned there, 2 Now when king Demetrius heard thereof, he gathered together an exceeding great host, and went forth against him to fight. 3 Moreover Demetrius sent letters unto Jonathan with loving words, so as he magnified him. 4 For said he, Let us first make peace with him, before he join with Alexander against us: 5 Else he will remember all the evils that we have done against him, and against his brethren and his people. 6 Wherefore he gave him authority to gather together an host, and to provide weapons, that he might aid him in battle: he commanded also that the hostages that were in the tower should be delivered him. 7 Then came Jonathan to Jerusalem, and read the letters in the audience of all the people, and of them that were in the tower: 8 Who were sore afraid, when they heard that the king had given him authority to gather together an host. 9 Whereupon they of the tower delivered their hostages unto Jonathan, and he delivered them unto their parents. 10 This done, Jonathan settled himself in Jerusalem, and began to build and repair the city. 11 And he commanded the workmen to build the walls and the mount Sion and about with square stones for fortification; and they did so. 12 Then the strangers, that were in the fortresses which Bacchides had built, fled away; 13 Insomuch as every man left his place, and went into his own country. 14 Only at Bethsura certain of those that had forsaken the law and the commandments remained still: for it was their place of refuge. 15 Now when king Alexander had heard what promises Demetrius had sent unto Jonathan: when also it was told him of the battles and noble acts which he and his brethren had done, and of the pains that they had endured, 16 He said, Shall we find such another man? now therefore we will make him our friend and confederate. 17 Upon this he wrote a letter, and sent it unto him, according to these words, saying, 18 King

Alexander to his brother Jonathan sendeth greeting: ¹⁹ We have heard of thee, that thou art a man of great power, and meet to be our friend. ²⁰ Wherefore now this day we ordain thee to be the high priest of thy nation, and to be called the king's friend; (and therewithal he sent him a purple robe and a crown of gold:) and require thee to take our part, and keep friendship with us. ²¹ So in the seventh month of the hundred and sixtieth year, at the feast of the tabernacles, Jonathan put on the holy robe, and gathered together forces, and provided much armour. ²² Whereof when Demetrius heard, he was very sorry, and said, ²³ What have we done, that Alexander hath prevented us in making amity with the Jews to strengthen himself? ²⁴ I also will write unto them words of encouragement, and promise them dignities and gifts, that I may have their aid. ²⁵ He sent unto them therefore to this effect: King Demetrius unto the people of the Jews sendeth greeting: ²⁶ Whereas ye have kept covenants with us, and continued in our friendship, not joining yourselves with our enemies, we have heard hereof, and are glad. ²⁷ Wherefore now continue ye still to be faithful unto us, and we will well recompense you for the things ye do in our behalf, ²⁸ And will grant you many immunities, and give you rewards. ²⁹ And now do I free you, and for your sake I release all the Jews, from tributes, and from the customs of salt, and from crown taxes, ³⁰ And from that which appertaineth unto me to receive for the third part or the seed, and the half of the fruit of the trees, I release it from this day forth, so that they shall not be taken of the land of Judea, nor of the three governments which are added thereunto out of the country of Samaria and Galilee, from this day forth for evermore. ³¹ Let Jerusalem also be holy and free, with the borders thereof, both from tenths and tributes. ³² And as for the tower which is at Jerusalem, I yield up authority over it, and give the high priest, that he may set in it such men as he shall choose to keep it. ³³ Moreover I freely set at liberty every one of the Jews, that were carried captives out of the land of Judea into any part of my kingdom, and I will that all my officers remit the tributes even of their cattle. ³⁴ Furthermore I will that all the feasts, and sabbaths, and new moons, and solemn days, and the three days before the feast, and the three days after the feast shall be all of immunity and freedom for all the Jews in my realm. 35 Also no man shall have authority to meddle with or to molest any of them in any matter. 36 I will further, that there be enrolled among the king's forces about thirty thousand men of the Jews, unto whom pay shall be given, as belongeth to all king's forces. 37 And of them some shall be placed in the king's strong holds, of whom also some shall be set over the affairs of the kingdom, which are of trust: and I will that their overseers and governors be of themselves, and that they live after their own laws, even as the king hath commanded in the land of Judea. 38 And concerning the three governments that are added to Judea from the country of Samaria, let them be joined with Judea, that they may be reckoned to be under one, nor bound to obey other authority than the high priest's. 39 As for Ptolemais, and the land pertaining thereto, I give it as a free gift to the sanctuary at Jerusalem for the necessary expences of the sanctuary. 40 Moreover I give every year fifteen thousand shekels of silver out of the king's accounts from the places appertaining. 41 And all the overplus, which the officers payed not in as in former time, from henceforth shall be given toward the works of the temple. 42 And beside this, the five thousand shekels of silver, which they took from the uses of the temple out of the accounts year by year, even those things shall be released, because they appertain to the priests that minister. 43 And whosoever they be that flee unto the temple at Jerusalem, or be within the liberties hereof, being indebted unto the king, or for any other matter, let them be at liberty, and all that they have in my realm. 44 For the building also and repairing of the works of the sanctuary expences shall be given of the king's accounts. 45 Yea, and for the building of the walls of Jerusalem, and the fortifying thereof roundabout, expences shall be given out of the king's accounts, as also for the building of the walls in Judea. 46 Now when Jonathan and the people heard these words, they gave no credit unto them, nor received them, because they remembered the great evil that he had done in Israel; for he had afflicted them very sore. 47 But with Alexander they were well pleased, because he was the first that entreated of true peace with them, and they were confederate with him always. ⁴⁸ Then gathered king Alexander great forces, and camped over against Demetrius. ⁴⁹ And after the two kings had joined battle, Demetrius' host fled: but Alexander followed after him, and prevailed against them. ⁵⁰ And he continued the battle very sore until the sun went down: and that day was Demetrius slain. ⁵¹ Afterward Alexander sent ambassadors to Ptolemee king of Egypt with a message to this effect: ⁵² Forasmuch as I am come again to my realm, and am set in the throne of my progenitors, and have gotten the dominion, and overthrown Demetrius, and recovered our country; ⁵³ For after I had joined battle with him, both he and his host was discomfited by us, so that we sit in the throne of his kingdom: ⁵⁴ Now therefore let us make a league of amity together, and give me now thy daughter to wife: and I will be thy son in law, and will give both thee and her as according to thy dignity. ⁵⁵ Then Ptolemee the king gave answer, saying, Happy be the day wherein thou didst return into the land of thy fathers, and satest in the throne of their kingdom. ⁵⁶ And now will I do to thee, as thou hast written: meet me therefore at Ptolemais, that we may see one another; for I will marry my daughter to thee according to thy desire. ⁵⁷ So Ptolemee went out of Egypt with his daughter Cleopatra, and they came unto Ptolemais in the hundred threescore and second year: ⁵⁸ Where king Alexander meeting him, he gave unto him his daughter Cleopatra, and celebrated her marriage at Ptolemais with great glory, as the manner of kings is. ⁵⁹ Now king Alexander had written unto Jonathan, that he should come and meet him. ⁶⁰ Who thereupon went honourably to Ptolemais, where he met the two kings, and gave them and their friends silver and gold, and many presents, and found favour in their sight. ⁶¹ At that time certain pestilent fellows of Israel, men of a wicked life, assembled themselves against him, to accuse him: but the king would not hear them. ⁶² Yea more than that, the king commanded to take off his garments, and clothe him in purple: and they did so. ⁶³ And he made him sit by himself, and said unto his princes, Go with him into the midst of the city, and make proclamation, that no man complain against him of any matter, and that no man trouble him for any manner of cause. [64] Now when his accusers saw that he was honored according to the proclamation, and clothed in purple, they fled all away. [65] So the king honoured him, and wrote him among his chief friends, and made him a duke, and partaker of his dominion. [66] Afterward Jonathan returned to Jerusalem with peace and gladness. [67] Furthermore in the hundred threescore and fifth year came Demetrius son of Demetrius out of Crete into the land of his fathers: [68] Whereof when king Alexander heard tell, he was right sorry, and returned into Antioch. [69] Then Demetrius made Apollonius the governor of Celosyria his general, who gathered together a great host, and camped in Jamnia, and sent unto Jonathan the high priest, saying, [70] Thou alone liftest up thyself against us, and I am laughed to scorn for thy sake, and reproached: and why dost thou vaunt thy power against us in the mountains? [71] Now therefore, if thou trustest in thine own strength, come down to us into the plain field, and there let us try the matter together: for with me is the power of the cities. [72] Ask and learn who I am, and the rest that take our part, and they shall tell thee that thy foot is not able to stand before our face; for thy fathers have been twice put to flight in their own land. [73] Wherefore now thou shalt not be able to abide the horsemen and so great a power in the plain, where is neither stone nor flint, nor place to flee unto. [74] So when Jonathan heard these words of Apollonius, he was moved in his mind, and choosing ten thousand men he went out of Jerusalem, where Simon his brother met him for to help him. [75] And he pitched his tents against Joppa: but; they of Joppa shut him out of the city, because Apollonius had a garrison there. [76] Then Jonathan laid siege unto it: whereupon they of the city let him in for fear: and so Jonathan won Joppa. [77] Whereof when Apollonius heard, he took three thousand horsemen, with a great host of footmen, and went to Azotus as one that journeyed, and therewithal drew him forth into the plain. because he had a great number of horsemen, in whom he put his trust. [78] Then Jonathan followed after him to Azotus, where the armies joined battle. [79] Now Apollonius had left a thousand horsemen in ambush. [80]

And Jonathan knew that there was an ambushment behind him; for they had compassed in his host, and cast darts at the people, from morning till evening. 81 But the people stood still, as Jonathan had commanded them: and so the enemies' horses were tired. 82 Then brought Simon forth his host, and set them against the footmen, (for the horsemen were spent) who were discomfited by him, and fled. 83 The horsemen also, being scattered in the field, fled to Azotus, and went into Bethdagon, their idol's temple, for safety. 84 But Jonathan set fire on Azotus, and the cities round about it, and took their spoils; and the temple of Dagon, with them that were fled into it, he burned with fire. 85 Thus there were burned and slain with the sword well nigh eight thousand men. 86 And from thence Jonathan removed his host, and camped against Ascalon, where the men of the city came forth, and met him with great pomp. 87 After this returned Jonathan and his host unto Jerusalem, having any spoils. 88 Now when king Alexander heard these things, he honoured Jonathan yet more. 89 And sent him a buckle of gold, as the use is to be given to such as are of the king's blood: he gave

him also Accaron with the borders thereof in possession.

11

1 And the king of Egypt gathered together a great host, like the sand that lieth upon the sea shore, and many ships, and went about through deceit to get Alexander's kingdom, and join it to his own. 2 Whereupon he took his journey into Spain in peaceable manner, so as they of the cities opened unto him, and met him: for king Alexander had commanded them so to do, because he was his brother in law. 3 Now as Ptolemee entered into the cities, he set in every one of them a garrison of soldiers to keep it. 4 And when he came near to Azotus, they shewed him the temple of Dagon that was burnt, and Azotus and the suburbs thereof that were destroyed, and the bodies that were cast abroad and them that he had burnt in the battle; for they had made heaps of them by the way where he should pass. 5 Also they told the king whatsoever Jonathan had done, to the intent he might blame him: but the king held his peace. 6 Then Jonathan met the king with great pomp at Joppa, where they saluted one another, and lodged. 7 Afterward Jonathan, when he had gone with

the king to the river called Eleutherus, returned again to Jerusalem. 8 King Ptolemee therefore, having gotten the dominion of the cities by the sea unto Seleucia upon the sea coast, imagined wicked counsels against Alexander. 9 Whereupon he sent ambasadors unto king Demetrius, saying, Come, let us make a league betwixt us, and I will give thee my daughter whom Alexander hath, and thou shalt reign in thy father's kingdom: 10 For I repent that I gave my daughter unto him, for he sought to slay me. 11 Thus did he slander him, because he was desirous of his kingdom. 12 Wherefore he took his daughter from him, and gave her to Demetrius, and forsook Alexander, so that their hatred was openly known. 13 Then Ptolemee entered into Antioch, where he set two crowns upon his head, the crown of Asia, and of Egypt. 14 In the mean season was king Alexander in Cilicia, because those that dweltin those parts had revolted from him. 15 But when Alexander heard of this, he came to war against him: whereupon king Ptolemee brought forth his host, and met him with a mighty power, and put him to flight. 16 So Alexander fled into Arabia there to be defended; but king Ptolemee was exalted: 17 For Zabdiel the Arabian took off Alexander's head, and sent it unto Ptolemee. 18 King Ptolemee also died the third day after, and they that were in the strong holds were slain one of another. 19 By this means Demetrius reigned in the hundred threescore and seventh year. 20 At the same time Jonathan gathered together them that were in Judea to take the tower that was in Jerusalem: and he made many engines of war against it. 21 Then came ungodly persons, who hated their own people, went unto the king, and told him that Jonathan besieged the tower, 22 Whereof when he heard, he was angry, and immediately removing, he came to Ptolemais, and wrote unto Jonathan, that he should not lay siege to the tower, but come and speak with him at Ptolemais in great haste. 23 Nevertheless Jonathan, when he heard this, commanded to besiege it still: and he chose certain of the elders of Israel and the priests, and put himself in peril; 24 And took silver and gold, and raiment, and divers presents besides, and went to Ptolemais unto the king, where he found favour in his sight. 25 And though certain ungodly men of the people had made complaints against him, 26 Yet the king entreated him as his predecessors had done before, and promoted him in the sight of all his friends, 27 And confirmed him in the high priesthood, and in all the honours that he had before, and gave him preeminence among his chief friends. 28 Then Jonathan desired the king, that he would make Judea free from tribute, as also the three governments, with the country of Samaria; and he promised him three hundred talents. 29 So the king consented, and wrote letters unto Jonathan of all these things after this manner: 30 King Demetrius unto his brother Jonathan, and unto the nation of the Jews, sendeth greeting: 31 We send you here a copy of the letter which we did write unto our cousin Lasthenes concerning you, that ye might see it. 32 King Demetrius unto his father Lasthenes sendeth greeting: 33 We are determined to do good to the people of the Jews, who are our friends, and keep covenants with us, because of their good will toward us. 34 Wherefore we have ratified unto them the borders of Judea, with the three governments of Apherema and Lydda and Ramathem, that are added unto Judea from the country of Samaria, and all things appertaining unto them, for all such as do sacrifice in Jerusalem, instead of the payments which the king received of them yearly aforetime out of the fruits of the earth and of trees. 35 And as for other things that belong unto us, of the tithes and customs pertaining unto us, as also the saltpits, and the crown taxes, which are due unto us, we discharge them of them all for their relief. 36 And nothing hereof shall be revoked from this time forth for ever. 37 Now therefore see that thou make a copy of these things, and let it be delivered unto Jonathan, and set upon the holy mount in a conspicuous place. 38 After this, when king Demetrius saw that the land was quiet before him, and that no resistance was made against him, he sent away all his forces, every one to his own place, except certain bands of strangers, whom he had gathered from the isles of the heathen: wherefore all the forces of his fathers hated him. 39 Moreover there was one Tryphon, that had been of Alexander's part afore, who, seeing that all the host murmured against Demetrius, went to Simalcue the Arabian that brought up Antiochus the young son of Alexander, ⁴⁰ And lay sore upon him to deliver him this young Antiochus, that he might reign in his father's stead: he told him therefore all that Demetrius had done, and how his men of war were at enmity with him, and there he remained a long season. ⁴¹ In the mean time Jonathan sent unto king Demetrius, that he would cast those of the tower out of Jerusalem, and those also in the fortresses: for they fought against Israel. ⁴² So Demetrius sent unto Jonathan, saying, I will not only do this for thee and thy people, but I will greatly honour thee and thy nation, if opportunity serve. ⁴³ Now therefore thou shalt do well, ifthou send me men to help me; for all my forces are gone from me. ⁴⁴ Upon this Jonathan sent him three thousand strong men unto Antioch: and when they came to the king, the king was very glad of their coming. ⁴⁵ Howbeit they that were of the city gathered themselves together into the midst of the city, to the number of an hundred and twenty thousand men, and would have slain the king. ⁴⁶ Wherefore the king fled into the court, but they of the city kept the passages of the city, and began to fight. ⁴⁷ Then the king called to the Jews for help, who came unto him all at once, and dispersing themselves through the city slew that day in the city to the number of an hundred thousand. ⁴⁸ Also they set fire on the city, and gat many spoils that day, and delivered the king. ⁴⁹ So when they of the city saw that the Jews had got the city as they would, their courage was abated: wherefore they made supplication to the king, and cried, saying, ⁵⁰ Grant us peace, and let the Jews cease from assaulting us and the city. ⁵¹ With that they cast away their weapons, and made peace; and the Jews were honoured in the sight of the king, and in the sight of all that were in his realm; and they returned to Jerusalem, having great spoils. ⁵² So king Demetrius sat on the throne of his kingdom, and the land was quiet before him. ⁵³ Nevertheless he dissembled in all that ever he spake, and estranged himself from Jonathan, neither rewarded he him according to the benefits which he had received of him, but troubled him very sore. ⁵⁴ After this returned Tryphon, and with him the young child Antiochus, who reigned, and was crowned. 55 Then there gathered unto him all the men of war, whom Demetrius had put away, and they fought against Demetrius, who turned his back and fled. 56 Moreover Tryphon took the elephants, and won Antioch. 57 At that time young Antiochus wrote unto Jonathan, saying, I confirm thee in the high priesthood, and appoint thee ruler over the four governments, and to be one of the king's friends. 58 Upon this he sent him golden vessels to be served in, and gave him leave to drink in gold, and to be clothed in purple, and to wear a golden buckle. 59 His brother Simon also he made captain from the place called The ladder of Tyrus unto the borders of Egypt. 60 Then Jonathan went forth, and passed through the cities beyond the water, and all the forces of Syria gathered themselves unto him for to help him: and when he came to Ascalon, they of the city met him honourably. 61 From whence he went to Gaza, but they of Gaza shut him out; wherefore he laid siege unto it, and burned the suburbs thereof with fire, and spoiled them. 62 Afterward, when they of Gaza made supplication unto Jonathan, he made peace with them, and took the sons of their chief men for hostages, and sent them to Jerusalem, and passed through the country unto Damascus. 63 Now when Jonathan heard that Demetrius' princes were come to Cades, which is in Galilee, with a great power, purposing to remove him out of the country, 64 He went to meet them, and left Simon his brother in the country. 65 Then Simon encamped against Bethsura and fought against it a long season, and shut it up: 66 But they desired to have peace with him, which he granted them, and then put them out from thence, and took the city, and set a garrison in it. 67 As for Jonathan and his host, they pitched at the water of Gennesar, from whence betimes in the morning they gat them to the plain of Nasor. 68 And, behold, the host of strangers met them in the plain, who, having laid men in ambush for him in the mountains, came themselves over against him. 69 So when they that lay in ambush rose out of their places and joined battle, all that were of Jonathan's side fled; 70 Insomuch as there was not one of them left, except Mattathias the son of Absalom, and Judas the son of Calphi, the captains of the host. 71 Then Jonathan rent his clothes, and cast earth upon his head, and prayed. 72 Afterwards turning again to battle, he put them to flight, and so they ran away. 73 Now when his own men that were fled saw this, they turned again unto him, and with him pursued them to Cades, even unto their own tents, and there they camped. 74 So there were slain of the heathen that day about three thousand men: but Jonathan returned to Jerusalem.

12

1 Now when Jonathan saw that time served him, he chose certain men, and sent them to Rome, for to confirm and renew the friendship that they had with them. 2 He sent letters also to the Lacedemonians, and to other places, for the same purpose. 3 So they went unto Rome, and entered into the senate, and said, Jonathan the high priest, and the people of the Jews, sent us unto you, to the end ye should renew the friendship, which ye had with them, and league, as in former time. 4 Upon this the Romans gave them letters unto the governors of every place that they should bring them into the land of Judea peaceably. 5 And this is the copy of the letters which Jonathan wrote to the Lacedemonians: 6 Jonathan the high priest, and the elders of the nation, and the priests, and the other of the Jews, unto the Lacedemonians their brethren send greeting: 7 There were letters sent in times past unto Onias the high priest from Darius, who reigned then among you, to signify that ye are our brethren, as the copy here underwritten doth specify. 8 At which time Onias entreated the ambassador that was sent honourably, and received the letters, wherein declaration was made of the league and friendship. 9 Therefore we also, albeit we need none of these things, that we have the holy books of scripture in our hands to comfort us, 10 Have nevertheless attempted to send unto you for the renewing of brotherhood and friendship, lest we should become strangers unto you altogether: for there is a long time passed since ye sent unto us. 11 We therefore at all times without ceasing, both in our feasts, and other convenient days, do remember you in the sacrifices which we offer, and in our prayers, as reason is, and as it becometh us to think upon our brethren: 12 And we are right glad of your honour. 13 As for ourselves, we have had great

troubles and wars on every side, for so much as the kings that are round about us have fought against us. 14 Howbeit we would not be troublesome unto you, nor to others of our confederates and friends, in these wars: 15 For we have help from heaven that succoureth us, so as we are delivered from our enemies, and our enemies are brought under foot. 16 For this cause we chose Numenius the son of Antiochus, and Antipater the son of Jason, and sent them unto the Romans, to renew the amity that we had with them, and the former league. 17 We commanded them also to go unto you, and to salute and to deliver you our letters concerning the renewing of our brotherhood. 18 Wherefore now ye shall do well to give us an answer thereto. 19 And this is the copy of the letters which Oniares sent. 20 Areus king of the Lacedemonians to Onias the high priest, greeting: 21 It is found in writing, that the Lacedemonians and Jews are brethren, and that they are of the stock of Abraham: 22 Now therefore, since this is come to our knowledge, ye shall do well to write unto us of your prosperity. 23 We do write back again to you, that your cattle and goods are our's, and our's are your's We do command therefore our ambassadors to make report unto you on this wise. 24 Now when Jonathan heard that Demebius' princes were come to fight against him with a greater host than afore, 25 He removed from Jerusalem, and met them in the land of Amathis: for he gave them no respite to enter his country. 26 He sent spies also unto their tents, who came again, and told him that they were appointed to come upon them in the night season. 27 Wherefore so soon as the sun was down, Jonathan commanded his men to watch, and to be in arms, that all the nightlong they might be ready to fight: also he sent forth centinels round about the host. 28 But when the adversaries heard that Jonathan and his men were ready for battle, they feared, and trembled in their hearts, and they kindled fires in their camp. 29 Howbeit Jonathan and his company knew it not till the morning: for they saw the lights burning. 30 Then Jonathan pursued after them, but overtook them not: for they were gone over the river Eleutherus. 31 Wherefore Jonathan turned to the Arabians, who were called Zabadeans, and smote them, and took their spoils. 32 And removing thence, he came to Damascus, and so passed through all the country, 33 Simon also went forth, and passed through the country unto Ascalon, and the holds there adjoining, from whence he turned aside to Joppa, and won it. 34 For he had heard that they would deliver the hold unto them that took Demetrius' part; wherefore he set a garrison there to keep it. 35 After this came Jonathan home again, and calling the elders of the people together, he consulted with them about building strong holds in Judea, 36 And making the walls of Jerusalem higher, and raising a great mount between the tower and the city, for to separate it from the city, that so it might be alone, that men might neither sell nor buy in it. 37 Upon this they came together to build up the city, forasmuch as part of the wall toward the brook on the east side was fallen down, and they repaired that which was called Caphenatha. 38 Simon also set up Adida in Sephela, and made it strong with gates and bars. 39 Now Tryphon went about to get the kingdom of Asia, and to kill Antiochus the king, that he might set the crown upon his own head. 40 Howbeit he was afraid that Jonathan would not suffer him, and that he would fight against him; wherefore he sought a way how to take Jonathan, that he might kill him. So he removed, and came to Bethsan. 41 Then Jonathan went out to meet him with forty thousand men chosen for the battle, and came to Bethsan. 42 Now when Tryphon saw Jonathan came with so great a force, he durst not stretch his hand against him; 43 But received him honourably, and commended him unto all his friends, and gave him gifts, and commanded his men of war to be as obedient unto him, as to himself. 44 Unto Jonathan also he said, Why hast thou brought all this people to so great trouble, seeing there is no war betwixt us? 45 Therefore send them now home again, and choose a few men to wait on thee, and come thou with me to Ptolemais, for I will give it thee, and the rest of the strong holds and forces, and all that have any charge: as for me, I will return and depart: for this is the cause of my coming. 46 So Jonathan believing him did as he bade him, and sent away his host, who went into the land of Judea. 47 And with himself he retained but three thousand men, of whom he sent two thousand into Galilee, and one thousand went with him. [48] Now as soon as Jonathan entered into Ptolemais, they of Ptolemais shut the gates and took him, and all them that came with him they slew with the sword. [49] Then sent Tryphon an host of footmen and horsemen into Galilee, and into the great plain, to destroy all Jonathan's company. [50] But when they knew that Jonathan and they that were with him were taken and slain, they encouraged one another; and went close together, prepared to fight. [51] They therefore that followed upon them, perceiving that they were ready to fight for their lives, turned back again. [52] Whereupon they all came into the land of Judea peaceably, and there they bewailed Jonathan, and them that were with him, and they were sore afraid; wherefore all Israel made great lamentation. [53] Then all the heathen that were round about then sought to destroy them: for said they, They have no captain, nor any to help them: now therefore let us make war upon them, and take away their memorial from among men.

13

[1] Now when Simon heard that Tryphon had gathered together a great host to invade the land of Judea, and destroy it, [2] And saw that the people was in great trembling and fear, he went up to Jerusalem, and gathered the people together, [3] And gave them exhortation, saying, Ye yourselves know what great things I, and my brethren, and my father's house, have done for the laws and the sanctuary, the battles also and troubles which we have seen. [4] By reason whereof all my brethren are slain for Israel's sake, and I am left alone. [5] Now therefore be it far from me, that I should spare mine own life in any time of trouble: for I am no better than my brethren. [6] Doubtless I will avenge my nation, and the sanctuary, and our wives, and our children: for all the heathen are gathered to destroy us of very malice. [7] Now as soon as the people heard these words, their spirit revived. [8] And they answered with a loud voice, saying, Thou shalt be our leader instead of Judas and Jonathan thy brother. [9] Fight thou our battles, and whatsoever, thou commandest us, that will we do. [10] So then he gathered together all the men of war, and made haste to finish the walls of Jerusalem, and he fortified it round about. [11] Also he sent Jonathan the son of

Absolom, and with him a great power, to Joppa: who casting out them that were therein remained there in it. ¹² So Tryphon removed from Ptolemaus with a great power to invade the land of Judea, and Jonathan was with him in ward. ¹³ But Simon pitched his tents at Adida, over against the plain. ¹⁴ Now when Tryphon knew that Simon was risen up instead of his brother Jonathan, and meant to join battle with him, he sent messengers unto him, saying, ¹⁵ Whereas we have Jonathan thy brother in hold, it is for money that he is owing unto the king's treasure, concerning the business that was committed unto him. ¹⁶ Wherefore now send an hundred talents of silver, and two of his sons for hostages, that when he is at liberty he may not revolt from us, and we will let him go. ¹⁷ Hereupon Simon, albeit he perceived that they spake deceitfully unto him yet sent he the money and the children, lest peradventure he should procure to himself great hatred of the people: ¹⁸ Who might have said, Because I sent him not the money and the children, therefore is Jonathan dead. ¹⁹ So he sent them the children and the hundred talents: howbeit Tryphon dissembled neither would he let Jonathan go. ²⁰ And after this came Tryphon to invade the land, and destroy it, going round about by the way that leadeth unto Adora: but Simon and his host marched against him in every place, wheresoever he went. ²¹ Now they that were in the tower sent messengers unto Tryphon, to the end that he should hasten his coming unto them by the wilderness, and send them victuals. ²² Wherefore Tryphon made ready all his horsemen to come that night: but there fell a very great snow, by reason whereof he came not. So he departed, and came into the country of Galaad. ²³ And when he came near to Bascama he slew Jonathan, who was buried there. ²⁴ Afterward Tryphon returned and went into his own land. ²⁵ Then sent Simon, and took the bones of Jonathan his brother, and buried them in Modin, the city of his fathers. ²⁶ And all Israel made great lamentation for him, and bewailed him many days. ²⁷ Simon also built a monument upon the sepulchre of his father and his brethren, and raised it aloft to the sight, with hewn stone behind and before. ²⁸ Moreover he set up seven pyramids, one against another, for his father, and his mother, and his four brethren. 29 And in these he made cunning devices, about the which he set great pillars, and upon the pillars he made all their armour for a perpetual memory, and by the armour ships carved, that they might be seen of all that sail on the sea. 30 This is the sepulchre which he made at Modin, and it standeth yet unto this day. 31 Now Tryphon dealt deceitfully with the young king Antiochus, and slew him. 32 And he reigned in his stead, and crowned himself king of Asia, and brought a great calamity upon the land. 33 Then Simon built up the strong holds in Judea, and fenced them about with high towers, and great walls, and gates, and bars, and laid up victuals therein. 34 Moreover Simon chose men, and sent to king Demetrius, to the end he should give the land an immunity, because all that Tryphon did was to spoil. 35 Unto whom king Demetrius answered and wrote after this manner: 36 King Demetrius unto Simon the high priest, and friend of kings, as also unto the elders and nation of the Jews, sendeth greeting: 37 The goldencrown, and the scarlet robe, which ye sent unto us, we have received: and we are ready to make a stedfast peace with you, yea, and to write unto our officers, to confirm the immunities which we have granted. 38 And whatsoever covenants we have made with you shall stand; and the strong holds, which ye have builded, shall be your own. 39 As for any oversight or fault committed unto this day, we forgive it, and the crown tax also, which ye owe us: and if there were any other tribute paid in Jerusalem, it shall no more be paid. 40 And look who are meet among you to be in our court, let then be enrolled, and let there be peace betwixt us. 41 Thus the yoke of the heathen was taken away from Israel in the hundred and seventieth year. 42 Then the people of Israel began to write in their instruments and contracts, In the first year of Simon the high priest, the governor and leader of the Jews. 43 In those days Simon camped against Gaza and besieged it round about; he made also an engine of war, and set it by the city, and battered a certain tower, and took it. 44 And they that were in the engine leaped into the city; whereupon there was a great uproar in the city: 45 Insomuch as the people of the city rent their clothes, and climbed upon the walls with their wives and children, and cried with a loud voice, beseeching Simon to grant them peace. 46 And they said, Deal not with us according to our wickedness, but according to thy mercy. 47 So Simon was appeased toward them, and fought no more against them, but put them out of the city, and cleansed the houses wherein the idols were, and so entered into it with songs and thanksgiving. 48 Yea, he put all uncleanness out of it, and placed such men there as would keep the law, and made it stronger than it was before, and built therein a dwelling place for himself. 49 They also of the tower in Jerusalem were kept so strait, that they could neither come forth, nor go into the country, nor buy, nor sell: wherefore they were in great distress for want of victuals, and a great number of them perished through famine. 50 Then cried they to Simon, beseeching him to be at one with them: which thing he granted them; and when he had put them out from thence, he cleansed the tower from pollutions: 51 And entered into it the three and twentieth day of the second month in the hundred seventy and first year, with thanksgiving, and branches of palm trees, and with harps, and cymbals, and with viols, and hymns, and songs: because there was destroyed a great enemy out of Israel. 52 He ordained also that that day should be kept every year with gladness. Moreover the hill of the temple that was by the tower he made stronger than it was, and there he dwelt himself with his company. 53 And when Simon saw that John his son was a valiant man, he made him captain of all the hosts; and he dwelt in Gazera.

14

1 Now in the hundred threescore and twelfth year king Demetrius gathered his forces together, and went into Media to get him help to fight against Tryphone. 2 But when Arsaces, the king of Persia and Media, heard that Demetrius was entered within his borders, he sent one of his princes to take him alive: 3 Who went and smote the host of Demetrius, and took him, and brought him to Arsaces, by whom he was put in ward. 4 As for the land of Judea, that was quiet all the days of Simon; for he sought the good of his nation in such wise, as that evermore his authority and honour pleased them well. 5 And as he was honourable in all his acts, so in this, that he took Joppa for an

haven, and made an entrance to the isles of the sea, 6 And enlarged the bounds of his nation, and recovered the country, 7 And gathered together a great number of captives, and had the dominion of Gazera, and Bethsura, and the tower, out of the which he took all uncleaness, neither was there any that resisted him. 8 Then did they till their ground in peace, and the earth gave her increase, and the trees of the field their fruit. 9 The ancient men sat all in the streets, communing together of good things, and the young men put on glorious and warlike apparel. 10 He provided victuals for the cities, and set in them all manner of munition, so that his honourable name was renowned unto the end of the world. 11 He made peace in the land, and Israel rejoiced with great joy: 12 For every man sat under his vine and his fig tree, and there was none to fray them: 13 Neither was there any left in the land to fight against them: yea, the kings themselves were overthrown in those days. 14 Moreover he strengthened all those of his people that were brought low: the law he searched out; and every contemner of the law and wicked person he took away. 15 He beautified the sanctuary, and multiplied vessels of the temple. 16 Now when it was heard at Rome, and as far as Sparta, that Jonathan was dead, they were very sorry. 17 But as soon as they heard that his brother Simon was made high priest in his stead, and ruled the country, and the cities therein: 18 They wrote unto him in tables of brass, to renew the friendship and league which they had made with Judas and Jonathan his brethren: 19 Which writings were read before the congregation at Jerusalem. 20 And this is the copy of the letters that the Lacedemonians sent; The rulers of the Lacedemonians, with the city, unto Simon the high priest, and the elders, and priests, and residue of the people of the Jews, our brethren, send greeting: 21 The ambassadors that were sent unto our people certified us of your glory and honour: wherefore we were glad of their coming, 22 And did register the things that they spake in the council of the people in this manner; Numenius son of Antiochus, and Antipater son of Jason, the Jews' ambassadors, came unto us to renew the friendship they had with us. 23 And it pleased the people to entertain the men honourably, and to put the copy of their ambassage in publick records, to the end the people of the Lacedemonians might have a memorial thereof: furthermore we have written a copy thereof unto Simon the high priest. 24 After this Simon sent Numenius to Rome with a great shield of gold of a thousand pound weight to confirm the league with them. 25 Whereof when the people heard, they said, What thanks shall we give to Simon and his sons? 26 For he and his brethren and the house of his father have established Israel, and chased away in fight their enemies from them, and confirmed their liberty. 27 So then they wrote it in tables of brass, which they set upon pillars in mount Sion: and this is the copy of the writing; The eighteenth day of the month Elul, in the hundred threescore and twelfth year, being the third year of Simon the high priest, 28 At Saramel in the great congregation of the priests, and people, and rulers of the nation, and elders of the country, were these things notified unto us. 29 Forasmuch as oftentimes there have been wars in the country, wherein for the maintenance of their sanctuary, and the law, Simon the son of Mattathias, of the posterity of Jarib, together with his brethren, put themselves in jeopardy, and resisting the enemies of their nation did their nation great honour: 30 (For after that Jonathan, having gathered his nation together, and been their high priest, was added to his people, 31 Their enemies prepared to invade their country, that they might destroy it, and lay hands on the sanctuary: 32 At which time Simon rose up, and fought for his nation, and spent much of his own substance, and armed the valiant men of his nation and gave them wages, 33 And fortified the cities of Judea, together with Bethsura, that lieth upon the borders of Judea, where the armour of the enemies had been before; but he set a garrison of Jews there: 34 Moreover he fortified Joppa, which lieth upon the sea, and Gazera, that bordereth upon Azotus, where the enemies had dwelt before: but he placed Jews there, and furnished them with all things convenient for the reparation thereof.) 35 The people therefore sang the acts of Simon, and unto what glory he thought to bring his nation, made him their governor and chief priest, because he had done all these things, and for the justice and faith which he kept to his nation, and for that he sought by all means to exalt his people. 36 For in his time things prospered in his hands, so that the heathen were taken out of their country, and they also that were in the city of David in Jerusalem, who had made themselves a tower, out of which they issued, and polluted all about the sanctuary, and did much hurt in the holy place: 37 But he placed Jews therein. and fortified it for the safety of the country and the city, and raised up the walls of Jerusalem. 38 King Demetrius also confirmed him in the high priesthood according to those things, 39 And made him one of his friends, and honoured him with great honour. 40 For he had heard say, that the Romans had called the Jews their friends and confederates and brethren; and that they had entertained the ambassadors of Simon honourably; 41 Also that the Jews and priests were well pleased that Simon should be their governor and high priest for ever, until there should arise a faithful prophet; 42 Moreover that he should be their captain, and should take charge of the sanctuary, to set them over their works, and over the country, and over the armour, and over the fortresses, that, I say, he should take charge of the sanctuary; 43 Beside this, that he should be obeyed of every man, and that all the writings in the country should be made in his name, and that he should be clothed in purple, and wear gold: 44 Also that it should be lawful for none of the people or priests to break any of these things, or to gainsay his words, or to gather an assembly in the country without him, or to be clothed in purple, or wear a buckle of gold; 45 And whosoever should do otherwise, or break any of these things, he should be punished. 46 Thus it liked all the people to deal with Simon, and to do as hath been said. 47 Then Simon accepted hereof, and was well pleased to be high priest, and captain and governor of the Jews and priests, and to defend them all. 48 So they commanded that this writing should be put in tables of brass, and that they should be set up within the compass of the sanctuary in a conspicuous place; 49 Also that the copies thereof should be laid up in the treasury, to the end that Simon and his sons might have them.

15

1 Moreover Antiochus son of Demetrius the king sent letters

314

from the isles of the sea unto Simon the priest and prince of the Jews, and to all the people; 2 The contents whereof were these: King Antiochus to Simon the high priest and prince of his nation, and to the people of the Jews, greeting: 3 Forasmuch as certain pestilent men have usurped the kingdom of our fathers, and my purpose is to challenge it again, that I may restore it to the old estate, and to that end have gathered a multitude of foreign soldiers together, and prepared ships of war; 4 My meaning also being to go through the country, that I may be avenged of them that have destroyed it, and made many cities in the kingdom desolate: 5 Now therefore I confirm unto thee all the oblations which the kings before me granted thee, and whatsoever gifts besides they granted. 6 I give thee leave also to coin money for thy country with thine own stamp. 7 And as concerning Jerusalem and the sanctuary, let them be free; and all the armour that thou hast made, and fortresses that thou hast built, and keepest in thine hands, let them remain unto thee. 8 And if anything be, or shall be, owing to the king, let it be forgiven thee from this time forth for evermore. 9 Furthermore, when we have obtained our kingdom, we will honour thee, and thy nation, and thy temple, with great honour, so that your honour shall be known throughout the world. 10 In the hundred threescore and fourteenth year went Antiochus into the land of his fathers: at which time all the forces came together unto him, so that few were left with Tryphon. 11 Wherefore being pursued by king Antiochus, he fled unto Dora, which lieth by the sea side: 12 For he saw that troubles came upon him all at once, and that his forces had forsaken him. 13 Then camped Antiochus against Dora, having with him an hundred and twenty thousand men of war, and eight thousand horsemen. 14 And when he had compassed the city round about, and joined ships close to the town on the sea side, he vexed the city by land and by sea, neither suffered he any to go out or in. 15 In the mean season came Numenius and his company from Rome, having letters to the kings and countries; wherein were written these things: 16 Lucius, consul of the Romans unto king Ptolemee, greeting: 17 The Jews' ambassadors, our friends and confederates, came unto us to renew the old friendship and league, being sent from Simon the high priest, and from the people of the Jews: 18 And they brought a shield of gold of a thousand pound. 19 We thought it good therefore to write unto the kings and countries, that they should do them no harm, nor fight against them, their cities, or countries, nor yet aid their enemies against them. 20 It seemed also good to us to receive the shield of them. 21 If therefore there be any pestilent fellows, that have fled from their country unto you, deliver them unto Simon the high priest, that he may punish them according to their own law. 22 The same things wrote he likewise unto Demetrius the king, and Attalus, to Ariarathes, and Arsaces, 23 And to all the countries and to Sampsames, and the Lacedemonians, and to Delus, and Myndus, and Sicyon, and Caria, and Samos, and Pamphylia, and Lycia, and Halicarnassus, and Rhodus, and Aradus, and Cos, and Side, and Aradus, and Gortyna, and Cnidus, and Cyprus, and Cyrene. 24 And the copy hereof they wrote to Simon the high priest. 25 So Antiochus the king camped against Dora the second day, assaulting it continually, and making engines, by which means he shut up Tryphon, that he could neither go out nor in. 26 At that time Simon sent him two thousand chosen men to aid him; silver also, and gold, and much armour. 27 Nevertheless he would not receive them, but brake all the covenants which he had made with him afore, and became strange unto him. 28 Furthermore he sent unto him Athenobius, one of his friends, to commune with him, and say, Ye withhold Joppa and Gazera; with the tower that is in Jerusalem, which are cities of my realm. 29 The borders thereof ye have wasted, and done great hurt in the land, and got the dominion of many places within my kingdom. 30 Now therefore deliver the cities which ye have taken, and the tributes of the places, whereof ye have gotten dominion without the borders of Judea: 31 Or else give me for them five hundred talents of silver; and for the harm that ye have done, and the tributes of the cities, other five hundred talents: if not, we will come and fight against you 32 So Athenobius the king's friend came to Jerusalem: and when he saw the glory of Simon, and the cupboard of gold and silver plate, and his great attendance, he was astonished, and told him the king's message. 33 Then answered Simon, and said unto him, We have neither taken other men's land, nor holden that which appertaineth to others, but the inheritance of our fathers, which our enemies had wrongfully in possession a certain time. 34 Wherefore we, having opportunity, hold the inheritance of our fathers. 35 And whereas thou demandest Joppa and Gazera, albeit they did great harm unto the people in our country, yet will we give thee an hundred talents for them. Hereunto Athenobius answered him not a word; 36 But returned in a rage to the king, and made report unto him of these speeches, and of the glory of Simon, and of all that he had seen: whereupon the king was exceeding wroth. 37 In the mean time fled Tryphon by ship unto Orthosias. 38 Then the king made Cendebeus captain of the sea coast, and gave him an host of footmen and horsemen, 39 And commanded him to remove his host toward Judea; also he commanded him to build up Cedron, and to fortify the gates, and to war against the people; but as for the king himself, he pursued Tryphon. 40 So Cendebeus came to Jamnia and began to provoke the people and to invade Judea, and to take the people prisoners, and slay them. 41 And when he had built up Cedrou, he set horsemen there, and an host of footmen, to the end that issuing out they might make out roads upon the ways of Judea, as the king had commanded him. 16 1 Then came up John from Gazera, and told Simon his father what Cendebeus had done. 2 Wherefore Simon called his two eldest sons, Judas and John, and said unto them, I, and my brethren, and my father's house, have ever from my youth unto this day fought against the enemies of Israel; and things have prospered so well in our hands, that we have delivered Israel oftentimes. 3 But now I am old, and ye, by God's mercy, are of a sufficient age: be ye instead of me and my brother, and go and fight for our nation, and the help from heaven be with you. 4 So he chose out of the country twenty thousand men of war with horsemen, who went out against Cendebeus, and rested that night at Modin. 5 And when as they rose in the morning, and went into the plain, behold, a mighty great host both of footmen and horsemen came against them: howbeit there was a water brook betwixt them. ⁶ So he and his people pitched over against them: and when he saw that the people were afraid to go over the water brook, he went first over himself, and then the men seeing him passed through after him. ⁷ That done, he divided his men, and set the horsemen in the midst of the footmen: for the enemies' horsemen were very many. ⁸ Then sounded they with the holy trumpets: whereupon Cendebeus and his host were put to flight, so that many of them were slain, and the remnant gat them to the strong hold. ⁹ At that time was Judas John's brother wounded; but John still followed after them, until he came to Cedron, which Cendebeus had built. ¹⁰ So they fled even unto the towers in the fields of Azotus; wherefore he burned it with fire: so that there were slain of them about two thousand men. Afterward he returned into the land of Judea in peace. ¹¹ Moreover in the plain of Jericho was Ptolemeus the son of Abubus made captain, and he had abundance of silver and gold: ¹² For he was the high priest's son in law. ¹³ Wherefore his heart being lifted up, he thought to get the country to himself, and thereupon consulted deceitfully against Simon and his sons to destroy them. ¹⁴ Now Simon was visiting the cities that were in the country, and taking care for the good ordering of them; at which time he came down himself to Jericho with his sons, Mattathias and Judas, in the hundred threescore and seventeenth year, in the eleventh month, called Sabat: ¹⁵ Where the son of Abubus receiving them deceitfully into a little hold, called Docus, which he had built, made them a great banquet: howbeit he had hid men there. ¹⁶ So when Simon and his sons had drunk largely, Ptolemee and his men rose up, and took their weapons, and came upon Simon into the banqueting place, and slew him, and his two sons, and certain of his servants. ¹⁷ In which doing he committed a great treachery, and recompensed evil for good. ¹⁸ Then Ptolemee wrote these things, and sentto the king, that he should send him an host to aid him, and he would deliver him the country and cities. ¹⁹ He sent others also to Gazera to kill John: and unto the tribunes he sent letters to come unto him, that he might give them silver, and gold, and rewards. ²⁰ And others he sent to take Jerusalem, and the mountain of the temple. 21 Now one had run afore to Gazera and told John that his father and brethren were slain, and, quoth he, Ptolemee hath sent to slay thee also. 22 Hereof when he heard, he was sore astonished: so he laid hands on them that were come to destroy him, and slew them; for he knew that they sought to make him away. 23 As concerning the rest of the acts of John, and his wars, and worthy deeds which he did, and the building of the walls which he made, and his doings, 24 Behold, these are written in the chronicles of his priesthood, from the time he was made high priest after his father.

The Second Book of Maccabees

The book presents a dramatic and embellished account of Jewish resistance against Hellenistic rulers, focusing on spiritual themes and martyrdom alongside the military campaigns found in its companion text. Composed in Greek and originally written as a summary of the five-volume work by Jason of Cyrene, this book covers a shorter timeframe than the First Book of Maccabees and emphasizes theological interpretation and divine intervention more explicitly.

This narrative provides a vivid portrayal of the events leading up to and including the Maccabean revolt, but with a focus that is more spiritual and less historical in nature. It begins with the events preceding the uprising, detailing the actions of the Seleucid ruler Antiochus IV Epiphanes, whose desecration of the Jerusalem Temple and persecution of the Jews are depicted with dramatic intensity. The text emphasizes the zealous defense of the Jewish faith, highlighting the martyrdoms of figures such as Eleazar and the mother with her seven sons, who choose death over transgressing the laws of their faith.

Central to this text is its theological perspective, which interprets the Jewish struggle as a manifestation of divine justice and mercy. Miraculous events, such as the appearance of heavenly horsemen defending the Jewish warriors, are described in vivid detail, reinforcing the idea that the Maccabean revolt was underpinned by divine support. This perspective serves to inspire faith and courage among its readers, presenting the endurance of suffering as a test of loyalty to God.

Moreover, the narrative structure of this book is designed to affirm the sanctity of the Temple and the rededication celebrated during Hanukkah, thereby linking the text closely with Jewish liturgical life. The author also makes a direct appeal to the reader for leniency regarding any inaccuracies, emphasizing the edifying purpose of the text over strict historical recounting.

The Second Book of Maccabees

1 The brethren, the Jews that be at Jerusalem and in the land of Judea, wish unto the brethren, the Jews that are throughout Egypt health and peace: 2 God be gracious unto you, and remember his covenant that he made with Abraham, Isaac, and Jacob, his faithful servants; 3 And give you all an heart to serve him, and to do his will, with a good courage and a willing mind; 4 And open your hearts in his law and commandments, and send you peace, 5 And hear your prayers, and be at one with you, and never forsake you in time of trouble. 6 And now we be here praying for you. 7 What time as Demetrius reigned, in the hundred threescore and ninth year, we the Jews wrote unto you in the extremity of trouble that came upon us in those years, from the time that Jason and his company revolted from the holy land and kingdom, 8 And burned the porch, and shed innocent blood: then we prayed unto the Lord, and were heard; we offered also sacrifices and fine flour, and lighted the lamps, and set forth the loaves. 9 And now see that ye keep the feast of tabernacles in the month Casleu. 10 In the hundred fourscore and eighth year, the people that were at Jerusalem and in Judea, and the council, and Judas, sent greeting and health unto Aristobulus, king Ptolemeus' master, who was of the stock of the anointed priests, and to the Jews that were in Egypt: 11 Insomuch as God hath delivered us from great perils, we thank him highly, as having been in battle against a king. 12 For he cast them out that fought within the holy city. 13 For when the leader was come into Persia, and the army with him that seemed invincible, they were slain in the temple of Nanea by the deceit of Nanea's priests. 14 For Antiochus, as though he would marry her, came into the place, and his friends that were with him, to receive money in name of a dowry. 15 Which when the priests of Nanea had set forth, and he was entered with a small company into the compass of the temple, they shut the temple as soon as Antiochus was come in: 16 And opening a privy door of the roof, they threw stones like thunderbolts, and struck down the captain, hewed them in pieces, smote off their heads and cast them to those that were without. 17 Blessed be our God in all things, who hath delivered up

the ungodly. 18 Therefore whereas we are now purposed to keep the purification of the temple upon the five and twentieth day of the month Casleu, we thought it necessary to certify you thereof, that ye also might keep it, as the feast of the tabernacles, and of the fire, which was given us when Neemias offered sacrifice, after that he had builded the temple and the altar. 19 For when our fathers were led into Persia, the priests that were then devout took the fire of the altar privily, and hid it in an hollow place of a pit without water, where they kept it sure, so that the place was unknown to all men. 20 Now after many years, when it pleased God, Neemias, being sent from the king of Persia, did send of the posterity of those priests that had hid it to the fire: but when they told us they found no fire, but thick water; 21 Then commanded he them to draw it up, and to bring it; and when the sacrifices were laid on, Neemias commanded the priests to sprinkle the wood and the things laid thereupon with the water. 22 When this was done, and the time came that the sun shone, which afore was hid in the cloud, there was a great fire kindled, so that every man marvelled. 23 And the priests made a prayer whilst the sacrifice was consuming, I say, both the priests, and all the rest, Jonathan beginning, and the rest answering thereunto, as Neemias did. 24 And the prayer was after this manner; O Lord, Lord God, Creator of all things, who art fearful and strong, and righteous, and merciful, and the only and gracious King, 25 The only giver of all things, the only just, almighty, and everlasting, thou that deliverest Israel from all trouble, and didst choose the fathers, and sanctify them: 26 Receive the sacrifice for thy whole people Israel, and preserve thine own portion, and sanctify it. 27 Gather those together that are scattered from us, deliver them that serve among the heathen, look upon them that are despised and abhorred, and let the heathen know that thou art our God. 28 Punish them that oppress us, and with pride do us wrong. 29 Plant thy people again in thy holy place, as Moses hath spoken. 30 And the priests sung psalms of thanksgiving. 31 Now when the sacrifice was consumed, Neemias commanded the water that was left to be poured on the great stones. 32 When this was done, there was kindled a flame: but it was consumed by the light that shined from the altar. 33 So when this matter was known, it was told the king of Persia, that in the place, where the priests that were led away had hid the fire, there appeared water, and that Neemias had purified the sacrifices therewith. 34 Then the king, inclosing the place, made it holy, after he had tried the matter. 35 And the king took many gifts, and bestowed thereof on those whom he would gratify. 36 And Neemias called this thing Naphthar, which is as much as to say, a cleansing: but many men call it Nephi.

2

1 It is also found in the records, that Jeremy the prophet commanded them that were carried away to take of the fire, as it hath been signified: 2 And how that the prophet, having given them the law, charged them not to forget the commandments of the Lord, and that they should not err in their minds, when they see images of silver and gold, with their ornaments. 3 And with other such speeches exhorted he them, that the law should not depart from their hearts. 4 It was also contained in the same writing, that the prophet, being warned of God, commanded the tabernacle and the ark to go with him, as he went forth into the mountain, where Moses climbed up, and saw the heritage of God. 5 And when Jeremy came thither, he found an hollow cave, wherein he laid the tabernacle, and the ark, and the altar of incense, and so stopped the door. 6 And some of those that followed him came to mark the way, but they could not find it. 7 Which when Jeremy perceived, he blamed them, saying, As for that place, it shall be unknown until the time that God gather his people again together, and receive them unto mercy. 8 Then shall the Lord shew them these things, and the glory of the Lord shall appear, and the cloud also, as it was shewed under Moses, and as when Solomon desired that the place might be honourably sanctified. 9 It was also declared, that he being wise offered the sacrifice of dedication, and of the finishing of the temple. 10 And as when Moses prayed unto the Lord, the fire came down from heaven, and consumed the sacrifices: even so prayed Solomon also, and the fire came down from heaven, and consumed the burnt offerings. 11 And Moses said, Because the sin offering was not to be eaten, it

was consumed. 12 So Solomon kept those eight days. 13 The same things also were reported in the writings and commentaries of Neemias; and how he founding a library gathered together the acts of the kings, and the prophets, and of David, and the epistles of the kings concerning the holy gifts. 14 In like manner also Judas gathered together all those things that were lost by reason of the war we had, and they remain with us, 15 Wherefore if ye have need thereof, send some to fetch them unto you. 16 Whereas we then are about to celebrate the purification, we have written unto you, and ye shall do well, if ye keep the same days. 17 We hope also, that the God, that delivered all his people, and gave them all an heritage, and the kingdom, and the priesthood, and the sanctuary, 18 As he promised in the law, will shortly have mercy upon us, and gather us together out of every land under heaven into the holy place: for he hath delivered us out of great troubles, and hath purified the place. 19 Now as concerning Judas Maccabeus, and his brethren, and the purification of the great temple, and the dedication of the altar, 20 And the wars against Antiochus Epiphanes, and Eupator his son, 21 And the manifest signs that came from heaven unto those that behaved themselves manfully to their honour for Judaism: so that, being but a few, they overcame the whole country, and chased barbarous multitudes, 22 And recovered again the temple renowned all the world over, and freed the city, and upheld the laws which were going down, the Lord being gracious unto them with all favour: 23 All these things, I say, being declared by Jason of Cyrene in five books, we will assay to abridge in one volume. 24 For considering the infinite number, and the difficulty which they find that desire to look into the narrations of the story, for the variety of the matter, 25 We have been careful, that they that will read may have delight, and that they that are desirous to commit to memory might have ease, and that all into whose hands it comes might have profit. 26 Therefore to us, that have taken upon us this painful labour of abridging, it was not easy, but a matter of sweat and watching; 27 Even as it is no ease unto him that prepareth a banquet, and seeketh the benefit of others: yet for the pleasuring of many we will undertake gladly this great pains; 28 Leaving to the author the exact handling of every particular, and labouring to follow the rules of an abridgement. 29 For as the master builder of a new house must care for the whole building; but he that undertaketh to set it out, and paint it, must seek out fit things for the adorning thereof: even so I think it is with us. 30 To stand upon every point, and go over things at large, and to be curious in particulars, belongeth to the first author of the story: 31 But to use brevity, and avoid much labouring of the work, is to be granted to him that will make an abridgment. 32 Here then will we begin the story: only adding thus much to that which hath been said, that it is a foolish thing to make a long prologue, and to be short in the story itself.

3

1 Now when the holy city was inhabited with all peace, and the laws were kept very well, because of the godliness of Onias the high priest, and his hatred of wickedness, 2 It came to pass that even the kings themselves did honour the place, and magnify the temple with their best gifts; 3 Insomuch that Seleucus of Asia of his own revenues bare all the costs belonging to the service of the sacrifices. 4 But one Simon of the tribe of Benjamin, who was made governor of the temple, fell out with the high priest about disorder in the city. 5 And when he could not overcome Onias, he gat him to Apollonius the son of Thraseas, who then was governor of Celosyria and Phenice, 6 And told him that the treasury in Jerusalem was full of infinite sums of money, so that the multitude of their riches, which did not pertain to the account of the sacrifices, was innumerable, and that it was possible to bring all into the king's hand. 7 Now when Apollonius came to the king, and had shewed him of the money whereof he was told, the king chose out Heliodorus his treasurer, and sent him with a commandment to bring him the foresaid money. 8 So forthwith Heliodorus took his journey; under a colour of visiting the cities of Celosyria and Phenice, but indeed to fulfil the king's purpose. 9 And when he was come to Jerusalem, and had been courteously received of the high priest of the city, he told him what intelligence was given of the money, and declared wherefore he came, and asked if these things were so indeed. 10 Then the high priest told him that there was

such money laid up for the relief of widows and fatherless children: 11 And that some of it belonged to Hircanus son of Tobias, a man of great dignity, and not as that wicked Simon had misinformed: the sum whereof in all was four hundred talents of silver, and two hundred of gold: 12 And that it was altogether impossible that such wrongs should be done unto them, that had committed it to the holiness of the place, and to the majesty and inviolable sanctity of the temple, honoured over all the world. 13 But Heliodorus, because of the king's commandment given him, said, That in any wise it must be brought into the king's treasury. 14 So at the day which he appointed he entered in to order this matter: wherefore there was no small agony throughout the whole city. 15 But the priests, prostrating themselves before the altar in their priests' vestments, called unto heaven upon him that made a law concerning things given to be kept, that they should safely be preserved for such as had committed them to be kept. 16 Then whoso had looked the high priest in the face, it would have wounded his heart: for his countenance and the changing of his colour declared the inward agony of his mind. 17 For the man was so compassed with fear and horror of the body, that it was manifest to them that looked upon him, what sorrow he had now in his heart. 18 Others ran flocking out of their houses to the general supplication, because the place was like to come into contempt. 19 And the women, girt with sackcloth under their breasts, abounded in the streets, and the virgins that were kept in ran, some to the gates, and some to the walls, and others looked out of the windows. 20 And all, holding their hands toward heaven, made supplication. 21 Then it would have pitied a man to see the falling down of the multitude of all sorts, and the fear of the high priest being in such an agony. 22 They then called upon the Almighty Lord to keep the things committed of trust safe and sure for those that had committed them. 23 Nevertheless Heliodorus executed that which was decreed. 24 Now as he was there present himself with his guard about the treasury, the Lord of spirits, and the Prince of all power, caused a great apparition, so that all that presumed to come in with him were astonished at the power of God, and fainted, and were sore afraid. 25 For there appeared unto them an horse with a terrible rider upon him, and adorned with a very fair covering, and he ran fiercely, and smote at Heliodorus with his forefeet, and it seemed that he that sat upon the horse had complete harness of gold. 26 Moreover two other young men appeared before him, notable in strength, excellent in beauty, and comely in apparel, who stood by him on either side; and scourged him continually, and gave him many sore stripes. 27 And Heliodorus fell suddenly unto the ground, and was compassed with great darkness: but they that were with him took him up, and put him into a litter. 28 Thus him, that lately came with a great train and with all his guard into the said treasury, they carried out, being unable to help himself with his weapons: and manifestly they acknowledged the power of God. 29 For he by the hand of God was cast down, and lay speechless without all hope of life. 30 But they praised the Lord, that had miraculously honoured his own place: for the temple; which a little afore was full of fear and trouble, when the Almighty Lord appeared, was filled with joy and gladness. 31 Then straight ways certain of Heliodorus' friends prayed Onias, that he would call upon the most High to grant him his life, who lay ready to give up the ghost. 32 So the high priest, suspecting lest the king should misconceive that some treachery had been done to Heliodorus by the Jews, offered a sacrifice for the health of the man. 33 Now as the high priest was making an atonement, the same young men in the same clothing appeared and stood beside Heliodorus, saying, Give Onias the high priest great thanks, insomuch as for his sake the Lord hath granted thee life: 34 And seeing that thou hast been scourged from heaven, declare unto all men the mighty power of God. And when they had spoken these words, they appeared no more. 35 So Heliodorus, after he had offered sacrifice unto the Lord, and made great vows unto him that had saved his life, and saluted Onias, returned with his host to the king. 36 Then testified he to all men the works of the great God, which he had seen with his eyes. 37 And when the king asked Heliodorus, who might be a fit man to be sent yet once again to Jerusalem, he said, 38 If thou hast any enemy or traitor, send him thither, and thou shalt receive him well scourged, if he escape with his life: for in that place, no doubt, there is an especial power of God. ³⁹ For he that dwelleth in heaven hath his eye on that place, and defendeth it; and he beateth and destroyeth them that come to hurt it. ⁴⁰ And the things concerning Heliodorus, and the keeping of the treasury, fell out on this sort.

4

¹ This Simon now, of whom we spake afore, having been a betrayer of the money, and of his country, slandered Onias, as if he had terrified Heliodorus, and been the worker of these evils. ² Thus was he bold to call him a traitor, that had deserved well of the city, and tendered his own nation, and was so zealous of the laws. ³ But when their hatred went so far, that by one of Simon's faction murders were committed, ⁴ Onias seeing the danger of this contention, and that Apollonius, as being the governor of Celosyria and Phenice, did rage, and increase Simon's malice, ⁵ He went to the king, not to be an accuser of his countrymen, but seeking the good of all, both publick and private: ⁶ For he saw that it was impossible that the state should continue quiet, and Simon leave his folly, unless the king did look

thereunto. ⁷ But after the death of Seleucus, when Antiochus, called Epiphanes, took the kingdom, Jason the brother of Onias laboured underhand to be high priest, ⁸ Promising unto the king by intercession three hundred and threescore talents of silver, and of another revenue eighty talents: ⁹ Beside this, he promised to assign an hundred and fifty more, if he might have licence to set him up a place for exercise, and for the training up of youth in the fashions of the heathen, and to write them of Jerusalem by the name of Antiochians. ¹⁰ Which when the king had granted, and he had gotten into his hand the rule he forthwith brought his own nation to Greekish fashion. ¹¹ And the royal privileges granted of special favour to the Jews by the means of John the father of Eupolemus, who went ambassador to Rome for amity and aid, he took away; and putting down the governments which were according to the law, he brought up new customs against the law: ¹² For he built gladly a place of exercise under the tower itself, and brought the chief young men under his subjection, and made them wear a hat. ¹³ Now such was the height of Greek fashions, and increase of heathenish manners, through the exceeding profaneness of Jason, that ungodly wretch, and no high priest; [14] That the priests had no courage to serve any more at the altar, but despising the temple, and neglecting the sacrifices, hastened to be partakers of the unlawful allowance in the place of exercise, after the game of Discus called them forth; [15] Not setting by the honours of their fathers, but liking the glory of the Grecians best of all. [16] By reason whereof sore calamity came upon them: for they had them to be their enemies and avengers, whose custom they followed so earnestly, and unto whom they desired to be like in all things. [17] For it is not a light thing to do wickedly against the laws of God: but the time following shall declare these things. [18] Now when the game that was used every fifth year was kept at Tyrus, the king being present, [19] This ungracious Jason sent special messengers from Jerusalem, who were Antiochians, to carry three hundred drachms of silver to the sacrifice of Hercules, which even the bearers thereof thought fit not to bestow upon the sacrifice, because it was not convenient, but to be reserved for other charges. [20] This money then, in regard of the sender, was appointed to Hercules' sacrifice; but because of the bearers thereof, it was employed to the making of gallies. [21] Now when Apollonius the son of Menestheus was sent into Egypt for the coronation of king Ptolemeus Philometor, Antiochus, understanding him not to be well affected to his affairs, provided for his own safety: whereupon he came to Joppa, and from thence to Jerusalem: [22] Where he was honourably received of Jason, and of the city, and was brought in with torch alight, and with great shoutings: and so afterward went with his host unto Phenice. [23] Three years afterward Jason sent Menelaus, the aforesaid Simon's brother, to bear the money unto the king, and to put him in mind of certain necessary matters. [24] But he being brought to the presence of the king, when he had magnified him for the glorious appearance of his power, got the priesthood to himself, offering more than Jason by three hundred talents of silver. [25] So he came with the king's mandate, bringing nothing worthy the high priesthood, but having the fury of a cruel tyrant, and the rage of a savage beast. 26 Then Jason, who had undermined his own brother, being undermined by another, was compelled to flee into the country of the Ammonites. 27 So Menelaus got the principality: but as for the money that he had promised unto the king, he took no good order for it, albeit Sostratis the ruler of the castle required it: 28 For unto him appertained the gathering of the customs. Wherefore they were both called before the king. 29 Now Menelaus left his brother Lysimachus in his stead in the priesthood; and Sostratus left Crates, who was governor of the Cyprians. 30 While those things were in doing, they of Tarsus and Mallos made insurrection, because they were given to the king's concubine, called Antiochus. 31 Then came the king in all haste to appease matters, leaving Andronicus, a man in authority, for his deputy 32 Now Menelaus, supposing that he had gotten a convenient time, stole certain vessels of gold out of the temple, and gave some of them to Andronicus, and some he sold into Tyrus and the cities round about. 33 Which when Onias knew of a surety, he reproved him, and withdrew himself into a sanctuary at Daphne, that lieth by Antiochia. 34 Wherefore Menelaus, taking Andronicus apart, prayed him to get Onias into his hands; who being persuaded thereunto, and coming to Onias in deceit, gave him his right hand with oaths; and though he were suspected by him, yet persuaded he him to come forth of the sanctuary: whom forthwith he shut up without regard of justice. 35 For the which cause not only the Jews, but many also of other nations, took great indignation, and were much grieved for the unjust murder of the man. 36 And when the king was come again from the places about Cilicia, the Jews that were in the city, and certain of the Greeks that abhorred the fact also, complained because Onias was slain without cause. 37 Therefore Antiochus was heartily sorry, and moved to pity, and wept, because of the sober and modest behaviour of him that was dead. 38 And being kindled with anger, forthwith he took away Andronicus his purple, and rent off his clothes, and leading him through the whole city unto that very place, where he had committed impiety against Onias, there slew he the cursed murderer. Thus the Lord rewarded him his punishment, as he had deserved. ³⁹ Now when many sacrileges had been committed in the city by Lysimachus with the consent of Menelaus, and the fruit thereof was spread abroad, the multitude gathered themselves together against Lysimachus, many vessels of gold being already carried away. ⁴⁰ Whereupon the common people rising, and being filled with rage, Lysimachus armed about three thousand men, and began first to offer violence; one Auranus being the leader, a man far gone in years, and no less in folly. ⁴¹ They then seeing the attempt of Lysimachus, some of them caught stones, some clubs, others taking handfuls of dust, that was next at hand, cast them all together upon Lysimachus, and those that set upon them. ⁴² Thus many of them they wounded, and some they struck to the ground, and all of them they forced to flee: but as for the church robber himself, him they killed beside the treasury. ⁴³ Of these matters therefore there was an accusation laid against Menelaus. ⁴⁴ Now when the king came to Tyrus, three men that were sent from the senate pleaded the cause before him: ⁴⁵ But Menelaus, being now convicted, promised Ptolemee the son of Dorymenes to give him much money, if he would pacify the king toward him. ⁴⁶ Whereupon Ptolemee taking the king aside into a certain gallery, as it were to take the air, brought him to be of another mind: ⁴⁷ Insomuch that he discharged Menelaus from the accusations, who notwithstanding was cause of all the mischief: and those poor men, who, if they had told their cause, yea, before the Scythians, should have been judged innocent, them he condemned to death. ⁴⁸ Thus they that followed the matter for the city, and for the people, and for the holy vessels, did soon suffer unjust punishment. ⁴⁹ Wherefore even they of Tyrus, moved with hatred of that wicked deed, caused them to be honourably buried. ⁵⁰ And so through the covetousness of them that were of power Menelaus remained still in authority, increasing in malice, and being a great traitor to the citizens.

5

¹ About the same time Antiochus prepared his second voyage into Egypt: ² And then it happened, that through all the city, for the space almost of forty days, there

were seen horsemen running in the air, in cloth of gold, and armed with lances, like a band of soldiers, 3 And troops of horsemen in array, encountering and running one against another, with shaking of shields, and multitude of pikes, and drawing of swords, and casting of darts, and glittering of golden ornaments, and harness of all sorts. 4 Wherefore every man prayed that that apparition might turn to good. 5 Now when there was gone forth a false rumour, as though Antiochus had been dead, Jason took at the least a thousand men, and suddenly made an assault upon the city; and they that were upon the walls being put back, and the city at length taken, Menelaus fled into the castle: 6 But Jason slew his own citizens without mercy, not considering that to get the day of them of his own nation would be a most unhappy day for him; but thinking they had been his enemies, and not his countrymen, whom he conquered. 7 Howbeit for all this he obtained not the principality, but at the last received shame for the reward of his treason, and fled again into the country of the Ammonites. 8 In the end therefore he had an unhappy return, being accused before Aretas the king of the Arabians, fleeing from city to city, pursued of all men, hated as a forsaker of the laws, and being had in abomination as an open enemy of his country and countrymen, he was cast out into Egypt. 9 Thus he that had driven many out of their country perished in a strange land, retiring to the Lacedemonians, and thinking there to find succour by reason of his kindred: 10 And he that had cast out many unburied had none to mourn for him, nor any solemn funerals at all, nor sepulchre with his fathers. 11 Now when this that was done came to the king's ear, he thought that Judea had revolted: whereupon removing out of Egypt in a furious mind, he took the city by force of arms, 12 And commanded his men of war not to spare such as they met, and to slay such as went up upon the houses. 13 Thus there was killing of young and old, making away of men, women, and children, slaying of virgins and infants. 14 And there were destroyed within the space of three whole days fourscore thousand, whereof forty thousand were slain in the conflict; and no fewer sold than slain. 15 Yet was he not content with this, but presumed to go into the most holy temple of all the world; Menelaus, that traitor to the laws, and to his own country, being his guide: 16 And taking the holy vessels with polluted hands, and with profane hands pulling down the things that were dedicated by other kings to the augmentation and glory and honour of the place, he gave them away. 17 And so haughty was Antiochus in mind, that he considered not that the Lord was angry for a while for the sins of them that dwelt in the city, and therefore his eye was not upon the place. 18 For had they not been formerly wrapped in many sins, this man, as soon as he had come, had forthwith been scourged, and put back from his presumption, as Heliodorus was, whom Seleucus the king sent to view the treasury. 19 Nevertheless God did not choose the people for the place's sake, but the place for the people's sake. 20 And therefore the place itself, that was partaker with them of the adversity that happened to the nation, did afterward communicate in the benefits sent from the Lord: and as it was forsaken in the wrath of the Almighty, so again, the great Lord being reconciled, it was set up with all glory. 21 So when Antiochus had carried out of the temple a thousand and eight hundred talents, he departed in all haste unto Antiochia, weening in his pride to make the land navigable, and the sea passable by foot: such was the haughtiness of his mind. 22 And he left governors to vex the nation: at Jerusalem, Philip, for his country a Phrygian, and for manners more barbarous than he that set him there; 23 And at Garizim, Andronicus; and besides, Menelaus, who worse than all the rest bare an heavy hand over the citizens, having a malicious mind against his countrymen the Jews. 24 He sent also that detestable ringleader Apollonius with an army of two and twenty thousand, commanding him to slay all those that were in their best age, and to sell the women and the younger sort: 25 Who coming to Jerusalem, and pretending peace, did forbear till the holy day of the sabbath, when taking the Jews keeping holy day, he commanded his men to arm themselves. 26 And so he slew all them that were gone to the celebrating of the sabbath, and running through the city with weapons slew great multitudes. 27 But Judas Maccabeus with nine others, or thereabout, withdrew himself into the wilderness, and lived in the mountains after the manner of beasts, with his company, who fed on herbs continually, lest they should be partakers of the pollution.

6

¹ Not long after this the king sent an old man of Athens to compel the Jews to depart from the laws of their fathers, and not to live after the laws of God: ² And to pollute also the temple in Jerusalem, and to call it the temple of Jupiter Olympius; and that in Garizim, of Jupiter the Defender of strangers, as they did desire that dwelt in the place. ³ The coming in of this mischief was sore and grievous to the people: ⁴ For the temple was filled with riot and revelling by the Gentiles, who dallied with harlots, and had to do with women within the circuit of the holy places, and besides that brought in things that were not lawful. ⁵ The altar also was filled with profane things, which the law forbiddeth. ⁶ Neither was it lawful for a man to keep sabbath days or ancient fasts, or to profess himself at all to be a Jew. ⁷ And in the day of the king's birth every month they were brought by bitter constraint to eat of the sacrifices; and when the fast of Bacchus was kept, the Jews were compelled to go in procession to Bacchus, carrying ivy. ⁸ Moreover there went out a decree to the neighbour cities of the heathen, by the suggestion of Ptolemee, against the Jews, that they should observe the same fashions, and be partakers of their sacrifices: ⁹ And whoso would not conform themselves to the manners of the Gentiles should be put to death. Then might a man have seen the present misery. ¹⁰ For there were two women brought, who had circumcised their children; whom when they had openly led round about the city, the babes hanging at their breasts, they cast them down headlong from the wall. ¹¹ And others, that had run together into caves near by, to keep the sabbath day secretly, being discovered by Philip, were all burnt together, because they made a conscience to help themselves for the honour of the most sacred day. ¹² Now I beseech those that read this book, that they be not discouraged for these calamities, but that they judge those punishments not to be for destruction, but for a chastening of our nation. ¹³ For it is a token

of his great goodness, when wicked doers are not suffered any long time, but forthwith punished. 14 For not as with other nations, whom the Lord patiently forbeareth to punish, till they be come to the fulness of their sins, so dealeth he with us, 15 Lest that, being come to the height of sin, afterwards he should take vengeance of us. 16 And therefore he never withdraweth his mercy from us: and though he punish with adversity, yet doth he never forsake his people. 17 But let this that we have spoken be for a warning unto us. And now will we come to the declaring of the matter in a few words. 18 Eleazar, one of the principal scribes, an aged man, and of a well favoured countenance, was constrained to open his mouth, and to eat swine's flesh. 19 But he, choosing rather to die gloriously, than to live stained with such an abomination, spit it forth, and came of his own accord to the torment, 20 As it behoved them to come, that are resolute to stand out against such things, as are not lawful for love of life to be tasted. 21 But they that had the charge of that wicked feast, for the old acquaintance they had with the man, taking him aside, besought him to bring flesh of his own provision, such as was lawful for him to use, and make as if he did eat of the flesh taken from the sacrifice commanded by the king; 22 That in so doing he might be delivered from death, and for the old friendship with them find favour. 23 But he began to consider discreetly, and as became his age, and the excellency of his ancient years, and the honour of his gray head, whereon was come, and his most honest education from a child, or rather the holy law made and given by God: therefore he answered accordingly, and willed them straightways to send him to the grave. 24 For it becometh not our age, said he, in any wise to dissemble, whereby many young persons might think that Eleazar, being fourscore years old and ten, were now gone to a strange religion; 25 And so they through mine hypocrisy, and desire to live a little time and a moment longer, should be deceived by me, and I get a stain to mine old age, and make it abominable. 26 For though for the present time I should be delivered from the punishment of men: yet should I not escape the hand of the Almighty, neither alive, nor dead. 27 Wherefore now, manfully changing this life, I will shew myself such an one as mine age requireth, 28 And leave a notable example to such as be young to die willingly and courageously for the honourable and holy laws. And when he had said these words, immediately he went to the torment: 29 They that led him changing the good will they bare him a little before into hatred, because the foresaid speeches proceeded, as they thought, from a desperate mind. 30 But when he was ready to die with stripes, he groaned, and said, It is manifest unto the Lord, that hath the holy knowledge, that whereas I might have been delivered from death, I now endure sore pains in body by being beaten: but in soul am well content to suffer these things, because I fear him. 31 And thus this man died, leaving his death for an example of a noble courage, and a memorial of virtue, not only unto young men, but unto all his nation.

7

1 It came to pass also, that seven brethren with their mother were taken, and compelled by the king against the law to taste swine's flesh, and were tormented with scourges and whips. 2 But one of them that spake first said thus, What wouldest thou ask or learn of us? we are ready to die, rather than to transgress the laws of our fathers. 3 Then the king, being in a rage, commanded pans and caldrons to be made hot: 4 Which forth with being heated, he commanded to cut out the tongue of him that spake first, and to cut off the utmost parts of his body, the rest of his brethren and his mother looking on. 5 Now when he was thus maimed in all his members, he commanded him being yet alive to be brought to the fire, and to be fried in the pan: and as the vapour of the pan was for a good space dispersed, they exhorted one another with the mother to die manfully, saying thus, 6 The Lord God looketh upon us, and in truth hath comfort in us, as Moses in his song, which witnessed to their faces, declared, saying, And he shall be comforted in his servants. 7 So when the first was dead after this manner, they brought the second to make him a mocking stock: and when they had pulled off the skin of his head with the hair, they asked him, Wilt thou eat, before thou be punished throughout every member of thy body? 8 But he answered in his own language, and said, No. Wherefore he also received the next torment in order, as the

former did. ⁹ And when he was at the last gasp, he said, Thou like a fury takest us out of this present life, but the King of the world shall raise us up, who have died for his laws, unto everlasting life. ¹⁰ After him was the third made a mocking stock: and when he was required, he put out his tongue, and that right soon, holding forth his hands manfully. ¹¹ And said courageously, These I had from heaven; and for his laws I despise them; and from him I hope to receive them again. ¹² Insomuch that the king, and they that were with him, marvelled at the young man's courage, for that he nothing regarded the pains. ¹³ Now when this man was dead also, they tormented and mangled the fourth in like manner. ¹⁴ So when he was ready to die he said thus, It is good, being put to death by men, to look for hope from God to be raised up again by him: as for thee, thou shalt have no resurrection to life. ¹⁵ Afterward they brought the fifth also, and mangled him. ¹⁶ Then looked he unto the king, and said, Thou hast power over men, thou art corruptible, thou doest what thou wilt; yet think not that our nation is forsaken of God; ¹⁷ But abide a while, and behold his great power, how he will torment thee and thy seed. ¹⁸ After him also they brought the sixth, who being ready to die said, Be not deceived without cause: for we suffer these things for ourselves, having sinned against our God: therefore marvellous things are done unto us. ¹⁹ But think not thou, that takest in hand to strive against God, that thou shalt escape unpunished. ²⁰ But the mother was marvellous above all, and worthy of honourable memory: for when she saw her seven sons slain within the space of one day, she bare it with a good courage, because of the hope that she had in the Lord. ²¹ Yea, she exhorted every one of them in her own language, filled with courageous spirits; and stirring up her womanish thoughts with a manly stomach, she said unto them, ²² I cannot tell how ye came into my womb: for I neither gave you breath nor life, neither was it I that formed the members of every one of you; ²³ But doubtless the Creator of the world, who formed the generation of man, and found out the beginning of all things, will also of his own mercy give you breath and life again, as ye now regard not your own selves for his laws' sake. ²⁴ Now Antiochus, thinking himself despised, and suspecting it to be a reproachful speech, whilst the youngest was yet alive, did not only exhort him by words, but also assured him with oaths, that he would make him both a rich and a happy man, if he would turn from the laws of his fathers; and that also he would take him for his friend, and trust him with affairs. 25 But when the young man would in no case hearken unto him, the king called his mother, and exhorted her that she would counsel the young man to save his life. 26 And when he had exhorted her with many words, she promised him that she would counsel her son. 27 But she bowing herself toward him, laughing the cruel tyrant to scorn, spake in her country language on this manner; O my son, have pity upon me that bare thee nine months in my womb, and gave thee suck three years, and nourished thee, and brought thee up unto this age, and endured the troubles of education. 28 I beseech thee, my son, look upon the heaven and the earth, and all that is therein, and consider that God made them of things that were not; and so was mankind made likewise. 29 Fear not this tormentor, but, being worthy of thy brethren,

take thy death that I may receive thee again in mercy with thy brethren. 30 Whiles she was yet speaking these words, the young man said, Whom wait ye for? I will not obey the king's commandment: but I will obey the commandment of the law that was given unto our fathers by Moses. 31 And thou, that hast been the author of all mischief against the Hebrews, shalt not escape the hands of God. 32 For we suffer because of our sins. 33 And though the living Lord be angry with us a little while for our chastening and correction, yet shall he be at one again with his servants. 34 But thou, O godless man, and of all other most wicked, be not lifted up without a cause, nor puffed up with uncertain hopes, lifting up thy hand against the servants of God: 35 For thou hast not yet escaped the judgment of Almighty God, who seeth all things. 36 For our brethren, who now have suffered a short pain, are dead under God's covenant of everlasting life: but thou, through the judgment of God, shalt receive just punishment for thy pride. 37 But I, as my brethren, offer up my body and life for the laws of our fathers, beseeching God that he would speedily be merciful unto our nation; and that thou by torments and plagues mayest confess, that he alone is God; 38 And that in me and my brethren the wrath of the Almighty, which is justly brought upon our nation, may cease. 39 Then the king being in a rage, handed him worse than all the rest, and took it grievously that he was mocked. 40 So this man died undefiled, and put his whole trust in the Lord. 41 Last of all after the sons the mother died. 42 Let this be enough now to have spoken concerning the idolatrous feasts, and the extreme tortures.

8

1 Then Judas Maccabeus, and they that were with him, went privily into the towns, and called their kinsfolks together, and took unto them all such as continued int he Jews' religion, and assembled about six thousand men. 2 And they called upon the Lord, that he would look upon the people that was trodden down of all; and also pity the temple profaned of ungodly men; 3 And that he would have compassion upon the city, sore defaced, and ready to be made even with the ground; and hear the blood that cried unto him, 4 And remember the wicked slaughter of harmless infants, and the blasphemies committed against his name; and that he would shew his hatred against the wicked. 5 Now when Maccabeus had his company about him, he could not be withstood by the heathen: for the wrath of the Lord was turned into mercy. 6 Therefore he came at unawares, and burnt up towns and cities, and got into his hands the most commodious places, and overcame and put to flight no small number of his enemies. 7 But specially took he advantage of the night for such privy attempts, insomuch that the fruit of his holiness was spread every where. 8 So when Philip saw that this man increased by little and little, and that things prospered with him still more and more, he wrote unto Ptolemeus, the governor of Celosyria and Phenice, to yield more aid to the king's affairs. 9 Then forthwith choosing Nicanor the son of Patroclus, one of his special friends, he sent him with no fewer than twenty thousand of all nations under him, to root out the whole generation of the Jews; and with him he joined also Gorgias a captain, who in matters of war had great experience. 10 So Nicanor undertook to make so much money of the captive Jews, as should defray the tribute of

two thousand talents, which the king was to pay to the Romans. 11 Wherefore immediately he sent to the cities upon the sea coast, proclaiming a sale of the captive Jews, and promising that they should have fourscore and ten bodies for one talent, not expecting the vengeance that was to follow upon him from the Almighty God. 12 Now when word was brought unto Judas of Nicanor's coming, and he had imparted unto those that were with him that the army was at hand, 13 They that were fearful, and distrusted the justice of God, fled, and conveyed themselves away. 14 Others sold all that they had left, and withal besought the Lord to deliver them, sold by the wicked Nicanor before they met together: 15 And if not for their own sakes, yet for the covenants he had made with their fathers, and for his holy and glorious name's sake, by which they were called. 16 So Maccabeus called his men together unto the number of six thousand, and exhorted them not to be stricken with terror of the enemy, nor to fear the great multitude of the heathen, who came wrongly against them; but to fight manfully, 17 And to set before their eyes the injury that they had unjustly done to the holy place, and the cruel handling of the city, whereof they made a mockery, and also the taking away of the government of their forefathers: 18 For they, said he, trust in their weapons and boldness; but our confidence is in the Almighty who at a beck can cast down both them that come against us, and also all the world. 19 Moreover, he recounted unto them what helps their forefathers had found, and how they were delivered, when under Sennacherib an hundred fourscore and five thousand perished. 20 And he told them of the battle that they had in Babylon with the Galatians, how they came but eight thousand in all to the business, with four thousand Macedonians, and that the Macedonians being perplexed, the eight thousand destroyed an hundred and twenty thousand because of the help that they had from heaven, and so received a great booty. 21 Thus when he had made them bold with these words, and ready to die for the law and the country, he divided his army into four parts; 22 And joined with himself his own brethren, leaders of each band, to wit Simon, and Joseph, and Jonathan, giving each one fifteen hundred men. 23 Also he appointed Eleazar to read the holy book: and when he had given them this watchword, The help of God; himself leading the first band, 24 And by the help of the Almighty they slew above nine thousand of their enemies, and wounded and maimed the most part of Nicanor's host, and so put all to flight; 25 And took their money that came to buy them, and pursued them far: but lacking time they returned: urned: 26 For it was the day before the sabbath, and therefore they would no longer pursue them. 27 So when they had gathered their armour together, and spoiled their enemies, they occupied themselves about the sabbath, yielding exceeding praise and thanks to the Lord, who had preserved them unto that day, which was the beginning of mercy distilling upon them. 28 And after the sabbath, when they had given part of the spoils to the maimed, and the widows, and orphans, the residue they divided among themselves and their servants. 29 When this was done, and they had made a common supplication, they besought the merciful Lord to be reconciled with his servants for ever. 30 Moreover of those that were with Timotheus and Bacchides, who fought against them, they slew above twenty thousand, and very easily got high and strong holds, and divided among themselves many spoils more, and made the maimed, orphans, widows, yea, and the aged also, equal in spoils with themselves. 31 And when they had gathered their armour together, they laid them up all carefully in convenient places, and the remnant of the spoils they brought to Jerusalem. 32 They slew also Philarches, that wicked person, who was with Timotheus, and had annoyed the Jews many ways. 33 Furthermore at such time as they kept the feast for the victory in their country they burnt Callisthenes, that had set fire upon the holy gates, who had fled into a little house; and so he received a reward meet for his wickedness. 34 As for that most ungracious Nicanor, who had brought a thousand merchants to buy the Jews, 35 He was through the help of the Lord brought down by them, of whom he made least account; and putting off his glorious apparel, and discharging his company, he came like a fugitive servant through the midland unto Antioch having very great dishonour, for that his host was destroyed. 36 Thus he, that took upon him to make good to the Romans their tribute by means of captives in Jerusalem, told abroad, that the Jews had God to fight for them, and therefore they could not be hurt, because they followed the laws that he gave them.

9

1 About that time came Antiochus with dishonour out of the country of Persia 2 For he had entered the city called Persepolis, and went about to rob the temple, and to hold the city; whereupon the multitude running to defend themselves with their weapons put them to flight; and so it happened, that Antiochus being put to flight of the inhabitants returned with shame. 3 Now when he came to Ecbatane, news was brought him what had happened unto Nicanor and Timotheus. 4 Then swelling with anger. he thought to avenge upon the Jews the disgrace done unto him by those that made him flee. Therefore commanded he his chariot man to drive without ceasing, and to dispatch the journey, the judgment of God now following him. For he had spoken proudly in this sort, That he would come to Jerusalem and make it a common burying place of the Jews. 5 But the Lord Almighty, the God of Israel, smote him with an incurable and invisible plague: or as soon as he had spoken these words, a pain of the bowels that was remediless came upon him, and sore torments of the inner parts; 6 And that most justly: for he had tormented other men's bowels with many and strange torments. 7 Howbeit he nothing at all ceased from his bragging, but still was filled with pride, breathing out fire in his rage against the Jews, and commanding to haste the journey: but it came to pass that he fell down from his chariot, carried violently; so that having a sore fall, all the members of his body were much pained. 8 And thus he that a little afore thought he might command the waves of the sea, (so proud was he beyond the condition of man) and weigh the high mountains in a balance, was now cast on the ground, and carried in an horse litter, shewing forth unto all the manifest power of God. 9 So that the worms rose up out of the body of this wicked man, and whiles he lived in sorrow and pain, his flesh fell away, and the filthiness of his smell was noisome to all his army. 10 And the man, that thought a little afore he could reach to the stars of heaven, no

man could endure to carry for his intolerable stink. 11 Here therefore, being plagued, he began to leave off his great pride, and to come to the knowledge of himself by the scourge of God, his pain increasing every moment. 12 And when he himself could not abide his own smell, he said these words, It is meet to be subject unto God, and that a man that is mortal should not proudly think of himself if he were God. 13 This wicked person vowed also unto the Lord, who now no more would have mercy upon him, saying thus, 14 That the holy city (to the which he was going in haste to lay it even with the ground, and to make it a common burying place,) he would set at liberty: 15 And as touching the Jews, whom he had judged not worthy so much as to be buried, but to be cast out with their children to be devoured of the fowls and wild beasts, he would make them all equals to the citizens of Athens: 16 And the holy temple, which before he had spoiled, he would garnish with goodly gifts, and restore all the holy vessels with many more, and out of his own revenue defray the charges belonging to the sacrifices: 17 Yea, and that also he would become a Jew himself, and go through all the world that was inhabited, and declare the power of God. 18 But for all this his pains would not cease: for the just judgment of God was come upon him: therefore despairing of his health, he wrote unto the Jews the letter underwritten, containing the form of a supplication, after this manner: 19 Antiochus, king and governor, to the good Jews his citizens wisheth much joy, health, and prosperity: 20 If ye and your children fare well, and your affairs be to your contentment, I give very great thanks to God, having my hope in heaven. 21 As for me, I was weak, or else I would have remembered kindly your honour and good will returning out of Persia, and being taken with a grievous disease, I thought it necessary to care for the common safety of all: 22 Not distrusting mine health, but having great hope to escape this sickness. 23 But considering that even my father, at what time he led an army into the high countries. appointed a successor, 24 To the end that, if any thing fell out contrary to expectation, or if any tidings were brought that were grievous, they of the land, knowing to whom the state was left, might not be troubled: 25

Again, considering how that the princes that are borderers and neighbours unto my kingdom wait for opportunities, and expect what shall be the event. I have appointed my son Antiochus king, whom I often committed and commended unto many of you, when I went up into the high provinces; to whom I have written as followeth: 26 Therefore I pray and request you to remember the benefits that I have done unto you generally, and in special, and that every man will be still faithful to me and my son. 27 For I am persuaded that he understanding my mind will favourably and graciously yield to your desires. 28 Thus the murderer and blasphemer having suffered most grievously, as he entreated other men, so died he a miserable death in a strange country in the mountains. 29 And Philip, that was brought up with him, carried away his body, who also fearing the son of Antiochus went into Egypt to Ptolemeus Philometor.

10

1 Now Maccabeus and his company, the Lord guiding them, recovered the temple and the city: 2 But the altars which the heathen had built in the open street, and also the chapels, they pulled down. 3 And having cleansed the temple they made another altar, and striking stones they took fire out of them, and offered a sacrifice after two years, and set forth incense, and lights, and shewbread. 4 When that was done, they fell flat down, and besought the Lord that they might come no more into such troubles; but if they sinned any more against him, that he himself would chasten them with mercy, and that they might not be delivered unto the blasphemous and barbarous nations. 5 Now upon the same day that the strangers profaned the temple, on the very same day it was cleansed again, even the five and twentieth day of the same month, which is Casleu. 6 And they kept the eight days with gladness, as in the feast of the tabernacles, remembering 27 For I am persuaded that he understanding my mind will favourably and graciously yield to your desires. 28 Thus the murderer and blasphemer having suffered most grievously, as he entreated other men, so died he a miserable death in a strange country in the mountains. 29 And Philip, that was brought up with him, carried away his body, who also fearing the son of Antiochus went into

Egypt to Ptolemeus Philometor. 10 1 Now Maccabeus and his company, the Lord guiding them, recovered the temple and the city: 2 But the altars which the heathen had built in the open street, and also the chapels, they pulled down. 3 And having cleansed the temple they made another altar, and striking stones they took fire out of them, and offered a sacrifice after two years, and set forth incense, and lights, and shewbread. 4 When that was done, they fell flat down, and besought the Lord that they might come no more into such troubles; but if they sinned any more against him, that he himself would chasten them with mercy, and that they might not be delivered unto the blasphemous and barbarous nations. 5 Now upon the same day that the strangers profaned the temple, on the very same day it was cleansed again, even the five and twentieth day of the same month, which is Casleu. 6 And they kept the eight days with gladness, as in the feast of the tabernacles, remembering that not long afore they had held the feast of the tabernacles, when as they wandered in the mountains and dens like beasts. 7 Therefore they bare branches, and fair boughs, and palms also, and sang psalms unto him that had given them good success in cleansing his place. 8 They ordained also by a common statute and decree, That every year those days should be kept of the whole nation of the Jews. 9 And this was the end of Antiochus, called Epiphanes. 10 Now will we declare the acts of Antiochus Eupator, who was the son of this wicked man, gathering briefly the calamities of the wars. 11 So when he was come to the crown, he set one Lysias over the affairs of his realm, and appointed him his chief governor of Celosyria and Phenice. 12 For Ptolemeus, that was called Macron, choosing rather to do justice unto the Jews for the wrong that had been done unto them, endeavoured to continue peace with them. 13 Whereupon being accused of the king's friends before Eupator, and called traitor at every word because he had left Cyprus, that Philometor had committed unto him, and departed to Antiochus Epiphanes, and seeing that he was in no honourable place, he was so discouraged, that he poisoned himself and died. 14 But when Gorgias was governor of the holds, he hired soldiers, and nourished war continually with the Jews: 15 And therewithall the Idumeans, having gotten into their hands the most commodious holds, kept the Jews occupied, and receiving those that were banished from Jerusalem, they went about to nourish war. 16 Then they that were with Maccabeus made supplication, and besought God that he would be their helper; and so they ran with violence upon the strong holds of the Idumeans, 17 And assaulting them strongly, they won the holds, and kept off all that fought upon the wall, and slew all that fell into their hands, and killed no fewer than twenty thousand. 18 And because certain, who were no less than nine thousand, were fled together into two very strong castles, having all manner of things convenient to sustain the siege, 19 Maccabeus left Simon and Joseph, and Zaccheus also, and them that were with him, who were enough to besiege them, and departed himself unto those places which more needed his help. 20 Now they that were with Simon, being led with covetousness, were persuaded for money through certain of those that were in the castle, and took seventy thousand drachms, and let some of them escape. 21

But when it was told Maccabeus what was done, he called the governors of the people together, and accused those men, that they had sold their brethren for money, and set their enemies free to fight against them. 22 So he slew those that were found traitors, and immediately took the two castles. 23 And having good success with his weapons in all things he took in hand, he slew in the two holds more than twenty thousand. 24 Now Timotheus, whom the Jews had overcome before, when he had gathered a great multitude of foreign forces, and horses out of Asia not a few, came as though he would take Jewry by force of arms. 25 But when he drew near, they that were with Maccabeus turned themselves to pray unto God, and sprinkled earth upon their heads, and girded their loins with sackcloth, 26 And fell down at the foot of the altar, and besought him to be merciful to them, and to be an enemy to their enemies, and an adversary to their adversaries, as the law declareth. 27 So after the prayer they took their weapons, and went on further from the city: and when they drew near to their enemies, they kept by themselves. 28 Now the sun being newly risen, they joined both together; the one part having together with their virtue their refuge also unto the Lord for a pledge of their success and victory: the other side making their rage leader of their battle 29 But when the battle waxed strong, there appeared unto the enemies from heaven five comely men upon horses, with bridles of gold, and two of them led the Jews, 30 And took Maccabeus betwixt them, and covered him on every side weapons, and kept him safe, but shot arrows and lightnings against the enemies: so that being confounded with blindness, and full of trouble, they were killed. 31 And there were slain of footmen twenty thousand and five hundred, and six hundred horsemen. 32 As for Timotheus himself, he fled into a very strong hold, called Gawra, where Chereas was governor. 33 But they that were with Maccabeus laid siege against the fortress courageously four days. 34 And they that were within, trusting to the strength of the place, blasphemed exceedingly, and uttered wicked words. 35 Nevertheless upon the fifth day early twenty young men of Maccabeus' company, inflamed with anger because of the blasphemies, assaulted the wall manly, and with a fierce courage killed all that they met withal. 36 Others likewise ascending after them, whiles they were busied with them that were within, burnt the towers, and kindling fires burnt the blasphemers alive; and others broke open the gates, and, having received in the rest ofthe army, took the city, 37 And killed Timotheus, that was hid in a certain pit, and Chereas his brother, with Apollophanes. 38 When this was done, they praised the Lord with psalms and thanksgiving, who had done so great things for Israel, and given them the victory.

11

1 Not long after this, Lysias the king's protector and cousin, who also managed the affairs, took sore displeasure for the things that were done. 2 And when he had gathered about fourscore thousand with all the horsemen, he came against the Jews, thinking to make the city an habitation of the Gentiles, 3 And to make a gain of the temple, as of the other chapels of the heathen, and to set the high priesthood to sale every year: 4 Not at all considering the power of God but puffed up with his ten thousands of footmen, and his

thousands of horsemen, and his fourscore elephants. ⁵ So he came to Judea, and drew near to Bethsura, which was a strong town, but distant from Jerusalem about five furlongs, and he laid sore siege unto it. ⁶ Now when they that were with Maccabeus heard that he besieged the holds, they and all the people with lamentation and tears besought the Lord that he would send a good angel to deliver Israel. ⁷ Then Maccabeus himself first of all took weapons, exhorting the other that they would jeopard themselves together with him to help their brethren: so they went forth together with a willing mind. ⁸ And as they were at Jerusalem, there appeared before them on horseback one in white clothing, shaking his armour of gold ⁹ Then they praised the merciful God all together, and took heart, insomuch that they were ready not only to fight with men, but with most cruel beasts, and to pierce through walls of iron. ¹⁰ Thus they marched forward in their armour, having an helper from heaven: for the Lord was merciful unto them ¹¹ And giving a charge upon their enemies like lions, they slew eleven thousand footmen, and sixteen hundred horsemen, and

put all the other to flight. ¹² Many of them also being wounded escaped naked; and Lysias himself fled away shamefully, and so escaped. ¹³ Who, as he was a man of understanding, casting with himself what loss he had had, and considering that the Hebrews could not be overcome, because the Almighty God helped them, he sent unto them, ¹⁴ And persuaded them to agree to all reasonable conditions, and promised that he would persuade the king that he must needs be a friend unto them. ¹⁵ Then Maccabeus consented to all that Lysias desired, being careful of the common good; and whatsoever Maccabeus wrote unto Lysias concerning the Jews, the king granted it. ¹⁶ For there were letters written unto the Jews from Lysias to this effect: Lysias unto the people of the Jews sendeth greeting: ¹⁷ John and Absolom, who were sent from you, delivered me the petition subscribed, and made request for the performance of the contents thereof. ¹⁸ Therefore what things soever were meet to be reported to the king, I have declared them, and he hath granted as much as might be. ¹⁹ And if then ye will keep yourselves loyal to the state, hereafter also will I endeavour to be a means of your good. 20 But of the particulars I have given order both to these and the other that came from me, to commune with you. 21 Fare ye well. The hundred and eight and fortieth year, the four and twentieth day of the month Dioscorinthius. 22 Now the king's letter contained these words: King Antiochus unto his brother Lysias sendeth greeting: 23 Since our father is translated unto the gods, our will is, that they that are in our realm live quietly, that every one may attend upon his own affairs. 24 We understand also that the Jews would not consent to our father, for to be brought unto the custom of the Gentiles, but had rather keep their own manner of living: for the which cause they require of us, that we should suffer them to live after their own laws. 25 Wherefore our mind is, that this nation shall be in rest, and we have determined to restore them their temple, that they may live according to the customs of their forefathers. 26 Thou shalt do well therefore to send unto them, and grant them peace, that when they are certified of our mind, they may be of good comfort, and ever go cheerfully about their own affairs. 27 And the letter of the king unto the nation of the Jews was after this manner: King Antiochus sendeth greeting unto the council, and the rest of the Jews: 28 If ye fare well, we have our desire; we are also in good health. 29 Menelaus declared unto us, that your desire was to return home, and to follow your own business: 30 Wherefore they that will depart shall have safe conduct till the thirtieth day of Xanthicus with security. 31 And the Jews shall use their own kind of meats and laws, as before; and one of the many manner of ways shall be molested for things ignorantly done. 32 I have sent also Menelaus, that he may comfort you. 33 Fare ye well. In the hundred forty and eighth year, and the fifteenth day of the month Xanthicus. 34 The Romans also sent unto them a letter containing these words: Quintus Memmius and Titus Manlius, ambassadors of the Romans, send greeting unto the people of the Jews. 35 Whatsoever Lysias the king's cousin hath granted, therewith we also are well pleased. 36 But touching such things as he judged to be referred to the king, after ye have advised thereof, send one forthwith, that we may declare as it is convenient for you: for we are now going to

Antioch. ³⁷ Therefore send some with speed, that we may know what is your mind. ³⁸ Farewell. This hundred and eight and fortieth year, the fifteenth day of the month Xanthicus.

12

¹ When these covenants were made, Lysias went unto the king, and the Jews were about their husbandry. ² But of the governours of several places, Timotheus, and Apollonius the son of Genneus, also Hieronymus, and Demophon, and beside them Nicanor the governor of Cyprus, would not suffer them to be quiet and live in peace. ³ The men of Joppa also did such an ungodly deed: they prayed the Jews that dwelt among them to go with their wives and children into the boats which they had prepared, as though they had meant them no hurt. ⁴ Who accepted of it according to the common decree of the city, as being desirous to live in peace, and suspecting nothing: but when they were gone forth into the deep, they drowned no less than two hundred of them. ⁵ When Judas heard of this cruelty done unto his countrymen, he commanded those that were with him to make them ready. ⁶ And calling upon God the righteous Judge, he came against those murderers of his brethren, and burnt the haven by night, and set the boats on fire, and those that fled thither he slew. ⁷ And when the town was shut up, he went backward, as if he would return to root out all them of the city of Joppa. ⁸ But when he heard that the Jamnites were minded to do in like manner unto the Jews that dwelt among them, ⁹ He came upon the Jamnites also by night, and set fire on the haven and the navy, so that the light of the fire was seen at Jerusalem two hundred and forty furlongs off. ¹⁰ Now when they were gone from thence nine furlongs in their journey toward Timotheus, no fewer than five thousand men on foot and five hundred horsemen of the Arabians set upon him. ¹¹ Whereupon there was a very sore battle; but Judas' side by the help of God got the victory; so that the Nomades of Arabia, being overcome, besought Judas for peace, promising both to give him cattle, and to pleasure him otherwise. ¹² Then Judas, thinking indeed that they would be profitable in many things, granted them peace: whereupon they shook hands, and so they departed to their tents. ¹³ He went also about to make a bridge

to a certain strong city, which was fenced about with walls, and inhabited by people of divers countries; and the name of it was Caspis. 14 But they that were within it put such trust in the strength of the walls and provision of victuals, that they behaved themselves rudely toward them that were with Judas, railing and blaspheming, and uttering such words as were not to be spoken. 15 Wherefore Judas with his company, calling upon the great Lord of the world, who without rams or engines of war did cast down Jericho in the time of Joshua, gave a fierce assault against the walls, 16 And took the city by the will of God, and made unspeakable slaughters, insomuch that a lake two furlongs broad near adjoining thereunto, being filled full, was seen running with blood. 17 Then departed they from thence seven hundred and fifty furlongs, and came to Characa unto the Jews that are called Tubieni. 18 But as for Timotheus, they found him not in the places: for before he had dispatched any thing, he departed from thence, having left a very strong garrison in a certain hold. 19 Howbeit Dositheus and Sosipater, who were of Maccabeus' captains, went forth, and slew those that Timotheus had left in the fortress, above ten thousand men. 20 And Maccabeus ranged his army by bands, and set them over the bands, and went against Timotheus, who had about him an hundred and twenty thousand men of foot, and two thousand and five hundred horsemen. 21 Now when Timotheus had knowledge of Judas' coming, he sent the women and children and the other baggage unto a fortress called Carnion: for the town was hard to besiege, and uneasy to come unto, by reason of the straitness of all the places. 22 But when Judas his first band came in sight, the enemies, being smitten with fear and terror through the appearing of him who seeth all things, fled amain, one running into this way, another that way, so as that they were often hurt of their own men, and wounded with the points of their own swords. 23 Judas also was very earnestin pursuing them, killing those wicked wretches, of whom he slew about thirty thousand men. 24 Moreover Timotheus himself fell into the hands of Dositheus and Sosipater, whom he besought with much craft to let him go with his life, because he had many ofthe Jews' parents, and the brethren of some of them, who, if they put him to death, should not be regarded. 25 So when he had assured them with many words that he would restore them without hurt, according to the agreement, they let him go for the saving of their brethren. 26 Then Maccabeus marched forth to Carnion, and to the temple of Atargatis, and there he slew five and twenty thousand persons. 27 And after he had put to flight and destroyed them, Judas removed the host toward Ephron, a strong city, wherein Lysias abode, and a great multitude of divers nations, and the strong young men kept the walls, and defended them mightily: wherein also was great provision of engines and darts. 28 But when Judas and his company had called upon Almighty God, who with his power breaketh the strength of his enemies, they won the city, and slew twenty and five thousand of them that were within, 29 From thence they departed to Scythopolis, which lieth six hundred furlongs from Jerusalem, 30 But when the Jews that dwelt there had testified that the Scythopolitans dealt lovingly with them, and entreated them kindly in the time of their adversity; 31 They gave them thanks, desiring them to be friendly still unto them: and so they came to Jerusalem, the feast of the weeks approaching. 32 And after the feast, called Pentecost, they went forth against Gorgias the governor of Idumea, 33 Who came out with three thousand men of foot and four hundred horsemen. 34 And it happened that in their fighting together a few of the Jews were slain. 35 At which time Dositheus, one of Bacenor's company, who was on horseback, and a strong man, was still upon Gorgias, and taking hold of his coat drew him by force; and when he would have taken that cursed man alive, a horseman of Thracia coming upon him smote off his shoulder, so that Gorgias fled unto Marisa. 36 Now when they that were with Gorgias had fought long, and were weary, Judas called upon the Lord, that he would shew himself to be their helper and leader of the battle. 37 And with that he began in his own language, and sung psalms with a loud voice, and rushing unawares upon Gorgias' men, he put them to flight. 38 So Judas gathered his host, and came into the city of Odollam, And when the seventh day came, they purified themselves, as the custom was, and kept the sabbath in the same place. ³⁹ And upon the day following, as the use had been, Judas and his company came to take up the bodies of them that were slain, and to bury them with their kinsmen in their fathers' graves. ⁴⁰ Now under the coats of every one that was slain they found things consecrated to the idols of the Jamnites, which is forbidden the Jews by the law. Then every man saw that this was the cause wherefore they were slain. ⁴¹ All men therefore praising the Lord, the righteous Judge, who had opened the things that were hid, ⁴² Betook themselves unto prayer, and besought him that the sin committed might wholly be put out of remembrance. Besides, that noble Judas exhorted the people to keep themselves from sin, for so much as they saw before their eyes the things that came to pass for the sins of those that were slain. ⁴³ And when he had made a gathering throughout the company to the sum of two thousand drachms of silver, he sent it to Jerusalem to offer a sin offering, doing therein very well and honestly, in that he was mindful of the resurrection: ⁴⁴ For if he had not hoped that they that were slain should have risen again, it had been superfluous and vain to pray for the dead. ⁴⁵ And also in that he perceived that there was great favour laid up for those that died godly, it was an holy and good thought. Whereupon he made a reconciliation for the dead, that they might be delivered from sin.

13

¹ In the hundred forty and ninth year it was told Judas, that Antiochus Eupator was coming with a great power into Judea, ² And with him Lysias his protector, and ruler of his affairs, having either of them a Grecian power of footmen, an hundred and ten thousand, and horsemen five thousand and three hundred, and elephants two and twenty, and three hundred chariots armed with hooks. ³ Menelaus also joined himself with them, and with great dissimulation encouraged Antiochus, not for the safeguard of the country, but because he thought to have been made governor. ⁴ But the King of kings moved Antiochus' mind against this wicked wretch, and Lysias informed the king that this man was the cause of all mischief, so that the king commanded to bring him unto Berea, and to put him to death, as the manner is in that place. ⁵ Now there was in

that place a tower of fifty cubits high, full of ashes, and it had a round instrument which on every side hanged down into the ashes. 6 And whosoever was condemned of sacrilege, or had committed any other grievous crime, there did all men thrust him unto death. 7 Such a death it happened that wicked man to die, not having so much as burial in the earth; and that most justly: 8 For inasmuch as he had committed many sins about the altar, whose fire and ashes were holy, he received his death in ashes. 9 Now the king came with a barbarous and haughty mind to do far worse to the Jews, than had been done in his father's time. 10 Which things when Judas perceived, he commanded the multitude to call upon the Lord night and day, that if ever at any other time, he would now also help them, being at the point to be put from their law, from their country, and from the holy temple: 11 And that he would not suffer the people, that had even now been but a little refreshed, to be in subjection to the blasphemous nations. 12 So when they had all done this together, and besought the merciful Lord with weeping and fasting, and lying flat upon the ground three days long, Judas, having exhorted them, commanded they should be in a readiness. 13 And Judas, being apart with the elders, determined, before the king's host should enter into Judea, and get the city, to go forth and try the matter in fight by the help of the Lord. 14 So when he had committed all to the Creator of the world, and exhorted his soldiers to fight manfully, even unto death, for the laws, the temple, the city, the country, and the commonwealth, he camped by Modin: 15 And having given the watchword to them that were about him, Victory is of God; with the most valiant and choice young men he went in into the king's tent by night, and slew in the camp about four thousand men, and the chiefest of the elephants, with all that were upon him. 16 And at last they filled the camp with fear and tumult, and departed with good success. 17 This was done in the break of the day, because the protection of the Lord did help him. 18 Now when the king had taken a taste of the manliness of the Jews, he went about to take the holds by policy, 19 And marched toward Bethsura, which was a strong hold of the Jews: but he was put to flight, failed, and lost of his men: 20 For

Judas had conveyed unto them that were in it such things as were necessary. 21 But Rhodocus, who was in the Jews' host, disclosed the secrets to the enemies; therefore he was sought out, and when they had gotten him, they put him in prison. 22 The king treated with them in Bethsum the second time, gave his hand, took their's, departed, fought with Judas, was overcome; 23 Heard that Philip, who was left over the affairs in Antioch, was desperately bent, confounded, intreated the Jews, submitted himself, and sware to all equal conditions, agreed with them, and offered sacrifice, honoured the temple, and dealt kindly with the place, 24 And accepted well of Maccabeus, made him principal governor from Ptolemais unto the Gerrhenians; 25 Came to Ptolemais: the people there were grieved for the covenants; for they stormed, because they would make their covenants void: 26 Lysias went up to the judgment seat, said as much as could be in defence of the cause, persuaded, pacified, made them well affected, returned to Antioch. Thus it went touching the king's coming and departing.

14

1 After three years was Judas informed, that Demetrius the son of Seleucus, having entered by the haven of Tripolis with a great power and navy, 2 Had taken the country, and killed Antiochus, and Lysias his protector. 3 Now one Alcimus, who had been high priest, and had defiled himself wilfully in the times of their mingling with the Gentiles, seeing that by no means he could save himself, nor have any more access to the holy altar, 4 Came to king Demetrius in the hundred and one and fiftieth year, presenting unto him a crown of gold, and a palm, and also of the boughs which were used solemnly in the temple: and so that day he held his peace. 5 Howbeit having gotten opportunity to further his foolish enterprize, and being called into counsel by Demetrius, and asked how the Jews stood affected, and what they intended, he answered thereunto: 6 Those of the Jews that he called Assideans, whose captain is Judas Maccabeus, nourish war and are seditious, and will not let the rest be in peace. 7 Therefore I, being deprived of mine ancestors' honour, I mean the high priesthood, am now come hither:

⁸ First, verily for the unfeigned care I have of things pertaining to the king; and secondly, even for that I intend the good of mine own countrymen: for all our nation is in no small misery through the unadvised dealing of them aforersaid. ⁹ Wherefore, O king, seeing knowest all these things, be careful for the country, and our nation, which is pressed on every side, according to the clemency that thou readily shewest unto all. ¹⁰ For as long as Judas liveth, it is not possible that the state should be quiet. ¹¹ This was no sooner spoken of him, but others of the king's friends, being maliciously set against Judas, did more incense Demetrius. ¹² And forthwith calling Nicanor, who had been master of the elephants, and making him governor over Judea, he sent him forth, ¹³ Commanding him to slay Judas, and to scatter them that were with him, and to make Alcimus high priest of the great temple. ¹⁴ Then the heathen, that had fled out of Judea from Judas, came to Nicanor by flocks, thinking the harm and calamities of the Jews to be their welfare. ¹⁵ Now when the Jews heard of Nicanor's coming, and that the heathen were up against them, they cast earth upon their heads, and made supplication to him that had established his people for ever, and who always helpeth his portion with manifestation of his presence. ¹⁶ So at the commandment of the captain they removed straightways from thence, and came near unto them at the town of Dessau. ¹⁷ Now Simon, Judas' brother, had joined battle with Nicanor, but was somewhat discomfited through the sudden silence of his enemies. ¹⁸ Nevertheless Nicanor, hearing of the manliness of them that were with Judas, and the courageousness that they had to fight for their country, durst not try the matter by the sword. ¹⁹ Wherefore he sent Posidonius, and Theodotus, and Mattathias, to make peace. ²⁰ So when they had taken long advisement thereupon, and the captain had made the multitude acquainted therewith, and it appeared that they were all of one mind, they consented to the covenants, ²¹ And appointed a day to meet in together by themselves: and when the day came, and stools were set for either of them, ²² Ludas placed armed men ready in convenient places, lest some treachery should be suddenly practised by the enemies: so they

made a peaceable conference. 23 Now Nicanor abode in Jerusalem, and did no hurt, but sent away the people that came flocking unto him. 24 And he would not willingly have Judas out of his sight: for he love the man from his heart 25 He prayed him also to take a wife, and to beget children: so he married, was quiet, and took part of this life. 26 But Alcimus, perceiving the love that was betwixt them, and considering the covenants that were made, came to Demetrius, and told him that Nicanor was not well affected toward the state; for that he had ordained Judas, a traitor to his realm, to be the king's successor. 27 Then the king being in a rage, and provoked with the accusations of the most wicked man, wrote to Nicanor, signifying that he was much displeased with the covenants, and commanding him that he should send Maccabeus prisoner in all haste unto Antioch. 28 When this came to Nicanor's hearing, he was much confounded in himself, and took it grievously that he should make void the articles which were agreed upon, the man being in no fault. 29 But because there was no dealing against the king, he watched his time to accomplish this thing by policy. 30 Notwithstanding, when Maccabeus saw that Nicanor began to be churlish unto him, and that he entreated him more roughly than he was wont, perceiving that such sour behaviour came not of good, he gathered together not a few of his men, and withdrew himself from Nicanor. 31 But the other, knowing that he was notably prevented by Judas' policy, came into the great and holy temple, and commanded the priests, that were offering their usual sacrifices, to deliver him the man. 32 And when they sware that they could not tell where the man was whom he sought, 33 He stretched out his right hand toward the temple, and made an oath in this manner: If ye will not deliver me Judas as a prisoner, I will lay this temple of God even with the ground, and I will break down the altar, and erect a notable temple unto Bacchus. 34 After these words he departed. Then the priests lifted up their hands toward heaven, and besought him that was ever a defender of their nation, saying in this manner; 35 Thou, O Lord of all things, who hast need of nothing, wast pleased that the temple of thine habitation should be among us: 36 Therefore now, O holy Lord of all holiness, keep this house ever undefiled, which lately was cleansed, and stop every unrighteous mouth. 37 Now was there accused unto Nicanor one Razis, one of the elders of Jerusalem, a lover of his countrymen, and a man of very good report, who for his kindness was called a father of the Jews. 38 For in the former times, when they mingled not themselves with the Gentiles, he had been accused of Judaism, and did boldly jeopard his body and life with all vehemency for the religion of the Jews. 39 So Nicanor, willing to declare the hate that he bare unto the Jews, sent above five hundred men of war to take him: 40 For he thought by taking him to do the Jews much hurt. 41 Now when the multitude would have taken the tower, and violently broken into the outer door, and bade that fire should be brought to burn it, he being ready to be taken on every side fell upon his sword; 42 Choosing rather to die manfully, than to come into the hands of the wicked, to be abused otherwise than beseemed his noble birth: 43 But missing his stroke through haste, the multitude also rushing within the doors, he ran boldly up to the wall, and cast himself down manfully among the thickest of them. 44 But they quickly giving back, and a space being made, he fell down into the midst of the void place. 45 Nevertheless, while there was yet breath within him, being inflamed with anger, he rose up; and though his blood gushed out like spouts of water, and his wounds were grievous, yet he ran through the midst of the throng; and standing upon a steep rock, 46 When as his blood was now quite gone, he plucked out his bowels, and taking them in both his hands, he cast them upon the throng, and calling upon the Lord of life and spirit to restore him those again, he thus died.

15

1 But Nicanor, hearing that Judas and his company were in the strong places about Samaria, resolved without any danger to set upon them on the sabbath day 2 Nevertheless the Jews that were compelled to go with him said, O destroy not so cruelly and barbarously, but give honour to that day, which he, that seeth all things, hath honoured with holiness above all other days. 3 Then the most ungracious wretch demanded, if there were a Mighty

one in heaven, that had commanded the sabbath day to be kept. 4 And when they said, There is in heaven a living Lord, and mighty, who commanded the seventh day to be kept: 5 Then said the other, And I also am mighty upon earth, and I command to take arms, and to do the king's business. Yet he obtained not to have his wicked will done. 6 So Nicanor in exceeding pride and haughtiness determined to set up a publick monument of his victory over Judas and them that were with him. 7 But Maccabeus had ever sure confidence that the Lord would help him: 8 Wherefore he exhorted his people not to fear the coming of the heathen against them, but to remember the help which in former times they had received from heaven, and now to expect the victory and aid, which should come unto them from the Almighty. 9 And so comforting them out of the law and the prophets, and withal putting them in mind of the battles that they won afore, he made them more cheerful. 10 And when he had stirred up their minds, he gave them their charge, shewing them there with all the falsehood of the heathen, and the breach of oaths. 11 Thus he armed every one of them, not so much with defence of shields and spears, as with comfortable and good words: and beside that, he told them a dream worthy to be believed, as if it had been so indeed, which did not a little rejoice them. 12 And this was his vision: That Onias, who had been high priest, a virtuous and a good man, reverend in conversation, gentle in condition, well spoken also, and exercised from a child in all points of virtue, holding up his hands prayed for the whole body of the Jews. 13 This done, in like manner there appeared a man with gray hairs, and exceeding glorious, who was of a wonderful and excellent majesty. 14 Then Onias answered, saying, This is a lover of the brethren, who prayeth much for the people, and for the holy city, to wit, Jeremias the prophet of God. 15 Whereupon Jeremias holding forth his right hand gave to Judas a sword of gold, and in giving it spake thus, 16 Take this holy sword, a gift from God, with the which thou shalt wound the adversaries. 17 Thus being well comforted by the words of Judas, which were very good, and able to stir them up to valour, and to encourage the hearts of the young men, they determined not to pitch camp, but courageously to set upon them, and manfully to try the matter by conflict, because the city and the sanctuary and the temple were in danger. ¹⁸ For the care that they took for their wives, and their children, their brethren, and folks, was in least account with them: but the greatest and principal fear was for the holy temple. ¹⁹ Also they that were in the city took not the least care, being troubled for the conflict abroad. ²⁰ And now, when as all looked what should be the trial, and the enemies were already come near, and the army was set in array, and the beasts conveniently placed, and the horsemen set in wings, ²¹ Maccabeus seeing the coming of the multitude, and the divers preparations of armour, and the fierceness of the beasts, stretched out his hands toward heaven, and called upon the Lord that worketh wonders, knowing that victory cometh not by arms, but even as it seemeth good to him, he giveth it to such as are worthy: ²² Therefore in his prayer he said after this manner; O Lord, thou didst send thine angel in the time of Ezekias king of Judea, and didst slay in the host of Sennacherib an hundred fourscore and five thousand: ²³ Wherefore now also, O Lord of heaven, send a good angel before us for a fear and dread unto them; ²⁴ And through the might of thine arm let those be stricken with terror, that come against thy holy people to blaspheme. And he ended thus. ²⁵ Then Nicanor and they that were with him came forward with trumpets and songs. ²⁶ But Judas and his company encountered the enemies with invocation and prayer. ²⁷ So that fighting with their hands, and praying unto God with their hearts, they slew no less than thirty and five thousand men: for through the appearance of God they were greatly cheered. ²⁸ Now when the battle was done, returning again with joy, they knew that Nicanor lay dead in his harness. ²⁹ Then they made a great shout and a noise, praising the Almighty in their own language. ³⁰ And Judas, who was ever the chief defender of the citizens both in body and mind, and who continued his love toward his countrymen all his life, commanded to strike off Nicanor's head, and his hand with his shoulder, and bring them to Jerusalem. ³¹ So when he was there, and called them of his nation together, and set the priests before the altar, he sent for them that were of the tower, 32 And shewed them vile Nicanor's head, and the hand of that blasphemer, which with proud brags he had stretched out against the holy temple of the Almighty. 33 And when he had cut out the tongue of that ungodly Nicanor, he commanded that they should give it by pieces unto the fowls, and hang up the reward of his madness before the temple. 34 So every man praised toward the heaven the glorious Lord, saying, Blessed be he that hath kept his own place undefiled. 35 He hanged also Nicanor's head upon the tower, an evident and manifest sign unto all of the help of the Lord. 36 And they ordained all with a common decree in no case to let that day pass without solemnity, but to celebrate the thirteenth day of the twelfth month, which in the Syrian tongue is called Adar, the day before Mardocheus' day. 37 Thus went it with Nicanor: and from that time forth the Hebrews had the city in their power. And here will I make an end. 38 And if I have done well, and as is fitting the story, itis that which I desired: but if slenderly and meanly, it is that which I could attain unto. 39 For as it is hurtful to drink wine or water alone; and as wine mingled with water is pleasant, and delighteth the taste: even so speech finely framed delighteth the ears of them that read the story. And here shall be an end.